Chithing

IN AT
THE DEEP END

Memoirs
of a Catholic Priest

Part 1

THE WAY WE WERE
1941-1976

Front Cover: Our Lady and the English Martyrs, Cambridge
Back Cover: St Mary's College, New Oscott

Published by Lidgate Publications
Wheelwrights, Lidgate, Suffolk

2013

ISBN No 978-0-9536091-1-6

By the same author

HAPPY LIDGATE
The story of a Suffolk Village
1899 - 1999

PREFACE

The following pages describe a world that has long gone. Village life has totally changed, both my schools are now closed, the training of future priests has ben radically overhauled and parish life is in a state of flux.

It could be said that some of the painful events recorded here are best forgotten but they reflect the growing pains (and my own) within the Catholic Church as the outcome of the Second Vatican Council gradually unfolded and its teachings still to be realised.

The sources of this book are my own personal diaries kept since my last year at school and letters home to my parents.

Anthony Foreman
Lidgate

September 2013

Dedicated to
my father and The Girls
and the extraordinary fellowship of clergy and lay people that make up the
Catholic Church

PROLOGUE

MY SUFFOLK &
LONDON ROOTS

LIDGATE, SUFFOLK

CHAPTER ONE

MY SUFFOLK AND LONDON BEGINNINGS

Some years ago I was pushing my shopping trolly around a well known supermarket when I encountered a parishioner. On seeing me she was rooted to the spot and exclaimed: 'Fancy seeing you here Father!' . A priest in those days was a bit of a mystery man who, like the proverbial Old Testament figure, Melchizedek, appeared from nowhere and disappeared just as mysteriously. The priest was taught that he is 'a man set apart', another Christ and in the past he was placed on a pedestal, the fount of all wisdom and knowledge - you did not expect to see him in a super market. Thankfully, the scandals besetting the Church have put paid to this. A priest is human like anyone else. He comes from a family; he is formed by his environment and the people he meets; he has his own strengths and weaknesses. He can sometimes fail miserably in his vocation but trusting that the grace of God will restore him once again. Perhaps the following pages will dispel some of the mystery surrounding the life, training and work of a priest as it was some fifty years ago. I always wanted to be a priest. Why, I am not quite sure. It was always a thought at the back of my mind without really knowing what I was letting myself in for. There would be rough seas and a feeling of drowning on many occasions but this was far from the tranquil beginnings of my story.

Family history is popular these days so here are my roots. My father, Humphrey, was born in 1889 the same year as Adolph Hitler; a detail of which he was quite unaware or if he was he was reluctant to admit. He was born in the small Suffolk Village of Lidgate on the Cambridgeshire border, noted for its Roman Villa, Norman Castle and birthplace of the prodigious medieval poet, John de Lydgate.

The family was rooted in the locality and my father was one of eight children. He came from a long line of wheelwrights, carpenters and beer sellers. His grandfather, William, had been estate carpenter to Lord North at Kirtling Tower as well as publican at the 'Kick and Dicky' Pub at Upend where he raised eleven children. His father, James, walked six miles to work every day in Newmarket and six miles at weekends to Great Bradley to court his future wife Fanny Dawson, daughter of a local farmer and on their marriage moved to Lidgate.

James's religious persuasion was Congregationalist. He played the organ at nearby Wickhambrook chapel. He also played the violin and it seems could dance a jig at eighty.

Fanny, on the other hand was 'Church' and my father was brought up in the Church of England. The 'mixture' of marriages in those days didn't seem to cause any trouble. Dad had only to cross the road to the village school where he was given a good basic education. His copper plate hand writing came in useful when called upon to inscribe the names of the deceased on the brass plates of coffins he occasionally made.

Times were hard at the beginning of the twentieth century and leaving school at the age of thirteen my father was soon apprenticed to his father in the trade, a trade that would be his for the next sixty five years. Many went abroad to seek their fortune and his uncle Ebenezer and aunt Hagar travelled to Canada and to the States to look for work. Great Uncle Ned had been a local cattle dealer and kept a shop near the village pond as well as being publican at 'The Star', Sunday School teacher and parish councillor. His trek to Canada was successful returning to encourage other young men to follow him. Great aunt Hagar along with her husband Bert Sparks trekked across the plains of the USA building a log cabin and begetting a child in each state. Tradition has it they were caught up in the Indian Wars and meeting with 'Sitting Bull' before finally settling in Portland Oregon where the family thrives to this day. Father's brother Charles, after a spell of driving out Lady Bristol at Ickworth Park also emigrated to Canada and brother Frank to the States. Tom became a baker in South London and Ted moved from home. Sister Effie married a farmer from Diss; Amy became a nurse and Eva a nanny. My father, being the eldest son, was left behind to carry on the family business. It was in the village that he spent his whole life and the furthest that he ever travelled was down to London, to Lincolnshire or Sunday school trips to Clacton.

My father's life was extremely hard and in old age he was persuaded to write his memoirs (now published in Happy Lidgate). It was work from dawn to dusk for in addition to his time in the workshop he had to maintain a small holding, working it sometimes after dark. Come the Great War he signed up at Newmarket recruiting office and took the King's Shilling, but luckily for me he was rejected on health grounds when a scar from a previous operation was discovered. His younger brother Ted was not so lucky being killed at the Battle of the Somme taking provisions to the front line. Brother Charles joined the Canadians and counted horses slaughtered in the offensive. He and his brother Frank both survived the conflict to live prosperous lives into old age.

After that brush with fate it was back to work for father. During the winter months he would help to plank trees in the village saw pit situated on 'The Meadow'. This was back breaking and unpleasant work as he was required to stand in the pit while pushing and pulling the end of the saw which covered him with choking dust for his efforts. As the years progressed he would develop a slight stoop with hands that were as hard and tough as old boots. On the death of his ageing parents in the 1930s, he made their solid oak coffins. By now in his late forties he was single and quite alone.

My mother, Irene Hilda Dean, born in 1904 came from Camberwell in South East London. She was one of six children who were to feature so much in my life – three sisters, Dorothy, Elsie and Vera and two brothers – Wilfred and Reg. Their forebears were from Bermondsey and Whitechapel. They were of solid Baptist stock and pillars of the local community. Alfred Dean, my grandfather, with delicate health and suffering from chronic TB worked for the SE London Gas Board, while his father George had been a lamplighter and his father before him a cordwainer. George had married a widow, Sarah, who ran a small millinery business. Her father John Read had been an artist. It is two small self portraits of John dating from the early 1800's that are the treasured possessions of the family. Unlike my father's grandfather, a country lad who had beautiful handwriting, George Dean, a contemporary, could not sign his name on the marriage certificate. This said much for the education of the country boys of that time. Grandmother's family were Nevilles. Her father had been a labourer in Penn's Iron foundry at Greenwich and his father James was a Birch Broom maker, whose brother reached the position of butler at the stately home of Knole in Kent.

Mother had been working as a secretary for Wallace Arnold, the travel agents, at Hayes Wharf Cartage in Tooley Street. She had learned to drive a car and was the proud possessor of an Austin Big Seven (with four doors) and this car was a family friend from 1939 to 1982 when she had to give up driving.

The Dean family came down to Lidgate for holidays. It was there that my parents met. Father would take mother out for rides on his pony but there was never any talk of romance at this time as mother already had a boy friend. They came from such different backgrounds and outlooks and it was not until 1939 when my father was nearly fifty and mother was thirty six that they decided to get married.

Some years before, mother's brother Reg, a brilliant student and former school captain of Haberdasher's Askes, Hatcham, had been an early entrant to Trinity Hall at Cambridge and, while a student, converted to Roman Catholicism. He had been greatly influenced by the Dominicans especially Fr Hugh Pope OP and was baptised at the University Chaplaincy. His brother Wilfred, a champion school boy boxer of England and Wales, found his route into the Catholic Church along a different path. Being a very argumentative type he had become involved with the Chesterton set. Both these boys were both committed Catholics until the day they died. Their arguments at home influenced both my mother and her sister Elsie. The Catholic clergy at Brockley were influential too; very pastoral men from the French order of Augustinians of the Assumption. My grand parents must have been unusually tolerant especially since being Baptists – how they coped with four children going over to Rome I can't imagine. Only Dorothy and Vera remained true to the Faith of their parents. Not only were the Dean family going over to Rome but other families too from the Church of England. Two, at least, would become Carmelite nuns and another joined the Dominicans. So upset were the local churches that to try and stop the rot a mission was held and letters from the local minister to my aunt warned her of the errors of Rome. In spite of all these upheavals they remained a very united and loving family. It is a great regret that I knew neither grandparent. Grandma died at the early age of sixty two, when grandfather came to live with my parents at the beginning of the war.

Before my parents' wedding could be arranged the cottage at Lidgate had to be brought into good order. My father had inherited an acre of land on which were four eighteenth century labourers cottages which had been combined into two. The smaller of them was derelict but had been converted into a workshop for the family business. In the four years since his father died the rest of the property had gone down hill and my father spent weeks getting the garden and house into order. Mother was certainly going to take on quite a job after her relatively secure life in London and on the verge of the outbreak of war it was some undertaking.

The day of the wedding came and father had been given some tea towels to wash to soften his hands for the big occasion. The marriage was celebrated in St. Mary Magdalene's Catholic Church in Brockley in 1939.

It was not until 1941 that I arrived on the scene and the war had been going for some two years. My father by then was too old to be called up but he did his part in the Home Guard and spent some of his time fire watching on the Belt Hill. His companion, John Turner, often fell asleep and he wondered what on earth he would do if the Nazis parachuted in. Grandfather had by this time come to live with my parents and also aunt Dorothy. She had always been the frail one of the family, had trained as a nurse and worked for some time in a London hospital caring for the children and wounded from the Great War, but she had to give up through ill health. She had spent some time as a child at the Great Ormond Street for sick children and had been treated for TB. At an early age she had been operated on by Sir Frederick Treaves, made famous by his friendship with Joseph Merrick, the Elephant Man. Her sister Elsie with whom she lived had moved to a flat in Wickham Road, Brockley and Elsie stayed there during the war to continue her work as teacher at Mantle Road Secondary School (now the John Stainer School). At

4

this school she would remain for the forty years of her career. Neither sister married, victims in their own way of the Great War- loves lost or a shortage of males. Two of their greatest friends George and Godfrey Crann had been killed in the war and a third brother Will had been badly wounded. Aunt Elsie had for a time been evacuated with her class to Bletchingly in Surrey but in the holidays would come down by train to Newmarket where we awaited her arrival with eager anticipation. She lived through the blitz and some of the essays written by her pupils were quite harrowing. The third sister Vera had married Charlie Smith, an Insurance Agent, amateur conjuror and member of the inner Magic Circle who saw active service as a member of ENSA. They lived at West Wickham, but much to their sorrow they had no children. They were all strong characters who would have a profound influence on my life.

The Old Rectory in the village was an important nerve centre for the military and was the home of Major General Dewing and his family. Nearby was Stradishall airfield, now Highpoint Prison and a decoy airfield had been set up at the far end of the village complete with search light to deflect enemy aircraft – almost to our cost since bombs were dropped around the village. Should they have exploded the church and I would not be here to tell the tale..

I arrive

We were in the flight path of planes on bombing raids to the midlands and on one occasion while mother was shaking her duster a Dornier flew over low to crash in fields nearby. The two occupants were soon rounded up by locals with pitchforks and whatever other weapons they could muster. In addition there was a gun emplacement near the pond and a defensive pill box. All these are gone now and there is nothing to recall those dark days.

Much to the family's joy, I arrived on the scene on 16th May 1941 in a nursing home in Springfield Road, Bury St. Edmunds – later to have the somewhat dubious name of 'Molly's Guest House'. I have no knowledge of the event. I don't even know what time of day or night I was born, how heavy I was or whether I was an ailing infant. I was just too embarrassed to ask; they weren't the sort of things to talk about in those days. I was baptised within the week at St Edmund, King and Martyr, Catholic Church in Bury. Mother was not well enough to attend and father was hard at work and so as far as I know only my Godmother – Hortense Linden, an ample and rather overpowering Irish Lady, (who had the distinction of being born in Bury Barracks) and my Baptist aunt Dorothy were present. My Godfather, by proxy was Uncle Reg. I was baptised by Canon Garnet, a descendent of one of the English Martyrs – so on the religious front I got off to a good start. Here then was my first contact with the Catholic Church which was to play such a part in my subsequent life.

My father was a loyal member of the village church and a member of the choir and in his Sunday best and trilby hat he would worship there each week. He had no doubt promised as was the requirement that any children would be brought up in the Catholic Faith and to the best of my knowledge he made no objection. Very occasionally he would come to the little church that mother frequented. This was at Kirtling, some four miles away and was the estate church for Lord North. It had been built on the occasion of his conversion to Catholicism in the 1870s. There I was brought in a Moses basket and no doubt to much billing and cooing. Fr Charles Davidson was parish priest at the time and later Fr Bill Burrows who would visit us on occasion. I remember his beret and his missing finger which he would produce to delight the children. The fact that mother and I went to a different church on a Sunday apart from other villagers tended to make her and me something of an outsider and feeling that she was not really accepted. However there was no real animosity that I was aware of but it was my first experience of the divisions in the Church and the need for ecumenism between the different denominations. Many years later I was to discover that Foreman cousins who worked on the North estate in the 1860s had in fact converted to Catholicism and eventually moved to Middlesbrough to become green grocers. Perhaps this 'betrayal' accounted for some of the antipathy by the local Foreman's to my mother's Catholicism.

Of those early years against the background of the war I can remember little except I was in a secure and loving environment. My earliest recollection at the age of two was spinning coins on the table with grandfather Dean and on his death at home I was reputed to have said on the way to the funeral that they were only grandfather's old bones going to be buried.

By modern standards life was primitive, but that was taken for granted. There was no electricity which was not to come until after the war. There was no running tap water – the mains were not to come through the village until the 1950s. For washing water we used the run off from the thatch gathered in butts – the water was a bit yellow with the occasional wriggly larvae but it had the bonus of being nice and soft. For drinking water we relied on a spring in nearby Cobbolds lane until a galvanised tank was installed in the village. From here dad collected two pails of water on his handle bars, spilling not a drop. Milk was delivered and ladled from a churn which mother scalded to prevent it going off. Sanitation was basic - that was not to come until the 1960s. We relied on an outside privy where we endured spiders, cobwebs and draughts. The necessary bucket father emptied on regular occasions to provide good manure for the crops. The newspapers and telephone directory provided the means to cleanliness until Izal arrived. For special visitors we provided a special Elsan in the cottage with chemical contents which one was

6

Waterbeach Walburga

not allowed to use. Since there was no electricity we depended on paraffin lamps and of course there was so no refrigeration. But food wise we were self contained growing our own produce, with occasional meat from rabbit or chicken and the weekly call on his bike for orders from Woolards shop at Wickhambrook, a certain Mr Littlechild. Mother had her car, but petrol being rationed made it difficult sometimes to get father to work on the various jobs he was called to do in the local farms and villages. Night driving was precarious and was something that mother avoided, nor in better times either and to save petrol she would often free wheel down Hail Hill into the village. Father began to learn to drive but the war scuppered those endeavours and he never took it up again afterwards. Meat was in short supply and in the end poor Percy, the pig, had to be slaughtered. I well remember his screams added to those being slaughtered across the road at Pear Tree Farm. His hams hung from the beams of the cottage to cure, but everyone was reluctant to eat what had become a family pet. We had a succession of cats and with them I came face to face with the reality of death. Dad only approved of 'working' cats and they were shooed out at night to earn their keep. Kitty the Pony was vital for transport, too, for collecting visitors in the trap from Newmarket station. We also acquired some goats from the Carmelite Convent at Waterbeach. These provided us with milk.

My father was a local man through and through with the local dialect and it was said that to begin with I spoke like a native. Sometimes it was difficult to understand what he said and how my parents really communicated I don't know. But he worked every hour that God gave him and there was no time for holidays or the usual pursuits that fathers these days share with their sons. Being in his fifties when I first got to know him had its disadvantages but then all my relatives were of an older generation and I was not to have any brothers or sisters. Father was a very shy man, with little social life or ambition. I would never know whether he held any strong views one way or the other so his influence on my life intellectually was minimal. He was not one to go to the pub, largely because his father had been that way inclined. He was essentially a craftsman who was good at his trade and I marvelled at his skill in constructing wheels and single-handedly creating ladders, hen houses and wagons. He was well known and respected in the local community and a valued member. Bringing up a little son, whom I am sure, had arrived so unexpectedly, was beyond his experience and I was left to mother to attend

7

to. He was a devout man and I well remember him kneeling by his bed and saying his night prayers.

Italian prisoners of war had been incarcerated at a nearby farm and they would come round doing jobs for us. One officer, whom I called Nini, invited me aboard their bus and I was taken for a ride down the village. They hadn't thought to ask my parents. As soon as I was found to be missing there was consternation – however I was returned safe and sound.

I must have been a trial to everyone. I didn't like food very much. Mother's anxiety no doubt communicated itself to me. She was a great worrier and used to get so anxious and worked up about things. The war years were difficult and money was tight. She would develop a high colour in her neck which was alarming. She took me to see a specialist in Bury. In the end they concocted some pudding containing every conceivable ingredient. I must have eaten it since it sent me into a state of rigidity - like a Dutch doll they said and much to everyone's alarm.

My only other recollections of the war were picking up handfuls of 'window' dropped to confuse the enemy radar, my Mickey Mouse gas mask and seeing a barrage balloon that had slipped its moorings as well as army transport through the village and the rattling of the front door as planes took off from Stradishall airfield.

But then the war was over. Auntie Vera and her husband Charlie Smith came to stay with us and we celebrated the first Christmas I can remember. Charlie, as related, had been in ENSA in the war in Stars in Battledress and was a good amateur conjurer. He was popular at children's parties which made a break for him after what must have been dull work at the Royal Insurance Company in town. We had a Christmas tree and lights and this tree, now of majestic proportions, to this day still stands in the garden.

'The Girls'
Aunts Dorothy, Elsie, Mother
& Dog

PART ONE

THE SCHOOL BOY

ALTAR SERVER
AT
KIRTLING

CHAPTER TWO

OFF TO SCHOOL

Thoughts now turned to my education and it was then that I made my first big journey on the steam train from Newmarket to London to stay with my aunts Dorothy and Elsie and with aunt Vera at West Wickham. I suppose I could have gone to the village school but mother had plans for me to attend a Catholic school. And until one could be found I was to spend a short time at an infant school in London. And so I was parted from my parents at a tender age. There was not much else they could do as work was scarce and father needed mother to take him to work if needs be.

36b Wickham Rd

Aunts Dorothy and Elsie rented a second floor flat in one of the big Victorian mansions in Wickham Road - a long straight road once lined with arching plane trees but long since replaced, at that time, with flowering cherry trees. The road linked Lewisham Way with Brockley and was once admired by Queen Victoria. Their's was the second floor flat with large bay windows and very high ceilings. This was to become my second home. We liked to say that we had both a town and a country house.

Each morning hand in hand with aunt Elsie I made the ten minute walk to school. By garages in Geoffrey Road I regularly got a stitch and declared my pain, but aunt E would have none of this and on I had to go. The short time that I was in the infant class seems to have been a happy one. I was very fond of my teacher Mrs Boyott and played the triangle when it came to some music. On one occasion I nearly got lost waiting for aunt to collect me from the senior school next door, but I had the presence of mind to stay by the railway foot bridge until I was found. But at the age of six I walked home with the friends that I had made and I remember banging on the metal advertisement for Camp Coffee on the wall of the railway bridge at Brockley Cross. Town life was so different from the countryside I had been used to but I seemed to adapt to it.

Childhood illnesses were inevitable. I had a brief stay in hospital to have my tonsils out. I well remember the pad put over my face, the ether spray and the sore throat that followed, but more serious was an ear infection that I developed due to an attack of measles. The doctor, on inspecting the spots, asked me how I had got them and I said – much to the embarrassment of the family- that I had been staying in the country and that they were flea bites. But my ear became very painful and I was given solace by the only two girl friends that I was to have – Anne Slatter – a baker's daughter and Susan White who sympathised with me in the play ground. This involved a more lengthy stay in hospital and my first real experience of complete separation from the family. Visitors were not allowed and all they could do was to look at me through the glass windows at the end of the ward. I was promised on my return home a Meccano Set and a tabby kitten. Both these I received. I named the kitten Cleopatra (appropriately) and she became the mother and grandmother of a great progeny through the years to come. My Meccano set absorbed my time and attention for many years as I added new upgrades to models that I would construct and very reluctantly disassemble. On occasion mother would travel to London to make sure I was OK and the letters father wrote to her were very touching missing both me and her and come the holiday season they would both travel up to London.

These were drab days after the war. Aunt had stayed teaching all this time during the blitz and some of her class had been killed or bombed out. There was a lot of bomb sites and destruction in this area of London. It was nice on occasion to travel to West Wickham to see my other beloved aunt Vera. She and her husband no doubt spoiled me but it was here that I first went to the cinema and saw Ali Baba and the forty thieves. Hawes Lane where they lived seemed a beautiful spot with the smell of the lilac in the spring and Uncle delighted us at Christmas with some of his conjuring tricks.

I was, then, brought up in an extended family with four mothers and a real and surrogate father. Having no grandparent living my aunts filled that gap but it was rather an isolated existence at home as regards children of my own age. Living in this former Victorian mansion one was rather cut one off from the neighbours. However those above and below were most friendly and firm in that relationship all through life. In the top flat were the Morrises. Peter was a dentist and Fay a most charming and attractive lady. They had a son Carey, a few years younger that I, who would later become a doctor. Immediately above were the Readers. Sid was a local head teacher and JP and with Kath his wife were leading lights in the scout movement. They too had one son called Nigel who to begin with was rather uncontrollable. Kath would regularly come down for a 'cuppa' each morning to keep aunt Dorothy company. Kath was a great character and full of fun. In the basement were the Mallers with whom we didn't have a lot of contact and I had to be careful not to stamp on the floors. But Nigel upstairs was given a drum and made a

Aged six

lot of noise. Stone steps lead down from our flat to the garden at the back divided up into plots and ending with what were the former Mews. In the Readers' garden was an old Anderson Shelter which remained there for many years.

On Sundays we went to the local Church, St Mary Magdalene, about twenty minutes walk away. We always went to the seven o'clock Mass on a Sunday morning and sat near the back. This got me used to getting up early on dark cold mornings in winter. We did this because with aunt Dorothy's fragile health her sister needed to get back to keep an eye on her. So we never got involved at all in parish affairs or events, novenas or devotions. Just occasionally we went to the sung Mass later in the morning but that was a rarity. The Parish Priest was Fr Patrick O'Neil. He was a Scot with a very fruity voice. Their housekeeper was my Godmother Hortense Linden. I always felt very embarrassed when she enveloped me with a truly Irish bear hug. Before the war the family were involved in ordinary parish life, in the Children of Mary and a trip to Lourdes and various Augustinian priests had been friends of the family. Parish life was even more tenuous at our church at Kirtling where the priest shot in at the last moment and shot out again before dashing off for another Mass at Haverhill. We rarely had a sermon and our contact with the main parish in Newmarket was marginal only going there occasionally for Holy Days of Obligation and for Confession. The family practice of the faith was fortunately not stifling – we weren't into devotions, first Fridays, holy pictures and attempts to say the rosary together ended up in giggles - though mother had a statue of St Therese of Liseaux and St Anthony of Padua. The family were very rooted in non-conformity and the practical site of Christianity and one of the first prayers that I learned was one of the psalms – the *'de profundis'* - 'Out of the depths I cry to you O Lord.'

By now my schooling in London was over and I returned to Lidgate. But what was my future academic career to be? Mother had made application to the local education authority in Bury St. Edmund's for assisted transport to St. Louis Catholic School in Newmarket seven miles away. She received a dusty reply saying that the authorities did not provide help for pupils attending denominational schools. The village school, in its own way, was probably very good but mother wanted better for me and there now came a period of uncertainty as to my future. It was then that we met up with an Austrian girl who had recently married into a village family. Her name was Ilse Murkin and for sometime she became what I liked to call my 'governess' and taught me along with General Dewing's children the basic skills of reading and writing.

One of the converts at the time of my mother's move to Rome was Marjorie Humphries.She had been secretary to Uncle Mac on Children's Hour on the radio. She became a Carmelite nun at Waterbeach near Cambridge. Her brother, Harold, was a rather eccentric but brilliant Dominican Deacon who took the name of Sylvester on joining the Order. Through his good offices we learned of a school run by the Dominican Sisters of the Congregation of St. Catherine of Sienna who were based in St. Leonard's – on – Sea in Sussex and it was to them that mother made application. So off we went, mother and I, down to Sussex by the sea for an interview with the Mother Prioress to assess my suitability. The house was certainly situated in a magnificent spot at the top of Filsham Road, overlooking the sea and Pevensey Bay and in the distance the misty outline of Beachy Head could be seen. The large parlour was sunny and the windows looked out on to a wide playing field. I was obviously rather nervous. The Mother Superior was the first complete nun that I had ever met close to. She wore this rather strange get up of a white habit and black veil with a string of large rosary beads about her waist but she was very friendly and when I stood with legs crossed she asked whether I wanted to go to the lavatory. I replied very decidedly that I did not want to go, thank you very much. So it was signed and sealed and to St. Dominic's I was to go.

THE LAST WHEEL

ST DOMINIC'S SCHOOL
ST LEONARDS - ON - SEA
1948 - 1954

Hill House, as it was originally called, had been occupied by the troops during the war and the only memory of that occupation was a warning scrawled on some paper and preserved in the bath room: 'You like it clean, so don't be mean and leave it dirty for others'. This was a lesson I have always taken to heart over the years. After the war the school had transferred from elsewhere along the coast and had not been long in operation when at the tender age of seven I was wrenched from the bosom of my family to start a new life by the sea. It was a traumatic experience and the ritual of the week or so before returning to school each term was painful for everyone and something I never really came to terms with until way on into my teens.

Proudly besporting my school blazer and cap - grey, edged in black and white with the Dominican badge and its motto *Veritas* (Truth) I joined the group of little boys with our little cases - trunks had already been sent 'passenger luggage in advance' - assembled at Charing Cross Station. Here Sister was waiting to collect us and shepherd us to our destination, West St Leonard's station, followed by the trek up Filsham Rd to the school. My first recollections were sitting on a trunk in the playroom and howling my eyes out. Naturally this initial homesickness gradually declined as the days went by and I settled in to my new surroundings and made friends.

It was a small school of barely a hundred boys including a small quota of day boys. Now, sadly, the huge playing field is a housing estate and the school a residential home for the elderly. The head teacher was a Sister Mary Benedict, a formidable lady and every bit the head mistress who ruled with a rod of iron and would administer the cane when she thought it necessary. Her second in command, was Mrs Joan Sargeant, the nurse. By modern standards she might have been had up for child cruelty when on occasion, if a child misbehaved, she would seize him by the hair and shake him vigorously. But on the whole she was OK if you remained on the right side of the law. Being a rather timid creature I was prepared to do that rather than risk the punishment that might be meted out. A prominent member of the staff was Sister Mary Walburga, with a red blotchy complexion, a lady of great artistic gifts being related to the artist, Lindsey Clark. Sisters Mary Magdalen, Conleth and Imelda are the only other Sisters that really have left an impression on me. They were really popular and always great fun. Many years later Sr Magdalene would help to found the Congregation in Bodo in Norway and I always regret that I never fulfilled my promise of saying Mass for her on her golden jubilee.

St Dominic's was by and large a good school giving an excellent foundation in the basics. There were none of the horrific tales of some convent schools that have surfaced in recent years. Sr Walburga encouraged our artistic skills and introduced us to the great characters of literature especially Dickens. How I loved *David Copperfield* and *Great Expectations*. I sort of identified myself with Pip. Perhaps it was because my father was a bit like Joe Gargery, the humble blacksmith who stayed at home while Pip tried to better himself. There the parallels ended but I teased aunt Dorothy that she was rather like Miss Havisham. My other favourite story was *A Tale of Two Cities* and I admired the heroism of Sidney Carton. I also became fascinated with things prehistoric and the radio programme, *How things began. The Lost World* by Conan Doyle was broadcast when I was on holiday and I regaled boys in the dormitory after lights out with my recollections of the story of dinosaurs and pterodactyls.

I was found to be somewhat musical and this together with drama was an area in which the school prided itself. Kenneth Brown, organist at Hastings parish church taught piano and his wife, Doris, elocution and together they produced some very fine operettas where I soon began to find my acting and singing abilities.

The very first play in which I performed was the *Pied Piper of Hamlin*. I played the little lame girl, Elsa – not the boy in the original story – who got left behind. I was doomed to play women's parts generally in my later career, which may not have been good for my psycho-

The Bells of Bruges

15

logical development! I got used to the smell of grease paint and hot and itchy tow wigs. It was to this first play that mother and aunt came from London to see and also to my First Holy Communion. But these were the only occasions in my academic career that they were able to visit me during the term time, due to the circumstances back at home. It was something I got used to as inevitable but it was rather sad. However, Uncle Charlie used to come down on a monthly visit and took me out for the day and so this was some consolation. We went to Hastings pier where I spent my pennies in the slot machines and occasionally took a bus along the coast to Bexhill. He was very good and I suppose I was some comfort to him and to Vera in their childlessness.

The plays, then, were a regular highlight of life. In addition we competed in the Hastings Music Festival. I was developing quite a good treble voice and competed regularly and winning on several occasions in my class at singing and piano – the highlight being the Bronze Medal. Taking part in the final concert at the White Rock Pavilion was daunting, the spot lights were bright and I remember singing flat. Poetry reading was another fruit of Mrs. Brown's elocution lessons and again I did very well on this score too, competing on several occasions on the stage of the Pier Theatre. We competed against all the major schools in the area and developed quite a reputation. One of my rivals was Paul Chevalier a relative of the famous Maurice. Since I was perceived to be 'inherently musical' Mr Brown offered to give me free piano lessons since the family could not afford to pay for this added expense and I am eternally grateful to him as it has stood me in good stead all through my life in so many ways.

During this period I was introduced to the Irish spirituality of the Sisters, as most of them were Irish and being brought up in an ecumenical family I found their attitudes to other denominations rather strange and upsetting. But I was attracted to the lives of the saints, holy pictures and the ritual of the Mass which I suppose sowed the seeds of a future vocation.

Each Sunday evening we trekked in crocodile fashion to the parish church of St. Thomas of Canterbury in Hastings where we served Benediction. We always vied with each other as to who could 'walk with Sister' and asked her searching questions. The church visit provided our first introduction to the opposite sex. This was not exactly promising for on one occasion when a group of school girls were assembling at the church we were told to look in the other direction. The natural curiosity of children which manifested itself on occasion in an innocent way was soon stamped upon very severely and gave an unhealthy approach to sex. The fact that we all had to wear shorts when having a communal shower, to preserve our modesty, also cannot have helped.

Uncle Charlie & Me

We used to go out for some enjoyable walks in crocodile mode and in the summer, very sensibly, we wore grey felt hats to protect us from the sun. It was great walking down to the beach and having fun there. The school chaplain, Fr Reginald Salter, a retired priest, occasionally took us out and treated us to ice cream and in one of my letters home I recalled that on a Monday evening we used to play cards with him. I really can't remember this at all and wonder what my folks back at home must have thought!

Letter writing home was a weekly operation. Our letters were censored, but having read adventure stories we all knew about invisible ink. I contrived to get some through the good offices of Uncle Charlie and penned a few lines home. The folks eagerly awaited the secret message to appear as they held it in front of the fire and if this was not enough I managed to write a message on a fragment of lavatory paper which I concealed beneath the postage stamp. I dreaded the possibility that the letter might be left on a hot radiator and my cover blown.

I was never really a sporty type but we played football and for awhile our coach was Harry Haslam, a future manager of Eastbourne and Sheffield United football clubs. He always spoke about the match we would, one day, be playing on a Saturday - that rather mystified me as we never played on a Saturday. We played cricket which I enjoyed and in the summer the inevitable sports day to which parents were invited - but of course no one came for me apart from Uncle Charlie. We had a gym with all its accoutrements and boxing which I quite enjoyed (thinking of my Uncle Wilf) and on my report it actually said that I was developing some style and then there was swimming down at the White Rock Baths. This was not such a happy experience. My first swimming costume was a one piece suite that covered everything and so I was rather teased for my 'Victorian' garment – and could they get me to take my feet off the bottom? In the end in desperation a rope was tied round my waist and I had to jump off the board at the deep end. I really thought I was drowning and would never come up again. By the time I left the school I was beginning to gain confidence and could swim a width. On one occasion one of the masters took us out to the old groin at Old Hastings that stretched right out into the sea. This was really scary as we had to jump over fissures in the rocks and in these safety conscious days such a thing would have never been allowed.

I also went riding. A friend of the family had offered to pay for lessons. This I really enjoyed on a Sunday morning at Beauport Park stables and the

Blaze

experience helped me to grow in confidence. On one occasion I lost an iron and was knocked off the pony by a tree branch – no safety helmets in those days - and on another occasion the horse, which was a full sized one bolted, when a train coming out of the mist, shot past us. I just hung on for dear life and squeezed with my knees for all I was worth and hoped for the best.

We had a regular film show and I aspired to be a deep sea diver after a film on the subject or to join the navy after a film about Dartmouth. A rather fierce Irish lay mistress, Miss Fleming, would threaten, as a punishment, 'you will miss the fillum' on Saturday.

For some boys not all was sweet and light. Three planned to run away. They smuggled onto their person the cream bun that we had as a treat on a Sunday evening for tea and made their escape. They planned to get a boat and cross the channel. Their plans went awry as their route took them past the chapel where the Sisters were singing their Office and were caught red handed. Punishment ensued! In fact punishment of the severest kind was enacted at assembly. There had been some misbehaviour on the buses by the day boys on the way to school (nothing changes) and the miscreants were called forward and received a thwack on the hand with a cane wielded by St. Benedict. How it swished through the air and, after dealing its deadly blow landed with a deep thud on her habit, entangling itself with her rosary beads. Day boys were always a bit of a problem for the public image of the school and on one occasion when my watch went wrong I gave it to a day boy, Philip Rix, to take home to his father a watch repairer – I was hauled over the coals for 'bartering with the day boys'. Comics were not allowed and when *The Eagle* comic came out, published by a clergyman, full of wholesome material, Aunt Elsie wrote requesting that I might receive it – but to no avail and the copies had to be saved up for the holidays so that I could get my dose of Dan Dare and his battles with the Mekon.

To broaden our horizons we had annual outings to places such as Dungeness lighthouse and the Dimchurch miniature railway, Ashdown Forest, Hampton Court Palace, Arundel Castle, Aylesford Priory, and Storrington with its community of Premonstratension Canons. Here I learned of the burial of Fr Tyrrell the priest excommunicated for his heretical Modernist views and how the Order had been put under an interdict because of their disobedience. This sounded really exciting stuff and introduced me to another aspect of Church life. When the weather was fine we had some great walks to the park or across the golf links (now a housing estate) to Hollington Church in the wood.

1949 First Communions with Sr Mary Benedict

We were of course prepared for the Sacraments. I made my First Communion at the age of eight. We made paper hearts in preparation putting down a black mark on one side for any sins we had committed and another colour on the other side for good deeds. I was Confirmed later by Archbishop Cowderoy, an experience I vividly remember. For some reason I was convinced that I ought to become a priest. There was no rational explanation and I really knew nothing about it apart from the ritual of the Mass and learning to serve, but I suppose that is how a vocation slowly comes to birth.

By this time I began serving Mass at Kirtling while home on holidays. It was always a ritual having banana sandwiches for breakfast. Mother was always concerned that they should be mashed up well lest they gave you indigestion. We then listened to *Chapel in the Valley* on the radio and the dulcet tones of Hazel introduced by nice Mr Edwards and this was the signal to embark on the four mile trip to Kirtling church where after picking up one or two people on the way we took our regular seat near the back of the church. Father Michael Kennedy was our new priest who arrived in 1953, as broad an Irishman as you can imagine. I served Mass with Geofrey Pavis who was somewhat older and bigger than I. It was quite an achievement hauling the heavy missal and its stand up and down the steep altar steps from one side to the other. It was an even bigger challenge trying to make my responses in Latin. Fr K would cut in before you had a chance to finish your bit: *Introibo ad altare dei - ad deum qui laetificat juventutem meum.* After Mass a group of us would go over to the neighbouring presbytery, which was looked after by Mr and Mrs Stalley, for a cup of tea and chat. Mr Stalley stoked the old boiler to heat the church and Edgar Pavis from the village rang the two bells that welcomed people while Sally Stalley, the daughter, generally kept the church in order and acted as sacristan. But Fr Kennedy had to dash off to celebrate another Mass at Haverhill so he was unable to join us. Fr Larry Howlin, the handsome young curate, impressed me by his general cheerful manner. The fascination of the ritual of the Mass and all that surrounded it lead me to make my play room into a little chapel complete with altar and aunt Vera made me a set of vestments – I look back now with much embarrassment! I liked experimenting with incense and finding suitable plants that might give off the appropriate smell. Perhaps the trip to Olympia to the Vocations exhibition was also an encouragement for the future. Here all the various religious orders displayed their wares to entice new recruits.

My experience with the sacrament of Confession was not altogether happy. We had been taught that the priest would never know who it was who went to Confession and of course would never divulge anything that he had heard. On this occasion I went to Confession in the sacristy where there was a portable *priedieu* and screen in place. I spouted my peccadilloes when, horror of horrors, the large crucifix in front of me suddenly collapsed with a bang and with that Fr Salter arose from behind the screen to see what was going on. This rather shattered my illusions of anonymity. The question of anonymity arose too when mother went to confession. She always wore a certain hat which I dubbed her 'confessional hat' as it came down a bit over her eyes. But then it didn't really matter since the confessional was usually shrouded in darkness. Strange, dark confessionals could be rather frightening for a youngster. On one occasion, having negotiated the curtain, there was a step inside which I failed to see, and went hurtling in at great speed narrowly avoiding crashing into the opposite wall. It was a blessing when all that changed some twenty years later.

My first experience of a death in the family came in 1950. My beloved auntie Vera had had a stroke while out shopping and had been nursed by her sisters at the flat but the news came through that she had died and this was announced to me by Sister Benedict. I was heart broken and I was advised to go to the chapel to talk to the Lord about it. This I suppose helped as it would in times to come when there was no one else around to confide in. But it would have been nice to have been with the family and perhaps have gone to the funeral. Uncle Charlie was of course bereft and his trips down to take me out were combined with his search for a new partner which he eventually found and married and lived with for many years afterwards. The same year saw the solemn definition of the Assumption of Our Lady by Pope Pius X11 amid great celebrations and to commemorate the event we built a Lourdes grotto in the garden.

There were some rather posh convent girl schools in the area and we joined with the school up the road and the Holy Child Convent in Hastings for festivals such as *Corpus Christi* and we enjoyed wading through the elaborate patterns of flowers laid out for the procession and the orange juice and biscuits we consumed afterwards as a reward for our serving.

It being the Festival of Britain in 1951 I well remember the train journey home as we crossed Charing Cross Bridge to the station and seeing the new

Festival Hall, the Skylon and the Shot Tower. But there were still the dreadful reminders of the war years with the bomb sites and the prefabs (or 'freefabs' as Nellie my aunts' cleaner called them) that had sprung up all over the place.

Although being a pretty law abiding boy, rather through fear than anything else, I did have one serious brush with authority one day during dinner. I was a monitor by this time and sitting at the end of a table when a particularly nasty piece of meat was served up complete with tubes and fat – which I abhorred. Other boys seemed only too keen to wolf it down and so I passed my dollop of the offending grease along the table only to be discovered. I was accused of being a bad example to the smaller boys and was quite out of favour until I went and abjectly apologised to Sr. Benedict. In those years after the war food was always a problem – powdered scrambled egg on toast sticks in my mind as particularly revolting. But I did like spam and we never really went hungry.

In the mornings as we emerged from sleep we could hear the scrunch of Sister's feet on the linoleum and the rattle of her rosary beads as she clapped to wake us up shooting us onto our knees to say the morning offering, 'Jesus through the pure heart of Mary I offer you....' And at night we all gathered together from our dormitories for night prayers before the statue of St. Rock on the landing. Our prayers concluded with what I thought were the following, 'most Sacred Heart of Jesus, take under your protection our hearts cooled and perished. St. Rock pray for us'. This always puzzled me as I grew older until I had the courage to ask Sister for an interpretation. She was amazed at my question and informed me that the correct rendering of the prayer was: 'Sacred Heart of Jesus take under your protection our hearth, school and parish....' I was also puzzled by the prayer to St Rock, whom I discovered years later, was the patron of those suffering from the plague - was it because Small Pox was again rearing its head in the neighbourhood? There had already been an epidemic of chicken pox to which I had succumbed so perhaps he was a suitable saint to invoke.

The Sisters wore a tight wimple around their head and one wondered what on earth they wore when they went to bed. I was never to discover this but was fascinated when I overheard Sister say that she would have to go to the barbers as her hair was getting 'rather bristly'. One wondered what on earth she would look like without her habit. For that matter did Sister have any legs? This problem was solved when, on one occasion, she had to climb a step ladder and we saw more than we had bargained for!

Religious instruction consisted, of course, in learning the catechism by rote and being tested by Sister. From time to time Fr Salter would come in to instructed us and on one occasion as we were getting towards the end of the catechism, someone posed him a very difficult question regarding the 'Four sins crying out to God for vengeance'. We understood what defrauding labourers of their wages was but what was the 'Sin of Sodom'? Fr Salter was embarrassed, made his excuses and left leaving us really none the wiser!

On one occasion I swallowed my tooth water which barred me from going to Holy Communion, because in those days one still had to fast from food and water from midnight. Sister remarked that she hoped I wasn't getting scruples – I had no idea what that meant and on a walk into town she pointed out another church where I might like to go to Confession if needs be. Why she should suggest this I had not the slightest idea. After all we had had no sex education or any warning about what the onset of puberty might mean!

We had our celebration of fireworks – but never on November 5th – as only along the coast was Lewis where they still burned the Pope in effigy.

On one occasion I was train bearer to Archbishop Cowderoy at a Confirmation. The train was about twenty feet long and I could hardly see the prelate at the end of it. When he suddenly swung around, unannounced, to give his blessing, I was swung round on the end of it and nearly came to grief on the altar step.

I was also introduced to the delights of the Greek language – how many children can say they have learned Greek at their Primary School – and this certainly proved to be of some advantage in the years to come – but languages were never really my strength.

Coming home for the holidays was a great joy and I counted off the days until the homecoming. Generally in the winter months I stayed with the aunts in London, my 'town house', and to the country for the long summer holiday. Here I got to know my father better and marvelled at his skills.

As already related our property consisted of an acre of land on which stood four 18th century labourers cottages made into two. The smaller was practically derelict and had been converted into a workshop for the family business. Farm carts, wheels and all sorts of farm implements to be repaired were brought in to the extensive yard at the rear. These would be brightly painted and Adrian Bell recalls them in his book, *The Flower and the Wheel*. There were large woodsheds at the back and front of the cottage where ancient planks of oak and elm were stacked and a small corrugated iron hut which comprised a small forge for the metal work required on the tumbrels and a wood turning lathe. The cottage had the smell of wood shavings and of pitch to caulk the coffins. Everywhere was covered with cobwebs. The steady sound of sawing could often be heard, clink of iron on anvil and the smell of glowing coke from the forge. On one occasion I remember sitting in the coffin father was making and handing him out the screws. But it was his skill at producing a cartwheel that was so amazing. This he did single handed apart from putting on the iron tyre which was tricky and he needed help. I remember pouring the water on the tire to shrink it and being fascinated by the rising steam; pouring boiling water on the coffin sides to warp them into shape and in addition there was the construction of many staved ladders which were much in demand before aluminium ones arrived.

The main cottage was quite large with a lean to at the back and a 'washus' and stable where the pony was kept. Ducks, geese, chickens, rabbits, bees, fruit trees, goats, were all part of the establishment, not to mention the cats.

We never went away for a holiday apart for a trip to Leigh-on-Sea to visit my mother's old work friends, Bill and Bunny Moore. They had a dingy and we sailed around some of the mud flats in the vicinity. Mother even made the attempt to put on a bathing costume and wade out into the water but I was none too keen as I had on an earlier occasion been knocked over by a wave and this had generally put me off water and swimming as has already been related. Living in the Suffolk countryside, I suppose, was a holiday in itself and there was always plenty to do although I missed the company of my school friends. Trips to Newmarket and Bury for shopping and the annual trip to see my mother's Carmelite friend at the Waterbeach convent were major operations and adventures and mother, ever hospitable, would welcome friends to come and stay for a week or two in addition to The Girls, as my aunts were called. My cousin Jonathan, Uncle Reg's boy from Horsham, the eldest of three, came down occasionally and that provided some company. At harvest time it was great fun watching the old binder cut the wheat and waiting for the rabbits to appear. We armed ourselves with some stout staves in order to whack one with the hope of providing a meal but we never succeeded. When the tall shocks, as we call them Suffolk, had been safely gathered in, the postmistress down the road, in true biblical style, would go round gleaning for her chickens.

Although we lived near Newmarket, racing never featured in our lives. We knew it was race week because the traffic through the village suddenly increased and the noise of cars would actually make us stand up from the table to see who was going by in their posh automobile. On race days the town was full of visitors and the notorious tipster, 'Prince Monolulu', decked out in his feather head dress and carrying an old shopping bag would take to the streets. 'I've got a horse', was his famous cry. I was terrified that one day we might meet this rather awe inspiring figure. And sure enough, one afternoon, we came face to face with him. He put his hands on my head and said: 'You'll be a jockey'. Well I might have had the build but his prophecy didn't come true – apart from my riding exploits at school already mentioned.

Visits to the Old Scotch Tea Rooms in The Avenue for coffee was a treat but I was terrified when aunt Dorothy, who did not take sugar in her tea, insisted on concealing her quota of sugar lumps in her hand bag. I was quite sure she would be arrested for theft. Another treat was a small portion of hard ice cream, from Dolfe's, rolled in paper which we consumed on cream crackers in the car on Duchess Drive. Once we went to the Newmarket Kingsway cinema to see *Seven Brides for Seven Brothers*.

On a Sunday afternoon father, in his Sunday best, would go visiting his sister Eva Docking in Bury Lane. Eva lived in very primitive conditions. The cottage, now Orchard Cottage, was cold, dark and damp and she really did put me in mind of Miss Havisham. A large print of Queen Victoria hung on the wall and there was a strong smell of apples coming from her pantry. I was consigned to a horse hair sofa whose contents pricked the back of me legs. Eva had been widowed early and had no family except my cousin Jim Seymour who would come down regularly to visit her. I liked Jim and his brother as they were nearer my own age and taught me how to fly a kite. Eva had been a nanny and worked in Gorlestone. I was rather scared of her. She was rather a grumpy sort of person who was not concerned much for her clothing, perpetually living in an overcoat complete with brown beret. I was struck dumb in her presence and no wonder as she would say: 'Hasn't the boy a tongue in his head?' She had an old piano and when I could play a bit I would have to give a rendering of *Jesus bids us shine*, while her bony hands appeared over my shoulders to show me how it should be done. She kept a large flock of chickens of which I was scared as already one of my father's cockerels had seen fit to defend his wives by attacking me on one occasion.

Although I had been learning the piano we had no piano at home, apart from my aunts' piano at the flat, and so I would go down to *The Star* public house in the village to practice. The publicans were Fred and Connie Kitcat. I was a little worried seeing the notice over the doorway that stated that no child under sixteen was allowed in the room. Again my law abiding sense and fear of the law came to the fore. My mother had a rather nice gramophone complete with cabinet and this was my first introduction to classical music with the *Il Seraglio* and *Marriage of Figaro Overtures*, *Minuet in G* and *O for the Wings of the a Dove* with Ernest Lough. There were records of Benediction and High Mass and other lighter records, perhaps reflecting my mother's youth - *Stop your tickling Jock, Turn it round the other way, Timothy* and *Ali Baba's Camel*. I liked finding out how things worked and sadly eventually the machine came to pieces and was turned into a storage box for blankets!

My father had acquired an old shepherd's hut and this became my playroom. As already mentioned I created a little chapel there for awhile but it was here that I constructed my Meccano models and played on an old harmonium that had been thrown out of a local chapel. It was at this point we first met the notorious Fr Oswald Baker, who came as a curate to our parish priest. He had formally been a Dominican Novice before joining the secular clergy. He was very kind and rigged up electricity for me as well as taking mother and me on our first trip to the Shrine of Our Lady at Walsingham.

1953 was Coronation Year. We heard the death of King George V1 announced on the radio and one of the Sisters commented on the poor misguided Protestant Archbishop of Canterbury. This did nothing to further my ecumenical understanding and was rather unhappy about her comments as most of my dearest relatives were Protestants. The great event was the arrival of the television and we all crowded around the flickering black and white screen to see the historic scenes of the Coronation. Television became a feature of school life and I was thrilled, on returning home for the holidays, to see an aerial sprouting from the chimney. To celebrate the Coronation we were all presented with commemorative books and lined the sea front at Hastings when the young Queen paid one of her first official visits as Warden of the Cinque Ports.

My exam results really weren't too bad. As I reached the end of my career at St Dominic's the problem was what to do with me next. There was the possibility of going to St Joseph's College at Ipswich but again there were going to be the problems of transport and the head teacher's reply was a little off putting. Through our Dominican contacts the possibility of Black-friars School at Laxton near Stamford was on the agenda but they didn't take boys until they were thirteen so letters were written to the prep school at Llanarth in Monmouthshire. But there again the upheaval for just one year or so was not really feasible and so I was to stay on at St. Dominic's until I was thirteen which was really far too old for the type of school St. Dominic's was. I had earlier passed the 11+ and I now sat for the Common Entrance exam along with Brendan Moran. Brendan would later join the Benedictines at Douai Abbey and become its prior. He was the brainier of the two. I passed and so was destined therefore to continue my Dominican education. And so I ended by career at St Dominic's as head boy and had the privilege of declaring: 'Three cheers for St. Dominic's as we left the front door for the last time.

CHAPTER FOUR

BLACKFRIARS SCHOOL
LAXTON
1954 – 1959

THIRD FORM   And now it was the move to the big school. I knew something about Tom Brown's School Days and was apprehensive that life might be along those lines. Strange to say, in these modern times, neither parents nor I visited the school beforehand and so had little idea of what it looked like (apart from photographs in the prospectus) or who the staff were. All we knew was that it was in remote Northamptonshire countryside some-where between Stamford and Corby. We had to rely entirely on the recom-mendations we had received from Brother Sylvester and our innate trust in the Dominican Order. The Dominicans, founded in 13th century by St. Dominic, popularly known as the Order of Preachers, were mendicant Friars before the Reformation. They were the intellectual big guns of the Church, so it was with some anxiety and trepidation that I began this next phase of life. My usual reluctance at being sent away from home received the kindly reply that, 'it wasn't as though you are being sent to 'The Front''. I had no reply to this as the folks had lost several close friends in the First War.

Parents could visit and especially at Whitsun for the annual Old Boys' cricket match and in letters home I hinted that it would be nice to see the folks, knowing that they probably wouldn't be able to make it. There were no parents' evenings and I stood in fear when the dreaded envelope appeared containing the end of term report. This was doubly burdensome as the report had to be sent to the local authority in order to determine the grant they would be willing to pay to help with the fees. The only time my relatives visited me was when mother and aunt hired a car to come and collect me and my belongings on the day I left the school. A visit would have been impossible since the school was in the back of beyond with poor communication and mother's old car would never have made the journey. It was a great shame and sadness, though, as I could never really share with them what life was like and during adolescent years, when it is usually difficult to communicate with parents anyway. The many hurts and knocks that are inevitable in such an establishment became bottled up. I had the feeling that since the parents had made so many sacrifices to get me to such a school it was incumbent on me to make the best of it and not to cause them further worry. My letters home give the appearance of optimism and I can't say that I was really unhappy though there were times when I was utterly miserable, going for long lonely walks on free afternoons. I suppose, in the end, the experience made me more resilient and reliant on my own resources rather than running home all the time to mother.

And so with trunk again sent Passenger Luggage in Advance (PLA) and wearing my brand new black blazer with the Dominican crest and its motto *Veritas* (Truth) crowned with a brilliantly red Cardinal's hat and with my little suitcase I joined the boys at Kings Cross Station. They were an assorted bunch with one very large rather arty looking family who were the Nuttgens. It was young Joseph that joined us. This family, I would discover, were skilled in stain glass window design and another boy, Gilbert Kilbride, from the distinguished family of weavers based at Ditchling. We were met by Fr Kieran Mulvey OP who was fondly known as 'Pongo'. I got off to a very bad start. I was the only boy in the group who had not been to the preparatory and there was the humiliating detail that I was still wearing short trousers, while everyone else was in longs! I felt terribly alone and for part of the journey I stood in the corridor biting my lip until someone thought of inviting me inside the carriage.

The journey took us to Peterborough where we changed stations for the branch line which tracked through some delightful countryside and villages, Kingscliffe, Nassington, Yarwell and, at last, our destination station at the twin villages of Wakerley and Barrowden. From here a coach ferried us to the school. For some reason or other, which I was to learn later, a great cheer went up as we passed the pub called 'The Stafford Knot' in Wakerley and then on through the dark gloom of Wakerley Woods, part of Rockingham forest, until, passing the old lodge gate, we reached the entrance of the drive to the house. What a drive it was – apart from the uneven surface which was full of potholes it was extraordinarily long and we bumped along until at last in the dusk the bulk of Laxton Hall loomed before us.

The building itself was a minor Georgian Mansion, designed by George Dance, the younger, and belonging originally to the Carbery family, formerly of Carbery, County Cork. Eventually it was sold to the Dominican Order and in 1924 Fr Jerome Rigby OP became the first head master, followed by Fr

Bertrand Pike and in 1932 Fr Henry St John succeeded. It was during his term of office that the school entered its, 'most richly creative and formative period of its modern history'. He would later found the preparatory school at Llanarth Court in Monmouthshire. The traditions of the school went back as far as 1659 being founded by the Dominican, Cardinal Howard, at Bornhem in Flanders for boys from England wanting to pursue a Catholic Education during the penal times. After several changes of venue it came to its final resting place here at Laxton Hall.

Laxton Hall stood in fine countryside and miles away from any human contact, compared with St Dominic's which was at least in the middle of a town. This had some advantages but of not much help when growing up as one needed to be integrated into a wider world. From the front of the house was a magnificent view over Laxton Park with the spire of the parish church in the distance framed by mature beech and oak trees. Here some important battle had been fought with the Romans. The author of the *Opium Eaters*, Thomas de Quincey, had stayed here as a boy while another worthy had noted that here was one of the most beautiful vistas in England. At night the glow of Corby Candle, part of the Stewart and Lloyds steel works, could be seen in the distance and whose great walking draglines scarred the surrounding attractive countryside by excavating for iron ore in the open cast mines. At the entrance to the park was the Wilderness with a variety of trees formerly planted for the leisure of the family and now the special preserve of the fifth and sixth formers. In the distance were Wakerley Woods and several playing fields marked out with rugby posts.

The main portico once columned, now filled in to create additional rooms, opened into a large central hall with a magnificent cupola that let in the light. Here we would assemble before meals for praise or correction from the head master and where on occasion a great scrum ensued when a team member was awarded his Rugby Colours, thrown down from a pillared gallery at the far end by the captain. It was also the setting for school plays until a purpose built stage was constructed elsewhere. There was a fine library of hundreds of books and the once grand sitting rooms had been turned into class rooms or refectory. A domestic staff of Italian maids lived somewhere in an adjoining building where the kitchens were situated. These were well off limits and out of sight though it was not unknown for a boy to make the occasional contact! The chapel was housed in what was originally the Orangery. The hallowed turf of the cricket field lay between the house and the park and one could see the uprights of the rugger posts of three other playing fields. Rugby, Cricket and Hockey were the only sports taken seriously although there were a couple of tennis courts, but there were no other sporting activities, neither riding, which I had so enjoyed at St. Dominic's, athletics or activities, usually associated with a senior school and there wasn't even a gym. In view of a lack of provision for such sporting endeavours there was no end of term sports day to show off one's prowess. The only athletic venture was the cross country run once a week which I could just about tolerate. If you wanted to swim – in the summer that is – then some hardy souls would go skinny dipping in the lake at a nearby ruined mansion, Fineshade Abbey. I never risked swimming until in my last year when I took the plunge in the river Welland near the railway station! Neither was there any prize giving at the end of term. But this seemed to be part of the philosophy of the school apart from the shear lack of human resources which would have made such events difficult to sustain. Fr Henry saw school not, 'just a machine for imparting information or a laboratory or gymnasium but the constant realisation of a vision and spirit - a family spirit. Religion, too, was not so much a subject to be learned but to be lived and there was encouragement of freedom of speech in discussion and formation of opinion with the emphasis on classics, literature and the other arts'. - so wrote Fr Gerald Vann OP, a former head as a tribute to him. But there was a realisation that science, too, was required in the modern world and the building of a laboratory plus dormitory witnessed to this and delayed our return to school that first autumn by a week or two.

So the lad, who had been head boy at his previous school, small for his age, was now just an unknown quantity. I felt bewildered and lonely and as I took in the architecture one boy, pointing to an overhead grating, informed me that it was from there that a previous butler had hanged himself as well as there being the 'Grey Lady' who haunted the place. My first impressions of the school, writing in my first letter home, were that 'it was huge with a creeper clinging to a classical cornice'.I knew not a soul among my peers. Two brothers, Jim and Joe Hopkinson, with whom I had been friendly at my last school were in the year above but the only consolation I had from them was that I would, 'soon settle down'. So I just had to grit my teeth and soldier on.

There was a shop where you could buy sweets, jam and sugar. The latter you could use at tea time and keep stored in a cupboard. We had films once a fortnight and there was a good variety and also a gramophone concert too, but we were not in possession of a TV. Our daily routine was up at 7 am and bed at 9.15 pm. And while at St Dominic's I was not allowed my favourite comic here I looked forward to getting *The Eagle* every week. Already one was faced with a choice of subjects – between Geography and Greek. I chose the latter as I thought it might be of more use in the future. Every morning after breakfast we were required to go for the morning walk – a stiff twenty minute walk up to the park gates and back. Not a bad idea but some boys always succeeded in 'skiving off'.

Blackfriars, like St Dominic's, was a small school with seventy six on the role. This enabled it to preserve a more intimate character and was good because apart from small classes you got to know the masters well and they you at a more personal level but there were obvious disadvantages too. Numbers, over the years, gradually rose to about a hundred and there were eventually big plans for the school's expansion but, sadly, in the 1960's due to lack of personnel and modern developments in education, the school had to close, sold to a rogue who short changed the sellers. But today it is back in Catholic hands as a home for retired Polish people

My first 'dorm' was the West Dormitory. It overlooked the park and the Penance Walk. The latter divided the front lawns from the cricket pitch with a sundial at one end. Here a prefect or master could send you for some misdemeanour or other and for a specified time. There you would have to walk back and forwards, with head bowed and hands behind your back in the full view of the house to contemplate you misdeeds and repent of your sins. I only spent one session there for a misdeed that I cannot now remember.

On our first night in West Dormitory, which held about a dozen beds, our priestly overseer summoned us one by one to his room. He was Fr Kieran Mulvey, who had met us at the station and taught French. We dreaded French on Fridays because he hated fish and this always put him in a bad mood. Summoned into his room we had to stand in a certain position so that we would know what to do if we were ever sent to him for a whacking. This was enough to put the fear of God into you from the start! But there were compensations because of the view across the park.

Lessons began and the inevitable sorting of books etc. My first bad experience in the railway carriage was now compounded further. I had done quite well in the Common Entrance exam but I was on the borderline of being put a form higher into the Fourth Form. The authorities decided that I hadn't quite made that grade so I was left in the Third Form. The unfortunate result was that I was placed at the top of the class and in those days we were seated according to our position in form. So there I was right at the top. This did not make me very popular since I was the only boy not coming from the Prep School and having quite a polished accent at that time – due to the good offices of Mrs Brown, it was all rather difficult. This did not give me much confidence in my self or my abilities and so much to mother's dismay I gradually drifted downwards in position during my progress in form! But anyway I got to work and into the routine and I made friends and acquired the nick name, 'Freddy', which was, I suppose, a good sign that I had been accepted and generally I got along well with people.

The fifth form, notoriously a difficult class, used to put new boys through something of tough time. We didn't have such a thing as fagging – but you could be 'common roomed'. If you offended some member of the fifth form or were a new boy you could be hauled off to their pad down in the old servants' quarters of the house in the basement. I was duly kidnapped and stood on the billiard table, surrounded by spotty teenagers wielding billiard cues and really not knowing what was going to happen. The word had got round that I could sing and mercifully all that was required was that I should demonstrate something of my skills. In my piping treble voice I rendered some ditty while these lads with half broken voices mocked my efforts. Whether my peers underwent any such initiation I known not – but stories went round that sometimes a boy who upset a fifth former was likely to be dragged down to the cavern, de bagged and a dose of black boot polish administered to his rear end! Whether the masters ever knew of this I don't know or even whether it ever actually happened – but the fear of the threat was there! In addition there was the rather painful experience of being 'hollybushed' - this needs no description!

Although religion was an important part of our lives it was not forced down our throats. We never had an end of term exam in the subject. According to good Dominican tradition we were encouraged to question and to think for ourselves. There was half an hour of RE / Scripture first thing in the morning and in the evening we all trooped across the lawn to the chapel and joined with the Fathers in the singing of Compline – in those days in Latin. This was something that we really quite enjoyed. The short walk across the lawn was always memorable in winter time, on a clear night, when the great constellation of Orion would dominate the sky. Even daily Mass was not compulsory - at least we weren't required to go every day but could choose a couple of days a week when we could have a lie in after putting our names down in a book the night before. This obviated the necessity for rough treatment by the duty prefect who roused us in the morning treating recalcitrant risers with a swift stripping of his blankets. On Sundays we would have a 'Conference' on some spiritual topic by a member of the staff and there would be a short Retreat at the appropriate time given by a visiting priest. We learned to serve Mass according to the now sadly defunct Dominican Rite. Daily Mass was a dialogue Mass and so we were quite advanced for the time in learning to participate in the Liturgy. The spirituality of the Dominicans *comtemplata aliis tradere'* (having meditated on the Faith, pass it on to others) was at the heart of life. That luminous spiritual writer, Fr Gerald Vann, had been head teacher for some years just before I came and that other great Scripture scholar, Sebastian Bullough, a great friend of my Uncle Reg, had also been a teacher. He was best remembered in his classes for teaching boys how to dismantle and reconstruct his Norton Motor Bike which he was famed for riding. There was, then, a very healthy approach to religion.

Weekly Confessions were held as was the custom or one could go at any time to one of the Fathers in their rooms. This trying time of adolescent development tended to be uppermost in many people's minds. The failure to keep pure for a week and the threat of mortal sin lead to the peculiarly Catholic requirement of abstaining from Holy Communion before a rush to Confession at the end of the week! This penalty was never spelt out by the Fathers and tended to be passed on by oral tradition. Here traditional Catholic guilt about sex had its perhaps sometimes negative effects.

We were encouraged to read and, apart from times for prep, an hour was set aside in the evening when we read some piece of literature of our own choosing and supervised by one of the prefects, who had a limited authority in dealing out lines or penance walks or referring more serious breaches of discipline to the head master.

Among the prefects at the time was Michael Astill. He was every inch a prefect and little did we realise that some fifty years later he would be the judge in 2007 who condemned the Blue Water terrorists to life imprisonment. These sixth form worthies had their own prefects' room and were allowed to smoke as were the fifth formers down in what was the Wilderness. I informed the folks back home about this adding, 'but some of the fourth form smoke behind the bushes'. This permission to smoke was, I suppose, 'enlightened' for those days and come the Christmas party at the end of term we were all given a cigarette to puff on. Some boys were already hooked on the weed and others, with some enterprise, would look for stalks in their baccy to send off to Players or Wills and received in return a brand new pack! Others started curing their own tobacco leaves. I succumbed on occasion but, fortunately, not in any big way.

My next challenge was to cope with games. At St Dominic's we only played football and cricket. Here, as already recalled, it was rugby, hockey and cricket and really no room for anything else- certainly not the game with the round ball. There were a couple of tennis courts but this was not taken seriously. As we had no gymnasium there was nowhere to exercise and so all the effort was put into these games and the weekly cross country run. This was a pity as some of us were not of the build for rugby and it became something of a cross to bear. For some reason I was always put on the wing and once nearly scored a try. To my amazement, with not much of a clue about rules except that one had to pass backwards, I was, on one occasion, made captain of a 'Small' game – as the junior game was described and horror of horrors even the hooker in a scrum. But I suppose this was all good for character building. Hockey wasn't much better but then most of the games were snowed off. But it was the sheer misery and dread of turning out on a cold day and standing there shivering waiting for the ball to be chucked in my direction. Cricket wasn't too bad, but I did miss the riding. We played all the surrounding posh public schools such as Stamford, Oakham, Uppingham and Oundle and on playing the Catholic Radcliffe College boys came back with tales of individual rooms for sixth formers and other civilised improvements.. There was none of that for us and we were in dormitories right up until the end. It was with some relief that I developed an in- growing toenail and athlete's foot and so had a legitimate excuse, for awhile, to get exemption from games from the prefects. Showers were compulsory after a match and we all piled in together. To begin with it was rather a shock to the system since at primary school we had all been modestly clothed in waterproof shorts and I had just not been used to seeing a seething mass of naked bodies of all ages.

The dormitories were the traditional lay out but two – Big Indian and Little Indian Dormitories were extraordinary in that some magnificent murals of Indian scenes adorned the walls. At the time we hardly appreciated them except for the bare bosomed beauties of the Indian King which introduced us to the opposite sex. Sadly when the school was sold these unique murals were torn out and presumably disposed of on the black market. In addition there was the famous painting of *Venus Rising from the Foam* by Botticelli that adorned the main master's staircase and was always a talking point.

It was then an all male environment and was something of a contrast from an all nun environment. However as I wrote home, 'I like the Fathers better than the Sisters because they ask you if you are clear about a subject and if not explain it again'. The only feminine input, then, were the aforementioned Italian maids who cooked and cleaned and the matron, Mrs. Hole.

The family managed to get their pennies together for me to continue with piano lessons. The master was an eccentric gentleman who came in from Stamford. He was a delightful character by name, Raphael Gabriel Gomer, and we had many happy lessons on the old Bechstein piano in the basement. On occasions we would go to his house in Rock Terrace in Stamford where his housekeeper, Mrs Saunders, would give us tea and we would practise our grade pieces. 'Gabby', as we called him, remembered seeing the young Sir Malcolm Sergeant walking past on his way to school. He would organise the occasional concert when we could show off our skills. Being a Dorset man he had a rich accent and his cousin, Father Adams with a wooden leg, was parish priest in Stamford. His main joke was to nudge you in the ribs if you made a mistake – it's <u>B</u> flat, son – with a knowing chortle and a twinkle in this eye.

One boy I became particularly friendly with in the first two years was Michael Murray Robertson who was a very gifted pianist. He left early as he was unhappy with the standard of music teaching – going to the Guildhall School of Music, he then studied the viola under Max Rostal. I stayed with him one holiday and we went to our first prom at the Albert Hall – The Planets, Enigma Variation and the Introduction and Allegro for Strings. We 'prommed' but I couldn't really appreciate the music as it was so tiring standing all the time.

Food was always critical for hungry boys. We always had brown bread and for breakfast it was porridge followed by bacon and fried bread and coffee. We never starved but there were the occasional near riot when the quality of the food did not come up to our standards such as when a batch of liver appeared to have green marks on it – a sure sign, to us boys, that it had been condemned and then there was the enigmatic. ''art done up'. Since the food had to make a long journey from the kitchens and then via the dumb waiter it was not always as hot as it might have been.

What am I to say of our teachers? Being Dominicans they were very much individuals - one might say even eccentric. The pressure of celibate men living together in community brings with it all sorts of problems of which the average person is unaware. The clash of personalities that sometimes occurred was soon picked up by us boys and a great source of gossip. They rarely wore their religious habit except on official duties and donned any old clothing that came to hand. However for the most part they were very popular and there was a good relationship all round. Being a small school we could get to know each other and there was informality between teacher and pupil outside school hours. The head master in the first year was Fr Ralph Hodsoll whose twin brother, another Dominican priest, was called Cyril, and as like as two peas in the pod. Ralph was the fiercer of the two. He was tall and ascetic and his pebble glassed spectacles added to the severity of his mien. His abrupt manner belied a gentler side. On one occasion a boy was sent up for six of the best. He put gloves on and assured him that it would hurt him more than the victim! But there was generally an enlightened apporach to corporal punishment compared with reports from other schools.

Fr Ralph always seemed formidable especially when coming in late for a Latin class having walked out the matron and her dog. He would curl up the dog's lead and peer at you through the hole with his pebble glasses while firing a question about an irregular verb. He told us about English words that derived from Greek ones and this could lead on to the more interesting red herrings such the construction of television valves, how to differentiate between species of trees and how to slim and keep fit.

Fr Hugh Nash was a former World War Two fighter pilot and newly ordained. He was very much a man's man with a shock of black hair and beetling brows. He had a suppressed vocabulary that would be unleashed on the rugby field and would sometimes threaten a ' blood bath' if certain matters were not satisfactorily covered in the maths class. Some years later Hugh after studying for a degree at Cambridge would leave the Order, return to his name of Kevin and raise a family. But he was popular especially with those who were keen on sports and he could be seen reading his breviary while walking around the sacred turf of the cricket pitch.

Fr Gerard Meath

Fr Gerard Meath, a graduate in English was a Mancunian, round and rubicund, with a fine resonating voice and an organist, succeeded Fr Ralph as head teacher. He was every inch the headmaster. Benign and yet a strict disciplinarian he could summon up a suitable temper when dealing with breaches of discipline and turning an apt puce. But he was a good authoritative teacher in whom one could have confidence. In later years he would become Provincial of the Order, work at the Catholic Communications Centre at Hatch End, do broadcasts and conduct retreats before coming to Blackfriars in Cambridge where I would meet him again later in my story. Gerard had acquired the nick name 'Yod'. This came about through his singing one of the psalms during Holy Week which began with that Hebrew letter.

Fr Vincent Pizzala, an Oxford graduate in classics, in his mid thirties and a competent teacher, with a pippin face and sometimes very stern with a stentorian voice when being serious. Classics were everything for him and he probably had the best academic head on his shoulders than any of the other masters.

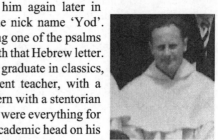
Fr Vincent Pizzala

Fr Aloysius Murray also joined the staff and acted as bursar. He was very popular when it came to celebrating Mass as he could get through the whole liturgy in fifteen minutes flat.

Finally there was Fr Anthony Ross. One can say he was the most popular 'Dad'. A short stocky Scot, he had been disinherited by his family when he became a Catholic. His teaching was not exactly inspirational and one could

Fr Anthony Ross

perhaps drift off during his spiritual conferences. However he had an excellent rapport with the boys. He loved a scrap as he had been an amateur wrestler in his time. He could often be seen under a pile of boys testing their strength in arm wrestling or the latest lock. He produced the plays and as with most of the other Fathers he held open house in his room in the evening when we could go in to have a chat, read his books, and have some quality time. On one occasion it occurred to him that I might need some sex education – but by then, I had learned most of the facts of life from my peers, from books and from the mating habits of butterflies and his description of the antics of the horse – since he knew I came from the country – was slightly bizarre. But this was a small point. He could engage with us and we could discuss the Faith if need be. In later years he would become novice master at Woodchester, Chancellor of Edinburgh University, Prior Provincial of the Order, a distinguished Scottish historian, and a worker among the poor of Edinburgh.

Winters were pretty hard in those days and with lots of snow. At least the latter meant that rugby games were abandoned and this enabled a little bit of sledging to be enjoyed down the steep slope in the park. A variety of sledges appeared as boys and sometimes the masters took the precipitous slide down to the little bridge, or rather a plank over the rivulet that claimed to be the river Lax. With the cold weather came a great deal of shivering especially when going to bed and being almost frozen to the sheets. The water was not exactly warm to wash in the morning as the antique plumbing system was hardly adequate and come November of my first term the system was on the point of breaking down with cold water to wash in and more or less the same with baths. In the new dormitory, the wooden building adjoining the main block, where the senior boys slept, the flannels had been known to freeze over night – and there was the question of keeping the windows open during the sleeping hours. It certainly toughened us up. However moving to the dormitory over the kitchen block, as we did in the fifth form, did have the advantage of some warmth coming from below even though in the summer months it could become oppressively hot.

As already recounted we were encouraged to read and books could be taken out from the extensive library and so our horizons were widened. *The*

Lord of the Rings had just been published and so I was soon engrossed in this great saga of Middle Earth. There were various hobbies and clubs we could join. For awhile I joined the printers in the old stable block. We set up our own letter heads and printed off small orders for notepaper. This was all done by hand compositing the type faces in the traditional manner. The music society attracted me and some evenings the old wind up gramophone with its huge 'His Master's Voice' speaker was wheeled out and we were introduced to the wonders of Beethoven and Mozart on the old shellac disks while someone was designated to sharpen the wooden needles. Others of a less classical bent started a Jazz Club and Skiffle group with tea chest and wash board and eventually the new matron, Marianne Catteral, formed a small orchestra where I played the treble recorder, though being such a small school we had rather a limited supply of talent to draw on. Occasionally Mr. Gomer would organise a concert when his pupils could show off their skills which was usually timed to coincide with St. Cecilia's Day, the patron of music. Another group did some taxidermy by skinning the occasional mole and preserving it while others went so far as to curing their own tobacco. My main interest was entomology and I would send off to L Hugh Newman's Butterfly Farm in Kent for caterpillars to raise and breed. Come the summer term it was a delight to go roaming in the Wakerley Woods with my butterfly net hunting down Pearl Bordered and Silver Washed Fritillaries, White Admirals and Marbled Whites. I even caught a Duke of Burgundy Fritillary. We didn't have much idea of conservation in those days. In the Fineshade Woods there was always the possibility of catching a Purple Emperor which luckily we never found. I had become friendly with a boy from Cambridge – Jo Ibbett whom I joined on expeditions. His brother John became a firm friend and we pursued the same hobby and kept in touch for many years. As we hunted in the woods there was nothing more redolent of an English summer with the smell of wild strawberries and garlic as in the distance the sound of ball on bat could be heard as the keen sportsman played some visiting team.

On occasion we enjoyed a 'month day', usually coinciding with the need to use the school premises for other requirements such as a clergy retreat. This was a day when we had to fend for ourselves. We were issued with regulation sandwiches and were told to go out and amuse ourselves. To begin with we could go into towns and by various means either by hitching, public transport, by bike or on foot boys disappeared to the four corners of the country. Later we were not allowed to go into any towns and had to use our own two feet. Three of us on one occasion walked the ten miles to Fotheringhay to visit the site of Mary Queen of Scots's execution. On another occasion I was on my own walking towards Uppingham when someone stopped and offered to give me a lift. Thank heavens I refused it. I might have become a victim of I don't know what atrocity. But in those days there was not much fear of kidnapping and the horrors we encounter today. The roads were largely empty. Other boys were more enterprising and a competition was held as to who could hitch-hike to London, York and Manchester. It seems they succeeded but didn't arrive back until after midnight.There must have been reprisals! There was a well equipped woodwork shop and for awhile I tried not too successfully to follow in my father's footsteps. Billy Bryce was a good teacher but I found I was not getting on too well chamfering squares of wood that would go to make up the feet of a lamp stand. I found I was much better at working in cardboard and Micromodels became a favourite. These miniature pieces of architecture ranged from the London City Gates to Old London Bridge and from the Globe Theatre to Hampton Court Palace which was quite a challenge and still adorn my shelves to this day. Eventually I started working on a model of the school itself. Model making became something of an obsession which continued throughout the years.

FOURTH FORM And so the first year passed and I moved up into the fourth form and into the Little Indian dormitory with about five beds and the magnificent murals. The classroom was over the front porch and so rather out of the way. Hormones were rising and some boys became over active. Bridget Bardot was the pinup but there were not many signs of posters concealed in lockers as I had seen when uncle Reg took me round Christ's Hospital. Fr Vincent had the habit of 'snooping' – standing outside the door listening for trouble and then suddenly bursting in to apprehend the culprits. However he missed out on the lad who set light to a waste paper basket which went into a tea chest and then in desperation thrown out of the window in flames and just missing the bike shed. Fr V had been in the scouting movement and some boys went with him up into the woods to help clear up fallen trees and dig out the drainage system.

Fr Gerard had become the new headmaster and we could now in the evening pursue our various hobbies, be that bookbinding, printing, or as it was described the 'destructive' pursuit of butterfly collecting. Milder pursuits such as stamp, match-box or cheese label collecting were carried on in the class room. However a great gap was any tuition in drawing, painting or art of any description. You were left to your own devices if you wished to pursue that course.

I commented, 'Nuttgens says that he says that he won't make a very good artist, and that he'll be a journalist instead, but we're trying to convince him that he is good, which of course he is.' Both he and 'Gillie' Kilbride left the school early and pursued a successful career in the stained glass and weavers' trade. One boy, Paul Colsell succeeded in passing Art at A level. How he achieved this is something of a mystery. He must have been very enterprising.

The only female influence in the school was matron. The first, Mrs Hole, appeared to be quite motherly and I commented that she was rather like the actress Betty Hardy. However one was not sure of her medical skills. Her main incantation over a boy going for some comfort in his illness was – *Oh you boys are all the same* – and in a famous poem that I wrote quite shamelessly for an English exercise and causing some mirth in the staff room, was based on: *I wish loved the human race, I wish I loved its silly face……*I developed lines such as *...I wish I loved old cook downstairs though food could do without her hairs and in the soup old fishy bones…… and then to matron we would go.. and with cascara dose our pains.* Yes, cascara was the main treatment. On one occasion this went too far when the boy was diagnosed with appendicitis and was rushed to hospital! She was not, then, exactly the motherly type which some of us younger boys perhaps could have done with. She presided over the laundry and we would get a clean shirt, two pairs of socks and two hankies each week and a clean vest and pants once a fortnight.

Come October we celebrated as usual the Feast of the Holy Rosary. An important Feast for the Dominicans as they always claimed that St Dominic had invented the Rosary and it also commemorated the famous sea battle of Lepanto that defeated the Turks in the sixteenth century. The Fathers, like the Sisters, always wore a large string of rosary beads from their belt. On this day, at Mass, a blessed rose was given to everyone – a petal of which to this day I have pressed somewhere in my prayer book. To celebrate the Feast we had tinned cherries and grapefruit for breakfast in addition to buns and cornflakes and there was a slap up supper in the evening followed by a gramophone concert. We were urged to be socially conscience, too, and a box for contributions to the Dominican Mission in Granada, which had been devastated by a hurricane, was on prominent display.

Mrs Hole, the matron, retired and her successor was Miss Marianne Catterall. She had a prestigious build and every inch the temperamental prima Donna. She had served in the RAF and was said to have been a rear gunner. She was a fine violinist and the daughter of Arthur Catterall who had been a distinguished violinist and conductor of the Halle orchestra. She had an equally famous sister, Yvonne, who was a concert pianist and whose husband, Hugh Dinwiddy, a former Cambridge blue, had once been a master in the school. Yvonne came on occasion to give us a fantastic recital of Beethoven's *Appassionata Sonata,* which inspired me in my love for that composer. She thought my playing was quite good considering I had rather small hands.

Matron

Marianne would from time to time throw temperamental wobblies and several times threatened to resign. She was known also to brew her own beer as the aroma of the hops would sometimes permeate the basement. As I commented home, 'She's like the nurse at St Dominic's, she thinks she runs the place'. And she probably nearly did!

A new lay master arrived, who replaced a very shy Mr Milne, who to everyone's amazement got engaged to a Spanish lady and became the scoop for the *Daily Weekly*, the form magazine run by Michael (Spike) D'Souza and Philip Durcan. This was in the person of Gordon Kerr. He was a rather dour Scot who received the uncomplimentary nickname of 'Slug'. He tried to enthuse us with English from our text book, *Pendlebury*. One day he would go on to become one of the most distinguished theologians and writers in the Dominican Order.

The Easter term saw a thick covering of snow and some short lived sledging. We experienced the coldest night since 1947 and I nearly froze to my bed sheets. Fr Anthony got some practice in public speaking going with the start of *Hat Nights*. Volunteers pulled a subject out of a hat and had to speak on it for two minutes. He led the evening with a dissertation on baked beans. I had become very self conscious and would not participate in this however I was roped in to my first play to take the part of Lucius in Shakespeare's *Julius Caesar* and with a second performance later in the spring I had graduated to that of Portia, Brutus's wife. I relished the words about being 'Brutus's Harlot – not his wife' – very daring.

A very exciting trip for those of us who studied Greek was to the Arts Theatre in Cambridge to see an all Greek production of the *Bacchae of Euripedes* which the sixth form had been studying as a set book. Although we could not understand very much of what was going on it was a most impressive performance and I was only sorry I could not have met up with the relatives who were only twenty miles or so away.

Easter was early and so we were at school for the Easter Vigil that year. It was most impressive as it was the first time that the revised liturgy of Holy Week came into operation. The Vigil was held later in the evening instead of first thing in the morning. A large brazier had been lit on the chapel steps and we all gathered round for the blessing of the new fire. It did not go without a hitch as the voice of Fr Gerard boomed out – 'Put that cigarette lighter out' –

someone had tried to be helpful in lighting their own candle instead of taking it from the Easter Candle. It was also the first time that we received Holy Communion on Good Friday. We started at 11 p.m. and were not finished till 1 a.m.

With the summer term of that year work began on replacing the ancient coal boilers in the basement and the redevelopment of the stable block to accommodate a spacious hall and stage and this added space allowed numbers to increase to ninety.

Mr Kerr left us to go to the novitiate at Woodchester Priory and he was replaced by Fr Aiden Deane, a newly ordained priest who had visited us earlier in the year to say Mass for us. He was a rather wan, languid and willowy figure and a French Canadian. He was very popular and we nicknamed him 'Trapper'. He would take French classes but was hopeless at keeping order. We also welcomed Mr Hurley from South Africa. He was the brother of the famous Bishop Hurley, who would be, in later years, as Archbishop of Durban, a voice against apartheid.

On Rogation days before Ascension we had the traditional procession around the walled kitchen gardens to sprinkle them with holy water and ask God's blessing for a fruitful harvest. I was cross bearer on this occasion and being misdirected I led the whole procession to a cul- de – sac. We had some difficulty retreating !

Something of a crisis now developed which lead to a desperate letter home:'Fr Gerard Meath informed us after lunch that the old tradition of forbidding of food parcels, except on birthdays, was to be revived, worse still was that he said that ALL FOOD OF ANY DESCRIPTION OR KIND TO BE GOT RID OF BY MONDAY MORNING. When he will come round and inspect our lockers. That means I shall have to get rid of ¾ of a jar of honey, two pots of paste, 3 boxes of cheeses, 1lb of sugar, ½ lb of marge, 2 packets of biscuits and 20 bars of chocolate and a few other things. What on earth shall I do? It's no good writing to him to say that the doctor says that I need more sugar because I know other boys' mothers will be doing the same. I am trying to think of a place to hide my chocolate. What am I to do with the wrest *(sic)* I don't know. Have you any ideas? Perhaps you could find a box so that I can send some of the things home. I don't know. Please answer by return if you have any ideas.' The box duly arrived and some of the contraband was returned.

The family were being loaded with other responsibilities for my livestock back at home,'You could give the frogs some live flies or spiders or anything like that if you see any'.

By this time my father was retiring and converting his old workshop into a habitable dwelling which would be occupied by my mother's cousin, Win.

There was also the excitement of main drainage coming to the village and I was sorry that I was not going to be around to pull the lever on our first inside low-flush lavatory – that would have to wait until the holidays.

I was finding history rather boring. I had come back late one term and missed a few weeks' lessons due to flue and had not really caught up. Such things as - the Irish Problem, and Salisbury's foreign policy (as far as I can see he didn't have one) did not really inspire me. But we did have an interesting talk by the actor parents of one boy, Simon Dyer, on the plays of Christopher Fry, which were in vogue at the time and several of which would be performed in the school and with *Xenophon's Anabasis* in Greek and *Caesar in Alexandria* in Latin our noses were really at the grind stone.

I dreaded the time when the exam results came because although at last mother got some help from the local authority this was conditional on my results. I had been drifting down to about half way in the class and mother was getting very uptight and anxious about my seeming lack of academic progress. Fr Gerard Meath, was very good in reassuring her that this was natural in the development of a boy. Having done well in the prep school, nature restored a balance as time went on and matters were made worse since some highly intelligent boys joining the class had pushed me further down – although in fact my marks were really quite reasonable. It took some time to convince mother that this was the reality - that it was the marks and not the position in class that mattered.

Another slight crisis was the loss of my clothes brush. Insignificant in itself it was important to me since I had been embarrassed by the fact that it took the form of what I described as a lavatory, or 'bog' brush in colloquial terms. This had provoked some ribaldry amongst my peers. I can't say I was sorry that it had gone but the relatives were rather upset – however much to my annoyance it did eventually turn up. But I never dared to use it for the purpose for which it was intended.

I had appeared to be growing just a bit as my trousers were now at 'half-mast' being four inches above my shoes and this was being remarked on. Come the summer term the weather became so dry that we were not allowed into the woods because of the possibility of fire no doubt remembering a boy who had burnt down a sizeable area of Wakerley Woods - smoking?

One major crisis erupted when a copy of Moravia's *'A Woman of Rome'* about the street women of Rome was found to be in circulation - just the thing to fuel the imagination of adolescent boys. What made it even more serious was that it was on the Church's list of forbidden books, *The Index,* and therefore penalties of excommunication could be involved. There was a certain panic until the book was retrieved and disposed of.My cricket prowess improved, being out for a duck against Stamford School and a scorer in the match again Oakham.

During the holidays my all American Uncle Frank over from the States. He had been appalled by the fact that at the age of fifteen I could still not ride a bicycle and so with his help I took to two wheels and never looked back. This really opened up a new world for me and borrowing a bike one summer's afternoon I cycled some twenty four miles – my furthest.

We made our annual trip to Waterbeach near Cambridge to see my mother's great friend Marjorie Humphries, the Carmelite nun, whose name in religion was Sr Mary Carmel of Jesus. As already related the Community had provided us with our goats. One was named *Waterbeach Walburga.* While at St Dominic's I had informed Sr Walburga that we had a goat by that name and for some reason she wasn't too amused! Converted to Roman Catholicism she had been disinherited by her mother until at the very end of her life she was allowed out of the convent to go and nurse her and reconciliation was effected. The Carmelites were a strictly enclosed Order of nuns. It always amused me after the challenging journey in the old car and finding the narrow entrance off the main road, scrunching over the gravel to the main door to be presented with The Turn. This was a sort of revolving cupboard set into the wall where you communicated with the Sr Portress. A quavery disembodied voice would respond to our ring on the bell to be told that the key of the chapel was on the Turn. This was most essential as it provided access not only to the chapel but also to the sole toilet. It was rather embarrassing gingerly tiptoeing over the echoing floor boards of the chapel to the toilet which went with a very loud flush, fearing that nuns were secretly listening or spying on the other side of the partition wall. It was then back to the little parlour and then into the room of 'the presence' to be confronted with an iron grill that extended the width of the room. Protruding from each intersection of the grill were large iron spikes that faced outwards. These were blunted and we were assured that this was not to keep the nuns in but to keep us out. Behind the grill was a wooden shutter behind which was a curtain. We waited in eager anticipation until we heard the rustle of rosary beads and the swish of the habit announcing Sr Mary of Carmel's arrival and first the curtain was drawn back and then the shutter and there she was framed in the grill. As mother was her only visitor she was allowed to see her face to face otherwise her veil would be down and you would see even less than a Muslim lady wearing a burka. Until the age of thirteen and the dangerous onset of puberty I was permitted to see her but after that I had to sit away from the main line of sight. Whose virtue was threatened by this operation I know not. Occasionally you would hear a little cough in the background. This was the Sister Chaperone who was always present at such interviews. During the conversation Sister never wasted a moment but worked away making rosary beads or embroidery etc. There were two draws under the grill through which you could pass objects, such as the latest photos of the family. From the other side might come rosary beads or the latest batch of kittens which would climb up the grill and be difficult to catch. Conversation was far ranging and the Sisters were well up to date on local and international news which provided an object for their prayer life. Sister was always interested in my Uncle Wilfred's large family – he had by this time eight of his own and one fostered - and I always had a sneaking feeling that in the dim past there may have been some romance between them. We were always regaled with a 'little tea', during our interviews, which mysteriously appeared in the outer parlour during one of our trips to the chapel. Sometimes it was a 'little lunch' provided at the lodge where the caretakers lived. The 'little' was always far more than we could cope with. When I had expressed, at some point, my interest in becoming a priest, I was immediately put at the head of their prayer list and with all that welter of prayer that would be ascending heavenwards in a sort of spiritual arm twisting spiral I really didn't stand a chance.

FIFTH FORM. Aunt Elsie was an expert curry maker long before it became the national dish. Before the war the founder of Veersawmy restaurant, a Mr. Palmer, an Anglo Indian established a curry factory at the bottom of the garden and the family developed a taste for it. Now it was a special treat for my cousins and me as a last meal before our return to school. On my return for the autumn term some of my peers thought I had grown a bit but, 'Dear old Father Ralph commented ' hm – he hasn't grown much has he?' At least I am no longer the smallest boy in the school and some only come up to my shoulder'.

The move to the fifth form did provide some privileges. We had our own common room in the old servants' quarters in the basement. We enjoyed a billiard table on which I had performed my solo of two years previous but not much else. The added privilege was access to the Wilderness garden and its magnificent trees adjoining the park where we were allowed to smoke. Fr Vincent had acquired a Jackdaw which one day flew off with a lighted cigarette in its beak and when on occasion I needed to go to Confession in his room the wretched bird had to be caught and confined under a waste paper basket – one hoped that it would be bound by the seal of Confession lest it picked up some of my misdemeanours and spread them round.

There were also confusing changes in the curriculum which were unsettling. Geography had suddenly become compulsory and there was now a choice between Greek and Science. Since I was now set on the priesthood and I had not been doing very well in Science I considered that I should stay with

Classics as being the most useful for the future. We were given anti TB jabs. Some boys came up with a big red patch and had to go off for an X-ray. I was lucky as all I got was a red ring with a yellow core which I assured the folk at home was due to needle reaction! A second injection followed some weeks later.

With numbers going up to eighty six the school was beginning to get very overcrowded especially in the chapel and plans were afoot to build an extension to take the side altars for the individual daily Mass. The sale of the old organ also helped to provide more room. My first introduction to the instrument had been through pumping air into it via a lever at the back. I dreaded failing in my duty which would have resulted in some very strange noises both from the organ and the organist!

In November I wrote home, 'Rats have been seen in the kitchen and matron says if she sees another one she will pack her bags, so several of the Fathers are setting mouse traps in their rooms. Fr Vincent has caught twelve mice and they all hope they catch a rat so they can plant it in matron's room.'

The sad news reached me that our friend Brother Sylvester had died and I got permission to go to the funeral. It was quite an adventure and I accompanied Fr Anthony down to Woodchester in Gloucestershire for the funeral. The countryside was beautiful and the priory was set in a valley. This has now been demolished but the church still remains. Sylvester stayed with us at home on one occasion and it was through him that I became interested in our heritage of English parish churches having been with him on several treks to view those in the locality. He was rather an eccentric character and this view was encouraged by his Dominican habit being far too short which displayed a pair of blue socks that hardly matched.

I had moved to one of the dormitories in a wing of the school that was immediately over the kitchens. This, as already related, became oppressively hot in the summer. Some boys succeeded in lifting a floor board and peering down through a grating into the kitchen below. It was none too pleasant watching the maids cutting up the meat on the table.

General Essays were now required of us. Mine was: *How to begin listening to Bach.* I'm glad that I didn't get: *Are the Americans politically hysterical?* We enjoyed one of our few educational outings. This was to the great Stewart and Lloyds steel works in Corby. Watching the great Bessemer furnaces at work and the strips of red hot steel on which men would fry their breakfasts was truly awesome. We were given a close view of the great walking drag line - the biggest of its kind in the world at the time. Now many years later with the closing of the works and the reclamation of the land it is difficult to imagine that the countryside had once been so devastated by the open cast mining.

The athletes foot and in growing toenail that had successfully excluded me from games had now cleared up so it was back to rugby again. Having not increased very much in bulk I commented, 'I could enjoy it but as there isn't much of me I always get knocked around with the result that it becomes an utter bore'.

Fr Gerard had started a junior branch of the Society of St Vincent de Paul for which I am very grateful. We met in Fr Gerard's room and after the suitable devotions we were allocated tasks for the coming week. This introduced us to practical Christianity. Occasionally a couple of us would visit an elderly lady, Mrs Hales, in Laxton village to weed her garden and were rewarded with tea and cake and strawberries in the summer time. Having now learned to ride a bike and being now the proud possessor of a new one I was able to visit further afield mainly some of the Irish families who had settled in the old huts on the disused airfield at Duddington some four miles away. This was my first contact with 'ordinary people'. They were real characters – the Regans, the Reilleys, and Gaughans. Towards the end of my stay we would catechise some of their children. I gained more experience in this 'parish visiting' than ever I was to do in later years at College.

Another group with whom we had some contact were the Distributists. Of Dominican origin they were a commune that lived in Laxton village following a sort of Christian/Communist ideal, farming the land without the use of modern mechanisation. These families would appear for the Sunday morning Mass which was open to all Catholics in the surrounding area. They had large families wore beards and were called 'Stribs' for short.

An innovation was the introduction of unofficial time for prep at the weekends. Very sensibly this was to get us used to working without the regimentation of the bell and encouraged us to use our own initiative as we would have to do in adulthood. Now the Middle East Situation dominated our discussions as the Suez crisis broke and there were heated arguments over whether Eden should have bombed the Suez airfields.

Fr Vincent, inspired by our visit to see the Greek play at Cambridge, was very keen to outdo Bradfield College which regularly put on a Greek Play in the original Greek. So since *Antigone* was the set book this year it was this play that we enacted. Some of the boys had prodigious memories to learn the lines in Greek. George Platen as Antigone was superb and Keith Howard as King Creon, equally so was Michael D'Souza (no relation to Edward De Souza, the actor and former old boy) as the blind prophet, Teiresias. I was given the part of the Queen Mother, Euridice. The six lines I had to declaim before I went off and committed suicides were really quite enough! We performed the work in the main hall since we had no theatre at the time and it received some good reviews. We were all dressed in various combinations of white sheets and the Chorus did their best to chant the music composed by Mr Gomer. As I wrote home, 'After the play we celebrated with some altar wine -it's all right it wasn't blessed or anything - and we only had half a glass and the alcohol content was only 18%.'

Fr Anthony, the producer of the plays and a great devotee of the playwright Christopher Fry now staged, *The Boy with the Cart* and *Thor with Angels* was next on the list.

But this was now the fateful 'O' level year and there was a great deal of swatting for exams. There was discussion about what careers we were going to go in for. The Dean, Michael Hawke, had won a scholarship to Dartmouth and would later rise to command a nuclear submarine. My friend Joe Ibbett, of butterfly exploits, had taken himself to the English College in Rome to train for the secular priesthood and this in some way inspired me to follow in his footsteps rather than joining the Dominicans. The thought of going on for the priesthood had been with me for some time and for which I seemed destined as there just didn't seem to be anything else, from my home experience, that I could put my hand to. I plucked up courage and told Fr Anthony and it seems the authorities were not too surprised. By this time at the age of sixteen boys were leaving and getting jobs and my father was met with the comment back at home, 'When's your boy going out to work?' and his brother Frank, in the States, was none too pleased when he learned of my intentions. His comment was that I should have joined the army or pursued a more lucrative career.

Another valuable school association was the Aquinas Society, named after that famous Dominican, St Thomas Aquinas. We had all sorts of outside speakers to broaden our minds – notably one, that stimulated much discussion, was by Fr Laurence Bright OP who spoke on *The Atom Bomb and the Moral Law*. He had been a nuclear scientist at Harwell and the implications of his research had led him to join the Order; Sir Tom O'Brien on *Trades Unions,* Professor Cameron on *Communism* and Dr Little on *Science Fiction*, to name but a few. A Medieval Disputation was also staged in its traditional form. Here arguments were put forward on both sides and the third participant brought the two together in a synthesis. There were also regular debates and the topics were far ranging: *That a classical education is most desirable, That modern warfare is immoral, That Lancashire and Yorkshire are the cream of England, That this house deplores boarding schools, That this house deplores smoking in the lower school* (some eyebrows were raised) and one fascinating event was the staging of a mock trial. Interest in music continued with the Musical Society at the highbrow end and the Jazz come Skiffle group at the other – who produced two tunes – *John Henry* and *The Saints*.

Our appreciation of the wider Church increased with the arrival of Abba Kidane, a Coptic priest. His Liturgy which normally lasted three hours was reduced to a comfortable three quarters and there was the added interest of being able to receive Holy Communion under the form of both bread and wine.

Some boys had been experimenting with explosives – sodium chlorate and sugar - and there were some rather alarming and dangerous explosions occurring. Fr Ralph had himself been up to something and succeeded in blowing a hole through his window at the top of the house!

An article in the local paper reported that two boys, 'risked six of the best for going to see an international wrestling match in Northampton, which was about twenty miles from here. They left at about 3 pm and left pillows in their beds. They didn't get back till one o'clock in the morning' – how it got into the papers I don't know.

Fr Anthony started taking classes in conversational Latin. He commented on my report that he, 'seems to understand - but doesn't say much'. This was a very accurate comment with emphasis on the word, 'seems'.

Fr Aelred Watkin, headmaster of Downside Benedictine Abbey, and a former old boy gave us the annual Retreat. He had us in stitches. One story was about an old monk who came in and said that he had found a host on the sanctuary floor and wondered what he should do (that was his stock question) he was told the obvious – so he summoned the nuns, lighted the candles, sang an appropriate hymn and put the said host in the tabernacle. The next day he came to consume it but being unable to he asked one of the Fathers to do the honours. He couldn't either – it turned out to be a milk bottle top.' Aelred was a great fisherman and left his rods behind so I had to cycle quite a few miles to Manton station in Rutland to put them on the train for him.

My model of the school was advancing and measuring the whole thing out and constructing it in cardboard was great fun. I got permission to go onto the roof to work out the chimneys. That was quite an experience as there was a maze of chimney stacks and it was rather scary looking down into the main hall through the cupola.

And so the holidays blighted by the anxiety of waiting for the GCE results came round again. My results were none too pleasing, and a great disappointment, having passed in only four subjects. I had passed the French Oral with Mdme Pomeroy, in spite of the distraction of her clicking dentures, as I had successfully learned the French names for the trees you could see from the window. This obviously impressed her. However I failed the French paper. This would mean that I would not be able to go into the sixth form until I had acquired a pass in one more subject. After a bit of French tuition with

Uncle Reg down in Horsham during the holidays, it was to be retakes in the autumn.

On my return to school my father always gave me a half crown and his one piece of encouragement, 'Learn all you can, son.' I was going to need it this term with the swatting required to get through my failed exams. It was now another term in the fifth form while most of my peers had moved up. At least I was now at the top of the class again after my slide to midway, but it was all a bit depressing. This term I was joined by cousin Jonathan, from prep school at Llanarth. It was nice to have one of the family at the school. As I wrote home, 'Fr Anthony has started a new scheme of weighing us at the beginning of each term. I went 7st 8½ lbs without blazer or shoes – I'm still several stones below the rest of the class.'The workmen were still installing the new central heating system but this upheaval which was nothing compared with the Asian Flue that struck in October. By the seventh of the month it was snowing hard to make life even more unbearable. Classes were suspended and the whole of the upper dormitories became a hospital. Those surviving seniors were on orderly duty and the juniors were occupied as far away from the source of infection as possible. Only about twenty were left on their feet and became expert tea-brews and dishwashers. But we were tough and by the sixteenth most were back in circulation again. I had been struck down and several of the masters and maids were also victims. Matron had her work cut out in the circumstances.

November saw retakes of the failed exams and luckily I managed to scrape through History and French. Exams engendered such a feeling of panic and were not my strong point; in those days there was no course work to take into consideration.

LOWER SIXTH FORM – My three month humiliation now over I had at last reached the top of the school and I was now in the Classical Sixth under the strict eye of Fr Vincent, who took our very small group for Greek and Fr Ralph for Latin. Our intellectual capacities were stretched by listening to a Medieval Disputation on the Third Programme on the theses that *Marriage is Indissoluble* conducted by eminent Dominicans who had been old boys of the school

Come February we were snowed up and the drifts of up to four feet deep meant that we were cut off from the outside world. Meat and milk were fetched on sledges by the prefects from the end of the drive and that meant wide detours into the surrounding fields. The intrepid postman walked up the drive with the mail and earned himself a slot on the six o'clock national news. By the next day classes in the upper school were suspended so that we could dig ourselves out to the main road. Fr Gerard sent six prefects to the 'Stafford

Knot' at Wakerely to get 18 pints of beer and two flagons of cider which were a just reward for their labour - no wonder there was always a cheer in the bus from the station at the beginning of term when we passed it. It was so cold at night that I slept in my dressing gown. Once the snows had gone and another month day came round I headed off into the unknown with another friend, Peter Noon, and by chance came across Kirby Hall. A once grand country house but now practically in ruins it was once visited in the sixteenth century by the famous Jesuit, Fr John Gerard who was one of the few to escape from the Tower of London. On the way back we were accosted by a local who accused us of poaching! He had a gun with him and after firm denials we beat a hasty retreat.

'I had made a resolution to eat at least two pieces of bread per meal, but the last two days it has been so stale I haven't been able to.'

But spring soon came and the snow forgotten and some of us went to meet the Student Cross Pilgrimage and we helped carry the large wooden cross they had been shouldering for many miles. The walkers slept overnight in the school so as to get to Walsingham in time for Easter.

It was into the play season again and Fr Anthony put on two plays *Poison Passion and Petrifaction* by Shaw and *Two Gentlemen of Soho* by A.P. Herbert in which I appeared as Lady Laetitia. The latter was much enjoyed but I hadn't expected so many 'wolf' whistles when I appeared on stage! The precision of my death was commended by the reviewer!

Fr Laurence Bright, in an article in the *Howardian,* our school magazine, entitled *The Science Sixth – A plea for Philosophy,* lamented the fact that boys would be condemned to spend two years in the sixth form doing very little but science to get through the exams for university when it should be a period of their lives when they acquired, 'a humane and balanced outlook' on life. He put in a plea for a study of philosophy that would underpin the other subjects being studied.

So life continued with its outside activities of forestry, photography, glee club and orchestra. My article on brass rubbing, a hobby that I had taken up with John Ibbett, appeared in the magazine including an account of our trip to Higham Ferrers to rub the enormous tomb brass of Laurence de Maur. I selotaped the rubbing on the wall of the study till its sheer weight pulled it down. This had been one of our furthest cycle rides. We called on the Vicar, the Rev Ford to gain his permission. He was most hospitable and gave us tea. This was my first experience of active ecumenism back in the fifties. Sadly he was knocked down and killed on a pilgrimage to Walsingham some years later. My greatest exploit at brass rubbing was during the holidays when our doctor's brother in -law took me on a trip to Stoke D'Abernon in Surrey where I rubbed the magnificent brass which still had traces of blue enamel on the shield. I have it to this day but it is too big to hang in the cottage.

A rugby match against Northampton High School elicited a paragraph home, 'before the game some were heard to remark – they're no good they're Catholics' – we soon beat them. They fouled awfully and were soundly beaten -if that wasn't divine judgment I don't know what was'.

UPPER SIXTH FORM Someone suggested that for our last year at school we should keep a diary and so now my diary proper begins and I have kept it ever since. I rejoined the school with my cousin Jonathan and his younger brother Philip to find that numbers at the school had soared by ten to 98. The chapel was so crowded now that we had to attend services in shifts. Fr Laurence Bright had joined the staff and was taking the senior school for science.

The new term saw a new Dean or head boy in the person of Michael Hawke. This was an ideal choice, as he was a very efficient character. There were a new batch of prefects from among my year and not being one of them I had some consolation in being created a librarian. This gave me more responsibility as I had to begin re-cataloguing the books according to the Dewey Decimal system.

My entomological pursuits were bearing fruit with the emergence of some of my exotic silk moths. These I tended like children keeping some of the cocoons on the radiator behind my bed lest I missed the excitement of their emergence. There was the more questionable operation of executing them and setting them for my collection, but I consoled myself with the thought that since they had no mouth parts with which to feed they really wouldn't miss out on anything and in any case they were not going to live very long anyway.

The round of SVP visits continued with trips to Laxton to weed Mrs Hales's garden with a glass of cider as a reward. There were the regular trips out to Duddington with Martin Davies (Claude) and Peter Stanyard to visit the Irish families on the camp and to catechise young Michael. My attempts at teaching him about the Trinity was rewarded by his drawing a sketch of a Triangle complete with its striker! It was scary cycling down Duddington hill as there were reports of local Teddy Boys trying to push people off their bikes but luckily we never encountered any.

I was even enjoying school meals on occasion and I actually had two helpings of,'liver, stringy beans and custard tart.' Sardines on toast were 'foul' and so was the 'vile' dry fish but, 'Matrons brew of rhubarb chutney did spice up the cold meat and potatoes.'

Classics classes were something of a struggle and rather a bore. I found it very difficult to memorise vocabulary apart from the grammatical structures, although looking back they proved a basis for interest now in things Roman and Greek. Coping with trying to translate Lucretius, Euripedes's *Bacchae*, Aristophanes's *Frogs*, not to speak of Horace's *Odes* was just beyond me sometimes. But the worst was attempting to translate Shakespeare or some other source into Greek verse that actually scanned. How on earth would you put, 'We have scotched the snake, not killed it..' into Greek verse? Ancient History, too, I found rather boring and was not too enamoured with Fr Vincent's approach to the subject. There were no visual aids or field trips to make the whole thing come alive, although he did show us some slides of his trip to Arles. If I hadn't been going on for the priesthood I might have gone in for something more creative or artistic which I had to pursue as a hobby.

In view of the fact that last term it had been suggested that I sat for the Roman scholarship I saw the Head about doing science. A pass in this subject was required but I felt that I couldn't possibly cope with that in under a year. His reply was, 'I wouldn't worry about that if I were you and I don't think they are offering a scholarship this year anyway'. My comment was, 'I don't know, after the number of interviews I've had with him about the wretched thing'! I was really not sorry as students away in Rome rarely came home for holidays and this was something that I would have found very difficult in the circumstances and academically I didn't feel up to it. However I did take up biology although there was not much hope of passing it in under a year's study. 'It will be food for the mill', said the headmaster on giving me permission and so there were a few field trips with Fr Anthony and AJ Martin. In the wood we met Fr Vincent, 'a lonely creature, cutting wood under a beech tree for his fire. We also saw where the mad cook had her den in the woods and where she sat for most of her time surrounded by her cats.' I helped to organise a Field Club with some of the younger boys and it was exciting using the microscope in Fr Anthony's room. We dissected broad beans as a preliminary exercise. He also went hunting round the kitchens for cockroaches – but matron hotly maintained that there was none to be found.

Orchestra rehearsals started again with me on the treble recorder, my cousin Philip on the descant and matron was first violin, the two L'Estrange brothers were second violin and cello with Bridge as conductor. We even had Cameron on the bassoon. Fr Hugh was also trying to get a Glee club going. A new boy, Martin O'Connor played the new organ for benediction. I thought he was excellent but considered that he had used 'excessive tremolo'.

The drama of the dying Pope Pius X11 now unfolded, 'Our Holy Father is dying after a relapse this morning and all hope of recovery has been given up', followed by the next day, the ninth October, by the news that he had finally expired after a cerebral haemorrhage. I tuned in for the latest news before enjoying a bowl of 'runny porridge and an apple' for breakfast. As well as this, 'The air today has been rank with the smell of matron brewing her beer – I think she roasts the hops or something.' However we got permission to cycle out to the Regans at Duddington to watch the burial of the Pope on the Television.

My article for the Howardian on *The Brasses of Northamptonshire* that had been absorbing my attention lead me to give a talk on the same subject to the school along with Gregory de Polnay on *Bull Fighting* and Paul Colsell on *The Development of the Parish Church*. John Ibbett and I had already cycled out to Geddington and Newton. The church was in the middle of a field and boasted one of the finest brasses in Northamptonshire – but it was covered with bird lime so we didn't bother. We had another trip to Little Casterton near Stamford but found the church locked. Nearer home on a Month Day we cycled to Deene, the home of the Brudenells of Balaclava fame and rubbed the brass there. Our efforts were preceded by lunch in a field – school sandwiches, and then a fry up – two sausages, two tomatoes and some baked beans fried in billycans over a meths stove - very tasty- in spite of the inclusion of a little of John's blood cut when he opened the tin. For a General Essay I did quite a good rubbing of Sr. Humphrey Stafford from Bulwick and when I had inked it all in with black indian ink it looked very impressive.

Fr Laurence Bright now left us to be replaced by Fr Arnold Plummer. He proved to be very popular. He was a photographer but more especially an expert lock picker and a member of the Magic Circle. So good was he at lock picking that the local police on occasion called on his services.

My cousin Philip (now chief executive of the Catholic Travel Company, *Pax*) was described by Gabby Gomer as 'an intelligent child' but Fr Vincent found him 'rather noisy especially when reciting Greek verbs. He starts off quietly and then works up louder and louder as the verb goes on.'

'The maids have now taken to not peeling the potatoes for meals – I suppose this was all good nourishment for us, but most of us peeled them during the meal. One of the boys has a ginger beer plant and brews every week - it really is very good. You can get cheap ginger in 2d cartons and you can use the lemon juice out of one of those squirters. We have been nearly frozen stiff in the dormitory. The thermostats on our side seem to have got confused and come on when the room is warm and go off when it is freezing.'

With November the new Pope, John XX111 was elected and we saw his coronation on the TV. 'It was marvellous wasn't it? I still can't understand why Holy Communion was brought to him at his throne'. Fr Vincent passed round sweets to celebrate. There were added celebrations when Fr Henry St John was elected as the new Provincial of the Dominicans of the English Province.

At the end of November Fr Anthony gave me a copy of Christopher Fry's, *'The Dark is Light Enough'*. He wanted to stage it for the St Thomas's day play next Spring and I was to take the part of Countess Rosmarin. The play had originally been written for Dame Edith Evans. It was going to be quite a task learning the seven hundred or so lines in time.

My comments on the staff weren't too favourable at this time. 'Vincent never teaches us anything as we have to read another dose of Greek history. The Head forgets to enter some boys for their GCE 'O' levels and, 'blows everything over with an innocent smile and 'Well lad you know.' It's a bit too bad', on top of this I made a comment that there was, 'dissension on dissension among the Fathers – it makes me sick'. There was always a certain conflict in our eyes between the staff. Fr Vincent, the academic was rather anti Fr Hugh and his sporting endeavours. In one of the good old 'hate sessions', as we called them, he made the observation that if rugby is supposed to create team spirit it should surely keep people quiet in the library where other people are trying to work. He was rather contemptuous of Fr Aiden as well. They had rooms adjoining each other on the top floor. Fr Aiden was unable to keep order during his French classes and these disturbed our classics tutorial in the next room. With some venom Vincent slammed down the window to make his feelings known to next door. However Vincent was soon appointed head of all the Tertiaries or Lay Dominicans in the Province and so this took him out a bit more.

And so the Christmas term drew to a close and we put on another little play at short notice: *A Husband for Breakfast* in which I played a Welshman called Isaiah Jones. There was no time to learn any parts so we just wrote them out and pinned them up at suitable vantage points such as inside my bowler hat. Exams came and went and I suppose 67% wasn't too bad for the Greek set books and so it was home to London clutching a large bunch of holly.

The three weeks holiday at home in Brockley was uneventful - staying with my cousins in Horsham for a few days where there had been a new addition to the family in the person of Andrew - meeting up with school friends entertaining relatives at home and usually relaxing. Mother had obtained a do-it-yourself rug making machine and with a constant clicking night after night and surrounded by balls of wool she succeeded in producing several yards of quite decent rugs for the cottage. However the day I was due to go back to school they were all struck down with colds and ailments and took to their beds and so I was none too happy leaving them to fend for themselves. On return to Blackfriars I found, to my surprise, that I had been made a prefect over others of my year whom I thought would surely have got the job. Now I had the privilege of being able to have my hands in my pockets and to shout at lesser mortals to take their's out, the luxury of the prefects' room - such as it was - where there was a constant fug of tobacco smoke - and the authority to dish out lines and minor punishments to miscreants. However with it went the responsibility of supervising the lower forms for reading and prep as well as waking the school up in the morning and serving very early morning Mass on occasion and being in charge of a dormitory. I was now responsible for the dormitory in the new outside building.

Fr Vincent, having celebrated his forty first birthday, had set up a roll of honour in his room for those who had passed 'A' levels and had gone to University and woe betide me if I didn't get on to it. Play rehearsals got under way and it was a horrifying to realise that it was due to be staged in March. How was it that I could learn 600 lines of text and not really do very well with my Greek and Latin vocabulary?

My comments on being a prefect were, 'Took the third form for prep. I must tighten up - I'm too easy on them....should have punished a couple - must get more self confident....I don't think I'm much of a prefect as there was an undercurrent of mutterings all the time, even though I dished out a few 'trots' (for the penance walk). They think it a bit funny that someone half their size is telling them what to do.' Indeed responsibility as prefect was becoming rather onerous as for one week I had to be up at 5.30 am to serve Mass and to wake the school. Some of us thought that writing out lines was rather unproductive and so on occasion we got miscreants to copy out poetry or some such text which might be of more benefit for them.

Needless to say Classics classes resumed and I was relieved that Greek verse had now been dropped. A General Essay on *The Origins of Life on Earth* was helped by the talk we had recently by Dr Bernard Towers from Cambridge on *Darwin and Evolution.*

With February another flue epidemic was in full swing and boys were going down like flies however I was lucky to escape it this time but we had the new experience of being vaccinated against the dreaded Polio. Apart from a sore arm there were no ill effects.

As I recalled, 'They have built a new Confessional in the chapel. I don't know what the workmen think of it, but it looks like a public convenience from the outside and it echoes.' This new Confessional was in use for the retreat given by a fierce Vincentian priest', Fr O'Neil. Every sentence was introduced with, 'it's a terrible thing....' It was on sin, Confession and death followed by Impurity, Holy Communion and Prayer. If you lead a bad life you will probably end up badly - it seems it's going to be pretty difficult to get to heaven - though he did say all this was to keep us awake during his conferences.' But we all enjoyed it apart from his lifting the curtain between himself and the penitent to have a chat which was most disconcerting and put some boys off from going. 'Foul supper of meat (?) mixed with rice and the gristle from the kidneys we had for dinner.'

It was then feverish rehearsals for *The Dark is Light Enough* which we performed on March 7th. The new theatre in the stable block was full and Bishop Leo Parker, our diocesan bishop, graced us with his presence. It was disconcerting as he kept making comments during the performance. But all in all it was a triumph but it was such a shame that, after all the work we had put into it, we only gave one performance. But we had rave reviews and I was particularly commended for my part as the Countess Rosmarin, and Simon Dyer as Richard Gettner, the fugitive. This was certainly the highlight of my acting career.

I had an 'interview' with the Bishop that weekend. This was the only interview I had with him in preparation for entering the seminary. Having stoked up his fire with some coal, he showed me plans of the Cathedral at Northampton which was being extended and spoke a lot about the expansion of the diocese. He said that there was not much fear of my going to Rome for training as he wanted 'quick returns' and that it would mean that I would be away from my parents for rather a long time – which extracted a rather painful 'yes' from me. 'In fact I almost forget he was the bishop and he seemed more like a fatherly old gentleman'. Little did I know at the time that he instilled fear into his clergy on visitations! But that was the sum total of my interview with him to be accepted for training. He also gave me a set of Davies's *Moral and Pastoral Theology* which he thought I would find useful. It looked deadly dull to me but I was rather interested that when he dealt with the sixth and ninth commandments the text suddenly changed to Latin and even with my classical education it was well nigh impossible to translate this ecclesiastical Latin!

The hockey season was now in full swing and we had one of the rather rare games and I was put on the left wing. 'It wouldn't have been too bad if I'd been able to stop the ball when it was passed to me.'

With one play over the big one was in motion for the tercentenary celebrations at the end of term. This was to be *The Strong are Lonely* by Fritz Hochwaelder about the Jesuit Missions in Paraguay. I was offered the part of the Spanish Ambassador but I had become rather type cast after my perform-ance as the Countess and I was not sorry not to get the part.

The uncle of one of the boys, the head of a Quaker co-educational school had been visiting. He was convinced that one sex schools were a hot bed of homosexuality. Fr Anthony tried to convince him otherwise and after he had gone we had a long discussion in his room about the pros and cons of his argument. There in fact didn't seem to be much evidence though I suppose there was the occasional 'crush' which was usually described as part of growing up.

Easter holidays at last and on return to Lidgate I found that great aunt Alice was well established in the converted cottage next door with daughter Win. She had been a Baptist lay preacher in her day. Father had made a nice bay window for her to survey the garden but she was not too interested but she was pleased with the company of 'Tiger' the cat, however she was going into decline and was beginning to refuse food. The main holiday project was going to be resurfacing the drive. A load of sand and shingle had arrived and I helped to shift barrow loads under the direction of dad and with the mixing of loads of concrete the task began. Here at last father and I had something in common as when I also helped him to paint the cottage windows. This took several days while trying to miss the showers. Mother as always joined in with great enthusiasm and worked like a navvy mixing the cement and helping to lay it. She was pretty good, too, at shinning up ladders to do the painting. In Suffolk terms she was described by my father as his 'slab'. The task was finished before I went up to London for the rest of the holiday.

Fr Kennedy, our parish priest, called. He was a Tipperary Man and was very popular. However his brogue was so broad that we just had to pretend that we understood when he related some Irish tales. He kept mentioning a person who's named appeared to be 'Sissy'. We eventually worked it out that the phrase was actually 'says he'. Serving his Mass at Kirtling continued to be a night mare as he took the Latin at great speed and it was all one could do to interject the responses. Bishop Leo would often go over to Ireland to recruit priests to come and serve in the growing diocese of Northampton since there were so few indigenous clergy of which I was to be a rare example. Fr Hugh came to Newmarket for some reason or other and I was called upon to serve his Mass as no one knew the responses and the form of the Dominican Rite. In many ways it was simpler than the Roman Rite.

While staying with the aunts I made a trip down to the old school at St Leonards. How it had gone down hill. There were only thirty boys there now and with the departure of Sister Benedict the school's reputation had sunk after a succession of inexperienced head teachers.

And so the summer term arrived with my last year at Blackfriars. I recorded, ' I have found a way of phoning from a phone box without paying – instead of pressing button A you speak down the ear piece and listen through the mouth piece – it worked, although being rather faint. You then press button B to get your money back!! I obviously had not begun to read Davies's Moral Theology text book.

On return to school for the summer term I found I had been made secretary for the SVP society and I was deputed to travel to Norwich as a representative of the Junior Section. The train journey on my own was quite an adventure but I succeeded in finding Notre Dame School where the meeting took place, and was addressed by the Governor of Norwich Prison. This gave me a new insight into the big wide world and the problems of life. SVP visits continued to the Irish families and we were beginning to say our goodbyes. My first under age drinking was a tot of rum at a pub at Easton-on- the Hill for a farewell party for Martin Davies. We managed to get bikes with lights and got back by midnight. It is not surprising that I felt I was floating on the mattress after one pint of bitter, a Guinness, half a pint of mild and to cap it the tot of rum! My only other drinking session was some weeks earlier when Fr Hugh had taken us over to the Regans in his old car for a party when I downed about six pints of beer. Drinking wasn't a real problem in the school and drugs had not yet arrived on the scene, however on occasions some lads found their way to the local pubs in the surrounding villages and one group had to make a quick exit through the back door when some of masters turned up unexpectedly. There were excesses sometimes especially after the Christmas party when some of the lower school were unable 'to hold their liquor'.

But now work was in progress for the tercentenary celebrations. A marquee for the play had been erected in the stable courtyard and Fr Arnold had been up onto the turret to restore the stable clock. He had recently been away giving a lecture to the Magic Circle on lock picking. The weather in May was glorious and I did a bit of sunbathing in the woods however it was not all relaxation as 'A' level exams loomed and an essay on, '*A critical estimation of the work of Thucydides*' got me scurrying off to the nearest encyclopaedia to find the answers. A new priest joined the staff - Fr. Philip Dominic Cetti.

An altar and canopy were erected on the library steps with the help of Fr Gerald Vann who was visiting and who was to play the organ at the celebrations and the servers were being put through their paces by Fr Vincent for the solemn Mass. It was my eighteenth birthday but it was hardly recorded except that I was given my first box camera, for the whole day was spent getting the anniversary exhibition ready in the old stable block and rehearsing the High Mass for the morrow. At home aunt Elsie retired after doing forty one sterling years in the same school and receiving a mantle clock with Westminster chimes for her efforts.

Whitsunday was the great tercentenary celebration of the school's foundation at Bornhem in Flanders by the Dominican, Cardinal Howard. Mass was celebrated by the Provincial Father Henry St John and many members of the Order joined us as well as Old Howardians. But the weather was dull and disappointing. There were exhibitions in the Old Stables. Jonathan and I planned an exhibition of our creepy crawlies and in the event a picture of myself appeared in the Catholic paper, *The Universe,* with my caterpillars crawling over my hand and where I was described as 'a young breeder'.

From the 'big top' in the stable yard could now be heard screams of Indians and the rumble of tom toms as final rehearsals took place. The play was first class with Michael D'Souza starring as the Father Provincial and Simon Dyer as the Spanish General.

The second day Whit-Monday dawned fine and warm with a Mass before our Bishop Leo when Fr Sebastian Bullough preached and a second performance of the play followed. I bumped into the Bishop. He told me that my fate had not yet been sealed but that I would probably be going to Oscott College. Then the seven hundred odd visitors, old boys and their wives, disappeared together with two thirds of the school for the rest of the week's holiday. I was rather sad since I had no one from the family to join in the festivities. But I had got used to that over the years and those of us who were left made the best of the break from classes and discipline had been relaxed. A group of us got permission to go to the Laxton pub for a pint - I was eighteen now so it was all legal. This was followed by another session the following day when Fr Aiden joined us at the *Stafford Knot* again and treated us to a pint all round. The junketing continued in this Whitsun week and having cycled to Stamford and back to get my photographs of the recent events I rejoined the gang at *The Swan*, at Harringworth, in the shadow of the great railway viaduct. We drank, recited speeches, sang Compline and played it all back on a tape recorder. Spike d'Souza of course said the most. The day ended by playing some of the rather dodgy songs by Tom Lehrer in the prefects' room. By this time the mob were returning and the peace of the school was disturbed once more.

Come June the weather was glorious and I look my life in my hands and went for a swim with Mark Dutton, Simon Halton and others in the River Welland near Wakerley and Barrowden station. It was a lovely spot where the river opened out into a pool. With no thoughts of possible contamination by rats we all went 'skinny dipping' and were joined at one point by a couple of the masters included Fr Ralph – wearing only his pebble glasses and a broad smile and Fr Aiden. I went in several times and my technique improved. They were glorious days..

Swimming in the River Welland
Simon Halton, Simon Dyer, Me, Mark Dutton

There was still no definite news as to where I was being sent for training in spite of what the Bishop had said. I was glad I was not joining the Dominicans as I reported, 'the novices are locked up at Woodchester for a year and are only allowed to write home once a month. Three other fellow prefects are entering the Novitiate in the autumn'. The news eventually came that I would definitely be going to Oscott and received a formidable clothes list from the College. However we were assured that the diocese would be paying for my training.

'Looking back on my career here', I wrote home, 'although it was pretty hard at first I am grateful that it was possible for me to have had a Dominican education, although it may seem to you that it hasn't produced very good results.'

The GCE 'A' levels were now upon us with the dreaded Latin, Greek, and Ancient History exams. In the event I passed two at 'O' level grade, but failed the Ancient History and the General Essay. So I have certificates with two passes in that subject which is rather strange.

Once exams were over life began to fall apart and a realisation that my days at Laxton were coming to an end. The prefects had their end of term 'binge'. Yes we had binges in those days and matron provided a good spread - fried tomatoes, bacon, eggs, sausages and chips followed by fruit salad and washed down with beer and sherry. All the Fathers joined us. The fifth form party that followed a few days later showed they were not so experienced in this kind of activity.

During my last music lesson Gabby Gomer looked at me oddly and said, 'Now I want to ask you a very personal question. Now you won't be cross will you?' I was wondering what on earth he was going to ask me, 'Tell me what sort of pants you wear? – The short kind? Well I've been given a silky pair

60

by an old friend who has lately died and they're a bit small for my boyish figure – so perhaps you might like them?' Well I've heard of dead men's shoes... but pants? The pants duly arrived - a treasured possession for several years.

And so the end of term came and at last, after so many years, mother and aunt Elsie came to collect me and my belongings and they were able to see the school for the very first time. Sad though that my dad had never seen either of the two schools I had attended but he would have been too shy and embarrassed to have coped with the experience. It was a glorious day and we had a picnic under the great copper beech at the front of the school. It was goodbye but it was not to be the end of my association with Laxton Hall.

At my homecoming a full blown crisis was working itself out. It was now that I had my first real experience of dying and death with the passing of great aunt Alice. Win, her daughter, was a very dominant character. She had had a tragic life. Her first husband had been a test pilot between the wars but had been killed on one of his flights. Her two sons had died tragically on taking his life and the other dying on the operating table. It was an act of charity by the family to give Win a home but relationships were never too easy. Aunt Alice was a long time a-dying. My father had set to work making a solid oak coffin for her but since she was a long time dying it had to be kept under wraps lest people got the wrong idea! Win's plan for the funeral date had gone by and Alice was being dosed up with pink pills - and there was even a hint of speeding her on her way. The whole process I found quite traumatic as I recorded in my diary. When the event finally took place, father's shiny oak coffin was at last revealed. It was a family effort to get her laid out and installed in her final resting place. This was the first time that I had seen a dead body. Since there was no local chapel of rest it was a team effort to carry the coffin the few yard to my play shed to rest until the funeral. The weather being so hot did not help matters but knowing father's workmanship the coffin would have been hermetically sealed with no worry about accidents. Aunt Win was jubilant, but perhaps it was through relief that the ordeal was over. Dad acted as undertaker for the last time as the coffin was wheeled on a bier from the house, as was the tradition, up the hill to the church. At a previous funeral the ducks had recognised his voice and followed the procession down the village. Father made a solid oak cross for the grave which is only now disintegrating after fifty years. Aunt Alice's last request to me was to find a copy of Tennyson's *Crossing the Bar*. One hoped that at last she had reached the shore.

Cousin Jonathan came and stayed for a few days and we went fruit picking up at Brooke's orchard at Wickhambrook. It was plums and greengages at 2s 5d and hour with a bonus of 3d a tray. Jonathan because of his age was paid less.

And now a great pall of depression settled over me about the future what with leaving school, the death next door and an unknown future into which I vas about to be thrust so immediately, I wondered whether I should continue ing to Oscott. There had really been no proper debate with any one about implications. I had had no discussions at school and the interview with ⅎ Bishop was hardly that. I was very unsure of myself and wondered ᵤether I should have a year off 'in the world' before plunging into some- ᵢing so irrevocable as training for the priesthood, even though this thought ᵢad been at the back of my mind for many years. I really wanted time to reflect and sort myself out before launching out into the unknown. I was very unhappy about the whole affair and at last plucked up courage to tell the folks. Mother was rather devastated and for the first time in my life suggested that perhaps I wanted to get married – this threw things into further turmoil in my mind and she phoned up Fr Kennedy to come out and have a chat with me. He did – not exactly setting my mind to rest but saying in his inimitable way, 'Ah so, Tony, it will just be a drop in the ocean if you try things out'. So I did and there was then the busy time of getting together my trousseau – cassock, cotta (square yoke, no lace), biretta, stock and clerical collar and sanctuary slippers which were required on the clothes list sent from the College. We purchased these items from Almonds, the tailors in Cambridge, and under the guidance of Mr Plumb, one of the old school, who had no problems in providing the necessaries.

The scorching summer days continued and there was much soul search- ing on my walks up Cobbolds Lane by the cottage as I reflected on the future

This bridle way through the surrounding golden wheat fields with its uneven sur- face became a symbol of my journey through life and a place to reflect on the glo- ries of God's creation and with the changing seasons the various joys and sor- rows I would encounter .

I was then packed and ready to go, still with some misgivings, for the next big step in my life. In the second week of September it was goodbye once more to the Suffolk countryside.

The old homestead - Cobbolds Vue

PART TWO

THE SEMINARIAN

THE STUDENT AT HIS BOOKS

CHAPTER SIX

ST. MARY'S COLLEGE, OSCOTT
1959 – 1965

First Philosophy Travelling up to London with aunt Elsie for an over-night stay at the flat we met up the next day with Simon Halton my contem-porary from Laxton, himself soon going off to the join the Dominicans. As with my last school it was a journey into the unknown not having visited the college beforehand. I travelled on my own and the Birmingham train headed into bleak industrial landscape which was so different from the Suffolk and Northamptonshire countryside. It was a gloomy prospect.

At the station I met two students, Pat Bailey, complete with pipe and Paddy de Wolff, complete with bow tie and a limp. Although some years ahead of me they were very welcoming to this nervous freshman. The bus trip gave no cause for encouragement as we drove through the wastes of the city and the suburbs of Aston until the Victorian Pile that was St Mary's College loomed on the horizon.

The red brick college was much as I had imagined it; an impressive appearance in the Gothic Revival style with banks of windows looking out over the parishes that students would one day serve. At least it was quiet and had extensive tree encircled grounds – an oasis of tran-quillity in the busy world outside. It overlooked fields with a farm attached and a cemetery. My room was on St Bede's corridor. My first impressions were positive - it was the first room I had ever had to call my own - a small corner room looking into the quad and very dark with just enough space for a bed, table, chair and bookcase and central heating pipes which terminated in a corner. There were no curtains, which rather upset the family, but I pointed out that

THE FRESHMAN

64

the room was so dark that I really didn't need any. I was not sorry to get to bed that night and so after evening prayers and meeting a few friendly students it was lights out by 10.30 pm only to be disturbed once in the night by the clanging of Pugin's bell suspended from its rather rickety 'Night cap' on the tower.

A cheery *'Benedicamus Domino'* by the student bell ringer roused me at 6.10 am. There were only twenty minutes for our ablutions and there being no hot or cold water in the room we all had to trek down several flights of stairs and corridors for a jug of hot water, passing similarly bleary eyed students on the way.

This first morning, we freshmen were confined to the chapel gallery from where we could view the destiny that awaited us for the next six years. Designed by Augustus Welby Pugin the chapel was impressive with its choir stalls, stained glass windows, and colourful Victorian wall paper. A large seven lamp *lampadarium* was strung across the sanctuary. Here Blessed John Henry Newman was Confirmed and from the high pulpit he had preached his famous *Second Spring* Sermon to the First Westminster Synod. Side chapels lead off to the right dominated by a large seated statue of our Lady, affectionately known as Queen Victoria. After half an hour's meditation, the like of which I had not experienced before there was Low Mass followed by breakfast – porridge, cornflakes and toast and marmalade - much better, as I recalled, than school days.

The twenty three students in our year were from a variety of backgrounds and ages- quite a record number and a sizeable percentage from my own diocese of Northampton. One, a sixty year old, had, insensitively, been placed right at the top of the house so he didn't last many weeks. Most of my year had been to the junior seminary at Grove Park or Cotton College in Staffordshire and all seemed a friendly lot. It was a relaxing first day with a walk with some students around the grounds or the Outer as it was called. This perambulation was to be our main means of exercise though there were facilities for tennis or volley ball, even a Rovers Den and playing field for the occasional games of rugger or soccer.

Without more ado we donned our cassocks and our clerical collars which were to be our garb through six years and straight into lectures the following day. These began at 8.50 am with short breaks when we could stretch our legs and midway through the morning a cup of coffee was provided in the Crush Hall near the Common Room. Without any preliminary introductions we were already into Sociology and started studying Pope Leo XIII's encyclical letter *Rerum Novarum* followed by *Quadragesimo Anno* and then hefty doses of Scripture and Philosophy - all strange stuff and in a difficult technical language. This was our first introduction to the professors who seemed pleasant enough. Fr Dennis O'Shea lectured in Sociology, Fr Peter Lawler in Philosphy and Mgr Richard 'Dickie' Foster the vice- rector, Scripture.

Later that afternoon, with Patrick Taylor from the Brentwood Diocese I was taken for a trip down into the big city to make a call at the Catholic Truth Society shop. We had to be back for a quarter of an hour's spiritual reading followed by two hours private study until supper. After the meal each grabbed a partner with whom to say the Rosary and we sped round the cloister telling our beads together. I was collared by Gregory Winterton, the son of a General and later to join the Oratorians, a very gaunt and ascetic looking man. Socialising in the Common Room followed when the first bombshell was dropped that we, freshmen, would be required to put on a concert the following Sunday for the whole college as part of our initiation. At nine o'clock there were night prayers or Compline with a bell at 10.30pm warning us of 'lights out'.

Essential books were now acquired, a *Noldin, Denzinger* and *Ott* and the *Liber Usualis* containing the Plain Chant for £2.10 d .These were put on a bill for the Bishop to pay. He sent me a cheque for £15 every quarter to cover expenses but begged me not to tell any of the other students. They had hefty grants from their local authorities but West Suffolk would allow nothing for denominational training! We also had to work out our own laundry bill if we wanted to keep clean. Mine came to 4/6d a week also paid by the diocese.

Now to meet the rector: Leonard S Emery, Proto Notary Apostolic *ab instar*. (This entitled him to wear a mitre when celebrating the liturgy). A bull of man, he must have cut a fine figure in his youth, now he was quite eighty five, but wore his years well. He was endearingly called: 'The Old Man'. His suite of rooms was situated on the 'Bees Wax' - the equivalent of the Long Gallery in a stately home. There were some fine rooms and furniture along this highly polished corridor with portraits of the illustrious forbears of the present incumbent. As I wrote home: 'I sat in a large chair at his feet looking up into his face and let him do the talking. He asked me various things and then remembered that you (mother) had written to him. He murmured, 'Oh old clothes, and all old clothes'. These were required, he assured me, for manual labour which featured twice a week. He was very nice and I should think that he's a good chap……..it takes him rather a long time to think of what to say and so you don't say anything. You usually can't hear what he says anyway, but the golden rule is that when he shuffles his feet you laugh – as that means he has cracked a joke'.

I hope the relatives were impressed by this description of the head of the college who was to be our leader and guide to the priesthood. 'Well you are now on the first rung of the ladder', he said with a twinkle in his eye. It was reported that he had asked one student whether he had ever kissed a girl and replying in the negative he was assured that he didn't know what he had missed!! But he saved me the embarrassment of having to answer that question.

The rector then addressed us as a group; he was largely incomprehensible. Remembering to laugh when he shuffled his feet we were touched by his endearing address which beginning with : *Carissimi* – very dear ones. This encounter was followed by an address by the vice-rector, Mgr Richard Foster. He had spent most of his priestly life at the college and was a well known scripture scholar having written a book on the psalms but was away so much from the college giving convert talks that he earned the nickname-'The Lodger'. He was a strict disciplinarian and his talk was on the importance of the house rules. We were issued with a long list of these - about not visiting each others rooms and not breaking the *Magnum Silentium* - that time between night prayers and Mass the next day when we were supposed to keep absolute silence. He didn't want to return late at night to witness the college looking like Blackpool illuminations when all lights should be out. We were not allowed outside the gates except in pairs but could go practically anywhere except to visit cinemas. Special permission had to be granted to go into the big city of Birmingham. A new rule had been issued forbidding nails to be hammered into the walls of our rooms, so :

'I have been busy getting them out. It will hit some students hard as some of them have 'luxuriously' furnished rooms with pictures on the walls.' His great emphasis was on obedience - a recurrent theme - obedience to the bishop and ultimately obedience to your future parish priest. Oscott had something of the reputation of being the 'Midlands Hotel', a reputation that he wanted to dispel. He also reminded us that it was forbidden to have 'coffee sessions' in each others' rooms – this rule was largely ignored and as I was soon to learn was an important way by which we could get to know each other in a more relaxed fashion. With that in mind a student gave me an ancient paraffin stove: 'it had been handed down from student to student - so that might keep me a bit warmer and I might even boil a kettle on it.' In addition another kind student bequeathed me some more cast offs - a table lamp and a mirror. The vice - rector's spiel was followed by one by the dean, the senior student in the college, in a similar vein and then the master of ceremonies who told us a little about what would be required on the liturgical front.

The chief professor for our first year was Peter Lawler. I had my first interview him and he asked me to translate a piece of Latin. He seemed to be an understanding chap, no more than in his mid thirties but with rather a sad expression. Lectures began in Epistemology – the theory of knowledge. I set my poor relatives the following question (in jest of course !):

'To what extramental reality, if any, does the Universal Concept correspond? Perhaps you could let me have an answer by return of post – though it has been troubling philosophers since Socrates (you know who he is DON'T you?). We have been studying, then philosophers' cracked theories since the time of Plato and we shall soon be getting down to Kant and Bertrand Russell'. Quite what the relatives made of this and what it had to do with studying for the priesthood I was not quite sure and half a century later I am still somewhat puzzled; it was never made clear why we were studying them and of what significance they would have in preaching the Gospel when we were ordained.

Frank Thomas, a recently ordained priest, hot from Rome's English College, was choir master and a very fine organist. A quiet, courteous, nervous man, prematurely bald and with a cherubic face he would later become rector of the college and Bishop of Northampton. He spoke to us about the importance of Gregorian chant which we would exclusively sing and some would join the more specialised choir.

The Liturgy was, naturally, at the centre of college life. No lie in on a Sunday. It was meditation, Mass and breakfast and back to chapel for a Solemn High Mass. We were decked out for the first time in cotta and birettas in addition to the cassocks and clerical collars which we wore day in and day out. (But when were we to wear the Sanctuary Slippers detailed in the clothes list?) This pom-pommed hat we had to raise every time the Holy Name of Jesus was uttered or the 'Glory be to the Father' was recited and to remember to wear it the right way round. The Liturgy was always celebrated with great reverence and dignity with each move by the appropriate minister choreographed as though it were a ballet and the celebration of Mass was indeed impressive. Sunday ended with more study and Vespers and Benediction.

Our freshmen's concert was upon us. I had practiced a lively Mozart Sonata. But I needn't have bothered. There wasn't much 'culture' among the average Oscotian and the piano had been stuffed with paper to put the participant off and this wrecking operation occurred for the other entertainers, but it was all done with much good humour and we realised that we had come through the initiation ceremony and were now fully fledged Oscotians.

Relationships with the professors were somewhat formal. This was one of the big differences I noticed between school and Oscott. Whereas at Laxton there was a certain informality between masters and pupils here the profs seemed very distant and we hardly got to know them even though they occasionally joined in our common room 'jollies'. I suppose this was part of the ethos of the secular clergy rather than the religious who had chosen to live in community.

Ken Collins

I was beginning to make friends. My immediate neighbour, overhead, was Ken Collins. A former Rugby educated boy and a convert with a military bearing and a dry wit to go with it he was highly intelligent. A year ahead of me he was most helpful when it came to discussing work and we became good friends. We communicated by taps on the pipes and he lowered down messages from his window. Later he would return to the college and lecture as Scripture professor for many years. His room like the rest on St Michael's corridor was bleak, with a lofty ceiling and high windows – and very cold. Originally the area had been one long dormitory in the early days of the college but now divided up into cubicles for the students. I was glad that I had my room despite its drawbacks. Dennis Hall was on my corridor, a former pupil of Cotton College, the junior seminary, he hailed from Hornchurch in Essex. We knelt next to each other from day one in the choir stalls and for the next six years. We were to become good friends through the years that followed and he was to spend most of his ministry in the East End of London, Canning Town, Manor Park and Forest Gate and Upton Park. Dennis in those days was a bit of a tearaway. Sensibly he escaped from the college as much as possible making various contacts here there and everywhere. On my left knelt Charles Crawford. A later vocation he had spent time as a monk on Caldey island and at Prinknash Abbey. He knelt bolt upright during meditation – obviously a man of some experience – did he perhaps look down his nose a little at us greenhorns?

Lectures came and went with a rhythm of their own. One subject, optional in the first year, was Hebrew with Mgr Richard Foster, the vice-rector. 'Dickie' was a short, bald headed man, whose cassock and cummerbund displayed an ample girth. He lived on his nerves being always in the shadow of the Old Man and attempting to keep the peace between him and the student body and probably the professors too. He was obviously a keen student of golf or bingo as one of his stock phrases was, 'head down - eye on the ball', and often raising eyes and hands to heaven with a, 'bless my soul'. He had a smattering of Italian from his Rome days and any knock on his door prompted the response *'Avanti'* at the top of his voice. His Hebrew lessons were hilarious and with great flourishes he would demonstrate how the Hebrew consonants were pointed with the vowels and he had no equal in the way that he would describe a *pathac furtive*. Uncle Reg, a hebrew scholar, set me a piece of Hebrew text once and I was able to pick out 'Absalom', so I knew a few letters.

Plays were a vital part of Oscott life, giving us the experience and the confidence of performing in public. I was soon given a part in one of the Whitehall farces, *Dry Rot,* and as ever I was asked to play a female part. So within a week of arrival we were having our preliminary reading of this great work accompanied by much hilarity.

Lectures in the History of Philosophy and Ascetical Theology were added to the curriculum. Peter Lawler, our lecturer, had a *gravitas* and studiousness about him that was impressive and a very sincere and devout man. He has been described elsewhere as 'dough faced' which is not a bad description but it was clear that he enjoyed bad health. One disconcerting habit was suddenly taking from his pocket a mirror and holding it up to his face. Was this vanity? We learned that he had eye problems and was trying to stimulate his tear ducts. Sometimes he would have to dash out of the room during a lecture or even during Mass when his malady afflicted him.

A week after our arrival we were summoned to one of the lecture rooms to be warned and advised about the forthcoming Retreat. For the next five days we went into a period of perpetual silence and introspection, which was really the last thing I needed. Anyway I recorded that the Retreat giver was excellent, rushing up the chapel at great speed to take his chair on the sanctuary steps. Although I did not record the substance of his conferences I did recall that the food had improved and was much better than school fare; we actually had pepper on the table. I missed the Dominican Rite of Compline from school days comparing it unfavourably with the Roman Rite. The climax of the Retreat was the ordination to the subdiaconate and diaconate of the top years. The auxiliary bishop of Birmingham, + Humphrey Bright, a nephew of the rector conferred the Orders. He had a voice like a nutmeg grater and little sense of ceremony. This lightened the solemnity of the occasion and nearly reduced the MC to tears. With other members of my year and after extensive rehearsals I made my first public liturgical appearance as a torch bearer. At the end of the Retreat I was shown the organ by the organist, Gerry Poole, one of the students. This was a fine instrument that I was to get to know over the years. Gerry was an accomplished organist and he entertained us with some fine playing of Bach after the Liturgy. This is more that could have been said for the hapless new deacon who hadn't a note in his head. His big moment was at the end of Mass with his singing of the *Ite Missa Est*. Rarely did one hear a rendering that was in tune. Being able to sing, it appears, was not a requirement for ordination. We let our hair down in the common room once the Retreat was over with a rousing game of Lotto when I won 3d.

1959 had been notable for a very hot summer and the 21st September was notable for a shower of rain. It also happened to be the Feast of Apostle, Matthew. On every Apostle's feast day we had the privilege of getting up that much earlier to take part in what was known as the 'bone walk'. In the centre of the chancel the 'Pugin Bird Cage' was situated. This consisted of a wooden gothic tower like structure into which, with much ceremony, were placed relics of the appropriate Apostle. Whether it was the same relic placed therein each time I know not. All I am aware of, as I served torch, was that I was glue eyed and only half awake and so was really quite unaware of what other ceremony was attached to this quaint ritual. And while on the subject of 'bones' I must mention the super 'bone march' that took place on the three Rogation Days before Ascension day, when a small casket containing the relics of local saints , among which were the relics of St Chad, the patron of the Cathedral, were processed with the whole college along the terrace at the front of the house. The locals in the nearby houses completely mystified by this ritual were quite convinced that this was a child's funeral, remarking that that was the 'third one buried this week!'

Not only was free time being taken up with rehearsals for *Dry Rot* but I was asked by John Molyneux, a student in the year above me and one of the college's great characters, to take part in the rector's concert that was to happen at the end of term. I was to play some duets with George Gould the deputy organist. He was a fine pianist, who was to eventually leave before ordination, and it was great to be able to play with him '*In a Monastery Garden*' and the '*Overture from The Hebrides*'. However real work was coming in thick and fast with Latin in groups translating texts from the Mass. Father Walter Joret introduced us to Patrology or the study of the early Church Fathers and informed us that we must produce an essay on one of the Fathers of our choice by Easter. I chose to write about St Ignatius of Antioch and spent a lot of time researching him in the extensive college library. Fr Denis Ryan, the procurator or bursar talked about forms relating to National Service exemption and then gave us an introduction to Manual Labour. We worked away at various tasks twice a week for a couple of hours in the afternoon and not only did it help to keep the wheels of the college turning but it got us out into the open air to do a bit of exercise. My first assignment was the joy of sweeping up and burning the fallen leaves and savouring the smell of autumn.

The half hour's meditation before Mass was already becoming a problem for me. They say that if the intention is there you mustn't worry - this was acceptable to the Lord. However sleep always descended very rapidly and it was all I could do kneel upright in the bench and to keep my mind on heavenly things. Once a week, the evening before, we were given 'medi-points' by Peter Lawler on some suitable theme to keep our minds occupied during the meditation period. But trying to keep my mind on this for any length of time just proved impossible. I don't know what the experience was for my companions but certainly the gentleman on my left put us all to shame. Obviously his experience as a former monk held him in good standing. He was able to kneel bolt upright without leaning on the bench in front - totally still and tranquil with just the hint of a smile on his face watching the struggles of us younger students. The matter came to a head one morning when I, nodding off, fell into Dennis my neighbour who set a whole chain reaction down the bench - yes they were in the same state as I - what a crash there was - the whole chapel woke up with a start! Charles, my neighbour, was unmoved. I tried to resolve things by getting up early and going for an early morning walk in the not so healthy atmosphere of a Birmingham dawn but this proved to be unsatisfactory. All this I suppose was to instil a discipline in us which, ideally, we would carry over into parish life.

One evening our study was interrupted by a visit from his Grace the Archbishop of Birmingham for his annual visitation of the college. +Francis Grimshaw was a tall athletic quietly spoken man. We were told that he would go for a weekly swim in the municipal baths to keep himself fit. However his students were never too happy as he never seemed to know them at a personal level. There was a tale that when asking a newly ordained priest – 'And who are You, Father?' the reply from the embarrassed student was, 'You ordained me last week, your Grace'. We Northampton students could always pride ourselves on our bishop, +Leo Parker, for although he was a fierce old bird he made a point of visiting his students every year and knew us all personally. And so the 'Arch' addressed the college on a suitably spiritual theme urging us to work hard and obey the rules.

The rector would, every so often, address the whole college in the Northcote Hall, the freezing lecture hall where the Theologians met for lectures. This impressive room had at one end a large stage and at the other a high rostrum from which lectures were given and dominated by an impressive statue of St Thomas Aquinas, the Angelic Doctor. We began to realize that the rector was beginning to need a change of scene. He had after all been rector for twenty five years and had succeeded Mgr Dey (later bishop). 'During Dey's regime the college had an open door to lecturers, scholars, musicians, and men from all walks of life' (John Coyne). This had been something of a golden age. As soon as Leonard Emery became rector the shutters came down and the doors were locked on the outside world and we were at the tail end of this stultifying regime. As his senility increased so did the quality of communication decrease. He would quote from a little spiritual book by a former rector and began his talk in a gentle touching way: 'Well

Carissimi' (echoing Cardinal Newman's mode of address)- 'well my very dear ones'. His talks eventually became quite incomprehensible - whether he was lacking his dentures I don't know, but occasionally he would chortle, heave his broad shoulders and shuffle his feet and we would dutifully laugh at his obscure joke. The only trouble was that, the following Wednesday, he would address us first philosophers, and question us on what he had been talking about a few days before. 'Well Mr. grrrrr what was I talking about last week?' The added complication was that we didn't always know whom he was addressing and invariably he had a college list that was at least a year out of date. Some brave soul would volunteer to stand up only to be told to sit down - 'Not you Mr..... Mr......', 'But he left last year Mgr'. Because of this horrific prospect of being questioned in this way the philosophers would always crowd to the front of the hall to hang on every word. One gathered a few *bons mots*, when talking about the five ways of prayer: 'Prayer is like a wind that gradually increases to a gale, or water which develops into a river' - presumably this referred to the Purgative Way!

We were told that each one of us should choose a spiritual director. He was the professor who would guide us on the right path through the years ahead. He would also encourage and advise us, suggest suitable reading material and make sure that all was well. I chose Peter Lawler who seemed a laid back sort of man and quite relaxed in many ways. It was said that his father made money in Michelin tyres and certainly, although not obese, he did give the impression of the man in the popular advert. He spoke a great deal about 'angst' and would cup his head in his hands with a rather soulful and concerned look on his face – 'Have you got a crisis. Tony?' I never found it easy to communicate with him. This was a difficulty I had at the best of times and would haunt me for many years. He was horrified when I told him that I was unable to get to daily Mass during the holidays as the nearest church was over four miles away. He had absolutely no conception of country life being born and bred in the big city. We sat in easy chairs in his room under a CS Lowery picture of pipe cleaner men walking too and fro in their industrial landscape. I knew that anything said to the spiritual director was always said in complete confidence and it was interesting to note that he was not allowed to make any comment when the staff were assessing a student's progress. This was puzzling as he was the only person that knew you at all well and I wondered how the staff could make a proper assessment of character apart from progress or otherwise in work, comportment on the sanctuary or how one performed in plays or read in the refectory or kept awake during meditation or lectures - I would certainly not score very highly in the latter regard. But anyway it was to Lawler that I went for the next six years on a more or less monthly basis.

73

By this time we were being loaded with philosophy notes by Lawler and I wondered how on earth I would master this very alien language. However I reported in my diary how quickly the time was flying and that I felt that I had been at the college for ages. I suppose it was just like a glorified school with its secure routine, summoned by bells and a meal on the table always provided. It was really a quite unchallenging environment. There were no individual tutorials with the lecturers to assess your work and give you advice as to the relevance of the material in your future life as a priest. Very rarely were there any essays. Lectures were just fed to us and the information was recorded in our notes to be regurgitated at exams. The one good thing was meeting up with so many different sorts of men. Some were straight out of school like me, while others had been working 'in the world' and had had jobs or had done national service. Discipline for them was far more tolerable than that which they had experienced in the forces. I felt that I was really growing up and for the first time meeting real human beings but I still had a long way to go.

Denis O'Shea was another of our lecturers. It was said that he had formerly worked in the Secret Service. He took us for Sociology as it was called. Not the practical sociology of day to day relationship but a highly theoretical approach studying the encyclicals of the Popes - *Rerum Novarum, Quadragesimo Anno* and various other documents. Dennis was a quiet sandy haired man. He was always very friendly with a wide smile but his lectures were - oh so boring. He would drone on and on in a thin quavery voice, largely on a monotone and his stock phrase was, 'as it were'. On one occasion referring to some incident during a strike he announced that people were 'standing on the housetops, shouting - we are Catholics, as it were.' This phrase qualified just about everything and was quite hilarious sometimes. It had been known for him, when the bell for the end of lectures sounded, to finish half way through a sentence and to resume the next lecture exactly where he had left off. It was also reported by someone, who went to him for spiritual direction, that he fell asleep during the middle of his direction and on one occasion both he and his student went to sleep to be awakened by the bell. Perhaps that was the most profound spiritual direction you could get!

In contrast 'Dickie' Foster was dynamic - almost action man throwing himself into his lecturing with abandon. He also took Comparative Religion lectures. This course was in essence, a critique of all the religions of the world showing how superior the Catholic Church was to any of them. We started at the beginning with Primitive Religions demonstrated with some complicated looking charts. We examined the religious beliefs of such exotic groups as the Coup-de-Poing and the Proto-Ugarit-Finns. To impress the folks at home, (I tried to keep them up to date in my weekly correspondence)

I told them that we had been studying the 'Exogomus monogomus totemistic patrilineal higher huntsman and also the early paleolithic coup-de poing civilisations who had the domestic dog'. In return mother impressed me by telling me that she had listened to the *Antigone* on the radio and I reminded her that I played the part of Queen Euridyce in our all Greek production at school. Matters reached a climax one day when the Rover Crew lead by the rather eccentric Paul Sankey, to illustrate the skill of these primitive civilizations, demonstrated how to make fire by rubbing two sticks together. This was an unmitigated success. Clouds of smoke billowed round the Northcote Hall and the lecturer sitting on his high dais disappearing behind a thick miasma of religious mist. The whole drama culminated in the lighting of a Roman Candle. If only all lectures could have been as exciting as this! Dickie's Hebrew lectures began to get exciting too and we were at last able to write out 'Coleman's Mustard' and 'Nathan is a good and holy man' in Hebrew characters.

As the rector sank further into decline, he gave up saying the community Mass and was now assisted by three deacons, who had to remind him what to do. One day it took him seventy minutes to celebrate Mass.

Manual Labour was the next operation. This was a 'joy' to celebrate twice a week. It gave us some exercise, reminded us that working with one's hands was no bad thing and was a welcome break from all the high faluting language of philosophy. Leaf clearing in the autumn gave way to potato picking. For three days in November we were let off lectures to gather in the six and a half acres of spuds. The top and the lower half of the college took it in turns doing three hours at a stretch. It was rather sureal with the college as a backdrop, the highly industrial panorama stretching in front and around us the farm with cattle grazing peacefully in the fields. After the main crop was lifted we had to glean the remainder going back and forward in lines with a sack between us. On another occasion I helped to move books from the extensive tower library or worked in the college museum, where I eventually ended up on a more permanent basis. This really was an Aladdin's Cave of wonders accumulated, largely by the great Pugin, over the years. Here were displayed in a rather random fashion a fascinating selection of artefacts from the penal days when priests ministered in danger of their lives. There was a miniature chalice that could be unscrewed into three parts and easily concealed. In pride of place was the priceless medieval Norwich Missal with its wonderfully illuminated pages and the entry for the feast of St. Thomas a Becket ruthlessly scraped out at the Reformation. These sat side by side with bits and pieces from the First World War including a bomb or two dropped from aircraft, fearsome bayonets, and the remains of some desiccated biscuits. Egypt was represented, too, with the mummified head of what was supposed to have been an Egyptian princess. She had been known to turn up in a student's bed on occasion! The wonderful Forbes Collection - large volumes of water colours of plants and animals by James Forbes from his travels to far off lands which were eventually sold to the British Museum; a nun's skull from the Middle Ages; an exquisite ivory crucifix with rubies for the drops of blood and above all the fabulous medieval lectern stolen by Napoleon from Louvain and eventually purchased by the sixteenth Earl of Shrewsbury. Its twin had ended up on the bottom of the river Seine during the Emperor's retreat. There I spent many a happy manual labour afternoon with Ken Collins and Roger Spencer. The well known art critic, Professor Bodkin, visited the college to assess the paintings but it seems he didn't think much of them! There being no 'health and safety' rules in those days for manual labour an occasional accident occurred such as when Terry Brain (the future bishop of Lancaster) fell off a ladder in the Lady Chapel, which he was decorating, onto the statue of the Madonna breaking off an arm of the Holy Child. It was remarked by someone that it was the first time that 'Our Lady had been brained' !

Philosophy notes were coming thick and fast with the philosopher Plato's *Universals*, and the *Allegory of the Cave*. Then I had to sort out my essay on St Ignatius of Antioch together with rehearsals for the forthcoming play and the rector's concert when I was to play duets with George Gould. All this began to make me feel very tired and what with the early morning rising into the bargain I was becoming rather jaded. Relief came with a celebration of the rector's Feast Day which visiting dignitaries attended - the Hierarchy dressed up in their accustomed finery with the vice- rector, a Papal Privy Chamberlain, displaying his cherry pink cassock with false sleeves looking rather like a superior Jesuit. It had a Victorian flavour and we attired our- selves in appropriate costume complete with side burns. The day after the nosh up there was a day's holiday with actually an hour's lie in. The time was spent walking round the grounds, the museum, having coffee and chat with friends and a final preparation for the concert in the evening which was a great success. This was organised, as were other events, by John Molyneux with whom I became particularly pally. He was a real character, very gifted, but rather teased and was known quite simply as 'The Moll'. He also acted as unofficial college barber.

The college had a Common Room where evening 'Jolleys' were held such as quizzes or 'housy-housy'. The latter consisted of three rounds for 3d, so it wasn't really gambling. The rector, it seems, excelled at whist but this was the least favourite among the students. The professors, normally forbid- den entrance into this sacred domain of the students, were allowed in on such occasions, otherwise as I reported home, 'they keep very much to themselves, don't mix with the students, so we don't get to know them all that well.' There were also opportunities to play table tennis and upstairs there were two snooker tables which in true style were always smoked filled. The one radio was in a smaller room as we were not allowed radios in our rooms let alone TV, but we did have a daily newspaper. My first duties relating to the Common Room was to light the fire for the evening which meant collecting logs with a fellow student, John Glen and trying to get the blessed thing to catch fire.

During October we had traditional devotions with a public recitation of the Rosary. The devotions concluded with the forty hours exposition of the Blessed Sacrament where the monstrance was displayed amid a sea of candles on the High Altar - it looked very spectacular. On the down side was that the forty hours carried on through the night and for my first effort I was roused at 2.30 am to 'watch' with two other companions for an hour or so. The strange liturgical climax was a Mass celebrated at a side altar with the monstrance still exposed on the main altar - a real confusion of symbols that needed disentangling.

We had our meals in the traditional refectory sitting on benches at long tables with the professors on a dais at one end - quite the medieval hall style. The food was reasonable and edible. A favourite was a sort of bread pudding that was nick named 'wet nellie'. Every so often a list would go up indicating new seating arrangements. This was to prevent, I suppose, forming 'particular friendships', and enabling us to mix together better. This was generally no bad thing except when you found yourself next to someone with whom you really didn't get on too well. During main meals we were read to from a pulpit at the far end. Fr Walter Joret, although with a French name, had a very Brummy accent, took us for a practice using the tape recorder. I thought my voice rather nasal and asked the folks at home whether I had had my adenoids removed. This gave good practice at throwing the voice and getting used to speaking in public. However some books were unbelievably boring. *'A Life of Ronald Knox'* by Evelyn Waugh was one and *'Three Cardinals by EE Reyonds'* stick in the mind. The length of the reading was dictated by the rector's mood or whether he had forgotten where he was at the time and the professors were afraid to tell him. A bell would then ring and the reader had to finish even if in the middle of a sentence. This could be very frustrating having to wait for another meal before the story was resolved. When the rector was in a bad mood the meal would, sometimes, go on longer than was endurable and we would get very restive. On occasion the reader would make a mistake - perhaps the mispronunciation of a word or he was inaudible. The bell would then ring furiously from the far end of the hall and the rector would correct the person - however, as with his talks you could rarely hear what he was trying to say and it was all the poor reader could do to comply - sometimes repeating the same mistake several times, with the bell ringing furiously and the students bursting with mirth. My turn soon came and Joret, whose daily Mass I had been serving, tested my voice again and he thought I was reading a little too quickly. I was very glad of the training I had had at St. Dominic's under the inimitable Mrs Brown. Supper was more relaxed when, to finish the meal, an extract from the *Menology of England and Wales* would be read. This was an ancient document relating the strange behaviour of some of our medieval and Anglo- Saxon saints - like one saint who as a baby would refuse his mother's milk on a Friday as a penance. This caused much hilarity among the students which was not appreciated by the Hierarchy at the top table.

For some reason or other Peter Lawler invited me to join what we called 'The Ont group'. This was a high powered philosophical discussion group. I didn't think I had exhibited any particular intelligence in this field. But anyway I went along and was privileged to sit alongside two of the most brilliant students, Peter Hocken and Nicholas Lash. Nicholas, the son of a brigadier and himself an ex army man, had an impressive intellect and would hold forth on the philosophy of Lonergan and others. Talking very rapidly with a slight twitch of his jaw, he was a lovely counterpoint to Peter Hocken who screwed up his face trying to focus his thoughts that would eventually be revealed in a slow and deliberate fashion. Both these students were for my Diocese and would eventually be ordained priests. Nicholas's academic career would eventually take him out of the priesthood and he would become the Norris-Hulse Professor of Divinity at Cambridge University and write many learned books. He however carried his erudition lightly and apart from being great fun was always willing to explain things to the less intelligent students such as myself. Peter would later lecture at the college and become an authority in the charismatic movement. So I sat through this session held in Lawler's room understanding some things but usually quite baffled and wondering at the intelligence of these luminaries.

And so I slipped into the day to day routine with the weeks passing by very rapidly. More philosophers such as Hume and Kant, Scepticism and Dreams followed. There was a dash of Existentialism and the plays of Marcel and huddles in discussion groups in the fug of the Common Room, unaware of the dangers of passive smoking. There were syllogisms and Stewart Mill and Camus and listening to the famous debate between Bertrand Russel and Copplestone. There were Totems in Comparative religion and a whole lecture on the meaning of 'highly favoured' in Luke. I was very pleased that I had studied Greek and found it more useful than Latin although we had still been having Latin sessions. Lawler was forever dealing with the 'crises' of his spiritual children which erupted from time to time. Play rehearsals for *Dry Rot* were in full swing and the fitting of dresses and high heel shoes for my female role. A student, Colin Trevor, a former professional actor came and gave us a critical assessment of progress.

For a short time I came into contact with John Cornwell, a student in the year above who would leave after a short time. He seemed a rather serious, quiet sort of chap who had been at Cotton with many in my year. Little did I know at the time the details of his home background which he describes in his compulsive book, *'Seminary Boy'*. I recorded in my diary that in one session I explained to him the *'Ontological Feminine Principal'*. (What on earth was that!!), and he lent me an alarm clock. He also gave a talk on 'Why nuns?'

November 5th came and went with the sound of fireworks all round us but our celebration only went as far as a banger in the cloister. Entertainments continued in the Common Room with the occasional 'beetle drive' and bingo but I had discovered the piano in the music room and would spend a lot of free time there, perhaps too much, practising (especially Mozart) and accompanying the occasional student who would come in. Sleep would dominate during meditation and a constant record in my diary that I, 'really must get down to some serious work.'

The day of the play at last came round and it was a resounding success with the audience in fits of laughter most of the time . When I came on I was expecting cat calls but people, I liked to think, were so taken aback by my appearance that there was a deadly silence! Well we had seen none of the opposite sex since coming here and I suppose I was the next best thing! The set was magnificent and the whole college seemed to crowd into the Green Room after the production. Photographs would eventually go up in the Common Room including one which was a view of my legs snapped by someone whose camera had slipped (accidentally?) and a close up of my holding hands with my erstwhile husband played by Charles Crawford. However one or two people objected to this rather 'obscene' picture and they were quickly removed. Nicholas Lash wrote a rave review in the College Magazine and my performance was described as giving a, 'vigorous, vivacious and verismilitudinous performance as Susan Wagstaff who was hotly pursued (by my companion in the choir stalls, the former Cistercian Monk), Charles Crawford. The future bishop of Lancaster, Terence Brain, who played the part of Beth the parlour maid was described as, 'a glorious six foot maniac with universal joints'. My neighbour from upstairs, Ken Collins, played my father Colonel Wagstaff, 'with apoplexy, pepper and a dash of green chili.'

The vice- rector practically came apart, one day, during the Hebrew class with his violent gestures. He was perhaps working up to the visit of our Prince Bishop, +Leo Parker, with the beetling brows and the royal 'we', on his annual visit. The bishop had been one of about twelve children and a native of nearby Sutton Coldfield. It had been pointed out in his early days that his legs were every inch a bishop's. He interviewed each of his students and, I must say, was very reassuring. I had last met him when he interviewed me at school and had been very enthusiastic showing me the plans of his expanded cathedral at Northampton while I stoked his coal fire. He started talking about the cause for the canonisation of King Henry V1, books he had written and whether I had all the clothes and money I needed. He fingered his cassock, pointing out its quality and that it had lasted him at least thirty years. On later visits we talked about the mission to the gypsies and bargees in the diocese and so I wondered whether he had something lined up for me on that score. One useful piece of advice was that one should take up smoking a pipe (even if it contained no tobacco) as this would keep ardent ladies at bay. He also advised possessing a silk topper. This was useful, he said, when one 'visited the houses of the poor' with Holy Communion. It would provide a suitably clean 'altar' on which to place the pyx and candles. Needless to say in later years I never tried out either of these pieces of advice - perhaps I should have done! I would learn later on that parish priests would quail when His Lordship came on visitation. He certainly oversaw a great expansion of churches and schools in the diocese and would make an annual trip to Ireland to recruit priests as there were few indigenous clergy for the ministry. It was a touching scene as he and the Old Man walked together. + Leo, although well on in years, was but a child compared with the Ancient Len who treated him as such. In one of the last great fogs of that era he was forced to return to the college and we had the pleasure of two more days with him. Indeed + Leo had the reputation of being one of the few diocesan bishops who regularly visited their students.

Then came a big outing to Birmingham Town Hall for the public reception of the Cardinal Archbishop of Westminster, William Godfrey (or 'Bloody Bill' as he was better known by the clergy). The rector had already spoken to us about his visit - 'he's coming here for a good meal and when he came here on Visitation in 1939 when he was Apostolic Delegate, the students fell in love with him and he visited the house from top to toe.' Actually at that time he had come to bless the new lavatories recently installed. The Archbishop of Birmingham gave a speech, a rather egoistical layman gave a speech and Bill lectured for forty minutes on what I believe was largely to do with what was to become the perennial subject of contraception. However we could hear little if anything as his back was turned towards us and it was more of a turn off than a turn on. On our return to the college we lined up in the cloister eagerly waiting his advent, the tension being relieved at one point by a cleaning lady clattering in with bucket and mop and appearing like a latter day John the Baptist preparing the way before him. When he did arrive he was deeply moved as we sang a popular Latin hymn: *'O Roma Felix'*... O Happy Rome. But the visit was worthwhile as we had a posh supper plus wine although we had to endure more speeches by the Hierarchy.

Although we were someway off the end of term the vice- rector gave us one of his regular talks. This was on how church students should behave during the holidays. We were, in fact, to spend it like little gentlemen. If we had to get work we should get employment that was compatible with our status in life so that meant no manual labour such as working on building sites. This it seems would be a threat to our vocations, presumably because of the company one was likely to keep. This riled me somewhat since my father worked with his hands and it appeared to be doing him down in some way. Chris White, a fellow diocesan student and a very practical man, also bridled as working on a building site was one of his main holiday jobs. We were also given the cautionary tale about the student who would go to daily Mass when, one day, an attractive young lady accidentally dropped her handkerchief – he picked it up and the rest was history. Although there was a grain of truth in all this most of the mature students were not amused and especially those who needed to get such work to make ends meet. Having been a term at college and having grown up just a little more and mixing with a wider circle of men with experience of the world I began to be critical of the whole college set up and with discussions relating to the Second Vatican Council that was soon to begin these feelings of criticism would more and more affect our way of thinking. We could see the need for a profound change in the whole outlook of the Church and so in our coffee sessions we would begin to discuss and criticise our training for the priesthood. Change would come, as we shall see, and Peter Lawler and Frank Thomas were of the same mind though they had to tread carefully. But a lot of water had yet to flow under the bridge and life would continue without health and safety regulations when I was detailed to climb up a dodgy ladder in the museum to clean the statues of Our Lady and St John and lowering them to the ground by an ingenious series of ropes under the supervision of Ken Collins.

End of term exams were looming and I wondered how on earth I was going to absorb all that was necessary. The fear that used to grip me at school with this prospect did so again and late night sessions with a torch under the bedclothes or getting up extra early to do more revision was not unknown. At the last spiritual direction session of the term Lawler thought that I was

81

suffering from 'Intellectual Scruples' regarding work. I didn't really understand what he meant by this. Perhaps I had been giving the impression that I understood more than I really did. But in the highly introspective atmosphere of the college it was not surprising that appreciation of life became somewhat distorted. We then went on to talk about the antiquated form of night prayers that we were using every evening.

Schopenhauer seemed a very appealing philosopher at this time. But I cheered up when I found a photo of the college soccer team in 1890 where a very youthful 'Old Man' was captain and holding the soccer ball. So the first set of exams was upon us. The vice- rector gave us the ideal pass mark to achieve: 'as long as you get your 40%!!'. This seemed the figure to aim for, below which, no doubt, one would be sent down or expelled. Lawler's oral passed off with Aristotle, Descartes and Kant but I floundered when he asked me what I would do if I should meet a Representationalist in Regent Street. He reassured me that I had passed and I was suitably comforted by Ken and Mol. A three hour Scripture paper followed and Sociology. In the event I needn't have worried because although the results weren't brilliant they were all in the sixties - apart from fifty percent in Latin - and to think I studied this at A level! But of course that was Classical Latin and not Church Latin – a somewhat different animal.

And so the climax of Christmas arrived with Midnight Mass followed by Solemn Lauds after which we were pretty fagged out with all the singing and praying and we didn't get to bed until 2.30 am At least we had a lie in until 7 am the next morning with meditation and Low Mass followed by a breakfast of bacon and eggs. It was then back again to chapel for solemn High Mass followed by the rector's farewell talk. Dinner was at 1.30 pm with turkey etc plus red and white wine and port which junketing went on until 3 pm. We carried on the celebrations in Ken's room with some more drink and a cigarette or two. The jollifications ended with the traditional pantomime which had been written by Peter Hocken and John Berry. Although very humorous in places it was generally agreed that it was rather a flop but one highlight was Gregory Winterton who made a lovely witch. The text was full of 'in' jokes about college life and this was one way that the students, through satire, could say what they thought about college life and those in power. This may account for the Archbishop's speech afterwards, who may not have approved too much of the incipient rebellion, as I described his comments as 'two edged' in my diary. John Molyneux who had produced the whole thing was very down in the dumps about poor reviews. The next day we were up at 5.40 am to catch the 10 am train to London and I had to stand all the way. So I was home once again after a very eventful three months.

I returned to the normal world of my family at Wickham Road, Brockley. Age was beginning to take its toll on the folks. The arthritis in my father's neck was becoming more pronounced, the aunts were frailer and mother had returned to her old job at Croydon doing some secretarial work for her old firm of Wallace Arnold. I met up with some of my peers from Laxton days who all seemed to be enjoying life. It would have pleased Fr Lawler that I was actually getting to daily Mass with the fifteen minute walk to St Mary Magdalene's and then the 7 am Mass on Sunday Morning. This was no hardship now after the excesses of Oscott. A trip to Horsham to visit my cousins and an outing to the West End to see the new film, *Ben Hur*, was an inspiring interlude. Fog and snow put a damper on outings except for a trip to St Paul's Cathedral and its whispering gallery. The old doubts of returning to Oscott soon surfaced again. I did not look forward to going back with any great enthusiasm or feeling that God had called me in a special way. Perhaps it was just a throw back to 'going back to school' as in the old days, but it was heightened by the knowledge that the next term was going to be for six months duration with no return home during that period. At least I had not been sent to Rome where students came home only once during their six year course and as the family had said, on a previous occasion, it was not as though I was going back 'to fight on the Front.' So events just had to take their course and I could see no alternative and on January 18th it was back to Birmingham and Oscott.

And so it was the same old routine into which I so easily slipped with a renewal of the friends I had made in my first term, Ken and Moll especially. A new delight awaited me in being elected to join the Shakespeare Society. It was a select group of only twelve members and met quite regularly when we, would be thespians, read Shakespeare's Plays and other authors to each other taking the various parts. Nick Lash had proposed TS Elliot's *Family Reunion* and we were to have a lot of fun ploughing through the plays of the bard and other writers. In fact it was really hilarious at times. Michael Jones - Frank whom we nicknamed 'The Admiral' as he had been in the navy at some stage, was a delight with his spoonerisms, so seriously dropped as he puffed away on his pipe. Manual Labour saw me still working in the museum and defying health and safety rules again by climbing back up onto a cupboard to fix back in place Our Lady and St. John after cleaning and oiling them.

The rector had had a fall during the holidays but was back in strength to give us a talk but complained that, 'Only the top year appreciate me; there will be green fields where I am laid'.

Dennis O'Shea droned on in Sociology, Dicky Foster's Scripture lectures were becoming a trial as they were so disjointed but at least we had moved from Epistemology in Philosophy to the joys of Metaphysics and with all the wonders of this learning to be yet unpacked for us by Peter Lawler. But the intermittent nag was still there - 'should I carry on?' However I was bucked up by a cheque from Bishop Parker for £20 and as his secretary, John Reffitt, said in his letter - 'a trifle to help you through until July'.

Oscott was becoming particularly bleak during these winter months with a great deal of snow, fog and rain and there was no incentive to go out - not that there was really anywhere to go even had you wanted to. It was a question of the daily Outer around the grounds or twice daily Outer in the opposite direction or inviting people to coffee in your room after lunch or being invited to someone else's room for a party. It was a hectic round. Even music was not exactly uplifting with a history of the Introit and the Kyrie, and singing a few, as I put it, 'ghastly hymns'. Moll was planning a pantomime for the end of the year and using his artistic skills to illustrate a Spiritual Bouquet for the rector's Diamond Jubilee. Len seemed to have bucked up a bit since last term and although his talks to us were intermittent one felt that he was there in control somewhere.

My duties as fire lighter in the Common Room continued sharing them with John Glen from my diocese. John was a great chap, played the guitar and sang and was always very cheery. He became a leading light in the catecheti-cal movement in the Northampton Diocese only to die tragically in a fire in his presbytery in the 1990s due to a faulty electric blanket. But the future then was not for us to see - *che sera.* Now we were on to Buddhism in Compara-tive religion and Dicky waved his arms around frantically when advising us that we must get off the wheel of Samsara if we are to achieve Nirvana - but it would have been so much more interesting if we had had a real Buddhist in to talk to us about his way of life. Music appreciation did continue at what was called 'The Amateurs club' when we could listen to some good classical music from time to time and Fr Thomas played some polyphonic Palestrina to broaden our appreciation of church music.

My typewriting skills were now enhanced through the good office of Michael Stokes from the Brentwood Diocese who lent me a do it yourself course on how to type. It rejoiced under the name of 'Mrs. Smith Clough's Short Course on Rational Typewriting' - I never looked back after that. Michael was a very serious minded and efficient type whom I'm sure would make a good bishop one day - however fortune has, to date, yet to bestow the mitre on him. My sessions of spiritual direction with Peter Lawler plod-ded on. He was pleased that I had started to say Prime, one of the hours in the Daily Office which was to disappear under the reforms. Of course it was all in Latin then and the Office was often called the *Onus Diei* (The burden of the Day) instead of the *Opus Dei.*(The Work of God). As a priest one would be obliged to say the eight offices of the day which were considerably longer than they are now and if keeping one's concentration in praying it in English was bad enough you can imagine what it was like trying to pray it in Latin! He also suggested that I spent a quarter of an hour extra visiting the chapel each day - as if our frequent times spent there weren't long enough already - I can't remember whether I followed out his suggestion. He was also working on the problem of my getting to daily Mass in the holidays.

One of the depressing features of Oscott life was the disappearance of students. On return to college you would find that you had moved up a couple of spaces in choir because one or two students had thought better of it and left during the holidays. 'Who's next?', one would ask. It also happened during term time as well which was disconcerting. On one occasion I recorded that there was much coming and going with rector and vice - rector seen in deep worried conversation and various people being interviewed with Lawler late for meditation points and a buzz going round the common room that some-thing was a foot. The following day the 'crisis' came to a head with one of the students leaving - I think it must have been John Cornwell. It was also announced that a student who had left about two years ago, because of an impending nervous breakdown and sent to a mental home as a voluntary patient had thrown himself under a train and was killed. Also someone had gone away for a few weeks as a breakdown was in the offing. Moll would be the Job's comforter being full of dire warnings about 'getting out while you can.' What was far worse was a priest leaving after he was ordained. On one occasion my attention was drawn to an old college photo and it was pointed out to me that 'he left the priesthood' - nothing could be worse - and yet in a few short years it would become commonplace. Such departures were unset-tling and a feeling of 'Will I be next?'. However the gloom was dispelled by the announcement of the birth of Prince Andrew and very patriotically we flew a flag from the tower and prayers of thanksgiving were said for the safe delivery of the new prince.

The challenge of Metaphysics, then, opened before us - potency and act, causality, essence and existence, substance and accidents. The Ont Group was regaled by a learned dissertation by Nick Lash on Lonergan's *Theory of Consciousness* - which sent the head spinning. This session, on occasion, provided another excellent venue for sleep and really I don't think many of my associates had much idea what he was talking about. Joret, who also came along, offered us the hospitality of his room and took the position of the plain blunt man and a 'Villa Supporter' and with his Birmingham accent he was quite the part but the most concern was expressed by Lawler as Lonergan's theories seemed to conflict with what he had been teaching us last term. So really it did become rather one big yawn. The vice- rector's jokes were still amusing even though we have heard them for the dozenth time and he gave us a very valuable talk on the use of our time. Say that again! But we were cheered up very shortly when one of the ethnic group of students put on a show in the Common Room. This time it was the Welshmen's turn to lead a sing song. They appeared suitably clothed in white sheets and wearing laurel leaves on their heads. At the end of this charade there was a triumphal crowing of the Bard. It was on occasions like this when we could all let off steam with raucous singing (what a contrast to the restrained plainchant - when we were not allowed to use our diaphragms and only a head voice) accompanied with loud guffaws. It was a real party night that would rival any post football matches celebration but without the violence. With Ken and Mol the trips to Sutton Park and the Bracebridge cafe, with its sandwiches and cakes, and its lake brought me back to the countryside once more though my companions were a little concerned that they might be accused of baby snatching as I was still very young looking for my years. Sutton park was a lovely stretch of land and a contrast to surrounding suburbia. Moll nearly lost his trilby hat in a gust of wind. He insisted on wearing this at all times when going out into the world, but it was relief that it was no longer compulsory for students to wear such a hat. However we had to wear our clerical collars black suite and more often than not a black rain coat.

We were now approaching Lent and the time of preparation for Holy Orders to be conferred. It was a tense time for students approaching these rites of passage to the priesthood. The big question was whether they would be 'on the list'. If you weren't on the list your Orders had been delayed for some reason, perhaps for some misdemeanour known only to the authorities. Perhaps you hadn't passed your exams with enough forty per cents or shown enough community spirit - who knows, it was a great mystery. But there was one notorious event when the librarians had installed two books in the library that were of very doubtful theological worth - it may have been a book by someone like Teillard de Chardin. This was a veritable black mark against them and as a way of punishment their Orders were delayed. Indeed a 'monitum', as it was called came from Rome, dictating that all books by that author were theologically suspect and had to be removed from the book-shelves. Nicholas Lash's Minor Orders were stopped because the question was asked in an exam paper whether, as an example, 'Tycicus's obligation to do such and such a thing was an obligation *in justice* or _merely in charity_.' The said student pointed out the theological dottiness of the notion of being 'merely' obliged to do something in charity. This was thought, by the authorities, to betray a dangerously subversive mentality and he was told that he would not be ordained to Minor Orders. The student advised +Leo about this who was furious and came down on Oscott like a ton of bricks. His words had an effect. Some years later the same student was chatting with the Bishop who said 'Do you remember that great week at Oscott? Monday, plus Leo; Friday, minus Len' ?!

It would be more than boring to recall the Lent Retreat with its continual visits to the chapel for conferences by the Retreat giver - some of which were inspiring but certainly designed to make one even more introspective. Fr Rourke who gave the retreat had spent the war in a Sumatra Concentration camp and gave some of the gory details. But a cheering note this year was the celebration of the rector's Diamond Jubilee - there were flowers on the table and a telegram from his Holiness.

The first event of the Ordination season was the Entrance into the Clerical state or Tonsure. The candidate went before the Bishop who wore what looked like a pouch around his waist used for fruit picking and the student, kneeling before the seated bishop, had a few tufts of hair snipped off by His Lordship – '*Dominus Pars, hereditatis mei*' 'God is my portion and cup' and these tufts were placed in the said 'pouch'. The amount of hair gathered from twenty or so men was then deposited in a hole in the sacristy floor, known as the *sacrarium*, together with the hair of countless generations of Oscotians and with all sorts of other detritus from Liturgical Worship that would accumulate during the year. There was some amusement when the near bald headed Jim Daly presented himself. In days gone by baldness could be considered an 'impediment' because of the levity it might inspire amongst the people and the said person might have to wear a wig to compensate. The following day Bishop Bright administered the four Minor Orders to First and Second Theology. Porter and lector and then exorcist and acolyte. The Orders of sub diaconate and diaconate were also conferred. The bishop had problems with some of his consonants and many an Oscotian was ordained as Acolyte not to carry candles but to 'climb up them' (ascendere instead of accendere). After this some of us dashed down to St Chad's Cathedral in the centre of the city to see the real thing - the ordination to the priesthood of some of our top year. However we couldn't see very much of what was going on due to the presence of Pugin's Great Rood Screen. Its removal some years later was to cause much controversy. A few days later the ordinands after their 'honeymoon' would return to the college to give us their first blessings. This was the event to which we all aspired and looked forward to and these newly ordained returned with an aura of sanctity and devotion which was inspiring. From then on they would say the principle Mass on the Sunday accompanied by the new deacons and subdeacons and during the week we would serve their private Masses in different rooms in the college. The talks by the Old Man on rubrics must have at last born fruit as we appreciated shortly afterwards when he tried to teach our year how to genuflect in the correct way.

This proved rather difficult for a man in his eighties and of some considerable weight but we got the message.

My interest in entomology was not to be snuffed out by city life and I had ordered some stick insects and silk moth caterpillars from L Hugh Newman which succeeded in breeding much to the amusement of my fellows. I even persuaded my neighbour upstairs, Ken Collins to take on looking after a few stick insects.

And so the first Easter was nearly upon us. The Liturgy of the Blessing of the Holy Oils on Maundy Thursday was the highlight of events. This was the day when the various oils used in the Sacraments were blessed and it seems that every geriatric hospital and nursing home had been raided to get a full company of clergy. One reflected that in not so many years one would be joining this throng of the halt, the lame and the blind as they tottered forward to bless the oils. It was an impressive ceremony with all the clergy vested but it was not without its humour. Each priest had to come forward and address the container of oil in plainsong: *Ave Sancte Oleum*: Hail Holy Oil and then breathe into the oil in the form of the Greek letter *psi*. This, for some mysterious reason, was deeply symbolic but one feared that false teeth might be lost in this manoeuvre or even with all the coughs and splutters some might actually be sick. They tottered and swayed up to the containers no less than three times: *Ave Sancte Oleum* for the Oil of Catechumens and the Oil of the Sick and *Ave Sancte Chrisma* for the Oil of Chrism. At least if anyone did have a heart attack the newly blessed oils would be there at the ready. The Good Friday Liturgy in the college was a disappointment for some reason, perhaps for the choir not joining in the responses of the crowd. The aftermath could have ended in tragedy as a group of us volunteered to clean the seven lamps of *the lampadarium* and when trying to repair a chain the large counter weight came crashing to the floor just missing our heads. In later years this ornament of the sanctuary recalling the Temple in Jerusalem was removed. Holy Saturday was not exactly holy as Ken and I planned a couple of pranks to play on Moll which went horribly wrong when a balloon full of water burst all over his floor. He was not amused but it did indicate that we were students like anyone else. The climax of course was the Easter Vigil and we were not in bed before 2.30 am.

Easter week provided some break from our usual routine and a certain amount of freedom. Terry Brain's father drove us over to Coventry where we spent some time with Moll's family and also a trip to Lichfield to admire its magnificent cathedral. But the highlight of the week was what was called Excursus Day. Although we were not allowed any holiday at home it was possible to go out for the whole day, other days we had to be in for lunch, so we prevailed upon Enda Smyth to drive John Glen, Bernard Hughes, Moll and me home. We dropped off John and Bernard on the way and having run out of petrol at one point Enda succeeded covering the one hundred and twenty miles to Lidgate. It was a glorious day that I shan't easily forget. The countryside was bathed in sunshine and was like heaven after the ghastliness of Birmingham. Mum had put on her traditional spread, including her famous trifle, for the visitors and she and dad were so pleased to see us. Moll was impressed with the cottage but it was, oh so short - just about three hours before being picked up again by Enda and shot back to Brum. The following afternoon we went to Stratford on Avon but I was not overly impressed by the town.

The rector was in a bad mood. It seems that some students whose rooms were over his had disturbed his peace and as a punishment the college was kept waiting for nearly an hour for lunch the following day. The student body was restive and all kept a deadly silence which only annoyed him further but we eventually escaped and then we sought his permission to go to Hawkesyard Priory. Poor Moll was elected to get permission from 'His Grumpiness'. 'Why do you want to go there?''Yes you can go but don't make it a habit'. It seems he had an aversion to the Dominicans. A group of us cycled to Hawkesyard Priory, which was at that time the student house of the Dominican Order near Rugely in Staffs and where some of my contemporaries from Laxton were doing their training. It was good to see them all but none of them survived the troubles that were to hit the Order not so many years hence when the storm broke. One was ordained eventually but left not so long afterwards. It was a lovely spot and the priory was next to Spode House which was a retreat centre that had connections with Josiah Spode of pottery fame.

A certain feeling was growing regarding the rector and unhappy relationships were beginning to build up between the student body and the Old Man. It expressed itself at Compline that evening when Enda deliberately pitched the initial call to prayer very high indeed in the hope that he would not be able hit the response - but by Jove he did - he might have been eighty five but he was still as strong as an ox. Unfortunately the college was still not in the rector's good books and by way of collective punishment we were denied our extra hour's lie in the following day. Our week's 'holiday' ended with my turn to clean the common room this time with a new polisher which was better than the old bumpers. The evening concluded in the common room with hilarious plots on how to 'do away' with the Old Man.

The growing senility of Leonard S. Emery manifested itself again the following day when he stopped his private Mass in the middle for ten minutes while the server was detailed to find out where some noise was coming from. Such was the decaying regime under which we were living. However the vice-rector, just to pour a little oil on the bubbling situation, informed us how well the college rules were being kept but we must tread more carefully across the rector's rooms.

Sociology restarted with a bang: 'When a couple has been together for forty years, as it were'.. And, 'It were, as it were'... Could we be sure of anything? It was noted that there was a great deal of hilarity coming from the profs' common room. They too must have felt the dead hand of the rector and it was possibly a relief for them that he had gone away for a few days to the Old Brotherhood Meeting, of which he was president in London.

The growing sense of paranoia surrounding the rector was illustrated shortly after. The rector, as has already been mentioned had turned the clock back from the college's earlier approach to the outside world. No visitors were allowed to any extent and certainly no women were permitted inside the college. The vice-rector had the sense to see that the museum was a gold mine of antiquities and rare books and so he invited an expert to begin cataloguing the Recusant library. But what a performance - it would have topped any cloak and dagger enterprise. Mr Pullen had literally to be smuggled in under the eye of the rector. His car was hidden behind some bushes at the front of the house while we were working in the museum which adjoined the rector's rooms. We were posted by Mgr Foster to stand guard and to warn if there was any sign of the Old Man in the vicinity. It was all getting very oppressive and, having failed to match up the museum catalogue with a search for the vertebrae of seven elephants and only finding the skull of a horse and the rector's old trunk, we were pleased to make a quick getaway leaving Mr Pullen to the wrath of the rector should he be discovered! The first of his successes and it seems unknown to the Authority was the sale of a rare atlas for £3,000 which was reported in the local newspaper - and this was only the beginning. Such pettiness would continue for some time with the denial of bits of free time here and there. Fr Lawler's Meditation Points at this time were perhaps apt: 'To worry is to have a lack of trust in God'. The execution of Caryl Chessman on death row in spite of a reprieve that came ten minutes late caused much discussion at this time but this was countered by the joyous news that Princess Margaret had married Anthony Armstrong Jones and although we were not granted a holiday the Union Jack was flown from the Tower.

One couldn't help feeling sorry for the Old Man as not long after he was found on the floor having slipped out of his chair. One really wondered how much longer he could continue in his position. However there was jollifica-tion a few days later as we celebrated his twenty five years as rector of the college. At least we had a good meal - ham, tongue, salad, charlotte russe, melon and wine.

We had been rehearsing for a second play and it went off well and we seemed to be back in the rector's good books. I had a small part in *Arsenic and Old Lace* - perhaps a suitable play in view of the unhappy relationships in the house at present. The St George's Day party was scuppered because we had to clamp down on the noise – in the event a St George's Cross with skull and crossbones was strung across the hall. The dummy used in the play - Mr Spinalzo - appeared from time to time in various places and some students had considered dressing him in cincture and cassock and throwing him off the tower at an appropriate moment. This rather tasteless enterprise did not materialise but it was symptomatic of the student mood. Such stresses and strains showed in the professorial body and the vice-rector admitted in his talk to us that he was not fitted to his job and as I wrote home, 'I should think it would be a good thing if he were moved out into the world as he has been in the college for the last twenty six years ever since being ordained.' This lead up to my first birthday at Oscott - my nineteenth. Rather sad really as I had never celebrated my birthday at home, since I was seven years old. It was duly celebrated by a dose of Kierkgaard in Philosophy, a trip to the dentist and caching five clothes moths in my room. However the following day marked the beginning of a couple of days off for the Old Oscotian reunion and so it was as good as a holiday and we went off to Sutton Park where I treated my friends to sandwiches and cakes. The college was full of old *alumni* and lead by our new manual labour dean, Gregory Winterton. We were given 'battle operations' for serving our guests at table. Great rumpus and guffaws could be heard on my corridor - the Northampton old boys had arrived in the persons of Harry Wace and Bob Manley, two great friends and notorious characters. Little did I know what an important part they were to play in my life in the years to come! In fact the Northampton students were noted for their good humour and sense of camaraderie, no doubt, this was because of the size of our diocese and other students rather envied this quality in us.

A memorable event was the all night pilgrimage to Walsingham. It was glorious weather and the dawn chorus in the chill of the morning air was stunning and such a contrast from the grime of the city.

We never knew when the end of term was to be. Technically it was the middle of July and there were always threats of going over into that month. The authorities, themselves, never seemed to know until the last minute. However the rector did manage to announce that the next term would begin on September 14th and there was a good likelihood that June 29th would see the last of Oscott for awhile. On this occasion it was customary to announce the name of the new dean or head boy which next year was to be Nick McArdle - not a job to be envied in the present state of affairs. During these last few weeks the weather had turned really hot and some of us sunbathed in the field by the old observatory and I wore my shorts under my cassock. The temperatures reached the upper 80's and were the hottest on record for that time of year. There was one student, Leo Woodward, a former parson and the splitting image of Cardinal Newman- even more so than Gregory Winterton - who succeeded in getting onto the glass roof over the museum to sunbathe. In those hot months he wore only his cassock under which was a brief pair of briefs so that he could quickly strip off for his favourite pass time. By a cunning system of string and attachments he was able to keep his collar in place by fixing it to his underwear.

Lectures rattled on: Jung, Hinduism and an attempt to solve the Synoptic Problem in Scripture. Peter Lawler had been away giving a Retreat to some Teddy Boys and had been trying to learn some of their slang so that he wouldn't sound too square. How I should like to have been a fly on the wall. Revising, exams, packing of trunks, a thirty five minute talk by the rector contrasting the Spiritual Priest with the Worldly Priest and announcing that next term now started on 7th September and after Compline we sang the *Te Deum*, and the *Itinerarium*. It was a tortuous cross country journey home by train but we steamed through some old haunts near school. The countryside was intoxicating and on Cambridge station I was met by my old friend from school days Joseph Ibbett with his brother John.

Home at last to the glorious Suffolk countryside away from the hot house of college life and Birmingham gloom. It was back to normal and the ordinary day to day events, free from philosophical speculation. Father had converted the old wash house at the back of the cottage as a room all to myself which was marvellous. I hunted around for a job - especially fruit picking but there was none on offer and there was no other employment in the locality so I fell back on the hospitality of the family. The time was peppered with visitors, old friends of the family who came and stayed for a week or too. The family was ever hospitable and it enabled mother to dispel some of the isolation she experienced in living in the country. Father just went along with things. He had retired and was in his early seventies but he was continuing to do what work he could. He was in the process of making, single handed, a thirty nine stave wooden ladder. His ladders were still being used on the farms and for the corn stacks. I wondered at his skill as a craftsman but he was ever quiet with little conversation and becoming more introverted with the growing problems of arthritis. The aunts were as strong and supportive as ever and there were numerous drives out into the country-side and local towns to show visitors the sights and sounds. Mother still had her 1939 Austin Big Seven, which was beginning to show signs of age and there was ever the danger and worry of imminent breakdown, so the extent

John Molyneux & Me

of our trips were somewhat limited. For a few days John Molyneux came to stay and borrowing another bike I was able to show him some of the local sites - a countryside so different from his native Coventry. There was a return to Laxton for a visit and to meet the 'Dads', as we called them, now on an adult level. There were great plans for expanding the school to bring it up to modern requirements, but I noted a decline in general standards. There were trips out with my friends the Ibbetts and very long lonely cycle rides on my bike. One hundred and two miles on one occasion was my furthest adventure to explore the richness of the local environment and the medieval parish churches which were the usual goals of my excursions and of course there were my usual walk up Cobbolds Lane to commune with nature. How lucky I have been! There was a memorable holiday in Sidmouth with my four cousins from Horsham and their parents. There had been a late addition to their family in the person of Andrew who was only four and also Stephen another brother who had not gone to Laxton. In fact it was the first real holiday that I had ever had away from home and, despite the rain, it was quite an experience. It included a visit to Buckfast Abbey and Exeter Cathedral, the cliffs at Salcombe, swimming in the sea and cornish pasties. On return home, no doubt due to mid holiday blues, I went into one of my depressions about the future. I noted in my diary that I felt that I had got little from my first year at Oscott except a knowledge of philosophy and that I felt I ought to get a job so that I could gain experience with people in different environments and walks of life rather than my own restricted experience. I was sure that if I didn't look out I should just drift along in the rut and be unable to get out of it. If only I could get out of this introspection. With the experience of family life with my cousins it made me realise that being an only child was part of the problem. I felt rather envious of them in the progress that they were making especially having outgrown me.

On return home there was the annual trip to see mother's Carmelite friend at Waterbeach near Cambridge. On this occasion I was 'privileged' to see her. I suppose that now I was potentially a chaste celibate I was no longer a threat, in spite of the grill and the blunted spikes that pointed outwards towards the visitors. Sr. Mary of Carmel was as ever very down to earth and knowledgeable about the affairs of the world.

93

SECOND PHILOSOPHY Sept 1960 - June 1961

September 14th arrived only too quickly and the painful process of saying goodbye took place as usual but the trauma of earlier years had, thankfully, passed. In those days you could get a cross country train to the Midlands travelling from Cambridge to Bletchley and thence to Birmingham. Here I was greeted by torrential rain which did nothing to lift my spirits. It was good to see old friends again and with Jim Lawless said an introductory rosary round the cloister and actually had a little chat with the Old Man who seemed fighting fit again and to Peter Lawler who looked as ill as ever.

I had changed my room from one end of Bede's corridor to the other. It had the advantage of giving me a little more light but there was no more room and it was still pretty gloomy. This, too, in future years would become a toilet/broom cupboard. And so it was back into the old routine. My meditation skills had not improved during the holidays and blissful sleep soon overtook me.

We had now moved into the second year of philosophy and we said goodbye to Peter Lawler as our philosophy professor. We moved lecture room to what was known as the 'Ice Box', next to the snooker room. It certainly deserved that name! We now faced the dreaded Dr Alfred Oddie and the daunting prospect of studying Cosmology and Psychology. The Doctor was a plain blunt Northerner with a caustic and abrasive humour. He was the one who knew it all and we students would jolly well have to know it too. Sometimes he was a brilliant lecturer, sometimes he was dreadful. One of his stock phrases was, 'I have a theory' and sometimes I wondered whether he composed his lectures around some of his jokes. He was good when he didn't use notes and especially when he went off onto one of his red herrings such as his mistrust of statistics especially when shown in diagrammatical form. He impressed upon us that we would have to work hard and the sort of terror of being asked questions in class that beset me at school returned - there was the feeling that one's ignorance would show and so suffer humiliation from the rest of the class! We covered philosophical concepts of Time and Creation and such Ancients as Thales, Anaximander, and Pythagoras. His followers, we were told, were to keep their hands off beans, due to problems of flatulence. There was also Zeno and his argument about 'Achilles and the Tortoise', not to speak of Heraclitus and the fundamental questions of Prime Matter and Substantial Form, or the mysteries of Ether. We enjoyed a short course on science and the atomic theory. His one catch question, in which he prided himself, was whether a piece of chalk was more than one substance. He was so pleased that another student class got it wrong yet again. His question times were fearsome and he would tie a nervous student in knots and as a punishment a couple had to write essays because of their ignorance. I was not to escape and I gave a rather inadequate answer on Anixemenes.

Doc Oddie, in spite of his very down to earth approach, was extraordinarily scrupulous when it came to celebrating Mass, which could sometimes take over an hour. The delay occurred purifying the vessels after Communion. The belief of the Real Presence of Christ in the Eucharist is fundamental to Catholic belief but he took this to a point of exaggeration when searching for particles of the Host on the corporal. He would spend ages scraping the Corporal with the Paten and holding it up to the light, lest any microscopic speck should be left thereon. It was interesting that in the Archbishop's address to the college he dealt with this very subject of priests who held everyone up at Mass by scraping the starch out of the corporal. I wonder if the Doc's ears were burning! That, I suppose, is what happens when one is a philosopher, but this was never Catholic teaching as these tiny specs certainly did not have the resemblance of bread and therefore cease to be a sign of the Presence.

Sociology droned on with a presentation of the list of encyclicals that we would be studying in the coming term and we began to deal with Hobbes's false theories of the State and some aspects of the United Nations. However Denis was suddenly very witty and we all laughed and we ended up with a 'raison d'etre, as it were'. During my first spiritual direction, Peter Lawler continued his thoughts on my 'intellectual scruples'. This involved going over work continuously that I already understood. I must say it was a pretty accurate analysis of the situation, but then in those days one was really not given any practical ideas on how to study, revise or organise one's time.

The college was getting very cold and I had developed a stiff neck from the draughts, a sore throat and a headache, even a mat placed over my bedclothes did not alleviate the condition but it gave me one advantage that during meditation I could actually sit down, feeling rather poorly, rather than kneel slumped over the choir stall. Meditation improved somewhat and I wonder why I hadn't thought of sitting down before. I suppose I considered that it was not the done thing. When the heating eventually went on in October I found the temperature in my room went to the other extreme and that I was about the only student who was able to keep his window open in the depths of winter so hot it became and this time round I had the benefit of some curtains!

Although there was only one radio in the house - at least in theory, I was determined to acquire one - my first act of rebellious disobedience ! I was fascinated by an advertisement for a kit for making one of the new fangled transistor radios. This appealed to my need for making something with my hands. Having acquired the kit and sending it back once or twice because of missing parts I succeeded in putting this primitive wonder of technology together and low and behold to my joy it worked but since I had no solder I got Paul Sankey, the Rover Crew leader, to solder it together for me. It was like a crystal set and I was able to get several stations going.

There were only sixteen new students this year compared with twenty five the year before and none from my diocese. It had been rumoured that +Leo would not be sending any more students here while the present regime was still going strong.

The Freshmen were put through their paces at the concert of initiation and now we initiates could sit back and enjoy their discomforts. A new professor had joined the staff in the person of Fr Dan Leonard. He was a big quietly spoken Irishman who was too shy to do a turn at the concert when prevailed upon by the students. He was a nice genuine sort of man who would take us for Moral Theology, but like the other profs we really didn't get know him very well.

John Spence, a more mature student from my year and a Scot, was made our Beadle or liaison officer. He seemed a very solid easy to get on with character, from the Brentwood diocese. He had brought with him a full 44 lb bow and arrows. So we had a go with this in the grounds and I was quite pleased with my strength. Looking back it was a highly dangerous operation as we could surely not have known who was doing a tour of the Outer at that time - perhaps there was the faint hope that the rector might have been somewhere in the vicinity - but he was continuing as large as life with only a few downward dips. Another student who joined us was Graham Adams from the Westminster Diocese. He was a real character and always prided himself on being related to royalty or at least to aristocracy and he had documents to prove it. But he was a very genuine and sincere man, although he was mercilessly teased for his 'tofness' which he would always play up to. He would eventually achieve status in the Northampton Diocese as a Mgr on the marriage tribunal. Another addition was a student from the Menevia Diocese by name John Lloyd. He was always a bit giggly but gave no hint of the dreadful catastrophe that would befall him and others under his influence, when, as one of an Archbishop's staff, he would be imprisoned for appalling child abuse many years later. While mentioning this sad and distasteful subject that thirty or more years later would come to the surface one must mention another student, Sam Penney, who had joined us - fresh faced and with curly hair he came from County Cork and could talk a hind leg off a horse in true Irish style. In later years in became a baleful influence in the Birmingham Diocese and spent many years in prison as a sex offender. On a lighter note we unearthed a uniform in the museum of someone in the Vatican Army who fought against Garibaldi - even I had a job to get into it !

College life naturally centred around the celebration of the Liturgy and its precise execution according to the rubrics laid down - how different from the relaxed way in which we celebrate today. As greenhorns we began to learn the intricacies of this 'sacred dance' by serving torch with other colleagues, making sure to keep in line, holding the torch exactly the same height as your neighbour and changing hands at the right time. It was rather like parade ground drill. After torch bearing this year one graduated to being a thurifer - swinging the bowl on chains that contained the smoking incense. You were on you own for this and procedures were far more complicated. I was shaking during my first efforts for it was far more nerve racking than appearing on the stage. The eyes of all the college were on you including the great rector himself presiding from the back of the chapel. I made a mistake at the *Asperges*, the sprinkling with Holy Water at the beginning of Mass, but I managed to right myself. I gained the approval of the vice-rector at Benediction - he liked the red charcoal to create a billow of incense that would create a holy fog and I evidently succeeded on this occasion. The contrast between me a mere 5.6½ inches and the MC John Bourke at 6.5 inches must have caused some amusement among the brethren. In addition to my duties as thurifer I had the energetic task of waking people up in the morning. This involved going round all the corridors and its multitudes of staircases ringing a hand bell. At night time this was replaced by checking that all the lights had been turned off.

The quaint night prayers we said caused me to quote to my folks at home, ' 'Look down, on this this seminary of living plants to adorn thy sanctuary – and do protect its inmates from evil'. I ask you, any one would think this was either a mental hospital or a greenhouse.' Heaven knows what they were making of my comments back home as I kept them up to date with the course of lectures and posed them impossible philosophical questions. One of my main hobbies, when not studying, was practising the piano in one of the side rooms off the cloister. I must have been overdoing this and beginning to irritate the professors in their nearby rooms for on one occasion Frank Thomas came in and asked ever so politely, as was his custom, to tone it down as the Fathers were trying to have their rest. The point was taken.

The worst floods in sixty years were hitting the SW where we had been on holiday earlier in the year and also in the north of England too. Indeed it had been the wettest October for sixty seven years with twice the recorded rainfall for the month of 12.76 inches.

The organist, Gerry Poole,asked me to consider the proposition of becoming his understudy and eventually his successor. At the time I declined because of the commitment involved but things would develop on this score

We seemed to have holidays at the drop of a hat - The rector's Feast Day for example - and the notable visit of a Spanish Coadjutor Bishop from Cadiz, Mgr Anoveros . His visited was heralded by 'Mr Spinalzo' the dummy that had already featured in our play *Arsenic and Old Lace* and had been doing the rounds of the college appearing in various inappropriate places from time to time. He suddenly appeared dressed as a toreador sitting astride the banisters in the Crush Hall pointing at a bull at the bottom of the stairs - papal or otherwise. Spanish music played in the background with a notice proclaiming: 'Welcome Mgr Anoveros, Ola!' This was a return visit for a previous contact by Mgr Foster who travelled to Spain to learn something of the running of their seminaries and so gain ideas for Oscott. The Archbishop welcomed him. There were flowers on the table and we sang *'Ad Multos Annos'*. He could not speak a word of English and his words of wisdom were interpreted to us by a very English person. The rest of the day was proclaimed a holiday. These non religious holidays were designated 'pagan holidays' ! The Mgr was supposed to visit our rooms but he never got to mine and Dickey panicked, as was his wont, when he saw the cut out of the Toreador in the Common Room, and it was quickly removed before our eminent visitor did his rounds.

As we drew towards the end of term another play was enacted – *Charley's aunt*. The former Cistercian, Charles Crawford painted a magnificent set, Pat Kilgarriff (a future rector of the English College in Rome) was convincing as Lord Fancourt Babberley and I had two rivals in female roles in the persons of John Glen and Michael Cunnigham who played Kitty and Amy. I had also delivered a paper to the Shakespeare Society on Christopher Fry. The interest had been my 'starring' in our school production of *The Dark is Light Enough*. This was given before our luminaries Nick Lash and Peter Hocken. I think they thought it was my original thought - no such luck - culled from other sources! Panto rehearsal were coming on a pace and I was spending more time rehearsing the songs with participants at the piano. Moll had put modern words to old songs - so we had a rendering of his text to *Just an old fashioned girl* by Eartha Kitt and *It's an itsy bitsy teeny weeny polkadot bikini*. So we were quite 'with it' for those days.

In the wider ecclesiastical world and as a harbinger of the dramatic events that would soon unfold was the visit of the Archbishop of Canterbury, Dr. Fisher, to see Pope John - the first since the Reformation.

As a practice run for exams Dr Oddie asked me to define an element and a compound. He was not satisfied with my reply. Charles was asked about Ether. A fearful battle then ensued with Charles facing a loosing battle against the lecturer's ruthless logic. Fr Thomas gave us a little oral exam helping us along with hints, such a contrast to the Oddie, whereas O'Shea was waxing eloquent about the principle of subsidiarity. In Scripture Dickie held forth on the Garden of Eden and gave a very vivid demonstration of the creation of man by using the angle poise lamp as Adam with God breathing life into the aforesaid lamp. I noted that my faith had been rather shattered (temporarily) by the revelation that the Book of Genesis was not to be taken literally and that there was no real conflict between that and the theory of evolution. Comparative religion caused some amusement among the brethren when we dealt with Confucianism. We were told that all the emperor had to do was to 'sit in a southerly direction and do nothing as God will work through him. If however things don't go well he can be removed from his position'. This seemed to us an admirable description of the rector whose room in fact did face south. Such were our stresses and strains as we approached another Christmas.

There were concerns that we were not really getting any practical training for life on the parish even though this was four years away and Ken was worried that no techniques were offered for interviewing strangers who came to the presbytery door. For a bit of fun we did a bit of role playing and took it in turns with Moll being the parish priest or the anonymous visitor. Such techniques would be learned, as I was to eventually discover, by hard experience on the mission but it would have been helpful for us to have had some back up assistance.

The dreaded exams were upon us. Dr Oddie announced that, from the answers we had given to his questions, he didn't think many of us would succeed in passing them. He said he wouldn't be worried if we just sat there in silence for the full half hour of the oral exam, though, of course, he might ask whether it was worth going on and naturally we could always retake the exam the following term. Such comments did little to inspire us and horror stories circulated regarding Alf Oddie's examination techniques which seemed designed to confuse and intimidate the candidate. One would enter his room and he might be nowhere to be seen until a disembodied voice would emanate from behind his large desk or from behind a curtain, 'Mr Foreman: Hylopmorphism.' And then you just had to do your best to say all you knew about this esoteric subject. Any way I survived with a 64% - very generous - however his remarks on the written paper I am sure were very fair, 'had a job to read your writing as it got on - immature phraseology and stuff not very well digested.

The pre - Christmas encounter with Peter Lawler was rich in range - we travelled from stigmatics to art and from hospitals to imbeciles. This, on reflection,was a warm up for his talk on sex, the content of which I have no recollection, but no doubt elevating it to a spiritual plane with plenty of sublimation into the bargain. In fact this was part two of his talks. He was under the impression that he had given me part one and so I had to struggle to pick up the threads but I recalled it was a very good talk.

So the climax of the season came with the pantomime which Moll had been writing. He had been practising with home made custard pies-on himself and he got the the lot. The Panto was performed at the orphanage at Coleshill and I had sixteen or seventeen popular songs to accompany – which rather lowered my standards. The children thoroughly enjoyed it and there were swarms of them all over the place. Little did we know, at the time, that a terrible scandal was brewing here which would only come to light some forty years later with the arrest of the superior of the home, whom we met, and who was abusing some of these poor kids. The Christmas day performance was a sell out and we celebrated its success in my room with Moll, Ken and Terry Brain. Needless to say the religious services were conducted with the usual dignity.

I made my debut at dinner reading a section from a book from the high rostrum while the college ate in silence. Fr Joret with his Brummy accent and whose title was 'Master of Sacred Eloquence' thought it went well and that I was quite clear.

Diary entry,'One of Ken's stick insects has died of malnourishment, although it has plenty of offspring, and is now lying in state in a transparent sugared almond box in my room.'

The diocese had a noble band of women known as the Catholic Needlework Guild, who knitted and provided clothing for us poor students. We had put in our order and two enormous parcels arrived with about £40 worth of stuff. I did very well with: 'two pairs of brand new vests and pants (St. Michael- double knit pure combed cotton) and a pair of similar make pyjamas and a pair of hand knitted socks and they all fit me perfectly'. I had also acquired a hand me down cassock from a student who no longer wanted it.

So I returned home from what passed for normality to what was normality as this was the way ordinary people lived their lives. It began to strike me more and more that our life at college was totally artificial and bore little resemblance to the lives of ordinary people that one day we would minister to and this worried me considerably and would continue to so do long after. Life was made up of usually very small and seemingly petty things and here we were at college in the realms of the unreality of the philosophers and theologians. Perhaps they taught us how to think logically, I don't know, but I began to wonder what was really the point of it all. It was good to be back to normal with one's family and meeting old friends but a growing sadness in the slow deterioration in their health which was more marked as they grew older. I took my father to the pictures, as he really didn't get out much. I don't know what he made of the film, *'The Miracle'*, about a Spanish nun whose place in the convent was conveniently taken by a miraculous statue of Our Lady. This enabled her to run off and have a gay time in the world. She eventually repented, returned to the convent and Our Lady in her niche as the nuns gathered round to sing *Ave Maria*. Was this a parable of my life? However religion was not very far away as I made a couple of treks to St Dominic's in Southampton Road to be enrolled in the Third Order of the Dominicans. This little ceremony was performed by Fr Kieran (Pongo) Mulvey OP from Laxton days. I now had the right to buried in the habit of the Order when I died and to wear a miniature white scapular under my clothes.

On return to Oscott a flue epidemic hit the students and staff which did not augur well for a happy resumption of routine but I escaped the bug and college life continued on its relentless way. The cloisters were being painted at last by the students and it was nice to see bright white and blue walls after the depressing chocolate and yellow. Dr Oddie's opening gambit to a new term was not encouraging. He informed us that we were not a particularly brilliant year and that although dogs might dig for bones in the garden he would not. Lectures were generally boring with the occasional flash of humour and brilliance in Doc Oddie's Psychology classes dealing with the philosophical side of the five senses. He said he disliked pianos and organs even less (perhaps he had been the one complaining about my practising!) and could not enjoy a concert as he would be too busy analysing the mathematical side of the music.

A new college Spiritual Director in the the person of Dr Nicholson was installed and Lawler wondered if I would like to transfer to him, but I declined as I really couldn't face baring my soul again. Perhaps he was disappointed but he respected my decision. Manual labour continued under the directorship of Ken as John Winterton had gone off to join the Oratorians and if it was not copying out index cards in the museum it was thinning out beet on the farm, or moving books around in the library. The rector continued to go into decline with his Mass taking longer and longer and someone standing by him to make sure that there was some semblance of validity. The vice- rector was getting more and more on edge with this difficult situation not knowing from one minute to the next what was going to happen. All this, of course, filtered down to us and caused much discussion about the state of affairs. By now Dickie was acting as rector and mealtime was going from one extreme to the other from lingering for ages over the meals to being in and out before we know where we were.

As related earlier I had now graduated from being a torch bearer at Mass to being a thurifer which was a far more complicated choreography though if you did make a mistake it was more easily masked than if you were marching along in a phalanx of six and suddenly turned the wrong way. + Humph

Bright's arrival for Ordinations cut all this down to size. On this occasion I carried the *bugia* (small candle) to illuminate his book and was told I looked like Wee Willy Winkie or Christopher Robin with the concomitant chaos that usually surrounded his celebration of the liturgy.

With one of the warmest winters on record I roasted in my room with temperatures reaching 70F and with the constant rattling of the water pipes I was nearly driven up the wall. The first real loss from our year took place at this time. It was always shattering when this happened and one wonders, 'Will I be the next to leave?'

Dr Oddie at last caught the flue although he had a theory that he couldn't get it for another fourteen years. This coincided with an eclipse of the sun and we smoked glass furiously. However next day, on the tower, we never saw a thing because of the cloud and as I recorded, 'we would have to wait till 1999 for another chance to observe it.'

About this time we all received the 'gift' of a tin locker for our rooms for hanging up our cassocks. There was really no space in my cubby hole for such an addition and so I managed to squeeze the 'green goddess' under my bed.

Bishop Leo made his annual visit to his students and was on top form and I was at least half an hour chatting to him. He wanted to know how I was getting on and whether I was happy. He said I could go to Upholland for the Theology Course but of course the train fare there was £10 single – and Old Hall, Ware was really no nearer. I think he was beginning to be worried about the state of the college under the present regime. In the end he said that I might as well stay as, 'Oscott is the best of the holes'. We talked a lot about East Anglia, its increasing Catholic population and this was one of the reasons why his new auxiliary bishop was going to live near Norwich in order to put the eastern counties on the map. He also remarked that they were looking for yet another site for a new church in Newmarket. I was not to worry about money but I was not to spread it around that I was getting a special grant as everyone else might want one too. He advised me to keep up with the piano and to learn the organ as well.

March 10th marked an historic day for the college when the vice- rector announced that the rector was going away for a good rest to Selly Park Convent, but as we agreed this move would either kill him or he would return invigorated for another ten years. But we were not to see him again. Then the 'rot' began to set in. Fr Thomas was seen showing visitors around the college - unheard of before and the vice-rector, trying to be amenable and relaxed about this new situation, went to the other extreme in granting permissions right left and centre. Before you could get your request out of your mouth he would just waive his arms and give the go ahead before really knowing what it was you were asking for - a very dangerous precedent! History was made when a 'generous' permission was extended to me when I asked if some of my former school friends from Hawkesyard Priory might come over and his response was, 'Marvellous, when are they coming.' After a cycle ride over to see them, come they did, five of them and the procurator actually went out and bought some posh cakes and we were able to entertain them in the refectory. Some time before when the great Fr Ives Congar OP visited the college he had to eat in the kitchen. Everything was now 'marvellous' or 'bless my soul', or 'avanti' - such a contrast with the stultifying atmosphere up till now. 'A wind of change was blowing' and two students from the Anglican college came over and stayed for Vespers. They were more Roman than we and thought we were very slow in recognising the validity of Anglican Orders and considered themselves 'in communion with Rome'. However, despite this new liberal outlook, one evening the acting rector announced that he was now the 'Board of Discipline' and proceeded to read what was the equivalent of the Riot Act, something that had not been heard in the college in living memory. It was on April 14th that the Archbishop announced the official 'resignation' of the rector.

Dr Oddie continued as ever to inflict mental torture on us by drawing names out of a hat and the victim having to stand out at the front of class and answering questions for twenty minutes. One student refused and left the college shortly afterwards - its becoming, as I noted, like 'Ten Green Bottles'!

Having driven all the profs. mad with my piano playing especially as I had sent away for a do it yourself course on learning the instrument, Fr Thomas was very pleased to see that I had taken up an interest in the organ.. + Leo had encouraged me to do this and so I was to spend many happy hours in the organ loft and having a few lessons from Gerry Poole, before he too left the college for the greener fields of the parish.

We were given the traditional holiday for St. Patrick's day and those of Irish descent appeared with great clumps of greenery attached to their cassocks. They put on one of their unintelligible plays which we all enjoyed and in the afternoon Ken, Mol and I took a trip down to Stratford - on - Avon and Henley in Arden. It made a nice break but the stale scones and cakes we had at a cafe were some of the most miserable I had ever tasted.

The betting continued on who was to be the new rector. There were now thirty three possible candidates with Mgr Foster still in the running coming in at number thirteen. It looked as though we were going to get someone from Rome. We just hoped that we would not get Mgr Tickle.

With the expansion of the Northampton diocese there was the need for an auxiliary bishop to assist the ageing + Leo. To everyone's pleasure Charles

Bishop Charles Grant

Grant who had been parish priest of Kettering was appointed and we made the trip to our Cathedral at Northampton for his consecration. This was a memorably impressive affair and we were all entertained afterwards at a feast at the Overstone Solarium. +Charles, very laid back and somewhat indolent by nature, was a good contrast to +Leo and provided a much gentler and approachable side of the episcopate. He stood on no ceremony and turned up afterwards in his old banger of a car. The only disadvantage was that he was too well known by some of his fellow clergy. Eventually he was to take responsibility for the eastern part of the diocese until +Leo's death when he became bishop in charge. Peter Marsh invited him to coffee after lunch and we all piled into his room. Charles said he thoroughly approved of after dinner coffee so we thought we had an ally in him. Charles had been a convert while a schoolboy at the Perse School in Cambridge, opposite the English Martyrs, and he liked to tell the tale of his first encounter with the Catholic Church when he received a clip round the ear by the then sacristan, Clarence Mills, while nosing round the church

A domestic crisis was now brewing below stairs. There had been a mass walk out by the maids and we were alerted to the situation by the procurator, Fr Denis Ryan. He was a big fairly easy going Irishman who would have been of great value in any rugby scrum. There would be no one to clean our rooms, a task we would now have to perform ourselves. The inimitable Paul Sankey, ever inventive, gave a demonstration on how the new hoovers should be used and one was to be placed at the end of every corridor and we would also be required to clear and set up the refectory for meals.

The college was badly in need of repair and decoration and so some of its real estate was being old off. Some pictures were the first to go. One day Dennis Ryan came up to the museum to look at the great lectern. This was not from an aesthetic point of view but simply because the ceiling in Frank Thomas' room was beginning to sag and he thought we ought to move this 'old wooden', Pugin artefact somewhere else. We bridled. Did he not know that this was medieval and the earliest and largest bronze and only bronze casting of its type in the world? That it had been part of Napoleon's booty and that its twin had ended up in the Seine during one of his retreats. So we demolished it. Fortunately it very neatly came to pieces and we eventually transferred it downstairs to a room next to the chapel to await an expert from the Victoria and Albert Museum to take a look at it. Some years later it was sold at a huge price and took up its abode in the Metropolitan Musuem, New York, and from the proceeds renovation of the college took place.

Rumours began filtering back that Len was making progress - to the grave? but also that he was becoming restive and felt that he had been kicked out of the college - so we quite expected a manifestation or *parousia* in the near future. But in the event he would not return. It was all very sad and he should have moved on many moons before. But then rumours began to circulate as to who the new rector might be. There had been much speculation. It was hoped that perhaps Dr H Francis Davis, a well loved professor of former years might be installed. Mgr Foster seemed overjoyed at the possibility of not being here much longer - after all this was a bit of a dead end for the staff and he had been here for years. We did hope that Fr Lawler would not be moved as he was holding the whole show together and taking most of the burden of the college's spiritual life on his shoulders. As the Archbishop suggested we might get a 'lettered man' rather than the un academic man that the former rector had been.

The Easter Excursus Day came round and once again some of us succeeded in getting a train to London and seeing the folks for however short a time. Mother had received a letter from my father's brother, Frank who had emigrated to the States many moons ago and was a member of his local Masonic Lodge and so very anti Catholic. He had written to mother accusing her of forcing me into the priesthood and pointing out that, 'no man comes to the Father except through Christ' and certainly not through any Roman Catholic Priesthood. I should have joined the army and he would have paid for my education. It was touching seeing him some thirty years later on a video brought back by my parish priest in Cambridge attending a Mass in the local Catholic Church for some celebration or other – he must have mellowed considerably. And the real world went on with trouble in Cuba brewing and with an American spy plane being shot down over the Soviet Union. The Queen visited the Pope on the feast day of St Pius V, the Pope who excommunicated her predecessor - how ironic !

Another coach load of us went off again to Walsingham. The weather was fine and the countryside glorious. Some hardy souls actually cycle all the way. One poor chap got a puncture and had to walk miles.

May 25th saw the announcement of the new rector. No one, in the end, was very surprised that it was to be Mgr Richard Foster and the news was greeted with thunderous applause as was the announcement of the new vice-rector - Dennis O'Shea. As I wrote home, 'It all came as an anti-climax. Many people were very disappointed and we had been hoping till the last minute that it would be Dr Davies. I suppose it's no good passing judgment yet and we can only wait to see what happens. It seems funny that Mgr Foster is the man. He's certainly a character and a great personality, but whether he's of the stuff that rectors are made I don't know. Perhaps now, having complete authority in the college, he may change as before he had to be so careful of anything he did because of the of old rector.' He had been at the College for practically the whole of his priestly life and we really had hoped that it would have been someone entirely new with fresh ideas. We were delighted by the new vice- rector. This had come as a complete shock as he wasn't even on our list of possible candidates. He and Dickie get on well together, but he always seems so vague and 'off the air'.

The term climaxed with the Eucharistic Congress held in the college grounds and hundreds of people swarmed in for this event. One wonders what Len would have thought of it all. The following day was spent clearing up the detritus. An aspiration *a propos* of the congress was unearthed written by the eminent convert William Faber: *'O Happy Pyx, O Happy Pyx in which Our Blessed Lord is fixed'* - how quaint were our Victorian forbears. Exams proceeded with my lowest marks, not surprisingly being in Philosophy - as the Doc commented, 'You were confused over many things !'

The bliss of the wide open spaces of Suffolk and home to the bosom of ones family cannot be overestimated returning as it was to normality and the day to day trivial things of life. But there was a restlessness. There was a feeling that I was exchanging one prison for another and that I should be relating to the world in which one day I would be working. There were more anguished walks up Cobbolds Lane. The holiday began with a trip to Laxton and a trip to Stamford to see my old piano teacher when we played a few duets and accompanied some songs.

On return I actually got a job - fruit picking in the next village at Justin Brookes. He was the first man to grow a peach in this country and had extensive orchards in the area. I had been here some years ago with my cousin so was not so unfamiliar with the set up. Starting work at 7.30 am it was a back breaking job picking strawberries followed by currants in the afternoon for which I earned the princely sum of 18/6. There were a lot of students boarding there. This employment was to last ten days but it got me used to the world of work! Sadly the typical British summer threw down a few torrential showers that disrupted proceedings and my confidence was given a bash when our supervisor was not happy with the number of leaves in my offering. In addition a party of muscular bronzed ladies descended like a swarm of locusts on the surrounding bushes and made my efforts look very feeble in comparison. Conversation with a fellow worker ended in silence, so there was not much opportunity to try out my philosophical and theological skills upon him. However at the end of that session my earnings had made the efforts worthwhile. - £8.9s

One or two historic events occurred during this holiday. The first was the winning by our village of the Best Kept Small Village Competition for the whole of Suffolk and Sir Ian Jacob presented the trophy. There was a service of dedication held down by the pond and as was the norm in those days I kept my mouth shut tight during the recitation of the Lord's Prayer, it being a protestant service. This was followed by an attempt to see the Queen who was making her first official visit to the county. By narrow byways the old car found a spot just off the A 45 and we waited in eager anticipation. She came and was gone in a flash with the detection of just a hint of a wave. We were satisfied with simple pleasures in those days.

My father's health continued to give cause for concern. After many years of shoulder breaking sawing and heaving wood around arthritis had set in to his neck and shoulders and he was practically fixed in the one position. They could do little for him at the hospital and simply prescribed some tablets. The pain was driving him more and more within himself and what little communication there was between him and my mother was becoming severely reduced.

Our parish priest from London, Fr Patrick O'Neil, came and stayed for a few days and for an outing we went for a trip to Hengrave Hall, a wonderful Tudor mansion near Bury St Edmunds. It was then a superior girls school run by the Sisters of the Assumption in their attractive mauve habit and cream veil. In later years it became an Ecumenical Centre for the diocese only to be sold off in the new Millennium as its financial upkeep could no longer be sustained. My cousin Jonathan came and stayed for a couple of weeks and we made out first attempt at camping. The effort ended in a thunderstorm in a field by a stream at Brent Eleigh. The second attempt was more successful as we cycled up to Walsingham, being given lodging by the hospitable parish priest of Fakenham, Fr Frank Hacon. He gave us an enormous meal and a roof over our head for the night. We tried the same ploy at Beccles where a visiting Benedictine, staying with his sister, the town mayor, gave us refuge in the apple loft. We actually put down our canvas on a camping site at Aldeburgh and on the road to Ipswich we were stopped by the police. It was all we could do to persuade them that we were not the two boys who had recently escaped from Hollelsey Bay Penal Colony!

Looking back on the holiday I recall now with some embarrassment that, 'I have neglected my spiritual duties through sheer sloth and seem to have lost interest in the things that should be the driving force in my life with no zeal or ambition or love of the Lord I should be cultivating. I seem to be living in two unreal worlds - that of Oscott where I seem perfectly happy and here at home with the family. I have a feeling that I shall just drift through Oscott and yet the prospect of leaving and finding other work is so daunting that carrying through to the end at Oscott seems to be what I am destined to do. Perhaps this is what vocation is all about. I wish I had someone I could really talk too. My father just wouldn't have a clue what I was trying to say and I really don't want to cause more worry and concern to my family.' But perhaps it was all due to a general feeling of frustration about conditions at the college and certainly it was becoming clear to the folks that all was not well. News came through that the old rector had died and had been buried at Oscott. Perhaps a new era was beginning at the college and preparation for the priesthood would improve. The holiday ended on a high note by clambering, with mother, up the three hundred steps of Ely Cathedral Tower for the fantastic view over the fens and with another exhausting cycle ride around Suffolk.

FIRST THEOLOGY Sept 1961- June 1962

So now I had entered the ranks of the Theologians - four years of theology lay ahead. The college had spent its money from the sale of some of its treasures slapping more coats of paint on the walls which were now illuminated here and there with fluorescent lighting. In addition electric bells had been installed on the corridors to wake us up in the morning. This made the life of the 'bell ringer' much easier though they tended to be rather erratic at the start. I had moved into a new room - Bedes 6 on the same corridor where I was to remain for the rest of the course. 'My room is a great improvement,' I wrote home, 'but everywhere there is thick grime and remnants of the previous occupant are scattered about the place'. Now I had a panoramic view over the city, 'here and there are great chimneys belching out smoke and we get the full force of winds up here. It doesn't look quite so bad today as the sun is shining but even so it looks pretty grim.' I could see Aston and as far as the Bull Ring in the centre of town. This surely would inspire my apostolic spirit as I listened to the tunes of the Ice Cream van doing its rounds about Kingstanding. My room was next to Billy Madden a very friendly Northern Irishman from the year below. He had difficulty getting up in the morning and I devised various means of helping him - the most effective was dangling a pair of his used sock in front of his nose.

Four of our year had left during the holidays including the possible deputy organist – so there was a chance for me again. Indeed I started practising seriously but found the pedals rather difficult as my legs weren't long enough and there were three manuals into the bargain. I really needed a pair of 'winkle pickers' to cope. We acquired one new student, Derick Smith from the Norfolk Broads who had spent some time with the Carthusians at

Parkminster. Although we were still in the 'ice box' for lectures gone was the dreaded Doctor Oddie to be replaced by a new lecturer, Peter Jones, for what was called Fundamental Theology. He was hot from Rome with a string of degrees and very young. He seemed promising but it was clear that he had no experience in lecturing and to begin with we spent time translating sections from the Latin text book. He was, I think, aware of our boredom and initiated little breaks from time to time so that we could recover our interest. He was a nice enough chap but did not exactly set us alive with the fire of the Spirit.

We were becoming alert to the real world with the appalling famine in the Congo and the tragic death of the Secretary General of the United Nations in a plane crash. We were not to be free of the vice - rector's drone and his qualification of every statement by an 'as it were' had now transferred to Moral Theology – which would put an interesting gloss on propositions and the new rector, resplendent in his new garb as a Domestic Prelate to the Holy Father, gave a lively discourse in the chapel. My duties during manual labour had now transferred from the museum to the adjoining cemetery where I moved some earth with Denis Hall who was now in a room near me. While cleaning his 'forbidden' stove one morning he had dropped half of it out of the window narrowly missing the procurator. On attempting to retrieve it we found both the stove and the proc had gone the latter being quite convinced that it had fallen from my window, but no action was taken, much to our relief

The concert this year was very different since it was the first time that the new students had shouted down the rest of the house and the procedures ended in pandemonium. For the first half we were quite content to shout rude remarks at the actors, blow trumpets and let off at least six alarm clocks not to mention a gramophone. The new professors had joined us and in the spirit of the new regime we turned our attention to them. Fr Jones was in the middle of us and we gradually pushed back our chairs in a circle around him and eventually he was persuaded to stand up and sing something funny. The new Scripture professor, John Greehy, refused as did the rector after cries of, 'We want the new boss.' No one had any voice left to sing the hymn after night prayers that evening.

With the heightened tension in the cold war and the threat of atomic warfare, the rector announced that a 'Bomb Woman' would come to address the college on what we should do if an atomic bomb were to drop. The diarist of the Oscotian magazine recorded : 'One September evening we had a frightening talk by Miss Reilly, WVS on where we should go if someone happened to drop a nuclear bomb on us. She was able to reassure a questioner that the alcoholic was less likely to suffer from fall-out if he didn't die of cirrhosis of the liver first. Among other recommendations were white-washing the common room against overheating, washing clothes, keeping track of the clergy and having a hide out in the wine cellars. The Dean promised to find out where they were.' This proved quite hilarious. Apart from having lots of pails of sand around to douse the flames we should, in preparation, whitewash all the windows of the college – a roar of laughter went up from the assembly!!!

We now began serious stuff - sermon preparation. We had to take it in turns to write and to deliver a sermon. This was either in the Northcote Hall or in the chapel from the famous Second Spring Pulpit. The session was usually taken by the rector. This was followed by a period of criticism and each student, in turn, was asked to comment. By the time we had had the tenth criticism there wasn't much more to say and the stock remark was, ' It was very good sermon, Mgr but.....' It was all rather daunting and my first effort was about Blessed Henry Morse, one of the forty martyrs of England and Wales. This was delivered from the high rostrum of the lecture hall, with the statue of St Thomas Aquinas breathing down my neck, having first submitted my effort to the rector. He made no comments which might have been helpful had he done so. There was great discussion as to whether the sermon should be delivered by heart, have your full notes in front of you and refer to them, as I did, or just take up the main points on a card. The new intake were now having lectures on how to prepare sermons but this was not for us and we just had to keep battling along on our own.

Renovations continued on the decaying structure of the bell tower and there was a lot of banging and crashing as the famous 'Night Cap', which was about to collapse, was removed. 'The rector informed us that there was enough stuff in the museum, if sold, to finance the building of a cathedral, so perhaps we shall see some badly needed improvements in the establishment.'

In the meantime we were on TV. An American gang was here to make a film for American TV about English seminary life, so for some days we had to contend with arc lights poised at various vantage points throughout the college. Resplendent in our clean white cottas we thought ourselves a good advert for Persil or for Scribbens 'Top Grade Cut Loaf.' How things were beginning to change.

Fr Thomas had continued his history of the Liturgy and now we had the visit of Dom Gregory Murray OSB, composer and authority on the liturgy, who gave us a most interesting lecture on the Gelineaux psalms and a fine recital on the college organ. He was to be followed by Clifford Howell SJ who similarly gave a lecture on the psalms. Clifford was to do so much in following years going round parishes encouraging greater participation in the liturgy.

By now, well into October, the college was getting perishing cold and I would go round swathed in a scarf and most people had coughs and colds. I noted that everywhere was terribly dusty and this tended to get on one's chest. The folks at home even sent me a duster to clean up my room! An appeal was made to the procurator to put on the heating but he said he was not going to be dictated to by the students - but the day after our protest on Oct 19th the central heating went on at last. The cold really was intolerable, much worse than I had experienced at home. The draught even started to rustle the pages of my missal in the chapel. Somebody very kindly lent me a long sleeved polar necked pullover which warded off some of the breeze.

The new scripture professor, Dr John Greehy from Dublin was someone who knew his stuff. He had several degrees and was fluent in about ten languages. He was tall dark and rather gangly with arms and legs waiving around in various directions but he was a veritable dynamo and full of enthusiasm for his subject.

There were now lectures in Church History given by the procurator, Denis Ryan. This burley Irishman had a great facility for obscuring his subject and dealt one by one with the various heresies in the early Church. It was my lot to give a short talk on *Arianism*.

The college had its occasional eccentric. Among them was Michael Jones- Frank (The Admiral) already mentioned. One afternoon I had been down to Malvern with him and had a marvellous walk along to Malvern Beacon and then on to Worcester Cathedral. As I recorded: 'He has taken to cultivating different species of cheeses. He has got all sorts of strange varieties which are maturing in a damp vest hanging up in his cupboard. He doesn't give anyone a taste of them though. He has also taken to making coffee in a percolator.' I was very privileged, eventually, to be given a taste of the said cheese and it really wasn't as bad as it looked or smelled. I might have been considered an eccentric myself since two people quite independently of each other said that I looked like a gypsy. It may have been that I hadn't had my hair cut recently and I certainly wasn't going to loose any in the bitter weather. The topic of gypsies came up when +Leo made his annual visit and I asked him whether there was anything done for them in the diocese but he said that they usually went to Church. Again he was rather concerned about my appearance and wondered whether I was keeping in good health. He said that a site for the new church in Newmarket had been purchased and was pleased that I had taken up the organ. He was concerned about my parents, wondering whether they were supporting themselves all right – 'Are they on a pension? – so are We but we don't go to the Post Office for Ours.' Later on I received the usual cheque from him for £15 with the usual note that I was not to tell the other students who were probably better off than I.

111

The term ended with an Old Time Music Hall, when we all dressed in suitable garb with me accompanying the songs. There was the traditional carol concert in the common room and the rector in very relaxed mood sang, *'Though poor be the chamber'* in his rich baritone voice . We had already had our quota of plays, *Tons of Money* and *Nothing but the Truth* and my playing the Fairy Queen in the pantomime at Coleshill.

Holidays really seemed like another world and I felt I was becoming more and more distant from the folks, much as I loved them very much. Their lives seemed so narrow and in some ways petty compared with the social interaction at college. As they were beginning to age, since they were now all in their seventies, except mum they tended to get on each others nerves and father who was getting more and more introspective with the constant pain and discomfiture of his arthritis rarely spoke unless spoken too. He was happy reading the daily newspaper or the westerns that mum would bring back from the library but I was never really able to share with him any of my experiences from college. However on an almost unique occasion we got him to reminisce about his life, which I recorded, and the first time in my life that I really had any decent conversation with him. Mother and I managed to get several outings in - to the Albert Hall for the Messiah and also again to hear Yehudi Menhuin play Beethoven's Violin Concerto conducted by Sir Malcolm Sargeant - what an experience! However it was during a trip to the Wigmore Hall to hear Claude Frank play Beethoven that I must have picked up a flue germ and disaster then struck with me laid up in bed and passing on the germ to everyone else. Sorting out sleeping arrangements was a bit of a problem. As ever aunt Dorothy, the most frail of the family, was a tower of strength in ministering to us until she too was struck down. We then resembled something of a hospital ward and our Dr Clark, one of the last of the good old fashioned family doctors was round to the house practically every day for the next three weeks, so concerned he was with the arrangements. There was no question of my returning to college and when I had recovered it was my turn to wait on the invalids and do the shopping and cooking. Not only was there concern over the flue but small pox was rearing its head again and large measures were being taken to vaccinate everyone. Depression which follows illness took hold again and a questioning of why I wanted to become a priest and my motives for so doing. 'I have feeling that I won't be competent doing anything else. But then how can I say this as I have little idea what is going to be involved in being a priest. The fact that it offers more security than the problematic question of what else I could possibly do ? Does this mean that I have no vocation? In many ways I feel quite trapped, fossilised even, and not really knowing which way to move.' I was now having meals alone with my father and it was all I could do to communicate with him which was really getting me down too and for most of the time we just sat in silence until he went out for his afternoon hobble down the road. I only wish that I could get out and meet a few people. Our neighbours in the flats above, as ever, had been very good.

It was decided that I should return to college at the end of January. However on the day chosen our local taxi man advised me that as the traffic was so bad I should postpone my departure for another day or so. On the last day of January I eventually got the train back to Birmingham. I found myself alone in the train with a very unpleasant man whose obsession with sex was only too obvious and he was over curious about my life style. It was with a sense of relief when he got off the train before I had to pull the communication cord.

My companions seemed pleased to see me back and glad that I hadn't left. This was going to be the term for receiving First Minor Orders – tonsure, porter and lector. I reported to the rector immediately. He gave me a form to fill in to formally apply for Minor Orders. As I wrote home, 'The trouble is that those at the top don't seem to bring home the importance of this step. You just appear as a name on a piece of paper. I suppose that they are so used to this event happening they forget that it has personal importance to the candidate concerned.' And as I recorded, 'In many ways I half hope that I shall be turned down but if I do go through then I have to accept this as God's will for me.' However doubts still plagued me, 'Having lived in a community environment for the last thirteen years and not having much normal social contacts with people of my own age - let alone girls. Everything seems so unreal and abstract here. The days go by in a sort of dream and the lectures don't seem to take on any real meaning and I don't somehow feel the equal of other people. The trouble is I couldn't see any ways of solving the problem. Looking back over the last three years and how quickly they had passed I dreaded to think of the next three.' To distract me from these reflections I was plunged immediately into the radio broadcast of Vespers celebrated by Dennis O'Shea - sounding as ever like Larry the Lamb from *Toy Town* - not the most audiogenic experience but Dickey preached a lively homily. I was in the gallery handing the organist the music, nearly dropping it on the key board at a crucial moment. Plaudits came in with an interesting one from an eighty year old in beautiful handwriting who remembered visiting the College and seeing Cardinal Newman.

There were pages of Moral Theology to catch up, due to my late return to college, with dull old stuff from Canon Law, but I eventually got up to date with lost studies and back into the swing of things and there was the added pleasure that the staff problem seemed to have been solved and our rooms were now being cleaned once more. There was also the joy of receiving another anti polio jab. Some people had nasty side effects but the scab on my arm soon fell off with no other problems. I continued to work in the cemetery for manual labour levelling off the earth of some of the graves and trimming others. I had a good old chat with Dennis Hall about the state of affairs in the college and our main gripe being the perception how very little real contact there was with the professors and a feeling that they never really know you or take a personal interest.

There was now something of a breakthrough into the outside world under the new regime when Frank Thomas suggested that I might like to have some organ lessons at the Midland Institute and that I shouldn't have to pay either. Frank consulted the rector about this possibility and it was all right by him. However after consulting the procurator this was a different matter. He didn't see this as an expense for the college and, if the college paid, it might create a precedent. The problem was that my local West Suffolk Council was still not awarding me a grant towards training. We did apply again but it was a negative response - It would have been a different matter if I had been studying for a non-denominational degree in theology. Other students were receiving very generous grants from their local authorities which was very useful for purchasing books and other necessities. I was relying on the £15 or so pocket money from +Leo. So unless the Council offered me a grant, or failing that the bishop, organ lessons were off the menu. It was so annoying. I think the proc thought the lessons were just for my benefit and not for the wider college - I really needed to have them now so that I could take a greater part in accompanying the Liturgy. Just to add insult to injury Frank gave me a copy of the Midland Institute syllabus but as far as I could see the whole thing looked hopeless and pretty disappointing. Chatting with him later he thought I would still be able to go but had better postpone it until September - months away! The college organ was soon to be rebuilt and, in the meantime, I began to play at Compline for one of the anthems. It was a nerve racking experience and trying to cope with the time lag between voices and instrument. Later, when this was no longer possible, due to the restoration, I was allowed to practise on the organ down the road in the Boldmere church.

The Fundamental Theology lectures which at first seemed quite promising began to go downhill. I don't know whether Fr Jones really enjoyed giving lectures at all. At any rate when you asked him a question or posed a problem all he said was 'yes, that's true', and made no attempt to answer it . We bombarded him with questions over the text : 'Do you love me more than these?', but we could still not get a satisfactory answer from him. We embarked on the Apostolic Succession but a good many of his arguments didn't seem too convincing and those for Papal Primacy seemed even thinner from an apologetic point of view. It was difficult to prove things from the outside when one was bringing in the Church all the time as an infallible teacher. We were also being asked some questions for a test - daft questions such as, 'how many times does *ecclesia* occur in the Gospel?' The only professor who seemed to know where he was going was Doc Greehy in his scripture lectures. However we got some good input from the practice sermons and Michael Stokes gave a very interesting paper on the Byzantine Rite, playing some excerpts from their chant.

I had been studying a book on Christian Yoga and was determined to try and follow out some of the ideas. The exercises might hopefully keep me fit and also help me to keep awake during meditation in the morning. I was resolved to go to bed half an hour earlier and get up half an hour earlier in order to find time for the exercises. Whether it had any appreciable effect I have my doubts but I did succeed in eventually standing on my head ! In the end an outer in the 'fresh' Birmingham air, first thing, seemed just as effective. However to cheer us all up and to help us realise there was a world out there or up there - the astronaut, John Glen, went round the world three times in a spaceship and we heard some of the excitement on Moll's radio. Most of the profs were late for supper as they had been tuning for the result of his safe return.

Fr O'Shea's Moral Theology lectures continued much in the same vein as his lectures in Sociology. How many moral principles did he qualify by his stock phrase - 'as it were'? We spent a lot of time discussing whether a thing was a sin or not and the various influences that could reduce the gravity of an action such as ignorance, fear, passion etc. It was cheering to learn that if you were forced into marriage against your will it would not be a valid union. It was all deadly dull.

There was consternation felt in the college at a Papal Bull that Pope John had just signed concerning the use of Latin in the Church. It proposed that once again Latin should be used for lectures in seminaries. There was much discussion. It was bad enough trying to follow some of the lectures in English how we would manage in Latin I just did not know. And what would the professors make of it ? I liked the way it said that all those professors who could not teach Latin would have to find other professions. It had been rumoured that students at the English College, in Rome, had burned the said bull in the common room fire - but then they had lectures in Latin anyway.

We rarely saw anything of the lay staff of which there must have been quite a few. There was a matron but you never saw her unless you were desperately ill and we had a student infirmarian, Bernard Hughes, of our diocese, who acted as a sort of liaison officer. However one lady came into prominence when the Archbishop came to present her with a medal from the Pope, the *Bene Merenti*, for long service. This was to Mrs. Dunleavy who was eighty six and had been working at the College since she was 14 and her grandfather had worked here since the college first opened in 1840s. She used to dust the old rector's room when he was a student and remembered the great Cardinal Newman when he visited the college.

Interest was growing about the forthcoming General Council that Pope John had called to open the windows of the Church onto the world, 'something we could well do with here, although if his Bull about Latin was anything to go by, the future didn't seem very promising.' A Mgr Montgomery came to give us a talk about some of the characters that would feature at the Council. Before he became a priest he had been secretary, before the war, to several British Ministers at the Vatican. He knew the last three Popes and many of the Cardinals. He was not a very good speaker and even, while using notes, he seemed to be in a bit of a dream and I felt, with the presence of the rector, he had to be a bit careful about what he said. It was fascinating to hear him speak about Mgr O'Flaherty, 'The Scarlet Pimpernel' of the Vatican, who did much to smuggle Jews and others out of Italy during the war. We even had a discussion, in view of possible Council deliberations, about the possibility of restoring a married diaconate.

We were now to be thrust into the real world by the advent of a Television crew which was now to disrupt just about everything. The first TV broadcast from the college was to go out on Palm Sunday and so we were to spend a lot of time practising the Palm Procession. Miles of wires appeared and the chapel was festooned with scaffolding and arc lights for the Mass. This was a pleasant distraction from lectures which were proving interminable and the almost interminable process of decorating my room with plaster and wall paper and a new carpet. In the event, despite problems with one of the lights that broke down at the last minute, it was all a great success and we were TV stars. The rector celebrated and Fr Lawler preached covering his favourite topics of tensions, global warfare and illness with Fr Geoffrey Tucker from the University giving the commentary. Later in the day we were able to see a recording of the ceremony on O'Shea's TV.

The climax of Easter this year was the solemn knocking over of the Paschal Candle. When moving the lectern the MC, Geof Bagnall, caught the foot of the lectern underneath the candle stand and over it went and down came candle and flowers and a great flood of water but with great liturgical aplomb the MC collected things together and the ceremony proceeded as usual - if you make a mistake, make it with conviction and no one will notice! On the Monday visitors and parents were allowed into the college for the first time. At the other end of the scale was the Excursus Day. The rector was getting nervous about the relaxation of some of the rules and he insisted that our one day out in the year should be curtailed so that we must return to the

PALM SUNDAY ON TV
Madden, Cunningham, Adams, Spence, White, Ryan, Hall, Me

college by 9 pm for night prayers instead of drifting in at all hours of day and night as previously. This had caused great consternation especially since we wanted to get down to London again. Graham Adams came to the rescue and after letters to the management of British Railways he managed to wangle us a special excursion ticket by pleading that we were poor students and that it was our only day out in the year - which was quite true! So it was up at 5 am taking the 7.30 am from Snowhill while Graham kept flourishing his letter at all and sundry on the station. Despite the dreadful traffic at the other end I managed to get home to see the aunts, since the parents had already gone back to Suffolk, and I spent a few happy hours at the flat, but it was all too short lived and we had to catch the 5.10 pm train back to Birmingham and were in by 9 pm although one or two people were late. Another sign of the rector getting cold feet was his refusal to grant permission for us to stay for lunch at Hawkesyard Priory when we went over to see our friends on another day. He thought it was becoming too much like another Excursus Day since, according to the rules, we were only allowed one of these a year to be out for the whole day. All these rather petty restrictions, which I suppose were to be for the good of the soul, were becoming very irritating. At least I had another escape since I had been having problems with eye strain and with Dennis had to go down to the eye clinic at Birmingham hospital for various tests and exercises and this made a few nice outings into the big world outside. This lead to another interminable discussion with Dennis about life here and the priesthood. We came to the conclusion that it was too much like school - the profs seem to take no interest in you as individuals and there was no real incentive to work. I still considered that I should have had a year out before I had come to the college. I may have increased in knowledge since I had been here but as to my own personal development and integration into a community I felt I hadn't advanced at all and Oscott was no more than an extension of school. All this had been brought to a head by the talk given to us by Dr Marshall of the Catholic Marriage Advisory Council. This was interesting but very disturbing. I knew nothing about marriage, except my parents marriage and I had never even been to a Catholic wedding in my life and this applied to Baptisms etc. as well. Dennis on the other hand, coming from such a different background and an East End Parish, was full of zeal and enthusiasm.

The decorators were gradually moving round the students rooms and so there was some chaos and I had to move back temporarily into the dreadful room I had last year. I had great fun stripping the walls and learning how to paper the ceiling. This was a job my father hated and he was quite pleased to learn that I had been doing something practical like this. There were holes in my ceiling that had to be plastered first and the movement of the front of the college due to its building on sandy soil had caused problems. Then I had to choose my wall paper but there were layers of paper, going back years, to strip and in the end some of the lads came along and papered the lot for me. The folk had paid for a carpet to be sent for my room, which was too small, and had to be sent back. In the meantime I sent them potted accounts of my studies and especially on the Arian Controversy and the Great Western Schism.

I was informed from home that I now had a mysterious benefactor who sent me money to buy a new cassock and to this day his/her identity remains a mystery.

Our rarified philosophical existence in the Intelligentsia group continued with a learned paper by Paul Tubb on Heidegger and another on Karl Rahner. It was very obscure until Lawler clarified things a little. This was followed up by a paper given by Fr Cornelius Ernt OP who had translated his works. His delivery was attractive and I didn't fall asleep at all but the whole lecture was really over my head.

And so I reached my majority on the sixteenth of May. People were very kind and I received cards from fellow students and even 10/- from Denis and

Paul Sankey with £10 from mother and £5 from the aunts, money they could ill afford. I even received a letter from dad - the first ever which was very touching. Ken organised a little celebration in my room and Nick Lash and one or two other students came along for an hour or so. The celebrations continued with a trip to the eye hospital for a ten minute exercise when I had to focus on putting a bird into a cage. This had coincided with the visit of the old Oscotians for their annual reunion with the usual noisy advent of the Northampton Clergy. A chamber pot had been doing the rounds and somehow or other it eventually got into Bob Manley's suitcase which he carried off unwittingly.

John Rust, meanwhile, had come to visit the college in response to a letter I had written. He was vice-principal at the Midland Institute in Birmingham and a friend of Uncle Reg from Christ Hospital Days. He was impressed with the college and he had leanings to become a Catholic. Fr Thomas spoke to him about organ lessons and he agreed to give me free lessons from time to time. He played the organ at the end of Vespers. And so I started my occasional lesson down in Brum. This was a real break through as far as the College was concerned and I was something of a pioneer in doing some extra mural activities. John was a very lively character and I benefited greatly from his teaching in the years to come. This also gave him an opportunity to question me about matters concerning the Catholic Faith he had been discussing with Thomas. In the end he never became a Catholic and sadly I lost contact with him in later years. It was so refreshing having a proper teacher with certain targets to attain instead of the wittering on of so many of the lecturers at college.

I was also getting excited with the prospect of going to Rome for a holiday with Denis Hall in the summer. This would be a great adventure. How appropriate was the book being read in the refectory, *'Abbot Extraodinary'* about the founder of the Caldey Island Monastery and his interesting career - it did show what was possible. There was also my breakthrough into the technological age with the purchase of a tape recorder for my 21st birthday present. What fun I would have with that!

While travelling on the bus for one of my several visits to the eye hospital we were accosted by the bus conductor who maintained that he was 'saved' and that our Church was wrong to use Bingo to raise money. We were not yet primed for a return evangelisation and were glad to get off the bus pretty quickly. This reminded me of Bishop Leo's comment that sometimes Catholic bus conductors would waive the fares of students into town (whether they paid or not,who knows) and +Leo was most upset when he had to pay the full fare on one occasion.

Some of us had watched the impressive ceremony of the consecration of the new Coventry Cathedral though it was somewhat spoilt by the intonation of Archbishop Ramsey of Canterbury. This inspired me to go down to St. Chad's Cathedral in town for the annual eucharistic procession. The precession had been introduced some years ago because of the anti Catholic eucharistic preaching of the then Anglican Archbishop of Birmingham, Bishop Barnes. It was a Catholic witness to our belief in the Real Presence of Christ in the Sacrament and was a wonderful experience as we processed down the main streets in the City Centre. I lead the Rosary at one point with Denis and Pat Kilgarriff. Luckily the showers held off and no passerby was antagonistic. In the cathedral Bishop Bright preached and Benediction followed. It was lovely to hear the voices of the boys' choir after all these years. There followed a binge at the church hall and having stuffed myself with all sorts of food we returned to college by 9.30 pm for a cup of coffee with Ken. I had also been down to town to do some practice on the impressive Cathedral organ and at the local church at Boldmere so I was beginning to broaden my horizons a little. It was at the Cathedral during one of my sessions that I encountered my first 'man of the road', an Irishman on the cadge for some money. I pointed out that I was only a student and he seemed to understand though I did feel rather guilty in not helping him. Not long after when taking my brand new tape recorder back, as it was not functioning properly, another rough looking gentleman clutching a mince pie asked me whether I thought the nuns would give him anything to eat. I didn't like to state the obvious and directed him to the presbytery. He then asked if I was an RC and, on being told so, he thought that six years was a long time preparing for God's work. Little did I realise that these encounters would feature on a grand scale in years to come.

The family were taking an interest in Cardinal Newman and reading lots about him. They were fascinated by the two volumes written by Meriol Trevor. I had written that I gathered his Cause for Canonisation wasn't going too well and it was unlikely that he would be made a saint as there was not much popular devotion to him, but that was belied my relatives' interest.

Ken announced to me that he was leaving Oscott at the end of term to go to the Beda College in Rome and to study for a degree in Scripture at the Angelicum University. He bequeathed me a table and a chair. It was very sad to see him go as he had been a very good friend over these years. But he would eventually return to Oscott and subsequently would spend many years lecturing in Scripture. His position as Manual Labour Dean was taken over by John Drury of our Diocese,.

The odd exam would take place during the term. I had a ten minute quickie with Denis O'Shea and he asked me such obscure questions that I am sure that I must have failed. One question was about 'habitual implicit intentions'. He said that I had scraped through but the following day commented on the poor standard of exams in general and that he would be changing the traditional format for the future. He then informed us that catching butterflies could not be considered technically as 'hunting'. However he did comment on my essay which he thought was 'well balanced' but didn't think much of my Latin quotations. However I was amazed when I received my mark 80% - the highest ever and marks in the other exams were in the 60% range so perhaps I was not so dumb as I sometimes felt.

We were then given what were called 'the Scrutinies' for the forthcoming Minor Orders. This was a sort of test to see if we were up to receiving them and it was over in a flash. The crucial question to me by the rector was, 'Suppose you install a £3000 organ and the Bishop moves you, and all there is at the new place is a harmonium what would you do ?' Ah the old question of obedience! In hindsight, there would be far more serious problems to contemplate in times to come. At any rate I passed.

Fr Robert Nash SJ gave the June retreat. One of his books was, *The Priest at his Prie-dieu*. He was excellent at painting vivid pictures of his subject and was particularly good on mortal sin and Judas. He proposed that if a line were drawn from where he was sitting down the centre of the chapel and into Birmingham on either side you would find 'mortal sin'. He was obviously a very holy man and spoke from the heart. He informed us that he was following St Ignatius's Spiritual Exercises. At the end he left us all a signed copy of a spiritual pamphlet he had written with individual quotations in each one - was mine prophetic? This retreat was the build up to receiving First Minor Orders. It was preceded on the previous evening by the conferring of the tonsure by the Archbishop of Birmingham. This was the first of the rites of passage which initiated you into the clerical state. If the Church had indicated that you were suitable then this was a sign that your vocation was genuine and not purely a subjective call. I suppose this helped to allay some of my doubts but they were never entirely to leave me. As related in a previous chapter we came up in single file to kneel before His Grace and hair was snipped off from the top and the four corners of the head. I was rather alarmed at the amount that this amateur ecclesiastical barber removed from my scalp. Into the *'sacrarium'* in the sacristy it went. A nice thought that my hair was joining that of so many illustrious predecessors. *'Dominus pars, heritatis mei'*. 'Lord you are my portion and cup'. We repeated phrase after phrase, snip after snip. So I entered the clerical state and was no longer a mere layperson. I was now exempt from military service too. During the war archbishops tonsured many of their candidates early to gain exemption. On the following day I received the first two Minor Orders - porter and lector. I was now a doorkeeper and could lock and unlock the church - which we did as part of the ceremony and also to ring the bell summoning people to worship which we also did. Then followed the Lectorship which enabled you to read the scriptures in church and to catechise. All these minor orders (together with the subdiaconate) were swept away in the reforms of Vatican 2 to be replaced by entry into the clerical state and the ministries of acolyte and reader. With twenty or more in my year to be done we were pretty exhausted and so were glad to relax during the afternoon. This coincided with the arrival of 400 Ecclesiastical Education Fund collectors who came for a tour round the college - so we really were beginning to open up to the outside world at last.

Denis Hall
In Rome

Home for the long break and the clean pure air of the countryside came round again and there was much activity getting ready for the judging of the best kept village competition once again. So it was down to a great deal of weeding and grass cutting. But it was the three weeks that Denis and I had in Rome that was to be the highlight of this holiday. This was the first time that I had ever been abroad and was a real adventure. We travelled by train changing at Paris on the way, staying the night there. The journey was long but spectacular. In Rome we stayed at a very basic Pensione called *Maraviglia* in the Via Napoleone III near the railway station run by a former resistance lady, Maria. Rome was fabulous. St. Peter's was incredible only spoiled by the seats being put in place in the nave for the forthcoming Council. The highlight was the general audience with the Pope and we had a good view of Pope John carried into the basilica amid great cheering and applause. The second highlight was travelling to the English College on the edge of lake Albano for the ordination of Chris Budd, by Cardinal Heard a friend of Denis (later to become bishop of Plymouth). His family were most hospitable and we spent some time being shown round the college and enjoying the marvellous views over the sultry turquoise lake. There was a trip to the baths of Caracalla to see a fantastic performance of *Aida* and a concert in the Basilica of Maxentius in the Forum under a full moon with the Colosseum in the distance. Pope John had tightened up on clergy visiting such places of entertainment so we wondered whether, we had been technically excommunicated. The holiday at home came rather as an anticlimax but it was nice to see ourselves in The Universe Catholic paper with Fr Budd giving us his first blessing. After this experience I suppose it was inevitable that depression set in again. However my mood was lightened when one of the local village louts shouted out to me - 'Hey where's yer dorg coller'. So the cat's out of the bag! But I managed to get away from this other 'prison' by a trip up to Hawkesyard Priory for a Lay Dominican Conference at Spode House. The Dominicans leading it were Frs Conrad Pepler, Felix Watts and Vincent. The participants were mainly rather elderly women and some eccentric men but it made an interesting change. And so the holiday continued with more cycle rides visiting ancient churches, making cement for the garden paths and digging up a few rows of potatoes. I had become quite expert after our session in the fields at Oscott. A visit from Uncle Wilf and Judy from Maidenhead was an event. He was quite a philosopher and thinker and very critical of things - especially regarding the Church. Mother was in her usual anxiety state organising hospitality for the visitors and at last Fr Kennedy took me on his promised trip to Walsingham. Mother was beginning to worry about the cottage. There was too much land to cope with - about three quarters of an acre and quite beyond my father's capability to maintain it as he used to.

SECOND THEOLOGY Sept 1962 - June 1963

So I was ascending the heights with the new status of Cleric as I moved into second Divinity. Frank Thomas was now our lecturer in Dogmatic Theology. He tried to enthuse us with the subject but, however much I liked the man, his lectures became unbearable and as recorded at the outset, 'I will need patience to stand three years of lectures from him.' The whole subject was so cerebral and however much we were dealing with profound spiritual realities they didn't somehow catch the heart as they might have done. His delivery was so hesitant and nervous and came at us as an unrelenting stream. Dan Leonard, the new addition to the staff, was a big gentle Irishman with a bit of a twinkle in his eye and something of a contrast with Denis O'Shea who gave us the basic course last year. This term we would be dealing with the theology of the Sacraments. Dr Greehy, alone, was full of his usual vivacity as we began to tackle the Pauline Epistles. Among the new entrants was Anton Mowat who was an old boy from Laxton and so I was pleased that we would have something in common. There was an intake of thirteen students for our diocese.

I had now graduated to the role of Cantor for Compline and for the first time had to intone the *Jube Domne Benedicere* at its start calling on the rector to give us his blessing. 'The rector addressed us and recounted his trip to Louvain where he saw all the Oscott College treasures which had been shipped there for display, including the magnificent medieval lectern which originally came from there - I suppose he could have saved himself a journey by visiting the museum here.'

Everyone had been developing colds and coughs and our student infirmarian, Bernard Hughes, suggested to the vice- rector that this might be due to the beds not being aired in our absence - he chose to disagree.

The rector had bought himself a new car - a mini- and was now learning to drive. 'He asked us all not leap out of his way in terror when he drives round the grounds. He said that at the moment he was having difficulty in distinguishing between the brake and the accelerator!' He failed his first test and Peter Lawler was seen speeding round the grounds in his mini to show just how it should be done.

Regular visitors came from outside talking to us about their work in various ecclesiastical organisations. One was a UN Telecommunications Officer who was working in Iraq just before the revolt. His talk on that country was fascinating and showed us a movie he had taken - the first at Oscott. The speaker also informed us that if only the Iraqis got together it would be quite easy for them to turn the desert into fertile land and that food for three times the present population could be produced without any bother. With the aid of modern technology a tape recorder was used to play us a talk by Charles Davis on Sacramental Theology.

Now I received quite a shock when I heard from John Ibbett that his brother, Joseph, had left the English College and had returned home. He seemed so sure in his vocation and so it was rather upsetting. Still the interminable worries about the future and how I would cope still cropped up. This came from reading accounts by students in a periodical about what jobs they were doing in the holidays.

Among the interesting discussions we were having in theology was whether one could baptise a complete stranger who had been knocked unconscious in a road accident and whether it was permissible to give a baptised non catholic Absolution and the Last Anointing if they were dying and unconscious. It seems that you were able to do this, provided that this did not cause scandal among the bystanders. The other important gobbet of information that I passed on to the folks at home was that,'Women don't have to wear hats in church if they just pop in for a moment. It was only a requirement during the regular liturgy!' We were also relieved to know that thin porridge or even cornflakes with milk could be taken within the three hours fast for Communion provided it poured and so could be considered a liquid! Such useful information as this and much more I relayed in my letters home each week and posed them moral questions and extracts from our Scripture course. What their replies were I cannot recall as sadly I did not keep their letters.

I could see how permanent community life could be so difficult and how little things can grow out of all proportion and dominate consciousness even in our limited experience. My companion in choir, Denis, was becoming more and more irritating. He seemed quite incapable of keeping still and insisted on saying all the prayers twice as quickly as everyone else. I was surprised there were not more murders reported from enclosed orders!

Events in the wider ecclesiastical world were moving fast and excitement was growing at the prospect of the opening of the Vatican Council in Rome. October 11th was the memorable day with two TVs actually installed in the Common Room and we followed avidly the opening ceremonies with BBC on one side and ITV on the other. We noted how many times the Holy Father wiped his nose with his finger and the number of aged bishops whom we thought might not outlive the deliberations, especially poor old Cardinal Godfrey. There was some concern, too, about the health of the Holy Father. However we were somewhat depressed by a programme on the radio by Hans Kung asking whether the Council was coming too soon. As I wrote home, 'The opening ceremony was a moving and a stupendous sight with all the bishops assembling with the Holy Father who stood up to things very well. It was all very wonderful and one can only hope that great things will come of it.' After the news we watched a *Saint* thriller followed by Holy Hour - so far had we come already in the liberalisation of the Oscott regime. It was with a certain feeling of excitement and pride that I walked down New Street to my organ lesson wondering how many of the thousands of people I passed had also watched the morning's programme. The televisions were not to stay for ever but we were able to listen - those of us who were keen enough- in the wireless room to the daily broadcasts from Vatican Radio. This we tuned into with some difficulty but Nick Lash was usually there and we were delighted by the Moscow style speke of the broadcaster who invariably got his English pronunciation wrong - the first being the Supreme Pasture rather than Pastor and we marvelled at the votes when they were cast where invariably there were two or three bishops who voted against just about everything and a regular number that spoiled their papers. We lived through the interventions of the famous Cardinals of the day and the reaction of the reactionaries. We really were living through history and we wondered how the changes were going to affect us in the future.

With one of the rector's liberal permissions for those of us who were erstwhile Dominicans - Anton, Pat Brannigan and I cycled down to St. Agnes's Convent at Erdington. There we attended a monthly meeting of the local group of Lay Dominicans and were regaled by the singing of among others one we christened 'Sister Squawks'. We actually met some real live lay people and had tea with them. This was a pleasant and entertaining break from lectures especially Dogma where the good Fr Thomas just, 'drones on and on and there is just no communication' - Van Roo's theory of causality in the Sacraments was really quite incomprehensible..

But against the optimism at the opening of the Council a world crisis was developing with the Cuba Missile incident and the threat of a nuclear war. Perhaps we were going to have to heed the warnings of the 'bomb woman' after all. Things were getting very tense but we tried to keep our spirits high. My trip to practice the organ at nearby Boldmere Church was overshadowed by the fear that I might be blown up by the bomb before I returned to college but at last Secretary Khrushchev pulled back from Armageddon and we could breathe again but we were not without our local nuclear explosion during church history lecture when Dennis Ryan attacked the 'horizontal layabouts' who were reading during his lectures. One wonders why they were reading - was it something to do with the content and the delivery of his lectures ? - I wonder. Mind you Moral lectures were beginning to pall as well and the casuistry therein was getting quite ridiculous. The proposed cures for scruples would seem to aggravate the problems that people had. I started to read *Theology and Sanity* by Frank Sheed, a layman, in the hopes that he would bring some down to earth commentary on what we are studying. Occasionally we would get a visiting speaker that was comprehensible. Bernard Leeming SJ gave us a talk on Baptism and the protestant tradition. He put it so clearly and so non technically that it was a joy to hear.

At another organ lesson I met John Cleobury, a cousin of my cousins and his two boys Stephen and Nicholas. John was a psychiatric nurse and had come to give a lecture on Psychiatry and Music. Both his boys would go on to do well with Stephen becoming conductor of the prestigious Kings College Choir in Cambridge. I now had a rival in Simon Bracken, a new, student, who was obviously a very fine organist and so I began to feel that I was likely to be marginalised. However Frank Thomas succeeded in getting me manual labour time to practice once a week which did not please the procurator too much. I was having problems with the pedals and not being very long limbed stretching the distances required was difficult. I was now beginning to play for Compline and Benediction. The new organist was not to last long as he would leave during the following Retreat - so my position seemed safe though I was told that most of the organists usually did leave!

By November it had begun to snow heavily and there it lay and the fog came as well and there were fifty missing from supper one evening since the journey from Birmingham that usually took twenty minutes had on this occasion taken three hours.

We were still busily rebuilding the lectern, now safely returned from its original home in Louvain and now standing incongruously at the back of the church. The Bird looked magnificent with all the black paint that had covered it removed, and standing in all its burnished bronzed splendour and none the worse for its trip to its home town. It awaited the visit of the Burgomaster of Louvain himself. He came on a return trip for the rector's recent visit. What he made of the exuberant Scottish sing song after supper I don't know. Two students did a sword dance in kilts and the rector sang the *Eriskay Love Lilt* to thunderous applause. He looked bewildered when we all joined hands and sang *Auld Lang Sine*. All this while we were enduring the worst smog for ten years and there was talk of going home before Christmas because of the lack of services at the time. Not all was well with the golfers, either, as the rector read a letter from the golf club complaining about people not paying their subs. Understandably he was most upset - his liberalising of the regime was beginning to back fire.

The Catholic Needlework Guild, that noble band of women who knitted for poor students, sent me a bumper parcel of underwear. In addition I was to find a parcel in my bed. While packing away items in the museum for the general turn out, as the whole place was going to be overhauled, someone had kindly deposited the jawbone of the 14th century nun therein !! This I deposited on the Admiral's pillow the next day when I woke him up. Mr Spinalzo from *Charlie's Aunt* turned up again this time during Dr Greehy's lecture - he thought it in rather bad taste and had him removed.

People were going down with flue and colds and arriving home I found that the family were ill and that Dad had almost died of pneumonia but timely action by the doctor had saved him. The others weren't in good health either. The flat was perishing cold with no double glazing for the large bay windows and it was snowing heavily. There were terrible draughts everywhere and I tried as best I could to block them out. The family were living permanently in overcoats and scarves but they were made of tough material and survived.

The family were becoming great readers. Dad liked his westerns which were his staple diet. He never discussed any of the plots but he was engrossed and it must have taken him out of the nagging pain of his frozen neck and shoulders. As already related mother and aunt Elsie were now stuck into Cardinal Newman and had purchased the two volume biography by Meriol Trevor. His life seemed to have a great fascination for them. They even attempted his *Apologia* at my instigation but I'm not sure how far they got with that. We were beginning to experience the worst snow conditions since the 1880s and it would go on and on. Trips to the Albert Hall for concerts, the inevitable shopping and a go on the organ at the Brockley Church and a couple of days with my cousins at Horsham soon made the holiday disappear. Mother was doing her daily slog to Croyden coming home armed with labels to be addressed. This little bit of money helped her to keep the old car on the road and to pay the rates. On top of the dreadful weather we were experiencing power blackouts due to a work to rule.

Back at college and the snow began falling relentlessly and there was not a lot to inspire us! Whereas my room was excessively hot the rooms of some of the students were like ice boxes. The trouble was the number of draughts in the place especially in the main lecture hall where most students were swathed in scarves and overcoats for lectures and it was all I could do sometimes to keep awake being given the occasional prod from my neighbour. I wondered whether I was beginning to suffer from hypothermia. We were advised by Frank Thomas that we ought to spend at least an hour on Dogma each day- one at least began to realise how much traditional doctrines had to be rethought and the 'Faith' one had received took on a deeper meaning. The rector began a scintillating tour of Christadelphianism and Christian Science and the wonders of Mrs Baker Eddy and Animal Magnetism and we were soon to get bogged down in Mass Stipends and Indulgences in Moral Theology– no wonder there was a Reformation! Interest in the Council was fuelled by the visit of Mgr Francis Davis (popularly known as The Ike) who gave us a wonderfully illustrated talk on the Council and about his contact with the non-catholic observers. And it just got colder and colder and continued to snow - news from home indicated that Lidgate village had been cut off and aunt Win next door had a drift up to her bedroom window - it was no wonder that we suffered from one or two burst pipes in the college with its concommiant devastation. We were getting cold meals - cold spam and cheese and biscuits. In addition we were beginning to get powdered potato instead of the real thing - what happened to all the ones we had pulled up on the farm ? Everyone was beginning to feel exhausted and blamed it on the lack of vitamins in the diet. In spite of that some students had the energy to venture to Sutton Park for some skating. And on top of the snow there was the fog that just seemed to penetrate everywhere. There were drifts thoughout the grounds – going down for a walk in the fields we tried to track some of the animals by their footprints. Such depressing weather seemed an apt background to our discussions on the theology of John Calvin. By the end of January two notable national figures had passed on - Hugh Gaitskell, leader of the opposition and Cardinal Godfrey, whose death seems to have been shrouded in secrecy. He had been ill for some time and it was sad considering all the criticism that had been heading in his direction. Canon Nicholson gave us a conference on how we should treat children in varying circumstances – a pity that I cannot remember the content of his talk now in the light of the scandals that so many years later would crash about our ears.

A TV was actually imported for the Cardinal's funeral and we were pleased to see other programmes of which we had been deprived for so long.

Archbishop Heenan preached a good eulogy – and the prophecy that he would follow in the Cardinal's footsteps proved to be true.

Afternoon coffee sessions proved very valuable as an aid to socialising and to discussing life in general. How important it was to get a job during the holidays in order to meet ordinary people, especially the opposite sex and how to deal with them. This was rather appropriate as I far as I was concerned seeing that I had had no contact whatsoever with teenage girls. Lawler was more helpful in his spiritual direction session – that I must just put up with the present situation and if I feel like running up the wall then to go to him and he will try and pull me down again!

The tape recorder I had for my twenty first birthday was proving invaluable for recording practice sermons and a great deal of fun. It was my turn again with David Lloyd who sparked much criticism and controversy with his attack on 'pious' holy pictures and most of the time was spent analysing his contribution – this was something of a relief as it only left five minutes for mine – however the rector's words were encouraging as he thought my contribution commendable. .

At least there was some effort to keep us in touch with contemporary events. A man from the Catholic Pictorial gave a very interesting talk on the Catholic Press and Eamon Casey – whose eventful life as a bishop would dominate the press a few years hence – enlightened us about the Irish immigrant problem in Slough, Wilfred Purney on Church Music and an expert on the Covenant Scheme. But however good these windows into the outside world were they simply piled on problems in the vacuum in which we existed here.

By the middle of February it looked as though a rapid thaw was setting in but it was not to be for the snow was soon back again. We did however have a visit from the students from St. Edmund's College at Ware. The rector gave us a pre visit admonition. He warned us not to give coffee to the visitors. He said that he does not approve of the custom, but overlooked it. He doesn't want us to give these innocent students a bad impression of Oscott. It was very difficult to understand his point of view. In due course forty students came – were any entertained? – I do not know.

And now it was Play Time again. Graham was for putting on *Traitors Gate* which we had to drop as it was out of print instead he plumped for, *'A Man for All Seasons'*. At first I was to play the Spanish Ambassador, Chapuys, but ended up in my usual female role – this time as Margaret, More's daughter with John Reville as More's wife. Alan Holtham was Thomas More. Rehearsals took up a lot of our time but it was well worth it.

By March the dreadful winter was melting away and the mild weather returned. It was time for outside manual labour and a spell in the cemetery helping to dig part of a grave. Feeling rather energetic I went on a run – the first for four years and did several Outers but I was to regret it a over the succeeding days and apart from the odd putting with golf balls and tennis my sporting days had really come to an end.

The excitements of the ordinations were upon us again and it was a great joy to see John Molyneux ordained at the Birmingham Oratory. This time I had a good view of proceedings as I was singing in the *schola*. While there I was able to visit Cardinal Newman's room and see the original score of *The Dream of Gerontius* and also the original notes of his *Second Spring* sermon. His handwriting was not too good. The ordinands were late back for a meal and so we didn't have the usual 'clapping in' ritual. The next day a group of us went over to Coventry for John's first Mass and reception. It was a tremendous event but after the seclusion of Oscott such a public happening was almost too overwhelming and I was glad to get back to the seclusion of the College. The good news on returning was that my cousin Andrew had been accepted at the Westminster Choir School- the beginning of a career in music that would see him eventually as musical director at Manchester Grammar School. Peter Lawler, once again, suggested that I should try and get a position in a busy parish during the holidays to see what it was like. This seemed a good idea but how to bring it about in practice was another matter. We began another book in the refectory – *'The Life of Cardinal Manning'*.

The round of ethnic entertainments continued with a holiday for St Patrick with solemn High Mass. The day was rounded off by an Irish sing song in the common room. Doc Greehy showed some unexpected versatility by playing some Irish reels on the piano and singing a song in Gaelic. The Irishman put on their annual play, which was, as usual, totally unintelligible. The new priests were back from their 'honeymoon' and regaled us with stories from the week – and there were high expectations, supported by Nick Lash, that the Abbot of Downside, Christopher Butler, would be the next Archbishop of Westminster. On March 19th the heating went off – Spring at last ? However it got no warmer in the house and it was back to overcoats and scarves again and with snow showers appearing yet again the proc was pressurised to put the heating on again. But at least the crocuses were undaunted and pushed their colourful heads through the snow. Ibsen's *'Dolls House'* seemed an appropriate play to be reading at the Shakespeare Society in these wintry circumstances. Matters were not helped by the food which continued to deteriorate with stew yet again and there were quite a few complaints which were rarely heard when first I came to the college.

Our bishop made his customary visit. His new secretary was Fr Michael Hazel who replaced John Reffitt. He was full of his experiences at the Council and distributed some leaflets – there was one anonymous document of which he highly approved which accused some of the theologians of being like, 'termites, gnawing at the very foundations of the Church.' He seemed to have become very anti anything across the water especially Germany and even the Irish and at my interview he spoke of a possible mission to the fruit pickers of Wisbech,which was a change after the bargees of last year. He presented me with a nice pair of kid gloves which were too small for him. He said that the bishop should know his students as a father – sentiments with which I wholly concurred. He spoke to us in the Common Room and had us in fits of laughter. He produced a post card showing all the assembled Fathers of the Council sitting in serried ranks in St. Peter's. We were instructed to hold the post card up to the light so that we could see where he had been sitting, 'We have pricked Our seat,' he demurred in typical Leonine fashion. He was one of the few bishops to attend all the sessions of the Council and was noted for getting St Joseph included in the Canon of the Mass – a huge innovation ! He suggested that I tried again to get a grant from the local Council. He said little else apart from the interesting remark that the new candidate to replace Cardinal Godfrey, 'doesn't have to be a bishop, you know.' This was significant as he presided over the meeting which selected the three names of possible candidates to be sent to Rome for perusal. Was he perhaps referring to Mgr Wheeler or even Dr Davies. He didn't seem too keen on Bishop Heenan being appointed, 'He'll make us all ROMAN Catholics.' Leo was very keen on us being ENGLISH Catholics. He thought I ought to go to Lourdes but that it cost a great deal of money and I had better wait until I could take my parish. Sadly that event never occurred in the years that followed.

Denis O'Shea, in his gentlemanly way, read the Riot Act at the beginning of April. He commented on the poor spirit in the house; that there was too much murmuring and complaint and some of an 'offensive nature' ! He was concerned, too, that there were unseemly jokes about the sixth commandment and the priesthood – these should be cut out. (What was going on ?) Coffee sessions were a good thing (Progress!) but not to be prolonged and turned into gossip sessions and that radios were still forbidden since there was some subterfuge regarding transistors (ears burning!). Then there was the proverbial danger of particular friendships (well there was some truth in that!). He also made the interesting comment that there were dangerous theological views circulating in the house about having only one Mass on a Sunday and with talk of Concelebration (how prophetic!). A few days later the rector announced that, because of the 'abuse' by students arriving home beyond midnight on Excursus Day last year, we would all have to be back for night prayers by 9 pm this year or the day off was in jeopardy– that he was distressed by the spirit of criticism in the house and with the inevitable lecture on obedience. Matters went from bad to worse when the rector was doing his rounds on Easter Sunday blessing the rooms and discovered that some students had electric fires therein – if it happened again he would be writing to the students' respective bishops. One could understand the fire risk – but then the heating could be turned up to compensate during the appalling winter months.

Easter celebrations passed with due solemnity and some relaxation ensued during Easter week. A bike trip to the Roman Baths at Wall was educational and Easter Monday was a time when parents were allowed in to see their offspring and to be shown round the college – but I had longed closed my mind, since school days, to any hope of relatives coming to see me, and having developed eye strain retired to my bed for the afternoon. Wednesday was the big day when Graham Adams organisational skills were tested to the limit. Since we were not entitled to a cheap day return to London because of the rule that we had to be back by 9 pm he had petitioned British Railways, again, for a special excursion ticket for the 5.10 pm return train - pleading that we were poor students and it was the one day in the year when we were allowed out. He succeeded and having got up at 5 am we caught the 7.50 am to London. The parents were back in the country by now trying to cope with the aftermath of the winter freeze up. They had found the boiler burst and and an inch of ice on the bathroom floor. And there was nothing that I could do to help. The aunts were none too special and aunt Elsie was in bed with bronchitis with aunt Dot still pretty weak. But they had knocked together my favourite curry. I only had about three hours there as I had to leave by 3.45 pm to get back to Paddington. There was panic at the ticket barriers as the inspector hadn't been informed about our concession. But all was well and we got in by the 9 pm deadline.

'Aunt Elsie has given me a lovely transistor radio for my birthday to replace my DIY effort – so that will be listened to under the bedclothes – whatever happened to 'obedience'? I suppose she could be accused of cooperating in the sin of another ! My family history researches took off with the arrival of my great grand father William's marriage certificate which showed his father was a Humphrey Foreman,too, from Wickhambrook and a carpenter to boot. His father in law, John Parker, was a brick layer – so I am very much rooted in the locality. The Easter Week celebrations ended up with a little cricket practice, a slide show by the rector on his visit to Palestine (one of his rare appearances – he is away so much that we might as well not have a rector) and a talk by Lord Longford. Just to crown it depression descended once again with a feeling that I should leave for a year – my eyes were playing up too – too much study? And I seemed to getting another cold.

I noted that, 'A discussion ensued in sermon practice as to whether one should use humour in homilies. Some people seemed almost puritanical but surely one should bring everyday experiences into one's homily.' Play rehearsals were coming on a pace and the producer was getting annoyed that people still did not know their lines.

One student finding himself locked out one evening climbed back through the common room window to be confronted by the rector who threatened to write to his bishop. My twenty second birthday was rewarded with £1 from my parents and the odd 5/- and 10/- postal orders from relatives including one or two cards from fellow students. The annual Oscotian reunion took place and ancient clerics turned up to revive happy memories of the college of long ago. John Rust continued with organ lessons and decided that he wanted to take instruction in the Faith. There was excitement with the latest voyage into space and putting my alarm on for midnight I listened to their return on my illicit transistor radio.

More -Alan Holtham, Alice - John Reville, Meg - Me

May 24th marked the first performance of 'A Man for all Seasons' and it was hailed as probably the finest production for many years. Alan Holtham as Thomas More was outstanding and Michael Cunningham as the Common Man kept the play moving. The following day thousands of nuns packed the Northcote Hall and twittered away at practically everything and were especially tickled when I appeared in my costume. It was turning out to be a very warm spring as the news came through that Pope John was dying and the accounts of his passing were very moving. Graham Adams was greatly commended for this production. The chance of a summer holiday job came up from Anton. This was work for a week or two at the St John of God's Hospital at Scorton in Yorkshire . He had been there before and knew the Brothers well. I expressed my concern that I might not be up to the heavy work, but aunt Dorothy, as wise as always, encouraged me to go for if she, as a frail 19 year old girl, could cope with nursing so many years ago I certainly would be able to.

Two more steps to ordination were taken in June when I received the Minor Orders of acolyte and exorcist. These were rather redundant as the former allowed you to serve Mass officially but you were not allowed to exercise the second since each diocese had an official exorcist. I was required to make application in my own handwriting to show that I was not

133

acting under any compulsion and there followed big meeting of the staff to discuss the student's application. The ceremony lasted two and a half hours since the other Minor Orders were conferred as well as the subdiaconate and the diaconate. We were exhausted and to unwind I went on a run – the fifth this term!

On a scorching day in June while we were sunbathing in the meadows we heard that Pope John had died and there was concern as to whether the Council that he had convened would continue. Although we had no access to a TV in the house we were able to skip back and forwards to one or two professors' rooms to catch a glimpse of proceedings. It was an exciting time and with the election of Cardinal Montini as Paul V1 we felt that perhaps the era initiated by Pope John would be continued. The college magazine reported that, 'Mr. Foreman now looks like a little Hovis', due, no doubt, to my sunbathing. This was better than the comment from a couple of students who had thought I must be of gypsy origin.

A whole book could be written about my holiday experiences at the St John Of God Hospital at Scorton in Yorkshire. I hitchhiked up the Great North Road with Anton and for the next three or four weeks I was working on a ward for very disabled people from stroke victims to patients with genetic disorders. It was all new and the steep curve of experience that I needed. The Brothers were very hospitable and the hospital had a good reputation in the area. There was a Mr.Wilson, discharged fit from the army, who was now reduced to a skeleton and I had to feed him everyday with toast and marmalade. Another man who had had a stroke had to be lead to the toilet , where I did the necessary for him and on one occasion for an hour or so I was left in complete charge of the ward !! It was heavy and tiring work but I learned a lot about humankind. The food was excellent but the reader in the refectory had to declaim whatever book he was reading in a monotone which was really very strange. I broke a tooth while there and the dentist did some emergency treatment. I found that I had just shared the chair with the famous Fr Borelli, immortalised in the book *Children of the Sun* by Morris West. He thought I looked rather thin and ill. We shared the common room with two Asian Doctors and were allowed into the operating theatre for several operations from varicose veins to a stomach removal – in all its gory detail. I also made a trip to the great Durham Cathedral and to Darlington where I was able to visit an old friend of the family who had herself been a hospital matron. I came home with many a tale to tell.

THIRD THEOLOGY Sept 1963- June 1964

The usual emotional farewell over –including a surprisingly emotional goodbye from dad, I had the tedious trek back to college once more. It was the case of the train from Newmarket to Cambridge across country to Bletchley with an hour's wait and then a connection to Birmingham arriving at 3.15 pm There were some improvements at the college with my corridor painted and strip lighting installed but nothing had been done to the gloomy old Northcote Hall where we spent most of our lecture hours.

So back to the usual round of lectures, accompanying Benediction on the organ for the first time and helping Frank Thomas trying to cope with bees coming down his chimney. The rector's opening gambit was the usual *fervorino* about obedience, tolerated coffee sessions of which he did not approve (and how many more times had we to endure this?) and the strange complaint that some students had more than one chair in their rooms – one could construe from that what one could. His talk was underpinned by the archbishop's exhortation –'work hard and obey your superiors' – but what was intriguing was there was no mention of the threatened introduction of Latin into lectures.

A new professor arrived in the person of Fr James Wigmore. He seemed pleasant enough but I would not benefit from his lectures since he would be teaching the philosophers. (Wigmore would later leave the priesthood and become a distinguished Judge). But life was improving as we were beginning to have practical experiences of administering the Sacraments eg. using a doll for a baby. This was interesting as I had never seen a baptism before and Extreme Unction where, as a trial run, David Keniry took to his bed and John Drury ministered to him. My personal finances had not improved and West Suffolk County Council had still not been forthcoming with a grant for my education here and I was advised to apply yet again..

We started a discussion on contraception in Moral Theology in view of the advent of The Pill. Dogma lectures were as incomprehensible as ever. As I wrote home, 'How on earth are we meant to be able to put these doctrines over to people when we leave, I don't know. I hope they reform the seminary system eventually – still that would be too late to be of any use to me.'

Newly ordained Michael Jones- Frank came back on a visit and said that one way to get rid of annoying housekeepers was to collect cheeses. That was not surprising considering my past encounters with his smelly creations.

Church history lectures were getting spiced up as we began to look at some of the wicked Popes in history and the procurator talked about the, 'varicose vein that runs down the leg of Italy', and having discussed certain Papal Bulls, we learned that the college bull was called 'Golden Briar'. We also started learning about St Patrick and spent an inordinate time discussing whereabouts he came from in England. We really learned little or nothing about Catholics in this country since the Reformation.

At last a reply came from West Suffolk County Council which agreed to allow me a grant of £45 a year, which was typically stingy. The procurator was surprised as some students get that amount per term. Sir Alec Douglas Hume become Prime Minister. We regularly tuned into Vatican Radio to get the latest information on the Council,which was always a source of great amusement with their quaint use of the English language. Discussion about the relationship between the Pope and the bishops and the need for collegiality were most interesting though some bishops thought this would undermine the position and authority of the Pope.

Whatever the dangers of particular friendships, humanly speaking, the need for a soul mate seemed very necessary. Ken and Mol had been great pals, but Mol had been ordained and Ken sent off to Rome to do a Scripture degree. I had been to Scorton with Anton and we were becoming more friendly especially as we had been old boys at Laxton and so we had quite a bit in common. However this relationship in the hot house of Oscott, intellectually at any rate became from my point of view somewhat obsessive. Anton was friendly with two other students to the point of cliquishness and I think I felt I had become something of an intruder. Perhaps it was jealousy on my part. November brought something of a crisis and as I wrote home, 'I'm afraid I am going through a bit of a crisis at the moment. Fr Lawler has been very helpful and says it is quite usual for these problems to arise at this time of the course. By this time one has had just about enough of college life etc. The trouble is living in a confined space with the same people for so long – it must be hell in a small religious community. At one moment I'm in the clouds and at another in the depths of despair . You know this is usually the case with me but it's been even more so at the moment. I expect I shall get over it.' Father Lawler's comments were perceptive. He thought that I had reached the stage of having had enough of this place, of wanting to assert my independence, which at the moment is in the mid way stage. This was exaggerated by the ecclesiastical impersonalism of the college. My fear of the parish was exaggerated by being isolated during the holidays but I must see this in the scheme of Providence and as a cure suggested a week in High Wycombe to get me used to parish life. He thought the personal relationship problem with Anton was all caused by these inherent difficulties. Oh for the old days of Ken and Moll when there wasn't any sense of cliquishness and suspicion.

But Fr Moll returning to the college again on a visit was none too happy about life in the parish and said that if he had had the choice he would have opted out of things. He was as harassed as ever and I think that he is going to have words with the rector about the training at Oscott. He was thrown in at the deep end in one of the busiest parishes in the city with any number of baptisms, marriages and night calls to the hospital. – 'get out while you still have time' was his encouraging advice. He was quite clear that the seminary had not prepared him for what was to come.

There was a welcome break with a trip down to London to the Victoria and Albert to see the embroidery exhibition which contained some of Oscott's treasures. I took the advantage of getting home for a couple of hours. Only aunt Dorothy was there as Elsie had gone down with their doctor to pick up the parents from home. But I had a good heart to heart chat with her - she seemed a different person to talk to on her own and with such good advice. I have a wonderful family. Another expedition was to a school reunion in Sutton Coldfield. Unfortunately there weren't many of my group there and on arriving back at the college quite late I found the lodge gates locked and had to squeeze through the boundary railings. Luckily someone had left the back door open for me.

Dr Charles Hahn, a former teacher at Christ's Hospital School, and a principal of Lichfield Theological College, a friend of uncle Reg and a prominent Catholic convert of the time gave us a brilliant talk on Anglicanism and I chatted to him afterwards. He gave a rather gloomy but perhaps realistic assessment of the state of ecumenism and thought that John Rust who followed him at the school would have to give up a lot if he joined the Church but meeting John a few days later he encouraged him in his course of instruction –'what are you waiting for? – why don't you come on over?' Moral lectures were enlivened by an interesting case quoted from a newspaper by Dan Leonard about the breakup of a marriage due to a dog. Someone circulated a Latin *Casus* during study entitled – *Quid sit canis?*

On the 22nd of November news reached us, just as we were going into supper, that President John F Kennedy had been assassinated. We were all shaken by this terrible news. As I recorded, 'The second great John we have lost in a year', and with the assassination of the assassin shortly afterwards the whole drama intensified and rather trumped the drama put on by the 'Underdogs' (First and Second Philosophy) by Chris Scott (who one day would rise high in the prison service) called *the 'White Sheep of the Family'*. My personal problems were intensifying again with a sense of utter frustration and a total loss of interest in everything and inability to talk to people and a feeling that I really must discuss the possibility of leaving with Lawler next term.

But then another great breakthrough - we actually got permission from the rector to go swimming in Kingstanding baths. He stressed that we should choose a time when there were no women present – how we were to do that heaven only knows. But with Graham Adams, Pat Kilgariff and some others we made several trips over the next year. After all we were told that the archbishop of Birmingham would do several lengths of the municipal baths before work so why shouldn't we. I hadn't really been swimming since primary school days except for a dip in the river Welland at Laxton and the odd trip to the baths at Newmarket. But I really gained confidence and did a width or two and then a couple of lengths. Two students were more adventuresome and went to the Turkish baths at Erdington.

Fergus O'Connell's father, an eminent Dublin Heart surgeon, gave us an interesting talk on modern moral problems.

With December, swatting for exams begin in earnest and burning the late night oil, hoping that the authorities would not see the lights on and even studying under the bedclothes or getting up extra early. The moral theology oral exam consisted in asking what marriages could be dissolved in the context of doubtfully baptised Anglicans.

Tension had been growing between me and Anton and on Christmas eve I had a bust up about nothing with him and there was a total breakdown which, for me, was a new and wounding experience and for which I could see no apparent cause. This hung like a cloud over Christmas and communications would not be restored before the holidays and my attempts to apologise were rebuffed.

And so it was down to London for another Christmas holiday and I was able to get to a seven o'clock Mass each day. The parish priest, Brendan Fox AA invited me to be deacon next Christmas.

I achieved national fame during the holidays. During a trip up to London, while visiting the sights, and seeing the films, *'The Cardinal'* and *'Ben Hur'* for the third time, I ended up outside No 10, Downing Street where a crowd had gathered awaiting the arrival of the cabinet to assess the Cyprus crisis, among them were Selwyn Lloyd and Quinton Hogg and in the evening I saw myself on the tele. I was even seen as far afield as Ireland by one of my fellow students. And so another holiday passed with growing concerns about the family's health. Dad was getting worried about his inside, probably due to all the aspirin he was taking, and just sits for most of the day. He did quite a bit of reading and hobbled out on two sticks for long walks but his rheumatism was pretty bad and of course couldn't move his head from side to side, a condition he had endured pretty stoically for years. To my amazement I found him engrossed in a novel about St Francis de Sales – I don't know what he made of it nor of my copy of the *'Imitation of Christ'* which he picked up. aunt Dorothy wasn't much better and suffering a lot of pain in her hips. Mother was still doing her commute to Croydon and bringing back loads of labels to copy. It was meeting up with cousin Jonathan and his fiance to see the *'Love of Three Oranges'* at Saddlers Wells and going with Charles Crawford and Denis to the Festival Hall for a concert which cheered things up no end. So it wasn't all doom and gloom. Cousin Stephen from Horsham also called in. He had decided to go to the Junior Seminary at Mark Cross to train for the priesthood and I only hoped that he wouldn't be stamped by the Mark Cross – Wonersh system. Aunts' weekly help – Nellie called in as usual – I don't know whether she realised that we were Catholics but she remarked that some black people had moved in overhead at her flat –'they were Cafflicks' and she could hear them 'mumbling'. This was very much in the old tradition of describing Catholics. She also commented that her sister had been given a lovely 'maternity ring' on the occasion of her engagement.

And so back to college once more for the final full year of my initiation into the priestly life. Frank Thomas's first remark was that he thought I looked like 'A Beatle'. I hadn't been aware that I was modelling my hairstyle on the fab four – but my hair had always been something of a problem and with the cold weather it provided me with some insulation.

The inevitable rectorial talk stressed the importance of obedience, as if it had been the only virtue and we were warned that dogma studies would be particularly hard this year. Would dear Fr Thomas' lecturing skills improve? The weather was icy again – the chapel was particularly shocking in the early hours of the morning and the water from the bathroom was not even as hot as my hot water bottle which I had taken to using.

Peter Jones who took us for Fundamental Theology two years ago appeared at the top table in a collar and tie. One didn't realise such things happened until you saw them for yourself. Of course it was the worse thing out to have been sent here to lecture after spending all his training in Rome. I don't know whether he had actually been laicised or had just got leave of absence like Stephen Fermoyle in *'The Cardinal'* that I had recently seen.

And now we were introduced to our first really practical piece of pastoral work. This was catechising local children on a Sunday afternoon in the church at Boldmere. Without any instruction or training on how to deal with children of that age, let alone how to impart the Faith to them we were plunged into this new experience. At least I had had some experience from school days, as a member of the Junior SVP catechising one little boy at Laxton. But this was totally different. Once the group was handed over to me bedlam broke out. Hassocks started flying hither and thither. I tried to press on but with no avail and couldn't hold their attention at all .We should have been prepared for this sort of thing years ago. I had the particularly young children whereas Denis down at Maryvale got on better with the older ones. It really was very discouraging and there was no one with whom to talk over these problems. I tried my spiritual director but he was not very practical and nearly burst a blood vessel when I shared my experiences. However as the weeks progressed things did improve and some of the children's questions were very sharp from the seven year olds like, 'Who made God?', 'Where was he when there was no earth or universe?' And as I recorded, 'These Sunday afternoons really seemed the only thing worth working at at the moment.' However these kids were just guinea pigs for our experiments in teaching and the sooner they introduced some course in teaching techniques and child psychology the better as teaching was to be one of our most important jobs as priests. A priest may know his dogmatic theology but it was not much good if he can't put it over to people in a language that they can understand. So a fog descended comparable to the pea souper that had descended on Birmingham this winter where traffic were turning into the college grounds thinking it was the main road. Graham Adams had been to see the new archbishop of Westminster, Cardinal Heenan, but despite his being mitre bearer at his installation (trust Graham), it was not a happy meeting and in the end he applied to the Northampton Diocese and was accepted by +Leo to become one of the leading clergy there. My relationship with a certain student was still on dodgy grounds – a bright 'good morning' from me received an icy, 'good morning' from him. Oh well.

My second session with the kids improved somewhat I gave them all the grizzly details of the martyrdom of the mother and her seven sons form the Book of Maccabees. This quieted them down a little though one or two troublemakers ended up actually inside the organ where the pipes were, and a burst hassock at the end rather scared them. The parish priest, Fr McEvilly warned my mob about hurling hassocks about. They were quiet for a few moments and being so unused to this experience it rather threw me. The only time I really quieted them was for the final prayer and giving something practical for them to do in the next week. If only I had had some visual aids.

A word of praise came at the vice- rector'sl talk when he said he hoped he wasn't living in a fools paradise about how well the rules were being kept at the moment. Moral theology lectures were hotting up apace and we were beginning to enter into the forbidden territory of the sixth and ninth commandments – 'The Blacks' – as they were euphemistically called. Here we began discussing the Church's disciplinary rules regarding the validity or otherwise of a marriage and we spent quite a long time on the problems of impotence and how this might affect the validity of a marriage. The month ended with an inspirational talk by a Fr Hanlon, principal of a college of education on, 'The Priest as Minister of the Word'. The questions afterwards showed the general state of mind regarding this subject in the college and some very forthright questions were asked about seminary technique and curriculum. One wondered how much the vice- rector, who was present, realised that this was a serious problem on our minds. At least perhaps the seminary system has shown one thing to us – how NOT to go about things.

There was some good news that Sr Romaine, a well known expert on catechetics was to give some lectures and we were told we could send two representatives from each year to hear her– that seemed decidedly odd, why could we not all hear her for ourselves?

By now I was doing much more accompanying of the Liturgy and had even graduated to High Mass. My organ teacher was still coming for instruction but was beginning to find all sorts of problems and I feared that he wouldn't carry things through.

Bishop Leo came up for his annual visit and seemed impressed at my musical prowess. My interview with him was a hoot. First he thought my parents might move to Kirtling to look after the church there and reiterated the wise advice that I should take up the smoking of a pipe (even an empty one would do) – it seems that it makes you 'self-contained' and keeps the women at bay. He appeared to be more 'progressive' than one anticipated and full of ideas about possible changes the Council would inaugurate but seemed determined not to actually speak at any of the proceedings. He again thought it was too expensive to go to Lourdes in the normal way and suggested working in some hostel near Lourdes for a fortnight, where they pay all your expenses – I could stow-away in a boat to avoid the channel fare I suppose. He seemed a real fatherly figure.

The weekly catechism classes continued and, although only having a few one week, I managed to get something over about Angels. They asked the most pointed questions – ones that I am sure never entered my head at that age. One of my colleagues was being asked some very awkward questions about marriage by his ten year olds. It seems wrong that these kids should be treated as guinea pigs for our inexperience over the years when that is the only religious instruction they are getting.

I had a boost from Charles Crawford for writing my diary. He noted that the authorities were at last waking up to the need for making historical records of the college for posterity and my diary would be part of it ! There was more work in the cemetery with Sean Conway on the dumper truck and sweeping the cloisters. This was a laugh from beginning to end and we were beginning to be convinced that Oscott was a mental home in disguise and we were all certified patients. I now had a good read – Hadrian VII –by Frederick Rolfe – a 19th century eccentric and student who was kicked out of the college. He wrote this novel about a very go ahead Pope who was eventually assassinated. It later had a successful run in the West End as a play.

Students from the northern seminary of Upholland visited to play us at soccer. Their college sounded awful compared with Oscott and the restrictions placed upon them seemed even worse than school. The rector of a seminary in Malta visited to learn something of the English system in order better to reform seminaries there. To my mind their system didn't sound as though it needed much reforming.

Easter ceremonies passed as usual but for me there was an historic moment when mother and aunt Elsie, at last, after begging them for so long, made the trek up from London to see me and the college for the day. I met them at Snow Hill. They were naturally impressed with the college and they stayed for Compline and Benediction for which I played .

John Mol, continuing his grim reports of parish life in Sparkhill, drove me down to London for Excursus Day where we had about three hours with the folks before the scurry back to be in by 9 pm night prayers. Students from Ushaw seminary visited during Easter Week too. From reports from the visitors it sounded even worse than Upholland. 'The discipline seems quite oppressive and they appear to have no outside contacts at all. In fact they seem to be living in pre-Catholic emancipation days. We classed the seminaries in this order: Oscott, Ware, Upholland, Ushaw. We don't know about Wonersh yet. Thank heavens I'm at Oscott – even so one mustn't be complacent as there is a lot that needs changing here. The archbishop celebrated one day but no word did he say to the house – I give up.' Dennis in typical fashion had escaped from the college at every opportunity but this time he returned looking absolutely haggard and full of the big wide wicked world outside.

The big event of this Easter week was the arrival of Mr Galloway, portrait painter extraordinary, who was to do a painting of the rector to join the rogue's gallery on the Beeswax. He turned up to supper complete in dinner jacket which tickled the staff - he seemed to enjoy his spaghetti and a plate of cheese on toast. He was seen wandering around the college looking for a suitable site to set up his easel but in the end he plumped for the rector's room. Later Dennis O'Shea discovered John Drury sitting in for the rector and posing in his cassock – 'Oh blimey –its you', he exclaimed – a pity John hadn't said there had been a *coupe d' etat* and that he was now in control.

And now the very important step that I was soon to take was upon me and the rest of my year – that was the step of the subdiaconate. We had, once again, to make formal application to receive this Order – 'Lawler pulled me over and asked if everything was all right regarding this step. All I can do is to make an act of Faith and take the plunge wherever it may lead me'.

Our lectures in dogma now proceeded to the Trinity and Frank Thomas gave us a quite unintelligible lecture. The Holy Trinity is the most profound mystery at the best of times but our lecturer succeeded in creating even more mystery. 'One's mind would have to be in top condition to be able to follow what he says day in and day out. The trouble is he can't put it over in clear points but it comes out at top speed and in a mass. I tried to incorporate some ideas into my next practice homily on the Trinity and was chiefly criticised for my use of the analogy of 'family life' in the Trinity – a pity as it was an idea I had taken from that great spiritual writer Gerald Vann OP '

'Charles Crawford who had been working on the archives showed me the register in which the record of John Henry Newman's Confirmation was entered and also the diary of Fr Ignatius Spencer – I wonder if my diaries will be in this condition in 100 years time!'

I had yet another session doing manual labour in the cemetery and had a very existential discussion with my companion about death and the absurdity of life. However two interesting characters, visiting their loved ones, entered into conversation – one woman, undergoing instruction, told us that she had: 'received God into her soul by means of a light that issued from her back kitchen.' Another man wondered whether the Latin inscription on archbishop Masterson's tomb was in fact Irish ! We then noticed an error in the inscription on one head stone : 'fortified by the <u>rights</u> of Mother Church'

Our artist visitor gave a very inspiring talk on portrait painting using his fast developing portrait of the rector as a prop. We thought it was very complimentary but that it didn't have enough tension in it. It seems Mr Galloway had to leave Ushaw for health reasons. He was so overcome by his experience here that he couldn't stop thanking the rector enough for letting him come.

April 15th was the big day when our year assembled in the chapel to take the various pre-ordination oaths. Bearing in mind it was a moment of some solemnity that would have repercussions for the rest of our lives it was treated with a certain levity. The oaths were taken in Latin and repeated all together which was not really a dignified experience. One oath was the famous *Anti Modernist Oath* introduced by Pope Pius X and the other was the promise of celibacy. The rector walked up and down waving his arms about – with his familiar incantations 'heads down – hands on your bibles.' It was all quite nerve racking and took nearly half an hour to get through it all. – at the end Dicky said, 'don't say you didn't know what it means – you can't run off with a woman now' – however Father Lawler was more spiritual and gave me a pre-subdiaconate *fervorino*. The heightened tension of this experience was relieved by a tremendous satire on Oscott Life, based on *That was the Week that was*. This concluded with, *'This is your life – John Drury'*. (One must mention that John from our diocese had now been created Dean of the college and was a very popular choice. He had the ability to pour oil on troubled waters where student - rector relationships were concerned.) The curtain went up on a portrait of John in the rector's attire, painted by John Bourke and modelled on the famous portrait. Also a 'shy Fr Thomas' was depicted and wheeled in peeping out of a trunk – his first day at Oscott. These occasions certainly released the frustrations that many students felt with the system. It was even getting to the professors too. Doc Greehy blew up his presidium of the Legion of Mary. It seems he is very frustrated. He was full of ideas and zeal but unable to put any of them into practice here.

This momentous April came to a climax with lectures by Sr Romaine. Her lecture was now extended to the whole student body. It was really stimulating and an eye opener on catechetics. 'She is really a great personality and her technique looks simplicity itself. How much we have missed by not having a proper course. She gave several specimen lectures on different subjects for different age groups with a great use of visual aids by using ordinary illustrations taken from magazines. It was good to see that some of the profs were present. This is probably the first time that there has been an outside lecturer to the college and a woman at that'. The last day of the month was another first with the celebration of Mass facing the people in Pat Brannigan's Chapel. It really was impressive and one had no need of a missal to follow things.

With Easter over again for another year it was back to lectures with a vengeance. Some people were getting very het up by some of the proc's comments in Church history which seemed to be rather anti-Semitic. As with marriage, banns regarding the forthcoming Ordination had to be read out in local parishes and mine were duly proclaimed at Kirtling – no one seems to have come forward declaring a liaison. But then I was hardly known in my own parish apart from the little community at Kirtling.

In spite of my enthusiasm for visual aids, inspired by Sr. Romaine, my Sunday group were less than impressed with my attempts. Only the girls took some interest in the doll I had taken down to demonstrate baptism. But there they had probably seen more baptisms in their short lives than I had ever seen in mine!

I received a touching letter from the Carmelites at Waterbeach which said that since Mother Rosario was nearly blind she would like to give me her set of breviaries – a pity now that it looks as though everything will be going into English. Our horizons on the seminary system were further broadened by an outing to the junior seminary at Tollerton where Fr Sweeney (later master of St. Edmund's House in Cambridge) was rector. He was very hospitable and gave us a good meal. We were impressed by the cubicles the boys had in their dormitories and with hot and cold running water.

We returned to discover that the Hierarchy had made a statement about The Pill, the implications of which we would be discussing in the moral lectures over the next few days. An editorial in the Guardian was described by Dan Leonard as the most virulent attack on the Catholic Church regarding The Pill business since the attack on Cardinal Wiseman's *'Out of the Flamin-*

ian Gate'. My attempts to mend the fences with Anton proved fruitless and fellow students who were aware of the situation advised me to dismiss the whole business as, 'incompatibility of temperament.

A new liturgical function was now open to us – that of pluvialist which involved wearing a beautiful cope for Vespers. I must have cut quite a figure next to John Burke the celebrant who was well over 6'5. The authorities always seems to put us together! Outings to the swimming pool were a great relaxation- the idea had caught on and fifteen Oscotians turned up one day. There was some horse play by Chris White and the attendant had to blow his whistle.

The retreat, given by a Franciscan, was very inspiring and laced with humour and I felt a little more at peace about the future than I had done for a long time. Those coming up for ordination had then to endure the 'Scrutinies' by the rector – a sort of exam. It was a question of in and out in typical Foster fashion. His main question was, 'if you've just installed an organ and the bishop tells you to move.....what would be your reaction?'   Take it with me Mgr?

The retreat hotted up with the conference on, 'The art of conversation and the need to increase one's vocabulary', 'the presence of God in creation', 'not to be a butterfly', and 'putting up with people's foibles.' He quoted someone as saying that enjoying bananas was the sign of a 'carnal person' – I got some looks from people in the refectory when I brought a banana in for tea. At least the weather was warm and sunny and we could do a bit of sunbathing down in the field – where I spent part of my 23rd birthday – however the rector was not too pleased and put up a notice about bare calves showing under cassocks. This was particularly noticeable when, at Benediction, the deacon had to mount steps to place the monstrance on its stand. The server, to aid him, would lift up his alb, only to reveal the offending calves. One afternoon session was about 'girls and chastity'. CS Lewis *'Four Loves'* as reading was proving very helpful all round.

Denis was beginning to look like a Red Indian after his encounters with the sun but I was not given the description of 'Little Hovis' received last year. With the hour of Ordination approaching Lawler called me in and asked again if I was all right. 'It's good that someone takes an interest in spite of what some people say. As he said all that I needed was a little self confidence and that would come.' The retreat Father's last conference was on Confession and he told us how he had been refused absolution as a boy. The evening concluded with the archbishop conferring the tonsure on the year below our's. And so to the subdiaconate ordination on May 19th when we made that dramatic and literally fateful step forward together denoting our commitment to celibacy. I thought I was going to have a stroke during the prostra-

SUBDIACONATE ORDINATIONS

tions but all was well. Anton actually congratulated me afterwards with his inimitable smile – oh well. And now of course we got the usual comments from the rest, 'how's the wife?' – referring of course to the breviary which we were now bound to say daily for the rest of our lives. But it was rather strange because only one of the professorial staff congratulated us after the

D Hall. J O'Neil. J Smith. S Lawless . G Ryan . C White. A McGavin .A Handforth. D Oliver
J Lloyd. D Smith. D Keniry. Me, P Evans, J Glen , J Reville

ceremony and that was Dennis O'Shea who actually called me 'Tony'. But having now made this step I was very happy in myself about things.

Now that we were subdeacons we had the privilege of singing the Epistle at High Mass and due instruction on how to do this was given by Frank Thomas. My first experience was to be on the feast of the Dedication of the chapel, when the rector was celebrant and Barry Buckley was deacon. What an experience! The gold vestments were very hot and heavy.

My entomological pursuits meanwhile were reaching a climax with the hatching of two Indian Silk Moth Pupae – all quite fascinating.

A Mr. Gretrex the chalice maker called touting possible designs for next year – all too fabulously expensive I am afraid. There had been, too, the advent of Miss Gleeson who had invented the all purpose clerical shirt. You could wear it as a traditional shirt or slip in a plastic collar for official engagements. She was greatly blessed by the clergy. In lieu of, or, due to loss of the said collar one could always cut a section out of a Fairy Snow washing up liquid bottle which admirably did the trick. We were a little worried in that we think she may have run a sweat shop for immigrants somewhere off Piccadilly and wondered, therefore, whether the said shirts were altogether moral. The glorious May ended in storms and June was to begin with the coldest and wettest day since 1940.

The annual Oscotian reunion was again upon us and we helped prepare for this event but many escaped for the day as it was rather depressing seeing some of the old boys return –lamenting the 'good old days' and how students today have never had it so good. And with the 'new' ideas coming out of the Council there was even more talk. Then looking at the visiting clergy there was the prospect of what we might turn out to be like in the future. This was not at all encouraging. The tables were set out in the quad and although the weather was a contrast to the last month it was an excellent meal and plenty to eat. Dr Hahn was there again talking about his conversion and commenting on the state of the Anglican Church and the rector was interested to hear of my connection with Christ's Hospital through my uncle. It was good to get away from this ecclesiastical gathering and make another trip to the swimming baths where I achieved a whole width on the bottom.

News came through one of the Northampton students that +Leo had evidently put his foot down about saying the breviary in English even though bishop Wall of Brentwood had allowed it for some clergy. The end of the week saw the Eucharistic Congress being held in the college grounds with Mass in a Marquee and hoards of people poured in from the city but the whole thing was nearly washed away in the rain and the procession was cancelled at the last minute. This must have put the procurator in a mad mood for, during church history lecture the following day, he went on a rant. 'He thinks that we are on the eve of another schism in the Church and likens the period now to the one shortly before the Reformation. Some people were very cut up about his remarks.' But in hindsight how right he was !

The students met from time to time to discuss the general state of affairs in the college and on this occasion there was an interminably long discussion about finances. Some people did not know when to stop talking, 'The main argument was that the Oscotian Society had too much money in the bank – some £800 and a feeling that it should go to a poor students fund. I'm afraid most of these discussions go over my head and am not so alert to the various undercurrents. It seems a lot of ill feeling was engendered.' Coffee session had again come under criticism and though they could be open to abuse they seemed a very necessary thing for socialising. There was a feeling that the spirit in the house at changed considerably and not for the better. But there was some good news and Anton suddenly burst into my room and apologised. That certainly relieved the tension that had been going on now for some six months or more.

Having made the step to the subdiaconate the next step was to apply for the diaconate which I did at the end of the month. At last this interminable term came to an end. I didn't shine in my exams which were a consistent 60% or so – at least I got my 40%. The rector's speech congratulated the outgoing year and hoped that our year would be as good. He urged us, if we had to get work to take a job that was compatible with our dignity as a church student – same old admonition

News came through that the church at Newmarket was going up at last, 'The design I gather is a disaster as far as modern needs are concerned. The only one who is an admirer of the architect, son of Sir Ninian Comper, is the bishop. One of the priests from Cambridge who was up here said that even Father Kennedy wasn't too happy about the plans.'

My stick insects had died of old age and I was left with seven hundred eggs and not knowing quite what to do with them. And so home again along the old railway journey via stations familiar to me from school days and at Peterborough Bernard Hughes and his ailing father picked me up to give me a lift home.

As usual it was bliss to back in the free and fresh air and it was not long before I was out in the garden helping dad trim the hedge and the ditch by the road and cutting down the old almond tree. Although his rheumatism is becoming crippling he can still use his arms and weald a reap hook.

The weekly family trips to Clare then began. They made nice outings for the aunts and they could wander round the shops and meet old friends ending up at the local tea shop. Even though I was on holiday I was still wearing my collar which caused a certain amount of surprise amongst the locals. Mrs.

Tom Smith, wife of one of the farm labourers looking like a piece of old tanned leather and the mother of five sons greeted me, 'Hello Antny', and then looked dumfounded when she caught site of the white strip. She was even more surprised when she saw me a few days later without the collar. And then it was off to our clerical tailor in Cambridge to get equipped with some more garb from Mr Almond. I called in at the English Martyrs church and noticed that a collecting plate had been left on the ledge of one of the confessionals - I wondered what impression that might give to visitors!

Uncle Wilf had bought a cottage at Ousden and I got to know him and his wife Judy very well. Some years ago I had a short break with them at their home in Maidenhead. They had eight children and had fostered a ninth and I was most impressed by the organisation in the home. It was my first real experience of a busy family life. But it was all too short. He was widely read in philosophy and theology and was always spoiling for an argument and so he was keen to probe me deeply about my views on the Church in general.

A surprise phone call came from our friend at Waterbeach Carmel - and she didn't half make the most of the call! - was a request to go over to the Carmel for a funeral of one of the sisterhood. The funeral, the next day, was quite an event with sister in an open coffin. Canon Diamond, from English Martyrs, celebrated the Mass and I was able to help with the singing and swung the thurible. When it was all over we went 'inside' for the carrying of the coffin to the cemetery. It ended on a somewhat bizarre note. The coffin, still open, was laid on the wooden supports, awaiting the lowering when suddenly Mother Rosario, the Prioress, who was half blind but tall and stately leapt forward and embraced the corpse. At that point the bewildered bearers who had been lurking behind the bushes suddenly emerged to screw down the lid and lower the coffin into the grave. But it was a watery end because, in that fen country, the grave was already half filled with water upon which the coffin visibly floated. I wondered if a special dispensation had been granted for us to enter the enclosure for the usual penalty was instant excommunication. My father who occasionally did work for the sisters, being Church of England was fortunately free from this penalty.

Then it was off to Sussex by the Sea again to check up on St Dominic's. Sr Benedict had returned as head teacher to try and salvage something from the ruins left behind by previous heads who had brought the school to its nadir. There was a pleasant reunion with my music teacher and some of the nuns I had known. Sr Walburga, now stricken with angina was full of the new catechetics of Sr Romaine and Hoffinger, sweeping through the Church and the boys, all very polite, were full of The Rolling Stones and The Beatles. On then to my cousins at Horsham for a few days and theological discussions with Uncle Reg who was certainly 'with it'. They entertained the curate, Fr.

John Hull, a young priest who must have found life very difficult with the rather old fashioned parish priest, Canon Stone. But my cousins were doing well with Jonathan receiving a diploma at the Wigmore Hall, Philip who had been at University College London back from checking marks and Stephen home from Mark Cross and Andrew, the Benjamin of the family, growing up fast. Their mother Marjorie, herself an accomplished musician, was as placid as ever. We enjoyed each other's company and played duets. To add to our enjoyment there was a postal strike which caused total chaos in the system.

On return home I started on some epic cycle rides around the churches of Suffolk and I delighted in the architecture and the history of these marvellous buildings. My furthest trip was some hundred miles into East Suffolk. The roads were so quiet and it was a miracle that I never got a puncture. But they were rather lonely rides and I hardly spoke to a soul.

Michael Kennedy called, full of woes about the plans for the Newmarket church, to tell us about the stone laying ceremony soon to take place. He had had a row with the architect Sebastian Comper. He had wanted the interior of this basilica style church whitewashed, but Kennedy would have none of it.

But then I had a little pastoral experience at last. I cycled up to Walsingham and there met up with Peter Hocken and stayed for the inside of the week. Here we helped out with the annual Pilgrimage and met up with the famous Hume brothers Tony and Gerald. Both were blunt northerners. Gerry was the parish priest, very rough and ready and wearing a worn out cassock. Mgr Tony was a complete contrast and very smartly turned out. For many years he had run the diocesan travelling mission. The caravan, towed by his car, had been converted into a chapel and he would tour around the diocese together with Frs Bob Manley and Bob McCormick to celebrate Mass in outlying villages. On a couple of occasions he celebrated in our house and local Catholics would gather together, much as in penal times. On one memorable occasion Mass was celebrated at the Tudor Mansion of Giffords Hall at nearby Wickhambrook, where the former Tudor owners, the Heighams had been relatives of St Ann Line. She had been the housekeeper looking after the Jesuit priests including Fr John Gerard who had ministered in this area, until she herself was hanged for her work. One felt very much linked to our Catholic past by these events. From these house Masses developed some of the Mass centres around the Diocese, which sadly, are now being closed down because of the shortage of priests. My stay was busy and enjoyable and we were guided by the two grand old retainers Mr and Mrs Pegg who ran the shrine and I was subdeacon at +Leo's Mass who enquired how my organing was going.

On returning home I paid a visit to the church where I had been baptised at Bury St. Edmunds with a view to having a go on their very fine organ. Here I met the famous Fr Houghton and was entertained in what can only be described as his boudoire. This room was later returned to its previous use as a chapel. In fact it was one of the earliest chapels in use before Catholic Emancipation. He had been a convert and was very much the Edwardian country parson. Very much a pastoral man he had done much for schooling in the diocese. On the demolition of Tudor Rushbrooke Hall he had acquired the marble fireplace surround with its caryatides and made them into the surrounds for the main entrance. He had also acquired a Roman bath for the High Altar. He could not accept the liturgical changes that were soon to burst upon the scene and eventually retired to his vineyards in the south of France. Anyway he gave me a warm welcome and I was able to do a little practising.

At this time of the year, with the coming of the harvest, the stubble in the fields was fired. This year it was particularly bad and the cottage was surrounded by a sea of flame. Mother got out the hose pipe and trained it on the thatch in the forlorn hope that it might prevent it catching fire should any sparks blow over our way. But it was a terrifying sight. Tom Smith, who was tending the flames, told us not worry as the wind was in the other direction but this hardly allayed our fears. It was with relief when, some years later, the practice was banned.

At this time we met up with a young couple who had moved into the village. He was Janos Stryk and his partner Barbara from Poland. They were a delightful couple. He was Hungarian and escaping during the 1956 revolution came to England. He was an artist and bronze caster and we became great friends. He later moved to Carrara in Italy where he continued his work and gained considerable reputation in his field.

By the end of August temperatures were up into the nineties and it was time for the laying of the foundation stone for the new church in Newmarket. On 27th August we assembled on the footings with the bishop where I again functioned as sub-deacon with Fr Harry Wace as deacon. We perambulated around the various outcrops with the bishop asking what part was what as he sprinkled the holy water in blessing and the stone was lowered into position. As no one was talking to the architect I tried to have a word with him and also to Canon Diamond from Cambridge. It was hard going as he seemed more shy than I was - little knowing that only a year hence he would be my first parish priest.

As I recorded, 'This blissful holiday is drawing to a rapid conclusion. One of the happiest I can remember. Aunt Win is convinced that Catholics are scared of death (she isn't) but aunt Dot (a good Baptist) put her right on that one.' But there was the bleaker side, 'Beginning to worry now about the

Laying of foundation stone at Newmarket
Harry Wace   Bishop Parker   Me

future of the family. Dad is so crippled with rheumatism and seems so depressed, he doesn't smile or speak much. Mum on the other hand still acts as though she were about fifty - and she only looks that anyway. She has great plans for the garden, but I fear it will soon be all too much. I don't know how I shall be able to help.' With all this ageing and illness the worry of whom among the 'Big Three', as my cousins called their aunts, was going to die first.

FOURTH THEOLOGY Sept 1964- June 1965

The most important year of my life and the last year at Oscott dawned. The ritual of the trunk packing took place overseen by mother. It went as usual PLA but this time round we were 12 lb overweight and had to pay an excess of 2/3d. I served Mass for the last time at Kirtling after fifteen years on the job. It had been a great holiday. The journey back to college was tortuous. Cambridge to Bletchley where I had one and a half hours wait. Another change at Rugby for 20 minutes. College was just the same but the numbers were down to eighty – the lowest yet and there were now no longer any top tables. One reason was that first year philosophy had been transferred to Grove Park – the former pre-seminary college – and Mgr Foster was now rector of both establishments. One of the privileges of top year was being allowed out into the city on our own! We were really grown up now at twenty three years of age! The rector's address – no drink, no wirelesses, obedience to your bishop and to your parish priest!! John Spence, of our year, was now the college dean.

The main preoccupation was to prepare a course of twenty four convert instructions for use on the parish. Having no idea what was involved in becoming a convert it was all very theoretical and no one gave any advice on how to proceed. Even Peter Lawler wasn't very helpful on this score. But at least I only had four children in my catechism class and these were the very young ones and it was bliss compared with last year's group. My friendship with Anton was now back on track so that was a weight off my mind.

There was a minor crisis when the rector, in some dismay, summoned the house together. The CID had contacted him as one of the students had signed his application form for a new passport as a 'minister of religion' and the police could find no reference to him in their directory. The Mgr was really in a terrible state – perhaps the police may have suspected the student was one of the escaped great train robbers!

In moral theology we launched into *de usu matrimonii* – this was the big stuff reserved for top year and at last I would discover what those untranslatable Latin passages on sex and marriage meant in Davis's text book that the bishop had given me some years ago. It was also time to think about ordering ordination cards for next year to commemorate the great event. Some students designed their own with appropriate words. I chose a standard black and white version and ordered 1000 copies. A student gave a slide show of his trip to Moscow in the common room and I had to give the vote of thanks. I had been trying to teach myself a little Russian (in case the Communists came!) and so bedecked in an astrakhan I was able to say one or two words.

Dan Leonard now delved into the anatomical side of sex – on slides. Very enlightening! With the general election imminent the Conservative candidate, Mr Dark, actually came along to address us and a brilliantly written satire on the election was performed in the Common Room with Graham Adams as the Tory candidate and Terry Luxon representing Labour. Paddy Evans brought the house down as Bessy Braddock.

The Third Session of the Council had opened in Rome and we were full of excitement with the possibility of new ideas breaking forth in the Church. There was even talk of restoring the married diaconate. I commented in my letter home, 'There has been some dirty play by the 'conservatives' in that they are trying to get things watered down about the Jews and Religious Liberty and claiming Papal support. Fr Alfie Bull, of our diocese, has written a scathing letter in the Herald about the introduction of the vernacular – I only hope that I am not appointed as his curate next year.' Some people were hoping to celebrate a Scripture Service but the rector sat on this for public consumption until he had received some directives from the Archbishop !! He would never take any initiatives without Archiepiscopal approval.

A trip to the seminary at Upholland gave me my first view of Cheshire. A school for Church students was attached with about 200 boys but a very low percentage of students get through to train for the priesthood. It was in a very pleasant setting but Oscott seemed a better place.

With Ordination not far away we began to learn the rubrics of the Mass. These were very complex as we were still basically using the Latin Rite – a proliferation of genuflections, signs of the cross and kissings of the altar. The rector who took us for these lessons got very excited when some students extended their hands in prayer beyond the confines of their shoulders, laterally and vertically, as this was not the correct gesture; in turning to greet the people with a *'Dominus Vobiscum'* we were to keep our eyes down and not look at the congregation. It seemed very restrictive and an obsessive concentration on the mechanics of celebration. There were also the penalties of venial sin or even mortal sin for the infringement of the rubrics. We were really looking forward to what seemed very legalistic burdens to be lifted and, indeed, intimations coming from the Council suggested that the Liturgy would return to a 'noble simplicity' and something more in tune with the celebration of the Last Supper.

A good article in the Catholic Herald criticised the seminary system – I hoped the authorities took notice. Someone from local government gave us a talk and as a student remarked it was easy to get a person like that to address us but when it comes to someone like Sr Romaine it was a different matter. Life was becoming unsettled again and perhaps cold feet about next year. I got it into my head that after the diaconate I would like a year out to work and help out in the local parish at weekends - I seem to have noted that one before.

The beginning of November was marked by a Halloween Concert with some items I feel shouldn't have got through the censor! Broadening my style, I accompanied David Ryan singing *'Swinging on a star'* and Wilf Breen on the drums. An innovation in the liturgy was that students below subdeacons were allowed to come up to Communion in any order they liked instead of row by row – though I couldn't really see that this made any difference here at any rate. One innovation about this time was the the replacing of the long formula for administering Holy Communion to a simple, *Corpus Christi.* The reforms in the liturgy were buzzing about but not a word yet from the powers that be. We were cheered up by dealing with suicide in moral theology lectures and discussed the morality of Captain Oates going out into the snow for the nth time.

Some students were now getting permission to say the divine office in English. We were back to discussing the morality of using The Pill again and it was surprising to learn how little Infallibility is used in defining doctrines.. Ecumenism took off a little with the visit of twelve Methodist students who came one afternoon and were shown around by twelve hand picked students.. The discussion in the Catholic Herald continued about seminary training and we concurred with many of the sentiments. We went from the depressingly sublime as I started reading, *'The Plague'* by Albert Camus to the ridiculous when the vice- rector gave the House a spelling test - a hundred words. Mind you my spelling was far from perfect and Frank Thomas himself admitted that he couldn't spell 'antimacassar'. As the college diarist remarked, 'one or two students hearing the words 'concupiscence' and 'antimacassar' thought they were new sins and incorporated them into their moral notes.' They were all having a good laugh at us at the top table. The result of the spelling B was announced – I got twenty three wrong – and that was not as bad as some!

I was finding preparing the convert instructions quite impossible and all I could do was to write down a lot of references. However the question of The Pill dogged everyone and John Glen suggested that we all had a proper discussion at the next pastoral lecture and try and thrash things out. There was an air of unreality about life in the college now as we approached the final stretch and our year seemed very divided with so many different little groups – it seemed a great pity. Seminaries were on the agenda at the Council and there would surely be fireworks again. Canon Nicholson gave us a recollection on the Sacrament of the Present Moment – giving as an example of his own eye trouble – he was half blind and showed a great deal of courage.

The news then broke that the archbishop had to go into hospital and there seemed some doubt about when the ordination was to take place.

The rector announced that Birmingham students could say part of the breviary in English but didn't want them to apply while still students. This seemed daft as Brentwood and Westminster had already given permission very easily. There was uproar in Rome on the vote on Religious Liberty but the Pope delayed a decision until the next session. We were given a lecture on childrens' Masses from Fr Stonier. Three of us tuned in illicitly to the final Congregation of the Council and heard the promulgation of the *De Ecclesia* document and there was an interesting discussion on Radio Eiran between Kung, Schillebeekz and Baum. 'The question of birth control is still causing a great deal of discussion and controversy and completely worn out with it as we don't seem to be getting anywhere. The only answer is a Papal Definition. It's all very worrying as we are on the threshold of next year and will have to be dealing with these problems'.

I had a chat with Denis about the 'period of adaptation' – this was still the most alarming thing. 'We go from day to day here in a kind of straight jacket, knowing what ought to be done, but not being able to do it and given no support in effecting it. It s a DIY course here and there seems to be an entirely negative attitude on the part of the authorities.'Dan Leonard as good as admits that the convert instructions are a DIY. We start discussing medical ethics and the lecture was immediately taken up again with questions on contraception. The new Liturgy is beginning to take shape with Frank Thomas saying the community Mass with as much English as was permitted.

Let's hope that it will all be in English soon - it certainly takes on a new dignity, though a saddened few think we have thrown out the mystery with the mystification.' Towards the end of the month everyone began to go down with sickness and diarrhoea and lectures were suspended.

Into December changes in the Liturgy continued with an Offertory Procession - 'Tweezers to handle the altar breads proved a failure and was too much like the straight line test. As the Pope arrived in Bombay for his historic visit we began to revive but everyone is feeling very depressed – not improved by Denis O'Shea's rendering of the community Mass in the vernacular.'

Graham started to work on next years's play – *The Lark* by Anouilh. He offered me the part of John of Arc but I turned it down because of the prospect of so much work in the last year. Denis had been on one of his many excursions and came back full of the *St Severin* plan for parish life and he was a little incoherent in his enthusiasm. As it was the anniversary of the *Wreck of the Deutchsland* we read Gerard Manley Hopkins's poem by the same name in Pat Kilgariff's room. A suggestion was put forward that we might sing Lauds before Mass in the morning but this was dismissed by the rector because, presumably, he would have to get permission from the Archbishop

'There seems to be a general decline in the spirit of our year. The conversation at table has deteriorated to petty bickering and cynical comments. And for about the nth time we have been talking about the 'Safe Period'. With the diaconate coming up shortly there seems to have been no proper preparation for this important Order. Doctor Greehy treated the form of the Orders exam with a certain amount of contempt and he seemed to be frustrated with the whole set up himself although he did talk a little about the theology of the diaconate.

Now confusion reigned as to where the ordination was going to take place next year as we were from different parts of the diocese. The parish priest of Kettering, Mgr Collins, who had the reputation of being a stern disciplinarian with his curates, was determined that his student should be ordained there and as a compromise we suggested that we could be ordained in the Cathedral at Northampton. In the event +Leo decided that four of us should be ordained at Cambridge which was very acceptable. +Leo in fact came for another visit. He was not very amenable to giving permission to say the office in English. He didn't like the American Breviary and, 'the trouble is that people don't understand the psalms these days' – which proved the point that it might be a good idea to pray it in English. However in typical fashion he addressed the Common Room in the evening and cheered us up no end. The rector – otherwise known as The Lodger suddenly got very excited and enthusiastic about 'Mass facing the people' and writing off to the archbishop for permission to have it in the chapel. It seemed very strange that there was no formal retreat in preparation for the diaconate. Six of our year organised their own – much against the authorities wishes but we did persuade Dr Greehy to give us a talk – which was most inspiring. We had to suggest it and it was the first time that the diaconate has been mentioned to us in any meaningful way. I suppose the subdiaconate was the most important step and the diaconate was simply a final transitional stage to the priesthood. 'I renew my resolutions before tomorrow – it is only with God's help that I can win through,' I wrote in my journal.

Once again we had to swear the anti-modernist oath; +Leo was very keen on this. Did this mean that the authorities thought we had fallen into heresy since the subdiaconate? However this was a prerequisite for ordination. On December 19th, Bishop Tickle, now bishop of the forces conferred the diaconate and it was done smoothly and unhurriedly, though there was always that rather fearsome admonition at the start of the service declaring that anyone who left before the end of the ceremony was liable to excommunication. There was not the panic as with the subdiaconate. Only Denis O'Shea made some attempt to congratulate us afterwards. But after this life changing event it was back to revising for the rest of the day. 'Everyone is very miserable and fed up to the back teeth about the authorities. Life at table is getting a little bitter all round. If only there was more contact between staff and students and liaison between the rector and the professors. Old, old story, again and again – *ad nauseam.*' Peter Hocken wrote to me from his placement in Corby-a very inspiring letter - we need it and with the gift of £1 – very kind of him.

The ten minute moral exam was three days before Christmas. We covered taxes, oaths, vows, servile work (ran me round on that one). The rest of the day was spent decorating the common room. The 'stained glass window' of the Nativity was a magnificent success and with lanterns behind the lights it looked a picture with the added greenery. Sadly the carol concert was a bit flat compared with other years. It had been badly organised by the Music Deanery. The rector wasn't present so there was no traditional rendering of *'Nazareth',* which he sang so well, and only O'Shea was there from the profs. except Thomas who accompanied one or two songs as I did most of the accompanying with John Smith. The following day it was over to the children's home at Coleshill for the customary pantomime which went down well as ever with the kids followed by a huge spread provided by the sisters. Sam Penney fell over and badly concussed himself rather seriously; he had a similar concussion a year or so ago.

On Christmas Eve and, after five years, I was home with the family for the first time and, acted as deacon at the Midnight Mass in St Mary Magdalen's, Brockley. I had to give Holy Communion for the first time to ordinary parishioners. On reflection it was a wonderful experience. It was great being home for Christmas Day and we had some snow. Part of the time we spent with the family's GP in the next road He was very good at taking the aunts down to Suffolk when the time came round for them to go on holiday.

In spite of ice and snow we made a trip up to London to get a cassock measured at Wippels and a pyx for taking Communion to the sick. The family had clubbed together to buy me a chalice and we collected it from the maker, Mr Clark, at Islington. The year ended with freak weather – heavy snow, a tornado in Manchester and thunder storms. 'Fr Patrick AA, came to lunch and offered to buy me a slip cassock – I wonder where he gets all his money as a religious.' The year ended with apprehension but with hope and confidence in the Lord and I tuned in to an interesting discussion between a Moslem, a Buddhist, a Hindu and a Christian. It was surprising to learn how much they had in common.

The beginning of the year saw a trip with the family to the Odeon at Peckham to see the magnificent film, *Laurence of Arabia*. They got in for 2/6d on their pensions and I for 5/-. Perhaps inspired by the interfaith programme the next two books I bought were an *Islamic Anthology* and the *Confessions of St Augustine*. 'Dad's rheumatism is getting progressively worse especially in his legs but he stills manages to hobble out for his walks and it is probably best that he keeps on the move. Treatment in the shops is now getting casual – it was a do it yourself job in the shoe shop with no attempt to help me fit them – the girl just stood gormlessly looking on. Our family doctor offers, appropriately, to buy me a sick call set with an upper limit of £20. Met up with Charles Crawford and went to see *Laurence* again and this inspired me to read his *Seven Pillars of Wisdom*. We went for a coffee in a Pakistani restaurant – 'only coffee? – it is not our custom' – but in the end we got what we wanted.'

And so it was back to Oscott, in thick snow, for the very last time and the build up to the ordination on the Ember Saturday in Lent with all the business of sending out invitations. Dennis had something like three hundred while mine were not much more than a handful. The first event was a trip to the Town Hall for a Christian Unity meeting. The speakers were the bishop of Crediton, Bernard Leeming SJ and a Methodist Minister. Fr Leeming was too scholarly and lecture like and the Methodist was the best speaker and a good cross section of the public attended.

And now letters sped too and fro with the family about arrangements for the ordination and first Mass. It was all very hectic especially with all the initial uncertainty as to where the ordination was to take place.

John Molyneux called in again – his consoling words, repeated so often before on his visits, encouraged us – 'get out while you have the chance.'

The 24th January marked two historic events. The first was the death of Sir Winston Churchill and the second was the first time we had Mass facing the people on a portable altar in the chancel area before the *lampadarium* – it really was most effective. We went to Communion at the Low Mass instead of the High Mass which was sad as this was supposed to be the chief Mass of the day. Our two bishops arrived for the consecration of the new Birmingham auxiliary bishop in the cathedral on the following day, + Leo and +Charles. +Leo sat at the table, +Charles in an easy chair. While +Leo rambled on about the 40 English and Welsh Martyrs, +Charles in a quiet voice carried on business at the same time. It was now a question of light under the bedclothes to revise until 11.30 pm.

The consecration of Joseph Cleary as an auxiliary bishop was a big occasion. The Apostolic Delegate, Archbishop Cardinale, was the consecrator assisted by bishops Tickle and Dunne of Dublin. Archbishop Grimshaw was there but now looking very ill and a shadow of his former self. + Joseph Rudderham of Clifton read his breviary all the way through the ceremony following the example of + David Cashman and +Leo Parker. This was not surprising, I suppose, as the Office was very long in those days.

'The weather continued very cold with snow and the temperature in the Northcote Hall being just over 50F and the temperature there and in the chapel eventually bottomed out at 48F. The central heating is very bad. How people survived in the old days I don't know but I gather they usually lost one or two students a year by death. The rector announced that the solemn celebration of Mass, in future, will be the community Mass facing the people on a Sunday. – so we are making progress though it looks as though we shall still be preaching the homily at the succeeding High Mass – oh for a little imagination to be employed.'

'I had quite a long discussion with Charles Crawford about what we have gained from Oscott and the prospects for the future. We felt that we should have had more individual tuition from the beginning and perhaps more could have been achieved. I can't see myself going to the rector at the end of term and thanking him for all he has done. We have actually imported two TV sets to watch the impressive state funeral of Sir Winston. Lots were drawn for those who would have to stay behind for the Easter ceremonies as against those who would be allowed out into different parishes. Unfortunately I drew the short straw and will have to stay back for the ceremonies here. The rector grants us an extension to watch the TV until 9.25 pm– what progress.'

Another student had moved into my circuit of recent months and this was Patrick Fell. He was a convert Englishman – very reserved. He was somewhat teased as he had an almost full size statue of St Patrick in his room and seemed to be more Irish than the Irish. Along with Anton I invited him to my ordination and first Mass. Bishop Cleary celebrated his elevation to the episcopate by a Christmas dinner for all the students saying that he owed everything to Oscott.

Small things amused fellow students especially when one was in the public eye in the Liturgy. On this occasion I acted as deacon at the High Mass and at the appropriate place incensed the thurifer by mistake instead of the subdeacon – such trivial things caused a great deal of mirth in the student body. The cold weather continued and people were down with bad colds – not surprising when the temperature in some of the rooms only touched 48F. Feeling exhausted I retired to my bed several times – it was bad enough dropping off during lectures. Our visiting speakers continued to come including Fr Murphy – Brophy who spoke on his work as a prison chaplain in Winchester and about the St Dismas rehabilitation centre – you would certainly need to be the right sort of person to take on that sort of work and also the University Chaplain, Geoffrey Tucker about work with undergraduates. Spelling B's continued and a list of things we have to know for the Orders exam – only five weeks away! A cycle trip with Anton to magnificent Lichfield Cathedral was inspiring and tea at the Angel Cafe where you could eat all you wanted for 3/6d cheered one up no end. I wrote to St Dominic's about saying Mass for the boys but the message came back that the Mass had to be in Latin, so I wrote to the Vicar General in Southwark about it. All was fixed too for Laxton. A dispensation also had to be obtained for me as I would not have reached the legal age of twenty five by the time of the Ordination; but that was forthcoming.

One of the privileges being in Orders was to wash the linen for the liturgy – the purificators had to be dipped a couple of times in one water and then rinsed in another before going off to the cleaners – and the water presumably went down the *sacrarium* to join my hair of two years ago. There was a certain amount of disgust when I won five prizes in the photo slide competition – 12/- wasn't a bad reward.

'One feels as though the college is worn out. Perhaps I'm merely describing my own emotions but there seems to be a general lassitude in everything and apathy to lectures and liturgy, although Denis tells me there is beginning to be an upsurge in the Legion of Mary and YCW. We were told only yesterday that we had to make something of the secular clergy stall at the Vocation Exhibition at Harbourne – with such short notice it's no wonder that only a few of the solid always willing people are ready to do anything. Most of the encouragement comes from letters about the ordination – if only the laity knew how things really go on here.' However there were bright spots like excellent meditation-points on the need to develop a social conscience among the laity and an excellent talk on St Paul by Canon Nicholson and how much he is neglected.

The birth control controversy was never far from the surface and Dan Leonard read us a letter from a young Divine Word priest, Fr McMahon, in the Birmingham Post. He brought up some valuable points but much of it was considered bad theology about the Church and misleading in many ways.

Organ lessons still continued and John Rust seemed willing to take on another student. I went to an organ master class lead by Ralph Downes of Brompton Oratory – a very humble man but a brilliant organist; as were some of his students.

An innovation was to have a regular discussion group in the common room and this was inaugurated by Sam Penney who lead the discussion on the problem of pain. 'It is surprising how superficial one's knowledge of fellow students is – really we are just acquaintances without ever really getting to know each other much more deeply. I do try to get to know people but it's not always easy.'

'Chris White has printed my ordination cards. He's a chap who gets things done and makes no bones about it. Everything is now building up in my own mind about next week. I have reverted for the first time since school days to solitary walks in Sutton Park but even there one cannot get away from the throb of the traffic.'

Lent did not get off to a good start with pancakes more like fritters so David Mead made some later in his room which were delicious. Dennis Hall was full of his trip to Coleshill where the nuns had presented him with a pyx. He has certainly made the most of his time at Oscott in bending the rules by going on extra collegial pastoral activities. The temperatures in the Northcote Hall for lectures dropped to 40F the lowest ever and there were blizzards throughout the country.

We were getting on to the real pastoral stuff now as Dan Leonard showed us how to do a baptism – with a doll! and for the first time in three months the rector gave a pre retreat chat to our year. Uncle Charlie's card to me was most appropriate - 'God give your courage'. Poor John Lloyd would go into retreat remembering the death of his hamster – probably from cold – and it received suitable obsequies.

161

And so it was the last lap with a week's retreat at the Jesuit House at Harbourne. It was noticeably warmer than at Oscott and we had running water in our rooms. The Retreat was given by Fr Leo Nolan SJ. He was rather dry and heavy and the conferences were heavily laced with St Ignatius's Exercises. His catch phrase was that we should do a great deal of 'pondering and praying' and to do that well. We certainly did that. The food was very good with bacon and egg for breakfast. The week ended on a high as we dashed back to college for the final packing and preparation for tomorrow – 'It all seems very unreal and by tomorrow I shall hardly believe it has all happened.' We four Northampton Diocese students, Charles Crawford, Graham Adams, Derrick Smith and I returned to the college by taxi. Meeting up with a priest ordained last year, with sleeves rolled up, and tucking into a hefty pancake, we accepted his offer of sustenance before retiring to a rather late bed after a final packing.

THE ORDINATION -12th MARCH

And now the life changing events for which we had been preparing for six years were upon us. The coach left at 6.30 am on the Friday morning. We arrived at Cambridge by 10 am It was a glorious warm, sunny, Spring day. We left our luggage at the University Arms Hotel before walking down to the church of Our Lady and the English Martyrs. This large gothic church, with its tall spire, dominated this southern end of the city and was known locally as 'The Cathedral or 'The Cafflick' otherwise simply as OLEM. All my expected guests arrived; Fr Gerard Meath OP, my former head teacher at Laxton, and now Prior Provincial of the English Province of the Dominican Order who was to be my assistant priest during the ordination ceremony; Frs Brendan Fox and Patrick O'Neil AA from Brockley and my various school friends who were students from Blackfriars at Oxford, and Bros Bertrand, William, Mervyn and Joachim from Hawkesyard, Fr John Molyneux, Anton and Patrick Fell and a contingent from Lidgate. The ceremony was straightforward enough but my thoughts through the ceremony were how to ease my aching back. The laying on of hands was the climax of the ceremony and I was consoled by Fr Lawler's parting words before leaving, 'don't worry if you don't feel any emotion it doesn't mean that you should have become an accountant .' There followed the anointing of the hands with oil and Fr Gerald Moorcraft bound the hands together with a small fillet of material. During the concelebration of the Canon of the Mass, when we knelt behind the Bishop, I was assisted by Fr Gerard. Bishop Leo was more doddery than usual but got through very well as he did the two succeeding days at Kettering and Shefford. He tried to lead the people in a Latin Lord's Prayer but he was drowned by the congregation in a resounding, 'Our Father' in English.

Although he used English in the address at the beginning and also in some other parts of the liturgy, the microphones were ineffective and no one in the church could hear him clearly at all. The singing was not inspiring with only parts sung in plainsong by Frs Harry Wace and Brian Nightingale and there was no organ music to create any atmosphere since it was the season of Lent.. Being a working day presumably members of the choir were unable to get time off. However Fr Harry Wace, one of the curates gave a rather truncated commentary from pulpit as the bishop had not been very keen on the last one that he had done. But since the public address system was hardly working no one could hear what he was saying either and on top of this the central heating system had broken down, too, and so people were shivering in the main body of the church. There were several of the local clergy present whom I would get to know in later years - Gerald Moorcraft and Brian Nightingale both curates at the church with Canon Diamond and Paul Hypher and his parish priest, Paddy (Titus) Oates from the nearby St Laurence's Parish. My invitation to Fr Oswald Baker, our former Newmarket curate, had been turned down because he did not approve of the changes that had already been introduced into the Ordination Rite. + Leo had forbidden any flash photography (which could have been very discreet in that large building) but then complained afterwards when he saw the rather grainy black and white photos that had been taken.The bishop insisted on reciting the thanksgiving prayers with us after the Mass which delayed us and this meant that many people had left the church before we were able to greet them or give them our first blessings. Derrick tried to give his first blessing in English to the Bishop but he objected. Then everyone that was left came forward for the blessing by the new priests and the kissing of our hands and then we were surrounded by hoards of school children and the Cambridge Evening News who had the additional interest in me being a local boy. I felt really quite unemotional and the events hardly sank in. A small reception took place at the University Arms Hotel which was well underway by the time I arrived. The bishop joined us and promised us a free holiday in Rome (which never materialised!). Aunt Elsie dropped some cream on the carpet which another guest dexterously rubbed in with her shoe and it all went like a dream.

Mother and aunt now returned to London while I was taken to Newmarket to stay the night at the White Hart Hotel in the High Street with Fr Patrick and Patrick Fell. The latter and I had a walk round the town before calling at the small Catholic Church in All Saints road where I was to celebrate my first Mass on the morrow. This seemed cold and depressing but we managed to fix up a tape recorder for the historic event. There was a Masonic ball in progress in the hotel on return which went on into the early hours and with the excitement it was very difficult to get any sleep. But then I used my new

First Mass - Our Lady & St Etheldreda, Newmarket

Ecce Agnus Dei

Patrick Fell, Fr Vincent, Stephen   Mother, Fr Patrick, Fr Kennedy

Fr Patrick AA, Fr Vincent OP, Mother, Aunt Elsie, Fr Kennedy, Patrick Fell

Aunt Eva   Robina &Uncle Charlie Win
Aunt Marjorie, Andrew, Mother, Me, Aunt Elsie, Uncle Reg

Cousins Jonathan, Stephen and Philip Dean

powers to bless many of the ecclesiastical gifts that I had been given and about 2.30 am. I said Lauds which eventually sent me off to sleep.

Next day, Saturday, mother and aunt, Kath Reader from upstairs and Mrs Janes the doctor's sister in law arrived by car from London as did Fr Vincent and uncle Charlie. I was very sorry that uncle Wilf and his family couldn't come but uncle Reg, aunt Marjorie and the four cousins from Horsham were all there. But of course my dad and beloved aunt Dorothy were unable to be present and kept each other company at home for aunt Dorothy's birthday. There was a contingent from Lidgate including our sculptor friend Janos Stryk and Jo Ibbett from Cambridge. Miss Anne Emery supplied the flowers which brightened up the drab and deteriorating church and one of the Sisters from the convent played the harmonium. Fr Kennedy, due to the pressure of building the new church, was not at all well with a heart condition and was not much help as assistant priest. Uncle Reg, with his distinctive univesity accent, read the lesson and his son, Stephen, served the Mass. Fr Vincent read a commentary in English as most of the Mass was still in Latin and Fr Patrick preached the homily. We processed in to the strains of *Come Holy Ghost* on the wheezy harmonium and it was as well I borrowed the Prinknash vestments from college as the local ones were really quite tatty. After the Papal blessing they all sang *Loving Shepherd* - rather falteringly as there was some disagreement about the tune. Mother had the privilege of coming into the sanctuary to receive Holy Communion and then everyone came up to the altar rails for my First Blessing except auntie Eva who, still wearing her brown beret, said to uncle Charles, 'Don' t you go up for no Roman Catholic blessing.' But afterwards she did when the church was empty. Aunt Lillie was heard to say in a loud voice, 'and with thy spirit' and we all went out to *Praise to the Holiest*.

On return to the White Hart place names had not been put out and the manageress, a lapsed catholic, was in a flap. We had rather fatty and tough roast beef preceded by a little sherry which was our only alcoholic beverage - expenses were mounting up ! - but Uncle Reg gave an excellent after dinner speech developing the analogy between a Newmarket horse race and the progress through the seminary with the different Orders as the various hurdles and much to my pleasure he ended up with a quote from our local poet John Lydgate. It was a pity that the Anglican rector, Canon Newell, from nearby Ousden could not make it. I made some sort of reply alluding to my encounter with the late Prince Monolulu in Newmarket at the age of six when, as I have already related, he told me that I would one day be a jockey. Then it was all over and people went their different ways and I was left entirely to myself. Aunt had gone back to London and mother taken home to Lidgate to be ready for the morrow.

I called at St Louis convent for tea and the nuns kept popping in and asking for my blessing and I thanked them for their gift of £3. And then I just went walking, buying newspapers recording the event and up to Warren Hill and the gallops and at the bottom the glow of the forge of Curtis's the farriers could be seen as they worked late into the evening on the horse shoes.

Back at the presbytery it was chop and baked beans for supper. That evening we just sat by the fire - Fr Kennedy, his curate, Fr Garvey and I and chatted softly to one another. Fr Garvey took out a book to prepare his sermon for tomorrow. Fr Kennedy commented, 'I don't want to scandalise young Tony here, but if you can't think of anything to say give it a miss - you can't do your parish visiting and preach a good sermon on a Sunday - you can't burn the candle at both ends.' As Fr Garvey continued to look for inspiration from the bookshelf Fr Mick observed, 'Ah so, Father, they're all a hundred years out of date.' Fr Garvey then inveighed against the modern trend in Scripture studies. So here was my first introduction to real parish life and something of a dampener on my youthful zeal.

Then it was bed after an exhausting day. It was rather primitive upstairs with one wash basin and no hot water. The housekeeper who comes in from down the road advised me not to use the WC upstairs as it was likely to cause the pipes to rattle all night. But in the event I passed a reasonably comfortable night.

The following day, Sunday, was cold and windy and this was to be my home coming to Kirtling Church. The parish priest was unable to come and so I was on my own like any visiting priest and accepted as such. Apart from my mother all the familiar faces of old were there - Edgar Pavis rang the two bells and took the collection and David Mayo, son of the dentist and his wife, with whom I used to serve now serving me and the usual Sunday congregation with the Stalleys and the Basterikas in evidence. After returning to Lidgate and visiting some friends mother and I were then ferried to the Carmelite Convent at Waterbeach.

Sr.Mary of Carmel

On arrival we had to wait about an hour in the parlour before Sr Mary of Carmel arrived by which time we were cold and starving. However there was now a sense of excitement as the Sisters kept coming in and going out again behind the grill to ask for my first blessing. Mother Prioress had at least two goes. We were at last rescued by Fr Bayliss, the chaplain, a sprightly old Jesuit of about eighty who conducted us to the nearby Lodge where the nuns had provided us with a splendid supper of roast chicken etc. Proceedings were brought to a conclusion with a

167

pleasant evening next door with the Hawkes, parents of Michael from school and Fr Wace who had come over from Cambridg.

On the morrow it was Mass at 7.30 am for the sisters. Again there was great excitement and a great deal of twittering and with more blessings and Communion being given at the grill. I am sure some of them had a little peak upwards to have a better look at me. After all I suppose they were entitled too since I had been at the top of their prayer list for so long! But it was on the move again and we caught the train down to London to the flat and to be welcomed by aunts Dorothy and Elsie and dad who had had to learn of things second hand. But there was no rest for then it was a dreary ride on the tube out to Hornchurch for Denis Hall's first Mass. Denis was surprisingly calm and self assured and said Mass facing the people and he actually said the Canon out loud! I really felt for him as I knew the sort of mistakes he would make having practised saying Mass together at college. As he was well known there was a good parish turn out. When it was discovered that I was newly ordained it was first blessings all over again. He got a good collection for himself - some £50.

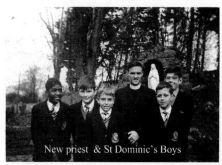

New priest & St Dominic's Boys

The next day was again pouring with rain and after an early Mass at Brockley Church I caught the train to St. Leonard - on - sea where a taxi was waiting to drive me in luxury to St Dominic's. After tea and a rousing reception from the nuns I went round to see my old music teachers, the Browns, and had tea again before returning for more tea and chat while the nuns did their embroidery. Mass, the next day, was in the gym with a special permission to have Mass facing the schoolboys. There had been some difficulty in getting this permission as bishop Cowderoy was not too keen. But it went well and afterwards I was swamped by youngsters who wanted my autograph and it was all very enjoyable and rewarding. And when it was time to set off again for London in the pouring rain the community all assembled to waive me off.

Come Friday of the great week it was my first public Mass at St Mary Magdalen's, Brockley where my parents had been married and there was a great turn out for the parish Mass. Even my father's brother, Tom, had come from South Norwood. Again we had Mass facing the people which I was told was very impressive. The choir sang a very powerful *Ave Maria* at the

Offertory which made me smile. A collection was taken and everyone thought it was personal for me and so were generous in their contribution. No such luck - the parish priest pocketed it for the parish!

The final day, after sad farewells to the family, it was up to the old school at Laxton to be met by Fr Aiden at the station. The Fathers were all very pleasant and welcomed me as one of the Community however they were not so keen to have Mass facing the people as they were not yet geared up for that. The following morning there was a downpour of snow but I managed to struggle over the park to see old Mrs Hales or rather her daughter as mum was in bed and was able to get some coal in for her. Attempts to hitch a lift into Stamford to see Mr Gomer were unsuccessful and the day ended with Stations of the Cross and Benediction over which I presided.

And so the great week week was over and having been delivered by Fr Aiden to Seaton station it was the dreary journey back to Birmingham where I was brought back to earth by the old newspaper seller by the bus stop outside the cinem and back to the college by 7.30 pm to the welcome of the students and one or two of the professors.

THE LAST THREE MONTHS

MARCH

After the week's 'honeymoon' it was lectures again with a vengeance. However I recorded, 'It seemed sad that none of the proffs made any comment or congratulated us on our ordination except Dan Leonard at the beginning of his moral lecture. Here we began the deadly tract on Justice in its manifold forms. A little later Peter Lawler did ask for my blessing which was very touching. The rector said not a thing and no doubt will be on tenterhooks till the end of term when we leave. I suppose once you are ordained he feels he no longer has any more control over us and the sooner we are gone the better. We have another outside speaker to talk to us about catechetics – he painted a rather a depressing picture about the state of affairs and didn't really suggest any remedies.'

Having experienced extreme cold we now faced temperatures in March of 75F. One afternoon was spent in the Rovers' Den where in true scouting fashion we lit a fire and cooked some crumpets. One privilege of being priests is that we are now let off one manual labour period a week.

Preparations were being made for the funeral of Archbishop Grimshaw, who in the meantime had died, and we awaited the arrival of three episcopal cars, Parker, Restiaux and Foley for the burial. Although the papers said otherwise in their tributes most of the Birmingham students said how little they had had to do with him and how remote he was – a shy man said the papers but very affable. +Leo saw all his students and speculated on who was to be the next archbishop – he must be one who can, 'drink anything, anywhere and at any time.' The funeral service in St Chad's cathedral was most impressive with a bevy of bishops presided over by Cardinal Heenan.

There had been mass blessings by the new priests in the chapel of the college and giving out of ordination cards. I preferred to go round on my own to students which made it a bit more personal – the rector gave me a cursory word and smile but then we had to endure – hopefully his final admonition to the house on obedience. Obedience to your parish priest took on a new strength as we approached our fate. Students from Heythrop College were coming to visit and on no account were we to give them coffee in our rooms after lunch otherwise future visits would be stopped. He said he would like to stamp out coffee parties but there was too much pressure from the professorial staff......if he mentions that again !! – but that of course was the last time, thank heavens.

APRIL

A final example of childishness was the visit of the Heythrop students to play us at soccer. 'A notice went up saying that spiritual reading would follow Benediction for the visitors. Nobody thought that this was forbidding us to see the visitors off. Unfortunately the rector thought otherwise and in a most forceful way a notice immediately went up on the notice board on 'obedience' and as a penalty for this 'lapse' those who were late were forbidden to go on the outing to Cotton College; not all those concerned were going anyway, but that was by the way. Such 'punishment' seems quite absurd and only goes to show the complete lack of understanding between the students and authority. The rector may be right and one must see both sides of the story on the other hand I have never seen so many students in the common room after supper with a common topic of conversation for ages – at one point we broke out into the Freedom March Song – *'We shall overcome some day'* ! One doesn't feel bitter but just sad at the whole situation.' However the rector lifted the ban some days later as he felt that not everyone had seen his notice on the board.

With April 1st out of the way - and had yesterday just been an April Fool - we proceeded in moral lecture to the final stage of *de usu matrimonii*. This was a 'practical' session and the mysteries of contraception were at last revealed to us – a box of real contraceptives were brought out. A great variety of mechanical devices were passed round and there was a great deal of amusement and discussion as to how some of these contraptions could be fitted into the female anatomy! It was enough to put anyone off marriage.

Historic First Concelebration at St. Chad's Cathedral

'I made a trip to Brewood near Wolverhampton with Pat Fell to meet his mother who was most hospitable. We visited the Dominican girls school afterwards. All the nuns came in and flopped down for my blessing. It's all a very strange experience.'

As I wrote home,'We say Mass every morning in English in our little chapels and it is quite like the penal days must have been. If these changes had been brought in four hundred years ago, perhaps we would not have had the Reformation. It's a pity they didn't bring in all the changes together as it will only confuse people.'

'One priest ordained at the same time as us, now working in an East End parish, paid us a visit and it was strange seeing him hobnobbing at the top table. It seems they have lost twenty students at Ware due to the tightening up there and the the complete reshuffle of the staff.'

'Three names have been put forward by the chapter in Birmingham for the new archbishop and they appear to be John Humphries, Bishop Cleary, H Francis Davies. But it seems likely that George Dwyer is to be the choice.'

'More English and participation is entering the Liturgy and one begins to wonder who is saying the Mass. However it is a big improvement. Various rites are springing up during the private Masses of the new clergy – are high and low Church parties developing ?'

With the fag end of the term approaching there seemed little incentive to get down to any studies and it was really difficult to concentrate. The weather continued to be freezing and everyone was back in overcoats and scarves for lectures. However there was one historic event in which we participated on Maundy Thursday and that was the first concelebrated Mass with Bishop Cleary. 'My, things would get moving if he were in charge.' It was a most impressive ceremony which took place in the cathedral. Many of my year peeled off afterwards to go home to their own parishes for Easter. Having drawn the short straw I had to remain at the college to do my bit at the Easter Vigil. In the event this was a great experience as I had to carry the Paschal Candle and sing the *Exultet*. The rector was very chatty afterwards and gave me permission to go home for my parents silver wedding.

Mgr Leboa from the Congregation of Rites was visiting the college and celebrated the Monday Mass – the rector was hoping that it would be in the true Roman Rite but as it was he had arms outstretched (rubric!) And almost said the Canon of the Mass out loud.

Appointments were now coming through - Charles was going to Northampton and Gerry Ryan to Slough. The Bishop mentioned in his letter to me about the Rome holiday that he had promised and if I still wanted to go – but that was the last I ever heard of the offer. For the Excursus Day Graham and I went up to Liverpool. We looked into the new cathedral that was gradually growing but was not impressed so far. The Anglican cathedral was a different matter. We ended the day by a trip to sandy Hoylake and dined at a hotel.

The last play to enjoy was *The Lark* by Anouilh. Graham had done a superb job producing it as he had done for a *Man for all Seasons* and Gerry O'Hanlon was magnificent as Joan of Arc. I felt a little bit jealous as I had been offered the part – but it would have been a tremendous slice out of my time and an amount to learn. But it was with some nostalgia as I walked over the stage wondering if this would have been my swan song after all the plays I had taken part in during my career. Now in my last year I was getting a bit bolder and with Anton disappeared for lunch and visited his brother who with the Divine Word Order at Droitwich. Luckily the rector hadn't noticed my absence at dinner.

At least there was one official pastoral visit outside the college and that was to say Mass at Maryvale for the Sisters as their chaplain had just died. It was at Maryvale that the college had first started as a school and orphanage before moving to Oscott. It was in the chapel where the 'new' devotion to the Sacred Heart of Jesus was introduced in bishop Milner's time. This had been Cardinal Newman's first Catholic home which he described as 'dismally ugly'. The rector ordered us back to the college immediately afterwards to prevent any lingering there otherwise this could lead to the rota being suspended. His other dictat was forbidding the use of surplices which were becoming popular with some students instead of the roman cotta. There seems to be a great fear about any change and our year were getting very restive and frustrated and straining at the leash. This restiveness was not helped by a further deterioration in the meals. No longer were we getting a second course and this was being substituted by a rather meagre cheese and biscuits. JR received a questionnaire from his bishop on seminaries for the Council and we hoped that we would all get one.

Even my spiritual director was showing signs of 'angst'. On request for some spiritual enlivenment from him he retorted that I wouldn't get much from him ! However I visited him the next day and we celebrated with a little sherry. 'I really let fly about the unhappy situation in the college. He was really quite surprised that nothing had been said officially about the ordinations. He agreed wholeheartedly with everything I said. He said that little can be done at the moment because of the mentality of those in charge. They were all good men and kind but there were problems with the basic questions of personal relationships. The fact that we were dealing with persons and not just 'souls' in bodies. We discussed the general apathy and lack of communication in the house. These were all things that had been worrying us and discussing for a long time now. Poor old Lawler. He obviously has divided loyalties and no wonder. He lends me an article on love and personal relationships. He tells me that it was 'dynamite'.'

Having informed the vice- rector about my visit home and trying to make conversation with him I set off on a warm sunny day.

MAY

The journey home by train was a great pleasure as we sped towards the fens and the bulk of Ely Cathedral rose through the mists. What bliss it was to be home again, but worrying as dad was getting more and more unable to do things and mother felt the loneliness so much, not really having anyone to talk to. But there was the pleasure of celebrating Mass on her 61st birthday in the sacristy at Kirtling along with dad, auntie Win and Sally Stalley who was the church caretaker. This was their only silver wedding celebration. I was not idle at home for these few days. The wire on the thatch was beginning to rust and the birds were beginning to get in and pull out the straw for their nests. So it was out with long ladders and plugging a few holes. The following day Sunday I celebrated Mass at Kirtling at 8 am and then it was off to London to see the aunts. For a pre birthday present I was given Pope John's autobiography – *A Journal of a Soul*. It was Mass facing the people at Brockley where they actually said the *Per ipsum* in English and then off to

Paddington and back to College. Just a dash of joy that passed so quickly and it was back to 'as it was in the beginning......'

Moral theology couldn't be worse as we dealt with 'Contracts' so my mood of depression soon descended again. Pope John's Journal was consoling as he had ups and downs too, although the piety he was brought up in – and we are still suffering from the aftermath of it here – seemed so narrow and introverted – though it did produce some results. The rector addressed us the next day. He did seem out of touch. The whole chapel was literally seething. He had obviously read the Council's Decree on Ecumenism, but his main comment was that we had all the doctrine buttoned up nicely and can prove it – read your text books and know the doctrine of the Church – don't be a periodical man. Its very depressing after reading some excellent articles in the *Furrow* periodical endorsing all that we had been saying about seminaries. Luckily we could laugh these things off but obviously our year was in his bad books. 'It seems that we Northampton Students had been particularly bad in seeking permissions especially in arguing with the bishop about the place for the ordinations – I should think next year they will put ordinations at the end of term. After supper was one of those rare evenings when we could let down our hair in the common room – 'laughter learned of friends'. The devil certainly does his best to destroy the Community. But still one must really stop complaining about the authorities.'

We still had some pastoral lessons to learn and this was how to hear confessions. One student had to act as confessor and another as penitent. The latter was given a list of possible sins which he 'confessed' and then the 'priest' had to sort it all out. It was rather daunting and artificial, and one dreaded having one's name pulled out of the hat. We were still in the position of having to ascertain the gravity and the number of sins committed –so what could possibly be the worst sin – raping a nun in the sanctuary by a priest and then murdering her with a chalice ? –how many mortal sins were committed ?– they might not have been on the list given but it was a good example and a bit of fun We were judges and dispensers of God's Justice and Mercy. There was really not much, if anything, on the counselling side. But it was a scorching May and plenty of time for sunbathing in the field and half the college was awake at 3.30 am to listen to the repeat fight between Sonny Liston and Cassius Clay – no doubt on illicit radios!

I was then to learn my fate with the arrival of +Leo. – he was sending me to Cambridge where I was ordained and he has given me permission to say Mass while I am at home. This really came as something of a relief as I would be on home ground. I also received a letter from Fr Wace to say that I was taking on his 'buskins'.

Bishop Parker and Mgr. Richard Foster

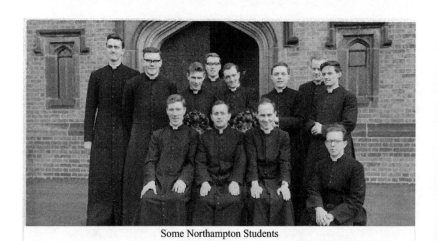

Some Northampton Students

Ken Lawrence   Chris White
John Smith, Gerry Ryan, Anton Mowat, John Glen, Derick Smith, Me
Bernard Hughes, John Drury, Peter Hocken Charles Crawford

JUNE

Old Oscotians poured in for the annual Oscotian Society meeting. It was a mirror of what we would be in a few years time and it was not very inspiring. We were all encouraged to join the Society. I attended the meeting -I wish I hadn't- it was all about providing three stained glass windows for three bishops. The rector proclaimed what a wonderful spirit our year had in that sixteen had joined the society (some things are better left unsaid). He also spoke about the outrageous letters to the press that said that seminaries were ghettos. These had been firmly scotched since Dr Greehy was to lecture at the university (what relevance was that to us ?). Unfortunately eleven students had skipped lunch yesterday and so a notice went up by the rector requiring them to report to him. By the evening half had done so. Another notice announced that if they did not report the holiday on Saturday would be cancelled and manual labour would be imposed instead. 'The poor man seems quite out of touch with the student body and he just does not seem to be able to cope with the changing mood and circumstances. It is so sad as he is a very good chap but one feels quite out of his depth and rather like King Canute. But the whole event has unsettled the college from top to bottom'.

The last retreat at Oscott was given by Abbott Thatcher who admitted that he had no experience of pastoral life- which was a good start, however it turned out to be very stimulating and the conferences of a high standard though somewhat overlong – one was nearly a whole hour. Pope John's, *Journal of a Soul* was being read in the refectory after complaints about Leo Trese's, *Tenders of the Flock*. However it was not the best book to be read publicly and I am sure he wouldn't have written half the stuff if he had known it would be – but then he was a child of his time. Frank Thomas dryly remarked that he was the 'seminarians answer to the Little Flower'. And so the round of ordinations continued with Bishop Cleary conferring the tonsure on first year theology and the subdiaconate on third year. Apprehension tinged with excitement follow in quick succession as my career at Oscott was coming to an end. Sometimes I felt I might end up in religious life. Aunt Dorothy wasn't too well, so I had to be prepared to expect the worst before too long. There was one final hurdle to cross and that was regarding the so called faculties exam. That is the exam that tests your competence to hear confessions.- Dan Leonard wanted a proper mandate from the bishop to examine us and the rector was annoyed because we hadn't asked to have the exam done here – how should we know? In the event I passed the exam which was on the questions of 'convalidation' and 'subsequent recourse'. The last great liturgical event for our year was a concelebration with nineteen of us taking part. It was a magnificent occasion and very impressive. John Spence, our dean, was chief celebrant and Peter Lawler joined us. It was a pity that rector and other members of the staff were not present. A couple of our year did not approve and did not join us – they remained a hard core of those who did not like the reforms in the liturgy. There were lectures right up to 19th June amid all the packing and final exams. There were fairwell speeches by Denis Ryan, the procurator and Dan Leonard looked glum. The rector thanked the now ex dean for his cooperation during the year. 'My room is really squalid. Managed to get through a fifteen minutes oral exam which covered – copyright, patent, usury, parvity of matter and the sixth command-ment. Play compline for the last time.' Ken Collins was home from Rome and it was good to see him and have a chat and he then helped me to roll up my carpet which he had helped me put down three years ago. And so 24th June marked the last day. 'Say goodbye to the rector - I don't know there's something wrong. He was quite pleasant but didn't seem really interested. O'Shea was very good and sincere. I was quite surprised what Dan Leonard said of me- this boosted my confidence no end and dear Lawler gave me a little chat – all very sad.' I ended up with a triumphal piece of organ music for the end of Holy Hour, apart from a few duff notes. Our garage man John Collin drove up to collect me and my luggage and he was impressed by the college and so my six years at Oscott were over and an unknown future awaited me at Cambridge.

Our Lady & St Philip Neri, Kirtling where I served Mass

PART THREE

THE CURATE

CHAPTER ONE

THE RAW RECRUIT

So the summer holidays, shorter than I had been used to during school days, were soon over and it was time to get my bags packed for this new phase of my life. On July 30th I arrived at the imposing door of the rectory, in Hills Road, and I wondered whether I would have turned back if I had known what lay ahead? It was rather like my first attempts at swimming at primary school, when despairing of my gaining any confidence and failing to have the courage to take my feet off the ground, in desperation, the swimming instructor tied a rope around the my waist and made me jump off the diving board into the deep end. I felt like a drowning man and wondered if I should ever reach the surface. That is how I felt at this moment and even after years of experience that same feeling would often come to haunt me. With little confidence, then, and with considerable trepidation I knocked on that formidable oak front door. John Collin, our garage man, had driven me over from home with my luggage and bicycle in the early evening and I was welcomed by the aged housekeeper, Lil Gunns. Lil had been a convert of a former parish priest, Canon Stokes and the present parish priest, Canon Frank Diamond, had inherited her along with the house. Lil, a rather bent and dumpy lady, with a shock of white hair and a rich Norfolk accent, hailed from Kings Lynn. To her I was just another new curate, one of a long line she had welcomed over the years; she had seen their comings and going as a matter of routine. Fr Gerald Moorcraft, M.A. the junior curate welcomed me warmly. He was a good looking young man of about thirty from Wales. An Oxford graduate he had trained at the French seminary of St. Sulpice and was imbued with its unique spirituality. He was followed Fr Harry Wace. Harry was a tall ex army man in his thirties with a personal bank balance and full of energetic enthusiasm. He had trained at Oscott and I had met him on a previous occasion. I was replacing him and he was soon to leave for his first parish in Kings Lynn becoming one of the greatly loved and respected characters of the diocese. Brian Nightingale made up the trinity - a big, gentle man and a former anglican from Rochdale. He was as someone described him 'without guile'. They were all excellent men with whom I became firm friends. Canon Frank Diamond, the parish priest, then arrived on the scene.

Canon Frank Diamond

He had recently recovered from the mumps. Softly spoken with a rubicund complexion I had already met him briefly at the laying of the foundation stone of Newmarket church and found it incredibly difficult to make conversation. He was a late vocation and had been in the banking world. He was, as I was to learn, a very caring and gentle person who was willing to listen to his curates and people. However he was so very shy, certainly as bad as I was. This would make it difficult, sometimes, to get onto each others wave length. As Harry Wace would say, 'he even has secrets from himself and on occasion would write letters to his curates.' He was always very aware of the 'image of the Church' which had to be preserved. A man of utter discretion he would, on returning from Chapter meetings at Northampton Cathedral, be totally committed to his oath of secrecy. Massaging the rear of his right ear was a sure sign that something was amiss and he was summoning up courage to speak his mind. However he was a good and excellent man and I must consider myself truly blessed at starting my career with such a fine body of clergy so well in tune with developments in the Church and with a keen pastoral awareness of people's needs. I could not have had a better start. This contrasted considerably with the accounts of contemporaries who were landed with parish priests who were still living in a bygone age and were not in tune with contemporary life. Some had a very rocky time and several were soon to leave the priesthood and find other work...

There was, as yet, no room for me to move into and I was housed in a tiny box room on the ground floor where there was just enough space to fit a bed but at least my tea chest had arrived with all my belongings. This was even smaller than the room I had at college. Here I was to spend several days and nights lulled to sleep, as I remember, by the Book at Bedtime which happened to be Thomas Hardy's *Mayor of Casterbridge* introduced with the haunting melody of Schubert's *Fantasia*. 'Well we have begun', I wrote in my diary, 'I must try and take each day as it comes.'

Our Lady and the English Martyrs, or OLEM for short is of Cathedral proportions and as such it is described by bus drivers as they drop off passengers before the chaotic cross roads known as Hyde Park Corner. It was built as an assertion of the Catholic Faith in the 1890's in a University City which had been the seed bed of the reformation and while building had to be defended by the navvies in the face of local opposition. It has the tallest spire in Cambridge and with a fine ring of bells featured in one of Dorothy L Sayers novels and with a clock chime based on the plainsong Easter Alleluia. Within, it does not hold as many people as you might expect but nevertheless it was awe inspiring for me just beginning my work. The large dining room overlooked what was once a pleasant garden but now taken over by the St Alban's primary school. Here meals were presided over by the somewhat melancholic portrait of the benefactress of the church, Yolande Lyne – Stevens, a former beauty and popular dancer in the Romantic Ballet of the 1830s and whose home was at Lynford Hall in Norfolk.

I said my first Mass the following morning at 8.15 am at the High Altar. This was situated at the far end of a sanctuary of collegiate proportions but so remote from the congregation. It was, then, into the deep end being thrust for the first time for real into the confessional box. All the training I had received, such as it was, over previous years, in the role playing exercises we had practised at college, was now supposed to come into action. In reality it was rather different. I soon became aware of my own inadequacy and lack of training in dealing with basic human psychology and with the great responsibility, thrust on my shoulders, of trying to help people in their spiritual lives. What struck me, in that first experience was people's great humility in telling their peccadilloes? And certainly those peccadilloes, some of which were hardly sins at all, would on occasions nearly drive one to distraction.

The parish priest was concerned that I couldn't drive a car so my first task, the following day, was to book up some driving lessons at the Cambridge school of motoring. It was so essential to be able to drive with the furthest Mass centre in the village of Linton some ten miles out. It was a pity that I couldn't have overcome that hurdle while still at college as there was certainly no way I could have learned to drive during the holidays. In the meantime I had to be ferried out to the different centres by Noel Hewings in the big old Austin Cambridge. The canon reminded me from time to time of cost and inconvenience of this - however I think this was only a gentle tease. Being told to take the wheel, by my instructor, for the first time in the middle of busy Trumpington Street was quite unnerving and it was fortunate that the car had dual controls. Avoiding cyclists and wobbly academic ladies of uncertain age were a great test of one's skills.

The other member of the household was Fr Joseph Creehan SJ He came each year to act as a supply so that a priest could get a holiday. An amazing character, he was a walking encyclopaedia of usually useless information with which he regaled us over meals. He was the ultimate academic spending most of his time in the university library doing research. Yet in many ways he was a very pastoral man and great entertainment. Most of his free time he would spend sunbathing on the rectory roof, except one August when he was deeply frustrated as it was a month totally devoid of any sun. Never a day passed without an early morning run, in singlet and shorts, down to the river Cam for a dip. He would come back and spin us tales of the students and their capers on the river after some late night celebration. One of his favourite walks was in the botanical gardens and was very knowledgeable about the plants. One favourite flower, rejoicing under the unfortunate name of *Lobelia Syphilitica,* he would check out every year. He was also an expert on the paranormal and followed in the footsteps of Fr Thurston S J who had been an authority in this field. So although uncle Joe was a bore he was a delightful bore and we welcomed his annual visit to the parish.

I was let off lightly my first Sunday and had a lie in with breakfast at nine o'clock and I was able to attend the Liturgy from the back of the church. I recall that I couldn't hear much because the loud speaker system was not very good and had hardly improved from the debacle of my ordination when it had broken down completely. As time went on this would be quite serious as we tried to introduce the new liturgy since congregation and the altar were so far apart. I recalled how people drifted into church right up to the homily and there, for the first time, I experienced the phenomenon of our Irish brethren who 'propped up' the west wall of the church. Once the distribution of Holy Communion began many were eager to make a quick get away to 'The Oak' across the road. My first public Mass at 5 pm, was packed to the doors and went without a hitch. At least on this first occasion I was not required to preach a sermon as one priest was delegated to preach at all the Masses on a Sunday. Earlier in the afternoon I looked on as Harry Wace celebrated a baptism. I think that this was the first real baptism I had ever witnessed in the Catholic Church apart from playing with plastic dolls in pretence baptisms at College. It all looked rather complicated and very different in practice dealing with real babies rather than with the inanimate varieties.

The next hurdle was being initiated into the mysteries of preparing couples for marriage and dealing with all the required documentation. Harry went through them with me but I ended up just as confused as when I started but he did provide me with helpful hints. Again I had never witnessed a marriage in the Catholic Church before and the only two I had ever attended was a wedding of a cousin in an Anglican Church and a friend in a register office a thing Catholics were really not supposed to do in those days.

Initiation was taken further by the canon with a trip round the district of Cambridge for which I was to have pastoral care. I had inherited Harry's area which was the western half of the city and the villages. This was the posh side of town - Girton and Newnham, Grantchester and out to Coton, Comberton and Caldecote. I felt a real idiot when Frank asked me what my particular pastoral interests were. Being greener that a piece of asparagus I really hadn't a clue having had no practical experience of parish life at all. It lead to something of an embarrassing silence which did not help in our relationship. The tour ended up with a visit to Bernard and Rosemary Christian's home and their daughter Brigid. These were a great lay support for the Canon and we relaxed there for some time.

Initiation was not yet complete for I had yet to do a tour of the various religious houses of the parish. We rejoiced in three convents. The first visit was to Hope Nursing Home in Brooklands Avenue or 'The Hope' as we called it. Teasingly we named the Sisters of the Holy Family of Bordeaux, the 'Little Sisters of the Rich' since they tended to take in the wealthier members of the community. But as it was pointed out the rich have souls to save as well as the poor. The Sisters, however, were delightful, Irish, and very homely. They mainly rejoiced with male names – Gerard, Charles, Michael, Aiden though there was a Philomena, a Clotilde and a Cecilia, each responsible for a different floor in the nursing home. One would have thought there were enough female saints to have taken as a patron. In years to come, though, they would return to their more feminine baptismal names. But it was Sr Aiden who was the general factotum and the equivalent of today's Parish Sister with whom I had most contact. She knew everything and everyone. Many would be the times when I sat in the pantry with a nice cup of tea and cake after doing my rounds and being brought up to date by Aiden on the latest parish gossip. The next port of call was at the other extreme - the grand sounding Canonesses of St Augustine in Grange Road which were situated in my district. These were very definitely Sisters of the upper echelons. Their chapel was attached to a large house near Newnham College and they provided a chaplaincy for the Catholic women students. The fairer sex were excluded from Fisher House, the main chaplaincy in Guidhall Street, by the famous Mgr Alfred Newman Gilbey (of the wealthy gin and wine merchants) who was chaplain at the time. Presumably they were regarded as too much of a distraction and temptation for the male students. The Monsignor was on the point of leaving after many years of service, to be followed by Fr Richard Incledon, and called in to see us. He was a most charming man, clothed in traditional ecclesiastical garb with spats and shovel hat. He would spend most of the rest of his days at the Travellers' Club in London ministering to the elite of society. The Sisters were very grand, among them being Sr Mary Paul and Sr Thomas More. In those days dressed in voluminous habits looking like characters from Chaucer's Canterbury Tales and one could imagine them riding out with hounds. On Holy Innocents Day each year, which fell a few days after Christmas, they would hold a Holy Innocents Day Party for the 'nice' children in the area. Sr Thomas More in later years would revert to her worldly name of Mary Berry, found the *Schola Gregoriana* for promoting Gregorian Chant and be rewarded with a medal from the Queen for her musical endeavours. In between these two Congregations of nuns came the Sisters of the Institute of the Blessed Virgin Mary - the Mary Ward

183

Sisters. They ran a very posh school in Bateman Street - St. Mary's Convent. They, too, could be rather grand. They still followed a sort of two tier system which most orders still employed - *viz*, lay Sisters. These did the entire donkey work of washing and cleaning and starching of wimples and the other mysterious fitments of a nun's trousseau. But, of course, they were very nice and one recalls them with affection especially the inimitable Sr Scholastica, a relative of Mrs. Lyne-Stephens, benefactress of the English Martyrs Church. She was affectionately known as 'Scholle'. Tall and willowy, she rode her bike round Cambridge like some bird of prey hovering over its kill. The Superior was Mother Gregory, who was nicknamed 'Smother', but, as I would learn later, was a lady of great distinction in her own right. There was Sr Jane with a swarthy complexion and perhaps a descendent of one of the Armada seafarers wrecked on the west coast of Ireland. She did a lot of pastoral work, and aged Sr Ignatius who ran the sacristy and would frequently have to ring up the rectory in a slightly angry voice demanding - 'Is anyone coming for Benediction' - Oh dear late again! Other religious houses I would visit later - the De La Salle Brothers in Brookside, The Franciscans in Trumpington St where Fr Alan Keenan was superior, The Dominicans in Buckingham Road and the Benedictines of which there was only one and of whom we saw nothing. So Cambridge was well populated with religious houses.

Having experienced this intensive introduction to the religious life of Cambridge, I had hoped for some respite but that was not to be. On return Fr Wace had a call to the maternity hospital to do an emergency baptism and since I was told I was to be chaplain there, as well, I should go round with him to learn the ropes. It was an interesting if unnerving experience. The child in question was to have an exchange transfusion and it was a matter of course to confer the sacraments including confirmation if the child was in really dire straights. I was struck by the fragility of the tiny baby and the problems of manoeuvring your hand inside the incubator around all the different tubes, terrified that I would dislodge something essential to life. But this was just the beginning as I was to perform such a ministry many times in years to come. Evening came and morning came the third day and I was glad to get to bed, 'The Canon is certainly very kind, courteous and helpful - but oh dear the times that lie ahead', as I penned in my journal.

The most important part of initiation came the next day with the counting of the Sunday collection. For two hours we struggled to bag those necessities for life and limb. As yet we had not delegated this chore to the laity but it was a real bind spending nearly the whole of Monday morning on this job. Having bagged and weighed the LSD we had to take the load to the bank in Cherry

184

Hinton Road in a large battered gladstone bag where it was all weighed again and we discovered how inaccurate we had been in our calculations;but, still, this was a fixed point of certainty in the week which was quite a pleasant change in its own way.

Having been initiated into the mysteries of the city of Cambridge I was then taken out by Harry to the country area. The first was to visit Elsie McNamara, a bed ridden lady at Coton, of whom more later and to a Miss Shepherd at Caldecote. Miss Shepherd had been a school teacher and had retired to this thatched cottage or what was left of it. What a cottage! Having needed a panga to fight ones way through the undergrowth to the front door you were presented with a cottage where half the thatch had blown off. With very little thatch left on the roof the rain came through into the bedroom (which of course she couldn't use) and into her sitting room below where there were bowls all around to catch the drips. Various plants in pots cut out what little light came through the windows and in winter small piles of snow collected inside the front door. But Miss Shepherd didn't seem worried and was quite happy. It was a long time before she could be persuaded to move into sheltered accommodation and when she eventually moved she didn't live long. The tour concluded with a visit to Maurice Wilkins and his wife at Caldecote. They were the pillars of the church in that area and prepared the Mass centre in the village hall once a month.

July ended, the wettest on record for eleven years, and I was exhausted with coping with all the new information and responsibilities.

My main concern and worry was preparing instructions to give to married couples and converts. At college we were supposed to have prepared a course as I have previously related, but this was now dealing with real people. We had no luxury of Marriage Care and the Catholic Marriage Advisory Council was not exactly flourishing neither did we have RCIA so we had to do the lot ourselves. Since I had never met an engaged couple before in my life, the whole exercise was rather academic as I was soon to learn. Nevertheless I set too with a will trying to work out what my words of wisdom would be to these imaginary people who would soon present themselves to me for instruction.

I thought I might then try my hand and do a little pastoral visiting. The canon had left a list of rules or do's and don'ts in my room. One of them was regarding parish visiting. He acknowledged that it was not always easy but that we should try and do some every week. Well I tried and as I was soon to discover this was one of the most frustrating parts of one's work and yet so important since it brought you face to face contact with people in their homes and with their problems. Sadly most people were out. This was frustrating as I very nervously walked up the long gravel drives to some of the big houses in the district. And not only out but my visiting lists were hopelessly out of date since many had moved away years ago or had died. So I spent most of the time crossing off names from my visiting book. At least I did one good turn for the day when an enormously fat lady fell over at my feet and I was able to help her up and onto her bus. I was successful with one family, Jim and Mary Prior and their daughter Ann who welcomed me warmly. So out of touch were some families with the Church that on one occasion the family asked how that nice Canon Marshal was. Well he had been two parish priests before the present one and had been dead several years.

In the evening, Gerard, who had a new car, took the canon and me for a spin to see the other Mass centres. The furthest was Linton village some ten miles out. Mass was celebrated every week in the village college and they were quite a well organised community. Once a month we had Mass in the Land Settlement hut in the nearby village of Great Abingdon and then weekly in St Bede's Catholic School in Cherry Hinton. There land had been purchased before the war for a future church which was eventually built some years later. Some four miles out was another Mass centre in the Village Hall in Fulbourn. In the opposite direction there was Caldecote, already mentioned and also Trumpington.

My responsibilities were not yet complete as I was to be chaplain not only to the maternity hospital but also to Hope nursing home, and the isolation hospital at Brookfields at the bottom of Mill Road. Here I was to don gown and mask and make my first visit to a Guadalupian recovering from chicken pox. This would be my hospital round for the time being.

As this was before the days of deacons and eucharistic ministers of Communion we each had our little round of taking Communion to the sick and the house bound. My main clutch was at Coton a short bike ride from base of some four miles. The most famous at the time was Elsie McNamara. Elsie, in her forties, appeared to be bedridden. She had been a convert of one of the Hope sisters and was extremely devout. She had an Irish husband Harry Wace had christened St Joseph, for apparent reasons since they had an adopted son, Robert. Elsie lived in a council flat in a large bed surrounded by articles of piety. After I had known her some years she executed an oil painting of me assisting at her deathbed. I was standing at the foot of the bed while Elsie's soul, like some ethereal protoplasm rose from her body. She would write impassioned spiritual letters to us with heavil underlined sentences and the constant cry being, 'use me, Father'. She would also supply us with little embroidered silk purses in which to carry the Blessed Sacrament to the sick. Elsie was very demanding and I must have spent many hours trying to give her support. She had every ailment under the sun and I would be given vivid descriptions of her gynaecological conditions which after 'St Joseph's' death would be attended to by her teenage son. The boy, naturally having enough of this experience, took flight on several occasions and once on dialling 999 in the middle of the night on her behalf, a road block was successfully set up round the city while the police searched for him. In the end they found that the cause of her ailments lay in her rotten teeth on which she had been self operating with a needle and after these were removed wholesale she took on a new lease of life and actually learned to drive a car. She lived on to a reasonable old age. Her son did quite well, married, joined the navy and settled down with three children.

Another on my visiting list was ninety year old, Ellen Marks, who was tended by her lodger, Jo Lott. Ellen was stone deaf and it was quite a challenge to negotiate her half full chamber pot at the side of the bed and to communicate with her in any meaningful way. I was reminded of the advice that Bishop Leo Parker gave to some aspiring cleric. He cautioned him, when visiting the homes of the poor, to be sure to take his top hat with him in order to provide a fitting and level surface upon which to place the Blessed Sacrament. I could have done with my top hat in those circumstances!

In those early weeks I was soon to come up against the great problem that was tearing the Church apart in those days and which had been beginning to worry us in my last years at college and this was the problem of birth control. In my own mind the Church's teaching had always seemed pretty logical but when coming out into the real world and meeting people facing this challenge in their married life I began to have my doubts. It was a constant problem in 'the box' and when couples came along to discuss their marriage arrangements. My first encounter had been a man wanting to 'put things right' before going on a plane journey. He was a physiologist and could honestly see no difference between the use of the 'safe period' which was permitted and the use of artificial means. The intention was the same in both cases. Since the Pope and his commission were discussing the problem in Rome at the time it was concluded by most people that there must be some doubt regarding this matter and so they acted accordingly. In years to come the 'problem' would disappear entirely from the list of sins since people had made up their own minds. Raw from the seminary I was to encounter similar problems on my visits to families which became increasingly difficult to cope with.

I was soon to get my quota of marriage instructions as OLEM attracted many during the year. I really felt quite inadequate in knowing quite how best to cope. One was supposed to give a course of instructions on the meaning of marriage. The habit of having children prior to marriage was a growing custom so there was no ignorance on that score and one or two of my first marriages had children as page boys. However it was mixed marriages that were the real problem - that is the marriage between a Catholic and a member of another faith or none. By and large one found that the Catholic party was usually 'lapsed' and the non- catholic quite indifferent or an enthusiastic Christian of another denomination. In those days the Catholic had to promise to work towards the conversion of the non-Catholic party and both had to sign a promise agreeing to the Catholic upbringing of the children. This, I may say, was something that filled me with dread on reaching the point when the couple were presented with the fateful dotted line on which to sign. I could quite see the Church's wisdom in this knowing that religion could be such a cause of division in a family. In fact Mixed Marriages were technically frowned upon, and one had to get a special dispensation from the bishop in order that the marriage could go ahead. It was best that these potentially divisive matters should be brought out into the open and discussed before a marriage took place. However falling in love rarely takes note of these sorts of problems and if a couple had not darkened the doors of a church for years they were an enormous hurdle to jump. More and more the non-Catholic partner balked at having to sign and the Catholic partner would be resentful. Sometimes they would sign just for the sake of the marriage. On another occasion it would be the last one would see of them and they would probably go off to a less demanding church or the register office. In later years of course all this would change and helpful questionnaires would be produced to enable couples to discuss their relationship; the declarations would be scaled down to be almost meaningless and the faith of the non-catholic partner would be respected but by this time fewer and fewer people would be married in the church anyway. At the time if one was really in trouble one could 'pass the buck' to the Catholic Marriage Advisory Centre which had been set up in town with varying success. It was difficult to get lay people as recruits as sometimes their own beliefs regarding the church's doctrine was rather problematic. But certainly one welcomed the gradual lay involvement of experienced married couples in this preparation programme. The girl in one of my first marriages was very pregnant. In fact she was still attending the sixth form at St Mary's Convent! The event had naturally caused quite a stir in the cloister that one of their nice girls should get in the family way and they were reluctant to admit the fact. It all happened - I don't quite know where - in the botanical gardens overlooked by the convent. Obviously the nuns had not been patrolling very efficiently! By the time of the marriage, fortunately for all concerned, she had ended her career at the school.

But back to my initiation. Lill, the housekeeper, had a cat called 'Marmy', an ancient moulting marmalade cat that was wont on occasions to do her business where it should not be done. The curates were not impressed and poor Marmy got the occasional boot. 'Don't you touch my little girl', was Lill's complaint and one was soon to learn the order of priorities in the feeding of the household. Her first concern was the parish priest, then the cat and then the curates. 'I've got a nice little bit of fish for my little girl', she retorted after shopping one day. Would that the curates had had a nice bit of fish from time to time! The food was pretty ghastly. The main meal was usually some sort of holocausted chop swimming in a thick gunge of gravy and incredibly tough into the bargain. Canon D was a fastidious man who liked his food and this was a great penance for him but like him we could not complain. However to make up for this trial on the big feast days or on the occasion of visiting clergy he would take us all out to a slap up meal at the Clayhithe hotel in the middle of the fens. There I had meals on a scale I had never experienced before and really felt quite guilty thinking about the folks back at home and what they were able to afford. But it was a welcome evening out and full of conviviality.

Lil had a deputy housekeeper called Florrie of about the same vintage. Florrie was rather simple and had been an orphan from Nazareth House. Lil was always worried when she went away on occasion that Florrie would not be able to cope with the cooking. In fact Florrie was an excellent cook and provided us with some very reasonable meals. One thing Florrie could not cope with was our erratic intercom system which summoned us according to different bleeps. We would be beeped if someone at the door wanted to see the duty priest. But she invariably got the number of bleeps muddled up. On top of this the mechanism would occasionally get stuck and no one would know what was going on. Florrie had the subtlety to distinguish between a 'man' and a 'gentleman'. A 'man' was someone on the cadge for money; a 'gentleman' was a respectable individual just visiting. One day the information coming over was Delphic like - 'I've put them in the first parlour'. Was it a 'man' or a 'gentleman'? Not quite knowing what to expect I went downstairs to find the parlour in darkness. On turning on the light I discovered in one corner a drink sodden man of the road smelling to high heaven and cowering in the other a terrified young young Irish nurse over in this country for the first time! On occasions the place would go mad with the front door ringing and Florrie on the bleep. Brian Nightingale seemed to fix all his appointments for 7.30 pm on a Monday evening. On one occasion there were not enough waiting rooms to house everyone and there were even bodies sitting on the stair case. We used to tease Brian on the time that he spent with

his engaged couples - sessions that would last long into the evening sometimes - was he giving them a few 'practicals' one wondered.

The parlours already mentioned lay on the ground floor. The rectory was
laid out with a corridor up and downstairs running the length of the building.
Three parlours, which were more like railway waiting rooms and the dining
room lay downstairs and our individual bed sitting rooms lay off the top
corridor. They were stark and functional. In later years and under new
management all this would change with the parlours becoming the clergy
sitting rooms and much more welcoming to visitors. Upstairs there was a bay
window where, having made our communal visit to the church, we would
assemble for awhile after lunch to watch the world go by. Two people would
usually come for Gerald at this time. One was doe eyed Mary Ida Smith
coming to do the flowers and the other was Jane, one of Gerald's converts.
She was a 'smasher'. I 'inherited' her after Gerald moved to finish off her
instructions. Her reception into the Church was grim with none of the family
wanting to join in but sat at some distance from the very private ceremony
and the man she married and whom we tried to dissuade her from so doing
treated her very badly. She was one of the many people I would have liked to
have kept in touch with during the succeeding years.

There were four confession boxes in the church. Three were in the gothic
style in tune with the church architecture. My confessional was a modern
wooden version by the main door of the church. Since it was by the main
door it would tend to attract visitors and give a novice curate more experience. In those days we were kept going during the main sessions on a
Saturday. The first session was after the morning Mass for half an hour which
could go on for an hour. There was an hour in the afternoon; another hour in
the early evening and a late session from 8.30 pm - 9.00 pm. Sometimes one
really felt that Providence was at work, but by and large confessions were
very routine and with minor peccadilloes to confess. Many people were still
under the illusion that you had to go to confession before you received
Communion on the Sunday. This was a strain of the heresy of Jansensim that
long persisted. It could become very wearing inside a claustrophobic box and
it was a set up with which I was never really happy. One never knew what
was going to happen. On one occasion someone wanted a Mass said for their
intention and attempted to push the money through the grill separating priest
from penitent which looked rather like a small louvre window. I tried to
dissuade the person at which point a pound note began to be pushed through
the door of my side. I was fearful that there might be witnesses to this
'transaction' with the person going away confirmed in the hoary old tradition
that you 'paid for confession.' On another occasion there was the most awful

grunting and groaning and scratching on the outside of the box. I thought someone was trying to gain entry by physically attacking the confessional. It turned out that a tramp worse for wear for drink had found a nice cosy spot on the radiator between the confessional and the wall. Sometimes there was a lull in the proceedings and one thought there was no one about and then jolted into action as someone out of the blue tripped and almost fell into the cubicle. The scariest occasion was when there had been dead silence when all of a sudden I detected a movement outside my door and looking down I could see an eye peering at me through the key hole. Evidently a child had wandered in. Children's confessions were always a great trial as they were marshaled in class by class and really had little to say. Either they had been primed by teacher or they didn't seem to know what they were doing there. But just on occasion it was worthwhile. The most unseemly venue for celebrating the sacrament was at St Bede's secondary school. Here there was no proper chapel or counselling room and one was lodged at the end of the stock cupboard with the smell of chalk and paper and with a horrible green curtain and a plastic crucifix separating you from the penitent. Again the teenagers were marshaled in and out by Sister Margaret, the deputy head. Here, on occasion, one could be of more help. But once, when more time was required, Sister's voice came over loud and clear, 'hurry up you're taking far too long.' Gradually one was moving from purely a judgement of a person's sin according to certain predetermined criteria to rather dispensing Gods mercy and expressing solidarity with the penitent. Sometimes it was just best not to say anything at all and leave it to the Almighty. In those early days Christmas Eve was a nightmare with a constant flow of people right up to the last minute and it was all one could do to extricate oneself from the box to begin Mass on time. The Poles who had a large community in the city had their own priests coming twice a year and it was a rather spooky sight seeing phalanxes of Poles arranged around the church in the semi gloom awaiting the 'OGPU' as we called the clergy - usually looking very sinister in dark glasses. It was not at all pleasant taking over from them and entering a very stuffy confessional reeking of strong after shave. With all the germs that must have been breathed forth one must have built up something of an immunity from the international body that were our penitents. After our mental exertions on a Saturday afternoon we often repaired to the television room and watched 'Giant Haystacks' and 'Big Daddy' throwing each other around the wrestling ring. You needed something to take your mind off things and help you to relax.

My first duty day was an unnerving experience. Each of us was allotted a couple of days a week when we would sit in and take responsibility for anything that might come our way either by door or phone. It might be just your luck if four weddings, a funeral, three baptisms, a couple of sick calls to the hospital, half a dozen tramps came your way and enquiry phone calls. Sometimes one nearly reached distraction levels trying to balance one demand against another. So I was really on edge that first occasion waiting for the phone to ring and not knowing what awful problem I might be confronted with. And then, on top of this, having to contend with Florrie on the intercom! It was most frustrating for if you sat around waiting for someone to call nothing happened and if you got down to some study or preparing your sermon then bells would start ringing all over the place. Not yet had we a lay secretary who could deal with many of these calls. Luckily on that first day I was let off lightly.

OLEM was a great centre for clergy dropping in at coffee time. The other parish was situated at St Laurence's in Milton Road. Its parish priest was the famous Paddy Oates -Titus for short - and indeed he was a very short man - even shorter than I. But he made up for it by a very loud voice and aggressive manner and was inclined to thump the table. His curate at the time was Paul Hypher. He was a 'high flyer' but, we were told, not in robust health for in a previous parish his PP had been a tyrant and on contracting what turned out to be meningitis he was at first refused permission to go home to his family where his father was a doctor. His tales of 'curate bashing' were very disturbing such as having to wrap himself in newspaper to keep warm in his bedroom or enduring a daily inspection of his room by the parish priest. Paddy seemed to have a great suspicion of 'converts' especially from the C/E who became Catholic priests - he regarded Brian as 'sinister' - anyone less sinister one could not imagine but we had a good laugh over the encounter. The other nearby parish was at Sawston, south of Cambridge whence came the parish priest, John Fennell and later Larry O'Toole. Clergy came from far and wide – even John Cureton from Sudbury called in to pick up the Rupert Tickets. For a time Rupert a great money spinner. The punter bought a ticket, tore it open, and if the letters inside corresponded to the first three letters of the Friday edition of the Rupert Bear cartoon then you were likely to win some 'fabulous' prize.

Cambridge was great place for birds of passage, clergy or otherwise. Another Jesuit, Fr Patrick Treanor, from the Vatican Observatory visited. He was attending the science week in the city. It was fascinating listening to him talking about this little known aspect of Vatican life. I was only sorry to have missed his sermon at the Masses the next morning but we had an enthralling astronomical discussion over dinner that night on the possibility of life on other planets.

Another aspect of parish life in addition to the weekly collection was what was known as the 'outdoor collection'. This arrangement went back years and mercifully didn't last much longer. Volunteer parishioners would, on a regular basis, visit homes to collect the dues parishioners had committed to the parish funds. The one benefit, apart form bringing in a useful income, was the contact with the non-church going flock. However it did give the impression that the only thing the Church was interested in was money.

We now had a house meeting, which became a regular feature of life, to sort out our allotted responsibilities. I was to be landed with three new burdens. The first was the 'Catholic Reading Circle', organised by the inimitable Miss Doris Brown, and the second was to   co-ordinate the Guild of St Stephen which promoted our altar servers . We were fortunate in having an excellent head altar server, Tony Sylvester, who was to carry on this task as well as sacristan for over forty years. The third was the Legion of Mary. Meetings were held regularly at St Edmund's House but they wanted to make it more parish centred. I was not too keen, for although it was a good apostolate for the laity its theology which seemed so centred on Our Lady, I found difficult to take. These were all Harry's pigeons. 'How I shall keep up the Wace Pace I don't know', I noted in my diary.

So the routine gained strength - the round of Communions to the house-bound on my bike, contending with the wind and weather and visiting the various hospitals that I had been allotted. There was the new experience of getting used to the pregnant mums in the maternity hospital and some, especially the Italians, with no inhibitions, feeding their babies in front of you On more than one occasion I was to be called out to sick babies to do emergency baptisms. If they were really ill I had, to begin with, to call out the parish priest to administer the sacrament of Confirmation. Later I was delegated to confer this sacrament and so felt rather like a bishop. There was also an undertaking to bring Holy Communion, early in the morning, to those who requested it in the hospitals. In those days the nurses were well trained to receive the clergy and had the patient prepared with bed table nicely arranged. I soon got the hang of deftly whisking the curtains round the patient's bed. In those days, before the Data Protection Act, when visiting the wards you were able to look through the admissions list or the ward sister would do it for you and thereby discover who were the Catholic patients - whether they wanted to see you or not. Generally speaking there were no problems and they were glad to see a member of the cloth and have a chat. On occasions one's appearance, especially to an Italian, might bring on a hysterical reaction as they quite thought that the priest was the harbinger of death! In our present climate all that has changed and it is now up to the patient or the family to let the clergy know if they want a visit.

In the wider Church we were now entering the final session of the Vatican Council whose deliberations were such a beacon of hope for change and development in the Church. Our bishop, + Leo prided himself on his attending every single one of the sessions of the Council and for him his most significant contribution to the reform of the Liturgy was the inclusion of the name of St Joseph in the Canon of the Mass. The full force of that *Decree on the Liturgy* would before long begin to affect us all in a very practical and not too happy way as we shall see.

From time to time we would have appeals by visiting clergy usually from someone who had worked on the Missions. Occasionally it was from someone nearer home. One was Canon Bill Hunting who was the administrator of the St Francis orphanage at Shefford. He was a real character with his gammy leg and down to earth manner. I believe he or his brother had been a second hand car salesman in his time and so was good at wheedling money out of people. Tragically the Canon was to accidentally run over one of his charges in a car accident and he never really recovered from this experience.

The clergy would meet every so often for a deanery meeting. This enabled us to talk over current problems and be presented with a moral case set by the bishop. It was usually some insoluble marriage problem or to do with the application of canon law. The two imaginary parties had usually got themselves into some tangle, Titius and Bertha were the two unfortunates. The case was presented in Latin and before we could untangle their dilemmas we first had to make sense of the ecclesiastical language! At least it was a chance to meet each other at a rather superficial level and ending the day with a good meal at some local hostelry. This was all change with the advent of the Liturgical reforms which were now to preoccupy proceedings. The first of these new style meetings was lead by Paul Hypher who celebrated what was called a 'Dry Mass' – i.e. a 'pretend' one so that we could see what was involved in the changes and to maintain some sort of uniformity in our presentation. On this first occasion I can't recall quite what happened but I noted, 'the outcome was chaotic.' Few of the clergy were enthusiastic for the revision of the Liturgy, though there were notable exceptions. The changes would be introduced piecemeal without any real sense of where we were going. Some saw the reforms as change for changes sake and instead of enthusing their congregations they were reluctant to implement the reforms until they had to. This was a great tragedy. At least at English Martyrs we did all that we could to catechise the congregation and intelligently introduce the new rites. But in spite of our best efforts this met with quite a bit of antagonism and hostility.

The Catholic Reading Circle was my next concern and I ventured out to visit Miss Doris Browne in Warkworth Street. She was a very apostolic lady very much concerned with raising the awareness of the general reader in Cambridge to Catholic matters. She had the unfortunate habit of not looking directly at you and as the canon would say, 'She would inspect your left ear!' She waxed lyrical about the great apostolate of visiting the bookshops and recommending 'Catholic' books in the hope that the shop owner would stock a few. There was even a little committee to vet what books were thought suitable to include on the list of recommendations. She had some success especially when it came to Mowbrays and Mr Fletcher as their's was of a Christian orientation and more inclined, in the growing ecumenical climate, to include Catholic publications on their bookshelves.

The canon had a late holiday this year which he always took with his good friend Edward McBride of the diocese, as different in character as chalk is from cheese, and as usual we succeeded in getting a supply for the statutory 'twenty six days holiday which was to include not more than three Sundays.' It was good to know that there was the custom of having the inside of a week off after Christmas and Easter as well. This was generous really considering that we were entitled to a day off a week too. On this occasion our supply was a missionary priest, Fr Adrian Hastings, who had ministered in Uganda. At this time we were not to know the dramatic part that Adrian was to play in bringing to the notice of the world the Portuguese massacres in Mozambique which would spark off civil war. We knew of his sister Cecily who wrote modern theology in 'paper - back' books which at the time were considered rather 'dangerous'. Adrian was a tall gangly man with specs and a cackling laugh but we got on very well. On collection counting days he would stack the pennies into little semicircular piles reminiscent, we thought, of the African huts he was accustomed to. Unfortunately during his mission-ary work he had contracted malaria and overcome with one of his shivering fits he had to retire to bed. The birth control issue was a growing concern and he maintained that there was a doubt regarding the present law and this would seem to apply to the use of artificial means. There was a feeling that the pope would reaffirm traditional teaching but permit the pill in certain circumstanc-es. In the years to come Adrian was to resign from the priesthood and, after working in Zimbabwe, take up the post of the Chair of Theology at Leeds University.

I was finding it rather difficult to 'socialise' and at least had this in common with the canon. Down the road at Cambridge Place was the Catholic

Social Club where I suppose most of the parish gossip took place. It was rather limping along at this time as social patterns were changing. I went down with Gerald for a pint and a chat but just did not feel at all comfortable with the small talk and perhaps only went there once or twice more. On other social gatherings in the school hall it was always a real penance wandering round to people and trying to make conversation amid the hubbub of general chat - but it was one of those things one was duty bound to do. We also made a special effort to stand outside the church after Mass to greet people - this was specially emphasised by the canon and I think was a recent innovation. One could see that it cost him a lot. Generally speaking people just swarmed out ignoring you on the way even if you had been preaching at that Mass. On occasion the regulars would monopolise you and it was difficult to maintain this contact. However with time it would bear some sort of fruit and after Christmas and Easter services one could manage to get in a hand shake or two.

Not being able to drive I was rather hampered on my day off. Luckily home was only twenty miles away. Sometimes I caught the train from Cambridge to Newmarket where mother picked me up. It was a sad sight seeing the huge Newmarket station, built for conveying horses, being demolished until it was a mere shadow of its former self becoming in time a mere halt with a single line rail. On occasion the canon very kindly took me home.

My father's health continued to deteriorate. He was now afflicted with arthritis in his neck and shoulders and with a growing problem of colitis. He was on regular dosage of aspirin and this eventually lead to internal ulcers. He became more and more withdrawn and unable to communicate with mother. My two aunts were a great help but they were getting on themselves. I was pleased, then, that I was able to give some support however small it was.

Even in these first few months of life at OLEM I was beginning to realise the impossibility of conducting an effective ministry in such a far flung and disparate community. Cambridge had such a fluctuating population with university students during term time and foreign students in the language schools during holiday periods. There was nothing for the latter who would often call at the rectory asking to meet English parishioners to better their English. But because it was the holiday period parishioners who might have been interested to help were away themselves. We had not the resources at the time to cope and we felt a little resentful having to deal with these folk on top of all our other commitments. So we concluded at our staff meeting that the current parish organisation was quite inadequate to deal with all the problems. In some ways we felt like a fire men being called out to damp down situations rather than making any positive moves to build a parish community. With the mobile population any structure we set up tended to collapse after a couple of years as people moved away. It was, then, very difficult to set our priorities as to what we were supposed to do apart from maintaining the existing structures of schools, hospitals, convents. Contact with the ordinary parishioners was very superficial and it was very difficult not to fall into the trap of befriending one or two special families.

My driving lessons were going on but I did not have regular practice in between except on days off when I went out in Mother's old Austin Big 7, the only car she ever possessed from 1939 to her dying day. This was somewhat different to handle compared with the Hilman Minx on which I had been learning. Now with students back from their holidays the city was crowded with cycles and new skills had to be developed to avoid knocking them off especially in the centre of town and down narrow Mill Road.

I attended my first clergy study day at St Edmunds House which was a regular feature to keep clergy up to date with developments at the Vatican Council and we learned that George Patrick Dwyer had been appointed the new archbishop of Birmingham - a colleague of Cardinal John Heenan from Catholic Missionary Society days. As I noted in the diary 'we had hoped against hope that he wouldn't be appointed!'

On October 10th we celebrated the 75th anniversary of the opening of the church. The canon was very pleased with the new lightning that had been installed for the occasion and the improved microphone set up. I was deacon at this Mass celebrated with all splendour at the High Altar where I had been ordained only a few months earlier. The sanctuary was incredibly long with choir stalls each side and it was so remote from the rest of the congregation. The stalls were filled by the choir, organised by Dr Richard Richens, director of the Commonwealth Bureau of Plant Breeding and Genetics. His particular interest was trees and in later years he wrote a treatise on the Elm Tree. The conclusions of his thesis, after his death, were questioned by his peers. He was rather a dry old stick but devoted to his choir who were equally loyal to him. It took some time to realise that the title Dr of which there were many in the parish did not refer to a medical career but to academic achievements. Such holders of the title did not like to be downgraded to a mere Mr. Dr Richens had quite a few men and boys in his choir (but as yet no ladies - technically they had to be out of sight behind a screen somewhere). They sang elaborate polyphonic settings at the morning Mass which was entirely in Latin apart from the readings that had now been introduced in the vernacular and some of the prayers. His plainsong was dreary beyond measure and so slow and lugubrious. We had an excellent organist, Ernie Peel. He was a local, non academic man, who had the facility of playing anything and everything at the drop of a hat. This he continued to do through the battles that were to come until his retirement many years later. Ernie was a great character and the salt of the earth. I had visited the Richens family on one of my rounds but only found wife Ruth at home. Very civilly they invited me round for a meal. This was my first outing, which was a very pleasant occasion, and I was entertained afterwards by their young family on various musical instruments. However it was clear that they were not at all happy with what he saw were potential developments in the Church's liturgy stemming from the Council.

The village of Grantchester was in my area. Here I had a regular communicant and there I made my first foray into things ecumenical by calling on the vicar at the rectory, made famous by Rupert Brooke's poem; and even more so in later years by the presence of Lord Geoffrey Archer. He seemed pleased that I had made contact as ecumenism was still in its infancy at this time. Later that day Gerald and I went down to the Senate House to hear Michael Ramsey Archbishop of Canterbury's lecture on Mission and Unity.

By now I had moved into my new bed sitting room on the corner looking across to Lensfied Road. I was told that one of my distinguished predecessors, Mgr Robert Hugh Benson, the famous preacher and author, once occupied this room. He noted that the outlook was 'heavenly' as it looked out on to a garden of trees and flowers. Now it was largely a car park and school buildings but I could still see the, 'angels and griffins grinning at me' attached to the church wall and could still here the clock's 'heavenly chimes every quarter of an hour playing the Easter alleluia.'

It became an increasing worry as to how to organise my time. In college everything had been laid out and organised by the bell. There was very little room for personal initiative. Now suddenly I was on my own trying to organise my time and priorities. There were so many disparate things to cope with that it became very frustrating. There was no coherent plan or direction in our parish work and we just reacted to events as they occurred. The basic framework was there of births, marriages and deaths; the daily routine of Mass and sacrament administered but one felt it was a question of keeping the show on the road and not really tackling fundamental problems. I got really dispirited and depressed at times wondering whether I was getting things right.

One of the major problems that were soon to confront me was the number of callers that we had on the door looking for a hand out of one sort or another. Sometimes it could be as many as half a dozen a day. They were mainly drifters, men or even women from broken homes or just out of prison or whose marriages had broken down. They could get no assistance because they had no address and they could not get an address because they had no money to pay for lodgings. It became very wearying listening to constant tales woven more often than not out of their imagination than from reality. We were discouraged from giving money but there was always the problem as to whether this person really was in need and so we were inclined to give them the benefit of the doubt. If you didn't give them money they could sometimes turn very nasty indeed. To this day there are scratch marks in the solid oak door of the rectory looking like the attack by some werewolf. This happened when one of these unfortunates picked up an iron bar lying there and almost attacked Brian Nightingale who just closed the door in the nick of time. But there were some real characters among them. There was Herman Schmidt, a tiny bearded individual who collected things like a magpie and lived in some sort of hovel outside the city. He would call at the door and before you knew where you were he was past you and into the house hoping to grab something on the way. Another local man we felt very sorry for arrived regularly at the door pushing a bike and carrying an old paper carrier bag. He usually wanted some help to mend his bike. Some years later he died and it was discovered he was very wealthy indeed and would carry some of his wealth around in the carrier bag. 'You call yourself a Catholic priest - you're not fit to wear that clerical collar', was the cry of some when one was hesitant to dole out yet another half crown. For a time we used a system of meal tickets. We had an arrangement with the fish and chip shop in East Road which would redeem these tickets, but the men were not really interested and what they wanted was hard cash. The idealistic students were a soft touch and the police told us that they could make quite a haul during the day. Locking up the church at night could be a rather scary experience going into that dark cavernous building looking round all the gloomy recesses and into confessional boxes. On one occasion there looked like a rolled up bundle of washing in one. I gingerly touched it with my foot and it moved - was it an abandoned baby? No just an old lag who had wrapped himself in a surplice. Brian was with me at the time and rather unceremoniously pulled the man to his feet - 'don't you realise you are wearing a sacred garment?' he expostulated - the man just looked bleary eyed and wandered off. One very useful parish apostolic group was the St Vincent de Paul Society. One evening in the week it gave out old clothing to men at the back door. Sometimes there was an almighty queue which got quite rowdy on occasions. However they were a useful group of dedicated parishioners to whom we could turn if we came across any really deprived families who were in need of practical help.

Acting as chaplains to the Catholic schools was another responsibility. Next door to the church was the primary school, St Alban's, with its long serving head teacher Mr Bates. He was very much of the old school and the teachers had been there since time immemorial. Gerald was acting chaplain so I was not greatly involved. He also acted as correspondent for the school managers. St Bede's was the secondary school in Cherry Hinton. Its head master was George Kent, a young man in his thirties, and brother of the famous Bruce Kent of CND fame. George always referred to him as 'my mad brother'. However when it came to religious education he was extremely old fashioned in his approach as were most of the other teachers and were very reluctant or frightened even to look into the new approach to catechetics especially in the light of developments in the Church. We did our best to provide help but there was the feeling they didn't want to know and it was a real on going problem to know what to do. Before long I was asked to take a class at the school. I might have enjoyed the experience more had I had a little more training. My only practical experience of teaching was, as I have already related, in my last year at college with my ill fated Sunday school class. But I had had no formal training in teaching or how to manage a class of lively children and what was I given but, what seemed to be, the remedial class and with little or no resources to help. It was all I could do to keep control sometimes and it all became something of a nightmare. I think the head thought that because you were an ordained priest you had special powers of control and ability to teach RE. One experience I did not relish was celebrating Mass with the youngsters, especially Mass for the whole school of several hundred. Perched up on the stage and with a sea of rather bored faces looking up at you was hard to take. Although attempts were made to get some singing going it was all rather half hearted and I felt that not a lot of effort had gone into preparing the celebration. Things did improve with small group Masses when there was more personal contact but overall over the years that followed I found it a rather depressing picture.

The convert classes began at the end of September. Each of us was allotted one section. Unfortunately none of my prospective converts turned up. Marriage instructions had begun to get going in full swing and although I was not at all confident in my presentation I was equally amazed at the lack of knowledge some candidates had about basic Catholic 'things'. One of the partners had only heard of the pope for the first time a few days previously! But what I found very irritating was the fact that many couples never bothered to inform you if they could not keep an appointment or were hours late –especially frustrating when one had other candidates in the pipeline.

Harry Wace had his send off one evening. It was the custom for a collection to be made and then the chap who had left would come back for a social and a presentation. This was very nice and I was able to meet a few new parishioners who were all very friendly. I did some successful visiting by calling on Miss Anne Parker and Miss Ursula Stearn, two maiden ladies who lived on Mount Pleasant and whom we had christened 'Bubble and Squeak'. This reflected their characters admirably but physically they were more like Laurel and Hardy. How cruel we were! They were however delightful faithful souls who found the ongoing 'changes' very hard to take. Down the road from them was the Cambridge Folk Museum whose curator was Enid Porter. I was to come to know Enid very well over the years as her health deteriorated and I took her Holy Communion regularly. She was an authority on local folk lore and had written several books.

By now I had covered the main Sunday routines. There were two country runs when we lived out of a suitcase for the morning. It was out to Linton Village College first thing, back to St Bede's School and then down the road to Fulbourn. Later, as ecumenical relations improved, hospitality was offered by the local Anglican church in both of these places. The other country run was an early Mass at Hope nursing home followed by Mass at Trumpington village hall and then to Caldecote village hall. Canon Stokes, a former parish priest, had been reluctant to open Mass centres. His argument was that since you were not obliged to come to Mass on a Sunday if you lived more than three walking miles from a church, opening a Mass centre in the locality would put more people in danger of committing a sin since they were unaccustomed to going regularly. An interesting logic! It was a pretty tiring round but in line with the travelling mission that was still in operation when Frs Anthony Hume and Bob McCormick travelled round the remote villages of the diocese saying Mass wherever they could in pubs, private houses or in the little caravan like chapel attached to the back of their car. Mother provided hospitality on occasion and it created a good community spirit and with local worthies working hard to gather the local people together for the quarterly event. It still smacked very much of the penal days. It was distressing for many when a few years later the mission was chopped almost over night without any consultation. Now in the present time, with the closure of many of these Mass centres, the need could arise again for such a ministry.

Perhaps the most gruelling session was preaching at all the Masses in the main church. - three in the morning and two in the evening. Every congregation was different and one became rather bored with one's own voice and the substance of the sermon became rather thin as the day wore on. It was quite an experience as there was such variety in the congregation - from the ordinary down to earth parishioners to high flying academics from the university, who chose not to go to the Fisher House, the University Chaplaincy. There were representatives from almost every nation under the sun especially when the students came to the language schools and it gave a great picture of the universality of the Church. I wish that I had developed a spontaneity in preaching without using notes but I hadn't at the time the confidence to do so. At least you had a critic in your fellow clergy who were celebrating the Masses. As the Liturgy developed this was lost since you then preached at your own Mass. One thing which the bishop could have done at his Visitation would have been to listen to his clergy preaching instead of naturally hogging the limelight himself - thereby getting a better idea of the state of preaching in his diocese.

The most tiring Mass was the 5 pm which was usually packed - many people seemed half asleep it being the end of the day and the opportunity of getting Mass in at the last minute. The 8 am was for early risers, the 9.30 am was one to which more families came and the 10.45 am was the traditional 'High' Mass with Dr Richens and his merry men pulling out all the stops. The choir had a second session in the evening at 6.15 pm when we had full Vespers, Sermon and Benediction. Vespers was painful as the choir had no idea of singing plainsong and it was lugubrious in the extreme. Another 'penance' was having to deliver a sermon at this service. This was a much longer one -perhaps fifteen minutes when you had time to develop the theme more extensively. There was an opportunity to do a trial run at Hope Nursing Home in the afternoon when the nuns celebrated Benediction. If they didn't fall asleep during your offering then it was quite likely to be thumbs up for the parish church.

I had now taken on the responsibility for the Guild of St Stephen. This was a sort of spiritual club for altar servers wherein one hoped to cultivate budding vocations. We would meet after the late Mass to discuss any problems under the leadership of Tony Sylvester and occasionally we would have an outing to the seaside. I would also train any up and coming youngsters. At least two of my protégés would go on to be ordained priests - David Bagstaff and Tom Murray. At one stage I was even giving them Latin lessons and a bit of Greek before they went off to college.

It was very nice, at this time, to meet up with one of my old friends from college days, Denis Hall. He had been appointed as curate to Saffron Walden - far away from the city life he so loved. We were to keep in touch over the years. He got his wish to go back to the East End and served for many years in Canning Town, Leighton, Manor Park and eventually Forest gate and Upton Park. So we had very different experiences to exchange as time went by.

Come October we were still enjoying temperatures in the 70's when Pope Paul V1 made his historic address at the United Nations and this created a great deal of media interest. His appeal for peace was deafening against the background of the ongoing Vietnam War and all its horrors.

Then occurred one of the unique Cambridge events . A woman ran up in a state of hysteria regarding her marriage. It seems that there was a Spanish priest in town who had joined the Anglican Church and was carrying out an apostolate among the Spanish au pairs by arranging their marriages. They were under the impression that he was a Catholic priest in good standing, but unfortunately, according to Catholic rules, the marriages he had conducted were invalid in the eyes of the Catholic Church while legally accepted. How many such marriages he had conducted I don't know but it certainly created a muddle. At least if the marriage broke down the Catholic party was free to marry – such are the strange effects of Catholic Marriage discipline!!

By October with the burial of John Biggs I had completed my first cycle from birth to the grave - the first of many more to come in the future. One of my relaxations in the evening was to go up to the organ loft and play the organ. It is a very fine instrument and although I regret I was unable to continue lessons after college or to put it to good use in the parish at least I was able to keep my hands and feet in good working order and it was nice to let off steam by pulling out all the stops in sight and making that great church resound.

Initial enthusiasm and the novelty of it all were beginning to wear off as I faced the realities of parish life, 'I wish I could get enthusiastic about things. It is incredible that I have been on the job for eleven weeks now. What about when it starts running into years... the problems seem insurmountable - what should one concentrate on in particular?'

Fr Kennedy dropped in at the end of October. He was in the throws of building the new church at Newmarket and it had put a great strain on his health. The final touches were now in progress and with the prospect of having Mass facing the people he was worried as to how he was to going to cope as the church was designed for the traditional form of worship. He was worried as to whether the bishop would allow him celebrate Mass in this way. The vicar general didn't think that he would be allowed. How things would soon change!

After one of my more successful visiting expeditions, calling on Poles, Italians and Bylo-Russian Orthodox into the bargain I made my first visit to Blackfriars in Buckingham Road. Having been brought up by the Dominicans I felt a special affinity with them and it was nice to meet such luminaries as Sebastian Bullough, Thomas Gilby, Kenelm Foster an expert on Dante,

Herbert McCabe and others. They 'serviced' their own area around Buckingham Road with their own special clientele.

I had my own small group of hospitals to look after but, from time to time, on duty days or in the middle of the night I would be called out to the main Addenbrookes Hospital in Trumpington Street. This would gradually be replaced by the new hospital that would rise some way out of town. But it was convenient at present as it was only a short distance down the road. It was a formidable building with lots of staircases and equally formidable nursing staff especially on one of the private wards where the sister tended to 'devour' incoming chaplains. So my first call on October 26th was to some poor old soul with acute jaundice. I did the necessary and it would be the first of many visits to this establishment.

Shortly afterwards I had a call to The Hope. One of the Carmelite sisters from Waterbeach was in for treatment. They had been finding it harder and harder to recruit novices and were delighted when they made this catch. She had been a former midwife at the maternity hospital and was a young thing in her forties who would be able to look after the older Sisters as time went by - I am sure her special skills would be very useful in the circumstances!! On the list too was a nun who was a sister of the Huddlestones of Sawston Hall. The family were famous for sheltering Mary Tudor on her way to rally her troops at Framlingham. Captain Huddleston was the last of the line of the Catholic family and it was very sad when his nephew, an unbeliever took over and converted Catholic chapel to other uses. An equally distinguished patient was Lady Walston. At the time I was unaware of her famous liaison with Graham Greene! On the next floor was Sister Julie who was on her last legs and I had my first experience of the ritual surrounding a death bed, even though I was not there to witness the end. It was very impressive with all the Sisters gathered around bearing candles, 'Go forth on your journey Christian soul.' I thought of all the poor souls who would not have the benefit of this support at their going forth. One of the good things when a religious or priest died was the good send off with a great meal afterwards for all the visitors. This duly happened a few days later when Sr Julie went to her Maker and she must have been pleased that we all enjoyed a five course meal at the University Arms Hotel.

The first Holiday of Obligation - All Saints Day came round. The phone did not stop ringing from one minute to the next with people wanting to know the times of Masses and there was a steady stream of confessions right up to the Mass, so much so that we had to come out leaving quite a few waiting. The practice had been for Confessions to go on all through the Mass. But we had been trying to gradually to prevent this confusion of more than one Sacrament being celebrated at the same time. The following day, All Souls, gave me my first experience of saying the customary three Masses for the departed - all quite exhausting.

The University Rag Day was soon in full swing and Gerald and I went down into the thick of it. Keeping up the old traditions there was a student suitably clothed in cassock and biretta outside Corpus Christi College 'selling Indulgences' and we were almost pressed into buying one or two. On the anniversary of Luther's famous declaration we actually found a copy of his 95 Theses nailed to the west door of the church!! Sadly all this jollification has now come to and end. We ended out trip at Brookside where the De La Salle Brothers had a small house.

The family had now moved back to London for the winter and I began my weekly treks down to see them. Dad's health was giving cause for concern and aunt Dorothy had to go to the hospital for tests.

Cambridge had a number of ethnic groups which also used our church. The Poles were a very strong community with their own chaplain. They had their own Mass at midday on a Sunday with patriotic and emotional hymns. Their chaplain at the time was Fr Zawidski, a very strong nationalist who preached (what sounded like) very political sermons - the one Polish word you could pick out, as he thumped the pulpit, was 'Gomulka' (Head of the Communist party in that country). There was a sizeable Italian community, too, that turned out in reasonable numbers once a month in the afternoon when their priest came over from Peterborough. Their fervour reached its peak on the major feasts, especially Palm Sunday, when they turned out in force to get their free palms. With our five o'clock service following on almost immediately it was total chaos with their community trying to get out and ours trying to get in and with fragments of palm branches strewn everywhere. It did not do a lot for good race relations. There was a much smaller Ukrainian group of expatriates. Their liturgy was even rarer. A few faithful souls turned up and it was interesting to participate in a liturgy so different from our western rite and yet bringing home the catholicity of the church.

November 27th marked an important date in the history of the Cambridge church. Up until now we had been celebrating Mass with our back to the people at the old High Altar. Now with the gradual introduction of the new Liturgical Rites inspired by Vatican II we were to take the plunge and give a lead in introducing Mass facing the people. This involved erecting a move-able altar just inside the altar rails - this was a rather cumbersome object on a platform but it served well. However, because the choir occupied the choir stalls at this point, the altar was demolished for their benefit after the first two Masses. The move was generally welcomed by the parishioners, since the altar was much closer to them, but little did we know at the time of the ructions to come.

Visiting us at this time and helping out with Masses - we could usually rely on priests studying at the University to help us out when we were short staffed - was Fr Gerald O' Collins SJ from down under. A very pleasant man he was reading history at Pembroke College, he would later lecture at the University in Rome and would become a distinguished writer in his field.

A trickle of marriage couples came along to prepare for their nuptials and although I was never too happy about the preparation and whether I was saying the right things, it was becoming less of an ordeal. There were interesting combinations - like Irish marrying Poles, or Italians marrying Fins. How to cope with these ethnic disparities we were never warned about at college. One had to face insoluble problems of divorce and remarriage, of looking for possible grounds for annulment which, luckily, one referred to the diocesan marriage tribunal. Celebrating marriage was of course very much an occasion where all one's reserves were called upon. Due to the tax breaks at that time Easter was a very popular season for them and on occasions we were so busy that as one couple was leaving by the great west doors another couple was coming in by the porch. There were gratings to the heating pipes near the altar rails and I always had the fear that one day someone would drop the ring to be lost for ever amid the cobwebs and spiders. Mercifully this never happened to me.

An American Jesuit Fr Pat Brennan now turned up and Gerald and they became great friends. December 7th marked another historic day in Church life with the final public session of the Vatican Council and the mutual excommunication launched in 1054 between Rome and Constantinople was rescinded. One felt full of excitement that a new era had begun in the life of the Church and its relationships with other denominations. I noted a growing frustration in the entries in my diary about the scope of my task and the need for the barriers that existed between clergy and laity to come down. We were too much on a pedestal and removed from the every day lives of our parishioners. We were still wearing cassocks in the house and looking very clerical but this gradually changed.

In order to promote more participation among the laity we began to introduce bible services as an alternative to Vespers. This was a Liturgy of the Word and a blessing of the people with the Bible. All new stuff but it seemed to go down quite well with the congregation. It was in English and they did not have to endure the painful rendering of the Latin plainsong Vespers. But this caused some resentment among the choir which did not augur well for the future.

The run up to my first Christmas was now in full swing. For about a week or so parishioners would don Middle Eastern Garb and in shifts stood in a Nativity tableau at the west front of the church while suitable music was played. This attracted quite a few onlookers and created some puzzlement among some middle eastern visitors. There was the round of the schools with the traditional and interminable nativity plays and concerts - but all good fun

Christmas Eve was unbelievably hectic. There was a constant stream of confessions and it was all one could do to get out of the confessional boxes in order to start the Mass on time at the stroke of midnight. On top of that there were the constant phone calls asking what time was midnight Mass – to which we replied 'Midnight'! The Mass was preceded by a sort of continuous sing along of Christmas carols. We tried to become more sophisticated as time went on with a sort of vigil service with readings or even part of the office. But this never became very popular and there were complaints that we did not have enough carols! After it was all over with exhaustion setting in we were treated to a glass of port and some barn brack which the good sisters of Hope sent up for us. However it was up early the next morning with Mass at Hope and then back for the nine o'clock where I had to distribute nearly 200 Communions on my own - no Extraordinary Ministers to assist in those days. The morning culminated with a solemn High Mass followed by a huge turkey dinner that one was too tired to enjoy. Collapse on my s bed for the afternoon followed and I am afraid I just did not have the energy to go round hospitals to visit people. Christmas Day falling on a Saturday could not be worse because it was immediately followed by the usual Sunday routine. The joy of Boxing Day was counting the collection as these were to be our perks. This year it came to the princely sum of £330 which was divided equally between us. A day at home to see the folks was welcome. The year ended on a bang when late at night there was a violent ringing of bells and crashing on the front door - at first we thought it was a tramp the worse for wear for drink. No it was only a pious soul wanting to be shriven. 'What a year this has been. The transition has been easier than I anticipated but new hurdles and responsibilities weigh heavily. Slackness can soon develop and a constant effort is needed in all directions.' Such were my comments ending 1965.

CHAPTER TWO

GROWING IN EXPERIENCE
1966

With the most significant event of the New Year having taken place, namely counting the Christmas Collection, I was able to open my first bank account. In addition I paid in part of my salary which was the annual princely sum of £60. Curates received this annual amount while parish priests received double. It's true that we received free board and lodgings and this amount was supplemented by the 'offerings of the faithful' to keep us going from day to day. These were Mass stipends and also Stole fees which, freewill offerings, were given on the occasion of a baptism or a wedding; though sometimes they were not forthcoming. These were all put into a common fund and shared out between the four of us. So all in all I was able to pay in £127. As I didn't, as yet, have problems running a car it was sufficient to keep me going and and to run my bike and I was able to buy my first record player for £19.99.

Mass at Hope Nursing Home was usually at 6 45 am on a weekday to enable the theatre staff to attend Mass but it was not so nice turning out of bed on a cold winter's morning for the trip down the road, however it was useful if you wanted to get away early on your day off. We were always given a very hearty breakfast afterwards of a couple of fried eggs and several rashers of bacon, sitting in grand isolated splendour at the huge polished table in one of the parlours; but not so isolated as Sr Aiden would come in and minister, standing a couple of paces behind and keeping up a constant flow of conversation. At the Canonesses of St. Augustine, in Grange Road a far simpler repast was enjoyed with the community who, even at that early hour, indulged in rather intellectual conversation. Boiled egg and theology didn't always scramble too well !

My days off were spent with a regular trip down to London while the relatives were there in the winter - a train from Cambridge after an early morning Mass at Hope enabled me to spend a few hours with the oldies before catching the 7.35 pm back from Liverpool Street. The thoughts I had implanted in mother about a possible trip to Rome in the summer began to bear fruit and she seemed quite keen. A useful contact was to be my cousin Stephen, who at that time was a student at the English College. On other days in the winter I would take the twenty mile trip to Lidgate taking my bike on the train and cycling the seven miles to keep and eye on the family home. As we were entitled to the inside of a week's holiday after Christmas and Easter I was pleased to spend them at home and regale the family with all my exploits. There were one or two interesting trips especially to see the exhibition of the Dead Sea Scrolls at the British Museum and the film *The Sound of Music* which would delight audiences for generations to come.

The Feast of the Epiphany was not propitious. I had been having a regular driving lesson and was making some progress through the mayhem that was the streets of Cambridge, but the first test came along on that day and I failed on a few technical points much to the chagrin of Canon Diamond.

Father Kennedy dropped in and he was full of problems with the new church in Newmarket. The Bishop wasn't getting on too well with the architect and there was some disagreement about whether the walls should be whitewashed and since the church was built in the more traditional style there was going to be some question, as mentioned earlier, of whether Mass facing the people was going to be a possibility. Both issues were eventually resolved but the church had been built just at the wrong time as far as the Liturgical requirements were concerned.

And now I was really going to be dropped in the deep end, much to the amusement of my colleagues. We were just settling down for the evening after the First Friday evening devotions, when there was a frantic phone call. A lady on the other end was in a state of near hysteria about financial troubles and was threatening suicide. Since it was my duty day there was no option but I had to go. On arrival it was like some scene from an Edwardian melodrama. She was robed in a flame red dressing gown and reclining on a *chaise longue* while her pet dog rested in her lap. She offered me lemon tea and reiterated her threat to commit suicide and I could quite imagine her there and then pulling out a dagger and doing the deed. She had got into debt about some anatomical improvements to her feminine persona and wondered what she should do. If I had been more experienced I might have detected a whiff of alcohol on the air, but not quite knowing what to say I just sat and listened which seemed to be the best policy in the circumstances. Then all of a sudden I heard footsteps stealthily pacing too and fro outside the door. 'That's my husband', she announced breathlessly. I thought at any moment the husband was going to burst through the door and accuse me of some nefarious deed but I managed to keep calm. It all ended as rather a damp squib - matters were resolved, the husband turned out to be an elderly gent much concerned with his wife's problems and when I returned to the rectory I learned that her phone calls were a regular feature in the weekly timetable.

And so the days ran into weeks and there was never a dull moment and rarely was there an idle one. It was dealing with a constant stream of wayfarers at the door looking for lodgings, wanting the fare to Lowestoft, couples who maintained their car had broken down outside Cambridge and wanted money for the petrol, some frighteningly aggressive. Then there was being called to the hospital in an emergency by a blind man with a heart attack. He was looking ' for help' but a doctor recognised him for the fraud that he was. The clergy always were taken for a soft touch. The night bell would frequently go - poor duty priest. On one occasion in the early hours we were awakened by two students who had picked up a drunken man with a bleeding head and had brought him round for us to deal with - luckily Brian was on call and took him round to Addenbrookes. With the proximity of the big mental hospital at nearby Fulbourn there were many callers with disturbed states of mind. And it can be said, without joking, that full moon was the dangerous time. On another occasion a group of students came round, badly frightened, as they had been experimenting with an Ouija board and something strange had happened. Apart from the external eccentrics there were the more resident ones within the church who were a daily challenge. One good lady, whom Harry had christened, 'The Iron Virgin', was a formidable character of a severe countenance enhanced by dark glasses who haunted the church and was, on occasion, to have 'mystical experiences'. She thought there was something sinister in my action of not enthroning the Monstrance on the high pedestal at the back of the altar for Benediction and was not quite satisfied when I said that I would have to grow a few more inches in order to reach those heights. On our traditional visit to the Blessed Sacrament after our lunch together, one of Brian's ladies would issue a whole stream of invective, which is quite unprintable, against us. And for some weeks the canon received a daily letter sometimes more than one, consisting of many pages which were quite unreadable. I attempted to unravel the story and it turned out to be a blow by blow account of the fortunes of one of the television soap operas with whom she felt intimately involved. It's no wonder that we felt that we were the only island of sanity in this city of Cambridge.

I did my regular visits to the maternity hospital, Hope Nursing Home and Brookfields Isolation Hospital as well as quite a big round of monthly Communions. A monthly trip out to Girton on my bike was about the furthest I had to go and this was to a Scottish family to take gran Holy Communion. I tried to do parish visiting but it became more and more problematical and frustrating as either the people weren't in, had moved, or had died. On one occasion I actually cycled as far as Long Stanton, along the now dangerous and congested Huntingdon Road, and met people who didn't seem to have seen a priest for donkey's years. I called on the vicar there, Hugo de Waal. He seemed a pretty liberal Low Church man, but very friendly and pleased to make a contact. He was later to become bishop of Thetford.

Duty days proved to be particularly frustrating. Marriage instructions would be booked in on that day but then invariably the phone would ring, interrupting the interview. Perhaps a sick call to the hospital and no sooner was one home again than there would be a man of the road on the doorstep or some other insoluble problem cropped up and the poor couple was left somewhat stranded in the waiting room not quite knowing what to do. At that time we had no secretarial staff to deal with such interruptions. Saturday Confessions were still crowded and I began to feel rather like a Sacrament machine dealing out the Lord's forgiveness. It certainly needed some stamina sitting and listening to people's tales of woe in my stuffy airless wooden box, which, as I have already related, was my seat of judgment at the back of the church near the main door. How I could have done with the inspiration of the Cure D' Ars who spent hours doing nothing but hearing Confessions. Dependence on Divine Providence was essential to see one through, hoping that I had said the right thing, but it is fortunate that one can largely forget anything that was said otherwise the burden could become too great. However I began to wonder whether this method of celebrating the Sacrament was really the best way of going about things.

However it was not all work and occasionally I could get out to a good concert in town. The most memorable was a performance of *Verdi's Requiem* in Kings College Chapel and also the *Dream of Gerontius*. For the latter it was magical sitting in the candle lit choir stalls as the dramatic music echoed round the fan vaulting. At the other extreme a tip to see the first James Bond Film, *Dr No* was thoroughly enjoyable.

As ever, one of the greatest problems was organising priorities. We had been programmed in college life to follow the bell, day in and day out - there was little room for personal initiative. Now there was no bell apart from Florry, the under housekeeper, whose finger seemed to be perpetually on the button of the intercom. Everything seemed so very fragmented and it was a question of keeping the main services going without much of what we call these days, 'outreach'. I was constantly being plagued by the idea that I was 'wasting time' - especially when it was calling on non existent parishioners or waiting for clients who did not turn up for appointments and did not phone to apologise. Trips round the hospitals were not always fruitful as more often than not a patient had moved on or the particular person did not want to see you. There was some criticism by staff that the Catholic clergy only visited their own flock. They failed to realise that the non Catholic chaplains to these establishments could do a full time job, impossible for us with all our other commitments. This in itself was frustrating as you felt you could never a do a job thoroughly but was perpetually flitting from one thing to another.

+ Leo, our bishop, appeared from time to time and there was a great celebration for his jubilee We all went over to the cathedral in Northampton for the solemnities. Cardinal Heenan and the Apostolic Delegate, Archbishop Cardinale were present as were old associates from college including Mgr Foster, the rector. We were treated to a slap up spread at the Overstone Solarium afterwards and Leo was presented with a cheque for £4000. Such a celebration was to lead into a pre Lent meal hosted by the canon at our hotel in the Fens at Clayhithe - curried prawns Bangalore followed by jugged hare and cream caramel and coffee and cognac. ' The poverty of the Church?' as I noted. However it was ' good to see how the other half lived from time to time'.

We were advised to get a spiritual director when we left college but I was never successful in finding anyone. Clergy in Cambridge especially came and went, and it was difficult to pin anyone down. However I did make occasional trips up to Blackfriars in Buckingham Road to be shriven and here I met Herbert McCabe OP. He didn't seem to be as unorthodox as he was made out to be. Sebastian Bullough, my Uncle Reg's Scripture friend, was also in residence. His mother had been the famous Italian actress Eleonora Duse who is still remembered in Venice and whose husband professor Bullough had given his house to the Dominican Order to be their first base in the city since the Reformation. He had been working on a new translation of the Psalms and still rode his Norton Motor Bike in his religious habit. And as related, when teaching at my old school, his pupils learned more about dismantling motor bikes than analysing Scripture.

So I began my first Lent. The canon had dictated, in correct liturgical style, that we should give a two minute homily each day on the readings so forty homilies lay ahead of us. It did become a bit difficult after a time to say something new each day.

The domestic situation was not without its crises. Florrie, rather simple and volatile, had a row with the lady who came to do the cleaning. She threatened to leave but as Lil, the chief housekeeper said, 'She goo, I goo too'. Florrie would come regularly to daily Mass and an old retainer by the name of Bill Stephens would come in every morning to unlock the church. A great character, he had been a railway worker in his early days. If any lady approached the priest before Mass he would keep her at bay saying, 'Let me take down your perticulers, my dear'. However Mass became something of a battle between Florrie and Bill. Florrie would answer very slowly in a bleating fashion and Bill would be rattling on ten to the dozen in anther register. It was a day when I was saying Mass with back to the people and so I could not see what was going on behind me. All of a sudden there was a terrible commotion in the pews. Evidently a parishioner had got so fed up with this dual act that she told Florrie to shut up and it ended with one pursing the other round the church - wielding a handbag?

28th February. Today was set aside for a clergy conference to discuss how we were to put over the developments of the Vatican Council to the people. Just as we were about to begin I had a sick call round to the maternity hospital to baptise a baby into whom oxygen was being pumped. I got back in time to read out to the assembled clergy the official rules governing the Jubilee Faculties, as a Jubilee Year had been announced by the Pope. The discussion on the Council really was desperate and nobody seemed to have much of an idea what to do and wanted all the directions to come from on high. In the end a committee was formed to draw up summaries of the Council documents. On locking up the church in the evening I had a chat with a solid Irish chap regarding the Church and the world. Here, I thought, was the real Church speaking- compared with this morning's fiasco - there seemed to be a great gulf between us, the clergy, and them, the laity. Unless talks on the Council were implemented by practical measures we would get nowhere. At any rate at OLEM we made a start with four introductory talks on the Council during Lent. The first was given by Fr Gerry O' Collins. SJ, which was really excellent but the little committee we set up comprising Frank Diamond, Paul Hypher and John Fennell from Sawston to work out some explanatory notes to be circulated didn't really get very far and I 'underwent mental torture' during this meeting. A priest from St Edmund's House gave a talk on the 'Church in the Modern World'. This was followed by a pretty hopeless discussion, especially as he hadn't even read the decree! Not long after the clergy assembled to hear a brilliant talk at the Royal Cambridge Hotel by Abbott Christopher Butler on the Council which was quite inspiring. Daily homilies for Lent had begun and it was not at all easy finding words each day to say on the Gospel. There were only three in the congregation and all of them had chosen to kneel behind pillars in the half gloom. It is very difficult speaking to people you cannot even see! The day was further marred by tragedy when Brian was called out to a pilot from Marshal's Airport who crashed somewhere on the A45. The tragedy was compounded sometime later when his wife in the first snow of winter skidded on the road coming in to Cambridge on the Gog Magog hills and was killed. Her two young children survived and were brought up by their grandparents.

There were more relaxing moments. We had the key to the Botanical Gardens where we could take a stroll sometimes and admire the plants in the tropical greenhouse. This was overlooked by St Mary's Convent where, on this first prize giving day, the address was given by one of the parents - Dr Conrad Swan who was the Rouge Dragon Pursuivent at Arms - one of the Queen's Heralds. Later he would rise to the heights as York Herald.

So the first anniversary of my ordination came round and I recalled that I had a lot to be thankful for and that things had been made terribly easy for me all the way along the line.

Doctor Beeching had not yet got to work on the railways and I was able to take a train to Oxford and Blackfriars for the ordination of one of my school contemporaries, Bertrand Callaghan. It was good to see some of my old friends from those days including Anthony Ross OP and the school matron, Marianne Catterall . However there were sad reports that the Dominican Order was in very low ebb with many people leaving. Bertrand was to join their number a couple of years hence. None of the five or more from my time at school who had joined the Order survived. It was all intensely depressing. The following day was even more depressing as I failed my driving test for the second time.

A Latin American Air force man from RAF Lakenheath called in with a persecution complex. It's surprising how little one has to say to make people feel better. I suppose most people just want a listening ear - however I recorded how more and more isolated I felt from normal life and from parishioners whose lives we should be sharing.

23rd March marked the dedication of the new church in Newmarket. Michael Kennedy had forgotten that he had asked me to be sub-deacon and in the event I sang the Proper of the Mass with Brian and Paul from the gallery. The Rural Dean, Brian Houghton, from Bury St. Edmunds celebrated the Mass. He was very much a traditionalist so most of the Liturgy was in Latin declaimed in his own inimitable style. In spite of his eccentricities he was a good pastoral priest doing much good work in Slough for the local schools. A good meal was had afterwards at the Bedford Lodge Hotel. All this coincided with the historic meeting between Pope Paul VI and Archbishop Michael Ramsey at St Paul's Outside the Walls in Rome which brought so much hope for possible reunion with the Anglican Church.

The developments in the Church were even affecting my dentist across the way from the church. Her name was Rosy O' Carrol and she took the opportuni-ty, when I was strapped down in the chair and with her drill about to strike, to let forth a tirade about the way that things were going in the Church. All I could do was to grunt while the torture continued.

Holy Week was an experience - my first ever in a parish. It was conducted with great solemnity and reverence. The Canon washed the feet of ten men on Maundy Thursday - he might have got in a couple of our vagrants for the other two! The choir sang well but for some reason the Canon chanted the Bidding Prayers on Good Friday in Latin. The Confessionals were bursting at the seams at the appointed times and once again we were helped out by Gerry O' Collins who gave a commentary during the Liturgy. The Easter Vigil was impressive, too, and there was almost a full church though nowhere like the crowds at Christmas. Tony Sylvester, the MC, was an expert at dragooning the altar servers and ran things like clock work. At the end of it all thank heavens for the slap up meal at Clayhithe and one really felt that it had all be worthwhile.

However relationships between the clergy were not always easy. Thrusting together four men of different temperaments and ages who did not choose each other's company is not easy and I sustained my first rocket from the Canon for being 'clam like' and 'uncommunicative' and giving the impression, so Sr Aiden told me, that I didn't like him, which was far from the truth. I'm not quite sure what he was referring to. The Canon had not yet resorted to writing letters to us but on occasion when we asked him about some event or other he would always refer us to the weekly news letter! The weekly news letter was something of an innovation introduced by him and Mass was always concluded by the admonition, ' take your weekly newsletter' and then to read out the contents to the congregation which rather defeated the object - or was it just a good teaching method? My discussion with Gerald regarding the state of the parish ended up by the comment - believe it or not, 'Communication, communication, communication.'

The hottest temperatures for May for twenty years reached 82 F and on my twenty fifth birthday I past my driving test, at last, much to the exultation of the Sisters at 'The Hope' who had been praying hard. I was now entrusted with the old Austin Cambridge parish car which was something of a tank compared with the up to date models on which I had been learning to drive. We had to write to the bishop to get permission to buy a car. This seemed rather strange since a car was a necessity in a parish like this, but I suppose it was to make sure we weren't taking on any debts. Our local garage man had come up with a mini which had only done 25000 miles on the clock. Although it had some teething problems I was now the proud possessor of my first car and at last had some independence.

Bishop Leo came for Confirmations with a seemingly very long pre-Council Train which was supposed to have been cut down and informed us that portable altars for Mass facing the people were 'going out'.

The old Forty Hours devotion was still in vogue and two hour long watches in the middle of the night did nothing to help the fatigue that I was beginning to feel from my exertions. Newly ordained clergy were also set an exam each year for a couple of years to keep our studies going and so this provided extra intellectual activity. The subject was to be the *'The theme of the Temple in the Old Testament'* and *'The Church's teaching on Conscience'*.

I was now introduced to the phenomenon of phantom pregnancy. It was the story of two ladies at the maternity hospital. One was as thin as a board; the other was as big as a house. The latter was entirely phantom the former gave birth to twins - the wonders of nature! Frustrations continued with parish visiting, but I always received a warm welcome from the people that I did find at home. This was especially so from those who had been living for many years in the parish and had never seen a priest in all that time. It struck me that such visits were very necessary and important. There was one ward in the hospital that was particularly dreary. On visiting one of our parishioners she was very upset, telling me that in the next bed was a lady who was having a termination of her pregnancy. It seems that such terminations were taking place before they were technically legal. One gynaecologist was particularly prominent as a pioneer and was well admired by the Sisters at Hope Nursing Home; surely unaware of this expertise at the hospital. Larry Howling, a very outspoken priest, had made a protest some years before but I was not of such stern stuff.

Deanery meetings continued on a regular basis usually ending in a good meal at one of the local hotels. At the Royal Cambridge you could help yourself to as much *hors d'oeuvres* as you wanted. However the starving clergy descended with such voracious appetites on these delicacies that the board was very rapidly wiped clean with the result that we were not at all popular with the management.

News came through that my old school at Laxton was closing down after forty years on that spot, although it could trace direct lineage to the original foundation at Bornham in Flanders. Fr Arnold Plummer, one of the younger clergy, had died suddenly and plans for developing and updating the school had fallen through. The Dominicans were going through a great period of turmoil, and changes in the educational system made it very difficult for small schools like this to continue. The Georgian mansion was eventually sold off to some no good developer who, it seems, fleeced the Order and removed some of the famous Indian Murals from the old dormitories. However it eventually came back into Catholic hands as a home for retired Polish people.

The summer was upon us and I had done a year at Cambridge. It was an overwhelming experience after six years at Oscott which began to seem more and more irrelevant and a period of wasted opportunities but I gathered there were changes in the air and I trusted that these would bare more fruit. But it was now off to Rome for a memorable holiday with mother. It was there by rail and back - nearly stymied by the seaman's strike. We stayed at the pensione, *Maraviglia,* near the railway station – a venue used by relatives of English College students and run by Maria who had worked for the resistance during the war. It was here that I had stayed with my friend Denis some three years before. We were shown around by a Dominican Lay Brother, David Lawson. He was a great character in his seventies and had been a member of the Ditchling Community and the Eric Gill set. He was able to take us into nooks and crannies which were largely off the usual tourist circuit. On visiting the excavations under St Peters I was mistaken for the guide by none other than the Bishop of Willesden, Graham Leonard, who was at the Anglican Centre. Later he would become famous by joining the Church. One great moment was celebrating Mass at the tomb of St Peter down in the crypt and of course a trip to the Opera in the Baths of Caracalla where we saw a spectacular, *Aida*. One memorable trip was with a young doctor, Gordon Reid to an ancient monastery at Allatri which was the home of Captain Jack Leslie son of the author Shane Leslie. Here we were waited on a by a former Yugoslav princess. It was all rather surreal. Another of Bro David's friends was an aspiring author, John Ginger and the estranged wife of the actor Marius Goring. Some Italians were all over us when they discovered that we were British - our win in the World Cup was still fresh in people's minds.

Back at the treadmill I had my first experience of prison. At least a solicitor rang me up wanting me to visit a young Irish lad. He was in the cells under the Guildhall in the middle of town and waiting to be arraigned for petty theft. It was quite an experience. He assured me that Canon Hunting had told him that if he was in any trouble a Catholic Priest ' would speak up for him'. I wish I could - but knowing nothing of the fellow's background or circumstances and the fact that his hour was very near - all I could do was to give him some ' consoling words'. Insoluble problems like this would keep presenting themselves and it was frustrating not really being able to do anything about them.

Another glaring problem, I soon discovered, was the question of children at non-catholic schools. There was little or no provision for them and any attempts to set up some sort of Sunday school was not encouraged since they should have been at the local Catholic schools provided for them. Parish visiting continued and although many people were very friendly others looked at you as though you were a being from outer space. Some thought you had come to read the meter or waived a walking stick at you through the letter box. It was sometimes a daunting experience approaching the front door of some of the big houses with their long gravel drives not knowing what sort of reception I might be given after my timid knock on the door. One family near Oakington lived in a caravan in the middle of a field and appeared to be gypsies but were quite lapsed. Another family denied being Catholics and another didn't know whether they were Catholics at all. Some with Irish names were probably descendents of those who had come over in the potato famine and had lost the Faith as there had been no contact with the Church in those days but at least I succeeded in finding some families at home way out in the country. Many of them had children who were receiving no religious education and nothing was being done for them. How in their circumstance they could have got to a Catholic, school, even if they had wanted to, I don't know. It seemed that we needed an army of catechists to bring them the Faith.

There was some cheer with the Guild of St. Stephen. David and Paul Bagstaff and Tom Murray had been enrolled and we all went out on a trip to Brancaster in North Norfolk. This was my first long trip in the car and so it was good experience. From the sandy beach there we moved on to Hunstanton where we all ended up with egg and chips. A few weeks later we included some of the choir boys and with Tony Sylvester at the wheel we drove up to the coast again. The somewhat precocious son of the choir master took exception to my putting a few coins in the slot machines on the pier and informed me that, 'priests shouldn't gamble.' I was very pleased to bowl him out at cricket on the beach. There was healthy rivalry on the bus on the way back as the servers drowned out the Latin singing choristers with a few rowdy songs!

With clergy away on holiday I had to fill in for their regular tasks, so my main consideration was visiting the Old Addenbrookes. One needed good leg muscles to cope with the steep steps. In those days , as already noted, you would visit the ward and ask the ward sister whether there were any Catholics in her charge. She would then scan the lists and you would visit any Catholic that happened to be there. Even those who were 'long lapsed' welcomed the visit. How different now with the restrictions of the Data Protection Act. It was pretty tiring going round all the wards and especially frustrating when you found the doctors were doing their rounds or patients were being 'attended to' and you had to come back again later. Arrangements for Holy Communion were made and you would return at some early hour the following day. Gerald, who was chaplain, was also responsible for the Nurses Guild and would go and speak to them on occasions.

Something, perhaps, of the initial enthusiasm was beginning to wear off as I realised that it wasn't going to be so easy to set the parish to rights and there were really periods when I felt I had just had enough and wanted to run away wondering why on earth God wanted me to do this job. I tried to preach an optimistic homily on how it was necessary for the Church, as it was at the moment, to die in order to be reborn.

There had been some discussion about having Mass in people's homes to bring the community together. At this time it wasn't permitted but we thought perhaps we could have a Bible Service or something similar to build up the local community. We needed to have some more idea of where our Catholic families were and to assess their needs. With that in mind I was sent to Holyrood House in London for a day course on parish census work. There were only about a dozen clergy their including Fr Wilfred Purney and the day was lead by Anthony Spencer. It was a fascinating course and I came back

217

equipped with ideas and a more scientific approach with specially constructed index cards for accessing information about people.

Another supply priest was Reggie Fuller of the Catholic Biblical Association. He was a friend of my uncle Reg and had wanted him to do a commentary on the prophet Jeremiah but due to school pressures he did not have the time. However uncle did keep us up to date with the latest in biblical scholarship and wrote a pamphlet for the Catholic Truth Society entitled - 'Why read the Old Testament'.

As autumn approached visits out home were somewhat nostalgic. The weather was perfect. The Michaelmas daisies were in full bloom and many Red Admirals and Painted Ladies were flitting too and fro. The potatoes I had helped to set in the spring were now ready for lifting and dad presided over mother and me in our efforts to lift them. Gerald Moorcraft drove me home so that we could collect a bag for the house. The grass needed cutting and there was quite a bit of ditch clearing to be done. I met up with Barbara and Janos Stryk down the road. He was the sculptor who had escaped Hungary during the revolution. He had been back to Hungary for a visit and it struck me then how lonely one's vocation was and how nice it would be to have the companionship of marriage. However their partnership was not to last and so not all things were rosy on that score With uncle Wilf staying at nearby Ousden there was on going talk about the crises in the Church and one wonders how many other families are similarly discussing things.

We took our annual trip to the Waterbeach Carmel to see mother's friend, Sr Mary Carmel of Jesus, who in her early days had been secretary to Uncle Mac on the children's radio and Mother Rosario, the prioress, who had been a professional artist and who's painting of St Laurence hung in the Chesterton church. In tune with Vatican 2 all the shutters and spikes had been removed and only the plain grill remained. One priest recalled that he had to take one of the Sisters to the doctor. She hadn't been out since the 1930s and was terrified at the speed he was going and the fearsome world outside. Mother's friend had been estranged from her mother when she joined the Carmel and now with her mother in her nineties she was concerned for her health. In the new post Conciliar atmosphere it was fortunate that she was eventually allowed home to nurse her mother in her dying days. Their resident chaplain was now Mgr Charles Davidson, one of the great characters of the diocese. He used to lead pilgrimages to the remains of the old town of Dunwich on the east coast of Suffolk where St Felix had been bishop.

With the gradual implementation of the reforms in the Liturgy feelings regarding the use of Latin were beginning to gather force. At the end of September I went round to Lady Margaret House as an observer at a gathering of about forty members of the Latin Mass Society. Fr Sebastian Bullough OP gave a really good talk mainly on the historical development of the Liturgy. Fr Oates from Chesterton was there shouting down all opposition. Mrs Richens produced a petition to send to the bishop to allow a Latin Mass in certain circumstances. Their objection was that the 'permission' of the Council for the vernacular has been made mandatory by the individual bishops. There were various University types there including Lord William Taylor and some of the usual old faithfuls from the parish.

The next Clergy Deanery meeting followed the same theme. Paddy Oates gave a paper on the Council's *Decree on the Priesthood*. His approach was very pre-conciliar and I suppose it was not surprising that most of the clergy were in agreement. Paul Hypher and Gerald Moorcraft and Canon Sweeney, Master of St Edmund's House, tried to push things a bit further forward but they were rather in a minority. But we had a good meal afterwards at the University arms- melon followed by *vols au vents* of turkey. The next day it was Aylesbury Duck at the clergy night arranged by the Catenian Association. There was an Anglican and Presbyterian Minister also invited. It is a bit of a mystery what these businessmen do but one is assured that they do a lot for the Church and it must be worth it for the excellent meal they gave us from time to time.

Enthusing people about the decrees of the Vatican Council, then, was now our main preoccupation. Canon Diamond had invited Fr Clifford Howell SJ to come and give a series of talks and liturgies. He arrived full of vigour and enthusiasm and the canon wondered who was going to get tired first, he or us. It was an uphill job for him. I attended his last Mass from the back of the church. The plainsong was uninspiring, people were still pouring in during the sermon and the Paddies were all leaning against the back wall telling their beads. No one sang - at least at the back! At the end of his visit his reaction was that he had never experienced anything quite the same as he had done in Cambridge and thought it was one of the most backward parishes he had been to! But once again we drowned our sorrows at Clayhithe with curried chicken and the next day, with the others, went to see the latest James, Bond film, *Thunderball*.

I was detailed to St Edmund's House to attend a Legion of Mary meeting that was to be transferred from the University to the Parish. It consisted mainly of Spanish *au pair* girls and a very keen Nigerian research student and headed by the president Margaret Mason who was secretary at St Bede's and quite a character, but she was soon to retire from this particular scene to train for the probation service.

The Guild of Ransom pilgrims now appeared on the scene lead by the indefatigable Mgr Goulder. These sturdy men were on their annual walk to Walsingham and he preached an appeal at all the Masses. He was very witty but some of his comments about the state of the Church were caustic and he envisaged great schisms to come in the community.

An interesting potential convert called in. His name was Benjamin Drage and a Jew. He had held a military position in Salerno during the war and the Liberation of Rome and in that capacity had met Pope Pius XII. Many years later, after getting married and having his first child, he had another audience with the Pope who asked him whether his child would be baptised and without thinking he said, 'yes'. And so his little girl was duly baptised and brought up a Catholic and was schooled at St Mary's Convent. He now at last took the step to receive instruction leading to baptism. This meeting would be the first of my growing interest in the Jewish Community and his Baptism was the first adult one that I celebrated. Following Benjamin I was given another candidate to instruct. He was a seventeen year old boy from the Perse school. We had many interesting discussion over the weeks ahead but it was when we came to the Church's teaching on marriage and divorce that he finally decided not to go ahead any further, but I put him touch with the chaplain at the University he was going to, but I heard no more of him. The theoretical course we were told to devise at college really wasn't of much use and I really wondered what was the best way to instruct these two very different candidates. It was all over to oneself without much advice from anyone else.

Every year the clergy Deanery met for a Requiem Mass for the deceased clergy. On this occasion there was the first election for the *Presbyterium*, a representative group of diocesan clergy to advise the bishop. We had to elect two members one over fifteen years ordained and one under. The canon and John Fennell from Sawston were elected. I picked up one vote. When the group first met at the rectory with the bishop some weeks later its outcome was shrouded in secrecy.

With the first Sunday of Advent the new changes in the Liturgy were introduced and much of it was now in English. However, strangely, the Preface was still left in Latin.

On 20th December came a bombshell and as I recorded in my diary, 'What may be of disastrous consequences for the Church in this country came to day with the announcement that one of our leading theologians, Charles Davis, is to leave the Church to marry. It seemed almost unbelievable when he was interviewed on the news. On the other hand it might buck up a few people's ideas in this country. The gloom that will descend on many particularly in the seminaries is easy to guess.' He had certainly done a lot through his books to popularise the Faith and make theology more approachable for the ordinary person. His criticism of the impersonal nature of authority in the Church had much justification and when talking to my friend Denis at Saffron Walden we felt it certainly applied to Oscott. His departure had quite an effect on the ordinary person and my family was full of it when I got home for a day off. Mother had gone to the library and got out his book , 'A study of Theology' and found passages therein to quote against himself and we had the picture of his face glowering out from the Sunday Papers.

But Christmas was upon us with the round of carol concerts in the schools and the live crib at the West Front of the Church. There was an ecumenical session out at Toft school which was most enjoyable where the Rev Smith gave the opening prayer and I did the blessing. Confessions seemed unending leading up to the midnight Mass and at one point we simply had to shut the main doors so that we could start the Mass. On this occasion I was sub-deacon. It was celebrated at the High Altar and about 800 people were present. It was a pity that we didn't have the Mass facing the people but the canon, although welcoming the reforms, was very cautious in his approach to implementing them. Come Christmas Day there was near disaster. I had been garaging my car opposite Professor Stopp's house. But could I get my new second hand mini to start? And I was due to go on the long country run to Trumpington and Caldecote. The noise brought Mrs Stopp out in her night wear. Mrs Stopp's sister said that I could borrow hers - but could I get it to go either? In the end in desperation we got in touch with the Ellwoods from Trumpington who fetched me just in time for the 8.30 Mass. Of course it was another bad servicing by John Collin as the battery was entirely flat. But with Tony Sylvester to the rescue it was soon in operation again.

'Two on a Tower'
With David Bagstaff

UNSETTLING TIMES AND NEW BEGINNINGS
1967

The Davis affair still dominated our thoughts and feelings as a new year arrived. I had a long discussion with myself about how to reduce the Church to its basic essentials especially regarding the papacy and authority in general and to speculate what was likely to emerge and these positive thoughts cheered me up but it was still something of a mystery as to why Davis had left the Church. There were arguments with my colleagues about parochial affairs and reorganising the parish and duty days. The world outside continued on its gloomy path with an American general saying that the war in Vietnam might go on for years while in the Universal Church a visiting Dutch priest said that at ecumenical gatherings in his country everyone was sharing Communion .

Meanwhile the Legion of Mary went into full gear now that it was transferred to the parish. A group from HQ visited the parish to drum up support. They were a very enthusiastic number of young people who 'witnessed' to a gathering of parishioners. They now set about visiting the parish. Canon Diamond was not too happy about this style of evangelisation but he let them loose. Fr Hanrahan, a missionary White Father, preached at all the Masses, imbued with the spirit of the Council, and his Legionaries stood outside the church afterwards taking names for a follow up visit in the afternoon. By the time they had left we were in possession of a whole host of names and addresses of people that needed a pastoral visit. That would be the day! The parish group certainly started off well with thirty parishioners and students coming along. I was given charge to be a sort of spiritual director for them.

Come the middle of January +Leo announced his resignation and there was great speculation regarding the new bishop and the possibility that this event would herald the splitting of our huge diocese into two. 'We teased the canon as to his prospects but, as ever, he was very reticent after his trips to Northampton and we don't even know who the Vicar Capitular is to stand in for the bishop. However we gathered that the Chapter had put forward possible names for his successor and we were also given the long overdue news that the Theatre Law had now been repealed.' This meant that clergy could now go to live theatre and even see Shakespeare without the risk of suspension from priestly duties! Although we had been allowed to go to the cinema the theatre law had been enacted before the cinema was invented and was to prevent clergy from frequenting such dangerous places as music halls and the like.

I made sandwiches for some men of the road but they threw them back at me and a group of four very ordinary blokes came in for a chat. We had a lively discussion. They were surprisingly articulate. They accused the Church of putting Our Lady above God, among other things, and it was a useful experience trying to translate Church language into terminology they could understand – 'whose the bloke that holds your cards?', said one of them. It really made one think how to get the Church's message over to ordinary people like this. One really feels that strange language such as 'Immaculate Conception' and 'Papal Infallibility' must put people off. After all Jesus used non technical language when communicating with people.

Two outstanding characters visited about this time. Archbishop Roberts, a former Jesuit archbishop from India, came to preach in Great St Mary's Church which was crowded to the doors. He was a man that stood on no ceremony and it was reported that when a certain lady craved permission to kiss his episcopal ring declared, 'It's in my back pocket, madam!' The other was Leonard Cheshire VC who came to supper. The latter was a most pleasant, charming and humble man. He spoke at the Unity Meeting in the Chemistry Lab theatre just next to the church. His theme was 'suffering'. The other speaker was Bishop Sansbury, the secretary of the British Council of Churches. We followed up with a Unity Mass and a get together of the local clergy in the rectory - this included Fr Barnabas, the Anglican Franciscan from down the road and Archdeacon Carey.

The next front page news was that Charles Davis was getting married in nearby Haslingfield Church and would be living with his wife, Florence, at Abington in our parish. He seemed quite happy so he would now come under the pastoral care of our Brian Nightingale!

An article in the periodical Blackfriars by its editor Herbert McCabe was in many ways sympathetic to Davis's position. But Herbert's description of the Church as being 'corrupt ' caused an uproar. This was largely misunderstood but he was removed from the editorship. I went for a chat with Brother James at Blackfriars who said that the phone hadn't slopped ringing because of the media interest and he felt the Church was in crisis. Shortly afterwards the big news was that Fr McMahon who was prominent a couple of years ago was also planning to marry and Malcolm Tudor, a fellow student from Oscott was resigning from the priesthood. He said he was resigning as a matter of principle and not because he intended to marry. 'In many ways this is all very unsettling and questions what one's own particular role is meant to be.'

I had long chats with Gerald. One just wonders what one is meant to be doing and where to start next. The situation seems really critical with a growing population, lapsing from the Church etc and we considered that there really should he an overall plan of campaign instead of just drifting along day after day.

About this time I discovered an old couple in their eighties on the farthest reaches of the parish at Monks Drive, Elsworth. They were really quite delightful but had lost contact with the Church over the years. She had been a communist in her day and espoused all sorts of socialist causes. But they came back regularly to Communion and I made the ten mile trek out to see them once a month. The time came when the old boy died and the coffin was placed in the front room. Mrs wanted to go to Confession so I suggested there and then - oh no - not in front of her deceased husband! She had secrets from him even in death which she would not divulge. So it was into the next room to be shriven!

At the last moment I was asked by George Kent, St Bede's headmaster, to come to the careers evening at the school to represent the clergy. It was a little embarrassing. All the other firms were there touting their wares with elaborate displays and handouts to encourage the youngsters to sign up. I was just presented with a bare table and chair and in the time available had nothing to offer or to create an interest - but I did have quite a useful chat with some of the pupils and their parents and the weather man from Anglia Television, who was at the next table.

But it was not all doom and gloom. A very well turned out lady used to come to Mass every day before going off to work. She was a Miss Hilary Clay and we were told that she was in 'ergonomics' - a top executive in a research council - something I thought that we badly needed in the parish. I was invited round to her house for a meal with her mother in Newton Road. It was a quite sumptuous repast but the most gruelling part was the chatter which continued non-stop still I left at 10.45 pm They were very pleasant people and I enjoyed their hospitality on a number of occasions. Mother, an American, spent most of her spare time playing bridge.

By the end of February we were in the news again. Archbishop Roberts SJ was invited to speak at Fisher House, the University Chaplaincy, about the current state of affairs in the Church and the question of freedom of conscience which had been hotly debated at the Vatican Council. I went down with Gerald and his American friend Patrick Brannan SJ who was staying with us. His talk was certainly very controversial, so much so that Pat walked out in the middle of it. The next we knew was that the acting chaplain, another Jesuit, Joe Christie, made a dramatic entrance, accused the archbishop of heresy, and ordered the meeting to close. There was something of a disturbance when the archbishop moved on to the vexed question of Natural Law and contraception at which point Joe appeared again (one detected a slight inebriated tone of voice) and brought the meeting to a halt. So the archbishop adjourned elsewhere to continue the discussions. It was all over the press the next morning. It was reported that ten priests had walked out and such was the disturbance that police had to be called! Fr Pat was in a state and had been up half the night with some students who had been worried about the lecture. What dramatic times we are living in! Matters, however, were put somewhat to rights when a TV confrontation between the two was broadcast. Joe withdrew his accusation of heresy and that it had only been made in a friendly way at a private meeting and the last thing they expected was press publicity. The controversy rumbled on in 'Varsity' where there was a full length article by Charles Davis and Joe Christie was really shaken by the criticisms he had received.

With the coming of Holy Week there was the question of the reading of the Passion. In past years it had been sung in Latin with the choir doing their polyphonic bits for the crowd. This year we were determined to read the Passion in English but to give some solace to the Latinists, as they were now being called, we agreed that they could participate in one of the evening Masses in Holy Week. In those days one of the other Passion narratives was read on a weekday in Holy Week. So we had a full polyphonic Mass for the Wednesday after Palm Sunday. A very reluctant Brian was celebrant at the last minute. I was the narrator and Pat Brannan, took the part of Christ. Little had we realised that this was the longest liturgy of the week with a Tract of inordinate length. The choir went to town - the plainsong was ghastly the polyphony was tolerable and the unsuspecting congregation was in situ for a full hour and a half! Sr Aiden gave me a good old telling off the next day and no doubt the canon also received a piece of her mind! The day concluded with two Irishman wanting to take the pledge but having no formal liturgy I had to concoct one on the sport.

Fr Drew, an aged Redemptorist, had been with us to comment on and preach at the Liturgy each day and we ended with the usual meal out, this time at the Red Lion al Wittlesford, where I had lychees for the first time as a desert. He had been baptised at the English Martyrs and checking the register we found that the record of his ordination had never been entered therein - he might have got away with getting married! The following day marked the historic announcement that Charles Grant, the parish priest of Kettering had been appointed as our new bishop. Canon Diamond was not amused as we got to hear the news before he did. But he became more cheerful when ecumenism made a leap forward and he was asked to preach the civic sermon at Holy Trinity Church.

April 1st marked my first family wedding. This was of my cousin Jonathan and with the family I travelled down to Tolworth in Surrey to conduct the ceremony. In some ways it was an April fool as the marriage, sadly, was to be short lived and for whatever reason his wife left him and Jonathan took up a new life as a teacher of the First Nation in Canada and, marrying an American lady, they lived happily ever after.

The annual trek for the family from the winter residence in London down to the country now took place. 'One wonders how much longer they can keep this going. Dad can no longer manage the stairs and so we rigged up a bed in the dining room which we didn't use much anyway. But they came back to a cold and damp cottage with mother getting into a terrible worry about the state of affairs trying to get the place habitable for the aunts to join them later. The news was not too good from London either as aunt Dorothy had fallen and fractured her wrist and this was serious for someone with her delicate state of health. I was glad to be able to get home for the Easter break to give the family some support.'

A resident priest was now installed at Kirtling as Sally Stalley whose family had been resident at the presbytery for many years as caretakers had been pensioned off. David Johnson was an ex-service chaplain and a member of the rather rare Society of St Edmund. He was beginning to work wonders getting the place tidied up and into order.

The 26th April was the historic consecration of Charles Grant as Bishop of Northampton and we all went over for the enthronement. A blow was nearly struck against ecumenism when we narrowly avoided running down the Vicar of Bedford on a bicycle; the mixture of horror and amazement on his face had to be seen. The enthronement was magnificent and we all concelebrated the Mass facing the people presided over by Cardinal Heenan. A reception followed at the Overstone Solarium and it was rather sad seeing +Leo handing over to his successor. He made a touching little farewell speech.

It was nice seeing some of my contemporaries including Mgr Foster who was recovering from a stroke. This had been brought on, no doubt, by one or two of his professorial staff leaving to get married. Bishop Charles gave us a very practical down to earth speech - the fact that we were all in it together and the atmosphere was far more relaxed than during the previous regime. He didn't think that the Diocese would be split for at least three years - in fact it would be nearly ten before that event happened.

My trip to the maternity hospital the next day was rather unnerving. The ward sister on checking the list of patients went out of her way to point out an American lady who had put herself down as 'Christian' - perhaps that description was unusual in those days. My suspicions were immediately raised and were confirmed when I caught sight of the name – Davis in the card index! It was a traumatic moment with the prospect of perhaps meeting the couple. Sure enough they were sitting in the corridor. I looked them straight in the eye and somewhat flinched, feeling awful as I passed them and later in the day looking back I should have at least have greeted them with a polite 'good morning'! On another visit the ward sister had said she had been doing a bit of probing about her description as being a 'Christian' and could only conclude that she was a member of one of those 'American Sects'. Her husband was a very well spoken man, she said, and a writer.

The altar servers were really keen on learning the Latin responses for the Mass but things were changing as, on 12th May, it was announced, that, at the discretion of the local hierarchies, the central prayer of the Mass the Eucharistic prayer could eventually be in English. The nuns were changing too. Sr Aiden was now resplendent in her new much neater and simpler habit. She told us how she had agonised as she surveyed the two habits lying side by side on her bed and wondered how she would cope now having to wear this new modern garb. But it was a vast improvement from the old habit. One wondered how the St Louis Sisters in Newmarket were managing. At least there was less chance of the race horses shying as they were inclined to do when they saw the good Sisters coming. With their habit it was a positive danger crossing the road as their wimple prevented them from looking left or right.

On my twenty sixth birthday the new bishop visited us and we concelebrated Mass – singing the Eucharistic Prayer. The Liturgy was sung complete with the choir and this may have kept people away. Some of the stalwart parishioners afterwards wondered why it had not been of a more popular nature but no doubt it was the canon trying to keep everyone, especially the choir, happy. Charles was very pleasant and I would think rather shy. He came with his new secretary, Michael Hazel.

With the coming of June the world was confronted with a war in the Middle East and Israel annexing much of the palestinian land. Routine continued and I made the observation that especially at Caldecote only 11 out of the 60 people present for a First Communion Mass actually went to Holy Communion. This was not just the presence of non-catholic friends but seems to be general state of affairs in this outpost. They had yet to catch up with Pope Pius X's 'new' rules about frequent Communion.

'My faith in human nature was dealt something of a blow today when a man, whom Brian and I had tried to help find accommodation, turned out to be pulling the wool over our eyes and had got through £13 in drink since calling here. How to cope with these many tall stories is a great problem and very taxing on one's patience and tolerance.'

Sr Aiden rather surprised me by telling me that the canon had confided in her that he thinks I am 'against' him or I am 'frightened' of him. This was just a bit shattering as I thought we had been getting on quite well together over the last few weeks since she had last mentioned the problem.

The feast of SS Peter and Paul on June 29th saw the introduction of more new rubrics relating to the Mass. We can now say the Eucharistic Prayer out loud in Latin and eliminating most of the signs of the cross etc. It looks as though this procedure will only be permitted once a month and on a Sunday.

The beginning of July was another historic first for English Martyrs when I celebrated an ecumenical marriage for the daughter of the Vicar of Teversham. He had come equipped with the SPCK pamphlet on Mixed Marriages. He said a few words at the end of the wedding and offered a couple of prayers.

The annual garden fete was celebrated at St Mary's Convent and raised £1100. But there I learned the sad news from Brother Bruno OP, a Grenadian, that Hawkesyard Priory was soon to close, and my contemporary Michael Callaghan whose ordination I had attended last year at Oxford last year had left the Order together with other contemporaries of mine. I am now the only one left of that group.

One respite in parish life was the annual clergy retreat. As much as anything it was an opportunity for the clergy of our far flung diocese to meet each other and compare notes as well as to receive necessary spiritual input. This year the retreat was held in Cambridge at St Edmund's House. The majority of the clergy present wanted to say their own private Masses each day which they did in relays. Ten of us chose to concelebrate which would eventually become the norm for such gatherings. Our spirituality must have been too fervent or the heat too much - it had reached 85 F -for our retreat giver, Fr Hamilton, on the last day promptly had a heart attack and I had to minister to him in Addenbrookes hospital. But summer was the silly season and I was approached by a mad opera singer who wanted to sing an aria during Mass. She said she had already met Dr Richens, the choir master, who was not over enthusiastic. But then thank heavens it was away again with mother by train to Rome and another memorable do it yourself holiday from 24th July - 10th August.

Even on return to work at the end of August, Rome was not too far away as Cardinal Dino Staffa had arrived to inspect the religious institutions in the city. He stayed at St Mary's Convent. He arrived with two crates of peaches and then promptly disappeared. The Sisters at the convent were buzzing with news about the Cardinal. Sr Scholastica remarked, 'Father, he couldn't even clean his bath after he had used it!' - no wonder the Church has been going to pot ruled by such curial characters.

Something of a crisis now developed in the Legion of Mary which had been doing great apostolic work around the parish visiting families. The vice chairman was insisting that they must take the Legion Promise or leave the group. I suppose they expected me to give a good example but I was was not too enamoured with the Marian theology of this declaration nor with the hard line taken by the officers. I impressed on them that their title to apostolic work was not in virtue of belonging to the Legion but because they were baptised members of the Church! With the departure of the student membership the group went into decline and the crisis regarding the 'promise' didn't help. We were left with just the president and the hard line 'Iron Virgin' as treasurer. As with other groups suffering from the 'Cambridge disease' it was thought best to close it down and think of something else to fill the need for outreach in the parish.

September was the month of ' autumn manoeuvres' when the bishop moved the clergy pawns around the chess board of the diocese. Gerald Moorcraft was to fall victim to this. He was a 'high flyer' and went off to Northampton as bishop's secretary and eventually settled in Princes Risborough where he remained for over thirty years or so as a Mgr and sitting on various diocesan commissions. We were sorry to see him move as he was a good foil to the canon and we became good friends during this time. Paul Hypher the curate at St Laurence's across the river was to take his place and we duly celebrated departure and arrival at the Clayhithe Hotel.

The celebration was followed the next day by an important deanery conference when we discussed the agenda for the newly formed Council of Priests and the various councils and committees which were to be set up. It looked as though we wouldn't have much time for anything else if we were for ever going to be on these committees. There was a lively discussion with everyone talking at once but the general tenor was constructive and John Fennell from Sawston had many important points to make. The canon also unloaded his district - the central area of Cambridge on to me. So he did have a district - it was always a bit of a mystery as to whether he had one or not. In addition to this I was also take a class of youngsters at St Mary's Convent on a Monday afternoon. These were children who were at non-catholic schools. I was to do this along with Paul Hypher and in going into the matter we found it to be a tremendous problem in view of the potential numbers involved. Sr Scholastica produced a list of the Catholic children at local non-catholic schools she had been surveying. If they all came to our classes there would be well over one hundred children!

'A dosser picked up a drunken women and brought her to the rectory plus a bottle of whisky. He was on the cadge and I could not get much sense out of her. In the end she decided to go not being convinced that I 'served Jesus'.'

A very friendly New Zealand priest, Ken Larsen, stayed with us for a few weeks and with him attended a multi-faith service in Great St. Mary's Church - I attended rather warily as this was all rather new ground. There was a small picket of protestors singing hymns in the rain- which featured on the TV news in the evening. The church was packed and Canon Montefiore, the University chaplain, preached a very orthodox and articulate sermon about dialogue with non- Christians. He was, after all, of Jewish origin and, I believe, married to a Catholic. It was a simple service of readings from the different Scriptures. Afterwards we met up with Canon Sweeney, and went along to the reception at Christ's College. We met the president of the 'World Congress of Faiths', Lord Sorenson, La Contesse de Pange and a Hindu monk in Saffron robes whom we couldn't understand at all. There was also there a white Sikh in traditional robes carrying a copy of Pope John's *Journal of a Soul* which was raffled. Anyway the congress seemed to have achieved something. There were, as expected, some negative comments from the parish about our attendance at this service. We had our own international gathering at the church next morning and I concelebrated with Ken, the New Zealander, an Argentinian Priest, and a lonely Franciscan friar back from South Africa who gave a demonstration of the Zulu language.

The next 'first' in these exciting times was the meeting of the liturgical commission at the rectory with a concelebrated Mass. The lay members were supposed to receive Communion under both kinds but the last concelebrant, who was not quite with it, downed the whole of the chalice and there was none left over for the laity. They sang a part of the Mass in English and part in Latin.

My first experience of a breakdown in communication was rather distressing. A sick call came from the hospital two hours late because they could not get in touch with us. Someone had died and Paul went round to the hospital while I was sent to comfort the grieving family. For sometime we were talking at cross purposes with me thinking they had been informed (surely after two hours) but then we realised, much to my embarrassment, that the news had not yet been broken to them. Luckily they took it well. As I noted, 'There is a danger of becoming rather desensitised in order to cope with these situations. You go from the happy celebration of a wedding or a baptism - the next minute to someone dying or a funeral. One's emotions tend to get rather strained and mixed up. I suppose it is the question of 'rejoicing with those who rejoice and mourning with those who mourn' , but it does take its toll.

The next real tragedy to hit us was the death of a little altar server, who was run over at a Cherry Hinton roundabout and killed. From what Paul gathered from the hospital his kidneys were removed without the parents' permission - in those pioneering days of kidney transplants. But there were the joyful times too as when my Jewish convert came to be received into the Church. It was my first adult baptism which preceded the Mass with his First Communion at St Mary's Convent. His wife and daughter were present and we celebrated with a chinese meal at the Pagoda Restaurant.

On the outskirts of Cambridge a new village was being developed called Bar Hill and I began visiting some of the families there. 'Discussions were in progress about building an ecumenical centre. It seems that the Free Churches aren't too keen about our participation. At a meeting of families it was said that the Catholics would not co-operate. The feeling is that the church should be non-denominational —which in practice would lead to a new sect. Hugo de Waal's line is very Low Church and questions the whole traditional Catholic theology of ordination. The problem of the Church in growing centres like this is certainly going to be great.'

We now started a regular Monday meeting to discuss work for the week. This was a very constructive idea, 'Paul is full of ideas and tends to dominate proceedings. After his experience with Paddy Oates, whom he had to shout down most of the time, he tends to do the same to us as well which rather irritates the quiet canon. However he has lots of constructive and positive thoughts.'

With the development in catechetics we thought we would like to help the teachers in our schools to keep up with the changing approaches to religious education so Derek Lance, an expert in the field, was invited to give a lecture. The response of the teachers was very meagre. It was a pity because the talk was really inspiring and we needed far more input like this. The teachers probably felt they didn't need to change and are threatened by all these new ways. The old way of the penny catechism was surely the well tried method. The editor and managing director of the Catholic Herald also addressed about forty assembled diocesan clergy. It was all enlightening but extraordinary how die hard some the clergy still are. Fr Baker from Downham Market also came. I hadn't seen him for years since he was a curate at Newmarket. He looked very sinister in his dark glasses and beret. He had refused the invitation to my ordination because it was in the 'hybrid rite' .

My weekly trips to London continued with the train fare rising to the extortionate sum of £1 return! It wasn't exactly relaxing with having to change trains and busses and then only having a very limited time to relax at home.

Parish life and worries about the family were beginning to get me down and I seemed progressively unable to cope with events. There were so many bits and pieces to do without being able to follow anything through and finish them off. This lead to considerable frustration. Elsie was very demanding and full of her woes which depressed me and living in community with the other clergy, however amiable they were, began to get on my nerves. Paul Hypher had incessant conversation at table which drove me into complete silence. The Catholic Reading Circle was on the point of collapse as fewer and fewer people came and yet dear Doris Browne was still ardent in her urgent vocation to get Catholic books into the local bookshops. I had another convert lady with whom it was most difficult to communicate. She had the most off putting habit of rolling up the whites of her eyes and could not remember from one week to the next what I had said. At the time I hadn't quite the experience to discern that she indeed had a drink problem. But we persevered until she was finally received.

One ambition was fulfilled when I was able to quote in one of my homilies from the prophet Amos, 'you fat cows of Bashan' not meaning anyone in particular of course, but the words did roll off my tongue and I hoped that Bubble and Squeak didn't take them to heart! But there were moments of relaxation with a trip to see the new film *Dr Zhivago* and a concert by Polish survivors of the concentration camps at Kings College on behalf of the Sue Ryder foundation. The famous debate between Ian Paisley and Norman St John Stevas enlivened things too - *'Roman Catholicism has no place in the modern world* was the subject of the debate at the Oxford Union. Ian, the ' black protestant', thumped his bible and

231

waved around an unconsecrated host emphasizing the ' blasphemy of the Mass.' The motion was heavily defeated.

Gerald called in for his farewell reception and received a handsome £80 present commenting on the ' utter disorganisation' at Bishop's House. He was soon followed by Bishop Grant himself who came on his first visitation of the parish. By a series of relays we managed to ferry him round to all the sick parishioners. I noted that: 'He really is a wonderful man and quite tireless, except for his bad teeth and shabby clothing'.

The First Sunday of Advent 3rd December marked an historic day as the English Eucharistic Prayer was introduced. + Charles found his sausages just a little too much for him at breakfast but he preached at the morning Masses which I celebrated facing the people, for the first time, at the 10.45 am Mass and this was to be repeated for the first time at the Christmas Midnight Mass. It was fortunate that the choir master was away sick and the choir was much depleted. We celebrated the event with some port and barn brack sent up from the convent.

The first Baptism

CHAPTER FOUR

ANNUS HORIBILIS
1968

My Christmas break was spent with the family and I met up with Dennis Hall in his new dockland parish of Canning Town where he seems to be in his element and making his mark. He had the sad news that several more of our contemporaries from Oscott had left the priesthood with one marrying a mother superior. All very cheerful but I did have a glimpse of an East End parish at work including Anchor House where we had lunch.

On return I found that the canon was to initiate a programme of house masses. I felt that this was very exciting and just what we needed to get more in touch with people in their own homes and I discussed the possibility of starting a few house groups with him.

Catholic clergy for some reason are mad about trains. Brian knew everything there was to know about the different classes and had set up a model railway in his room. Occasionally he would take some of his senior parishioners for a car ride and this inevitably took him to the main London line at Huntingdon to watch the train tear through. He was rather a speedster himself and some of his 'oldies' were a little shaken up by the experience. When caught by the police, on one occasion, for speeding he gave the excuse that he thought that it was all right to break the speed limit when overtaking.

Trouble began to loom after the introduction of more English in the Mass and a very long missive came from the choir master's wife demanding more Masses in Latin.

The Week of Prayer for Christian Unity got off to a good start with Bishop Grant coming over for a joint gathering in the Cavendish Laboratory with Bishop Brown of St Edmundsbury and Ipswich and Gordon Rupp, the Methodist President Elect. The last outshone them all and was particularly interesting regarding the Anglican - Methodist conversations and also those with Rome. The climax came when mother and I went to Westminster for the historic meeting between Cardinal Heenan and the Archbishop of Canterbury. The Cathedral was packed but outside there was a fare size picket of Paisleyites singing good old protestant hymns while we in the Cathedral drowned them out with a great waive of sound which increased as Canterbury advanced up the aisle . The whole place burst into prolonged applause as the Archbishop embraced the Cardinal. It was a really moving and historic occasion and one felt very privileged to be there. We didn't forget the Orthodox churches and a Serbian Orthodox Liturgy at St. Benet's, sung in English, was most inspiring and was a reminder of our historic links with the East.

While keeping an eye on the family at home one day I discover to my alarm that a thread I had put across a gap between the staircase and the outside wall had snapped and this could only mean one thing that the wall of the cottage was gradually moving outwards. This was due no doubt to the various windows that had been put in over the years that had weakened the ancient structure. Quite what we would do I just didn't know.

An end tail for this season of ecumenism was a visit to Great St. Mary's Church to listen to the Apostolic Delegate preach. It was quite an event but his sermon was more like a theological treatise and I really wondered what the average person made of it.

There were still quite a few derelict houses in Cambridge where some of the vagrants decamped. At this time, due to the prevalence of the down and out situation in the city, the Simon Community were trying to establish a centre in the city and Martin Wright their leader gave a very enlightening talk at the Catholic Nurses Guild. Before long this house would be established in an old pub in East Road. It would be a 'wet shelter' for those at the 'bottom end' of the problem and they would begin to do great work in the city. It provided the most basic accommodation and, on a regular basis, volunteers would take out hot soup in the middle of the night to some of the locations.

An ecumenical venture was set up called, 'People next door'. It seemed an excellent idea. The city was divided up into wards with street wardens who would keep an eye on people in their area. If anyone was in need they could put up the sign of the fish, the secret sign of the early christians, in their front window to attract attention. There was joint visiting around the areas, but how embarrassing it was when, at the open meeting, it was announced that when certain Catholic houses were visited the response was – 'We don't take part in this sort of thing, we are Catholics'.

Mass facing the people and English in the Liturgy was now the norm and generally people were very appreciative of being able to understand the Liturgy in their own tongue. There were even some rumblings among the laity about the amount of polyphony and Latin that we were still having at the 10.45 am Mass. The canon had put out a notice in the news letter asking for people's comments. One letter came back which was a great tirade against the use of English in the Eucharistic Prayer and a criticism of our 'Idiot Sermons'. Another came from the choir master inveighing against the bishop for not allowing a polyphonic Sanctus during a silent Eucharistic Prayer. There was nothing constructive in the letter at all and totally hostile. One could see this was very hurtful to the canon considering the gentlemanly and understanding way in which he, together with us, had been introducing the revised Liturgy.

In February our proposed house Masses began. My first celebration was at the Hall's in Comberton. About a dozen people came along but few went to Holy Communion. However I felt that this was something that we should have been doing for years. There followed simple refreshments and an opportunity to discuss parish life. It drew in people who otherwise might not have had much of a say and it was encouraging that so many were interested and enthusiastic. A month later there was to be another Mass which I celebrated with the Goodchild's at Girton - again there was a very positive response. This was to be followed by one at Professor Sheldon's (Professor of Japanese History). This too went well but a disappointing response to all the personal invitations that had been sent out.

Some times most peculiar situations arose. A strange French domestic working at Hope Nursing Home came for a chat - I didn't realise my French was so good! The upshot of it was that I had to go with her to the antique shop over the road to try and make the proprietor understand that she wanted to change her silver tea set. To add to this we received a circular from a priest in Aylesbury who wanted to set up a society to fight against the Neo Modernism that was supposedly destroying the faith of the people.

Our deanery meetings were becoming a little more relevant. We had abandoned the imaginary marriage problems of Titius and Bertha to take on more world wide issues. Pope Paul had issued an encyclical letter *Populorum Progressio* which was to become a classic in papal social teaching. This was to be the subject of discussion. Here was a new approach with everyone showing their ignorance of the problems and the need for us to respond to the issues raised.

The threat of nuclear war was never far away from our minds as the war in Vietnam rumbled on. A documentary film on nuclear war had been produced, *The War Game,* which was considered too horrifying to be released to the general public but it was shown at various smaller venues. Paul and I went to a showing at the Friends Meeting House together with clergy of other denominations. It was a most sickening and fearsome film about what would happen if a nuclear bomb dropped on this country. I was sorry I had to leave before the general discussion took place.

In response to an invitation from the Vicar of Girton, Anthony Leighton, I presided with him at said compline and then held forth on the Church and Sacraments to about 60 people. This was the first time since the reformation that a catholic priest had preached in the church. It was all very historic in those days. There followed an interesting discussion at someone's house with the vicar and the Baptist minister sitting at my feet!! The discussion got very theological - the development of doctrine etc - but none the less stimulating.

The canon's Silver Jubilee was a great event with quite a full church for the celebratory Mass. It was in Latin - but he insisted on celebrating at the temporary altar facing the people. Deacon and subdeacon were still in operation and afterwards the school hall was crowded out with people for the presentation which amounted to £500.

Easter went with a swing. The choir did its stuff but some people remarked that they were dying to join in but were unable to because of the elaborate Mass settings. My cousin Jonathan and his wife who were staying at home brought mother over for the Holy Week services which she enjoyed as she really had had no opportunity to take part in them before. This took her mind off the collapsing cottage that was giving real cause for concern. On top of this her car was out of action, due no doubt to the incompetence of our garage man, and she had walked to Mass at Kirtling - four miles and back and even got out her ancient bike. This was as much a cause of concern as with dad who was progressively loosing interest in the world around him.

It was shortly after Easter that we heard the disturbing news that Canon Diamond was to be moved. This was very unsettling as we were just getting to know him and him us. Who would come we just had no idea - and there were certain people we would rather not have! He was obviously destined for higher things - Vicar General or Bishopric?

It was not long before we learned that the canon's successor would be a Canon Paul Taylor at present parish priest of a parish in Peterborough. He was a science graduate of St John's College and so would have some knowledge of the town and university. He came over with his housekeeper, Maureen Harding, to reconnoitre. She was much younger than Lill. The canon seemed pleasant enough though perhaps a little brusque. Maureen seemed to think that she could manage the house alone - 'That's what she think', said Lil.

Meanwhile the bishop was talking about the possibility of an auxiliary bishop to assist him in this vast diocese. In the spirit of the times he consulted the clergy as to the sort of bishop we felt we needed. This was quite a revolutionary move and we had a deanery conference to discuss matters. Another revolutionary move by the bishops was the launching of the New Pentecost scheme. Every parish was canvassed as to its talents and expertise. But the whole thing was badly organised. In spite of the bishops' wishes that a lay person should give the appeal the whole thing arrived at such short notice that there was no time to brief anyone. On top of that all our leaflets went to St Edmund's House and their paltry few came to us. In the event the congregation filled in the forms with a generally poor response and we sent them off. But the lack of inspiration behind the whole enterprise, however good an idea it might have been, was more a, 'No New Pentecost', non event than that which was intended! It was not helped by the banner on the envelopes asking for donations: 'Your donation has made the New Pentecost possible'. The money went towards the setting up of the various national commissions throughout the country. The whole scheme was thoroughly criticised at the council of priests' meeting at the rectory with the bishop but Charles didn't seem too perturbed.

The 5th of June was a dreadful day and I nearly went crackers on duty with the number of marriages, tramps, baptismal certificates and telephone calls - the lot. You were halfway dealing with one problem when another totally different situation was presented and on top of this there was the tragic news that Senator Robert Kennedy had been assassinated. Everyone was touched with grief and felt involved as with the tragic death of his brother. The Solemn High Mass, the following Sunday, was for the repose of his soul. But generally the world seemed to be in ferment with serious student revolutions in France and not unaffecting students here.

A few days later, with the rain pouring down, Canon Diamond, after a good farewell meal at Whittlesford and a very joyous Mass with hymns, we sent him off on his way to Northampton. We were sorry to see him go. He had done a lot for the parish and although personal relationships were not always easy he was a very fatherly and approachable man and I was fortunate to have had him as my first parish priest. Frank would spend several more years as Administrator and Vicar General at the Cathedral before retiring to Great Billing where he died. Apart from a meal to which he invited us when he settled in at the Cathedral and other occasional visits we saw little of him in the years to come. This seemed to happen with clergy moves and we just pass each other like ships in the night.

Canon Paul Taylor DD

The Canon had hardly gone, when,with some apprehension, we awaited the arrival of the new canon - Paul Aloysius Taylor, with a Double First at Cambridge and for some years parish priest of All Souls church in Peterborough to which he would often refer in times to come. As Paul and Maureen arrived, Lill, Florrie and the unfortunate Marmie with pitiful mews were sent on their way and never to be seen again. So it was all change and, after a welcome meal at the University Arms, we got the impression that he was quite friendly and open and ready to communicate (so far). He was bald headed and a man in his fifties with a few eye sight problems and with a nervous cough. We were exhausted after settling him with all his impedimenta and were a little perturbed when he went round the rectory, at quite an early hour in the evening, locking and bolting every door in sight. We felt that this didn't augur too well for the future. Was he going to be strict in enforcing the 11 o'clock rule whereby all curates had to be in by that time? There was an incident recorded when one man in the diocese who was out late and, finding the door bolted on him, climbed up a drain pipe to get in and was badly injured in the attempt! But we curates had the advantage of knowing where everything was and who did what so, for the time being, we had the upper hand.

The new housekeeper seemed an efficient soul and the food was a great improvement and especially deserts for which the canon had a penchant. We showed him round the parish and a couple of weeks later he was inducted by the bishop into this prestigious church.

A new parish priest had taken over from Paddy Oates at Chesterton. This was Norman Smith, an easy going sort of chap, and he came in to discuss parish boundaries. He wanted us to take over St Vincent's Chapel, a tin hut (the original church of St Laurence's Parish) in Ditton Lane, and for us to give him Girton and district, thereby losing half my area. But it seemed logical to make the river the boundary and in the event things worked out satisfactorily.

Most people can remember, those who are old enough, where they were when President Kennedy was assassinated. The same question could be put to the clergy, who are old enough, 'Do you remember where you were when Pope Paul issued his famous Encyclical - *'Humanae Vitae'* ? - and so not long after Canon Taylor arrived the storm broke. For some time we had been expecting a statement from the pope after the discussion of the commission set up to look into the whole situation of contraception. The majority of the group came out in favour of some change in the discipline. Most people thought that, logically, there could be little change, but half hoping there might be some development in this teaching. Well, where were we when the news broke? We were counting the collection on the morning of 29th July and as I wrote in my diary, ' It was couched in terms far severer than any of us expected, having gone completely against the majority decision.' Of course the media were full of the news and we were all rather bewildered, to say the least, especially as the official commentator said that it was not an infallible pronouncement. The following day the press gave full coverage. Most of it was hostile though some admired the pope's courage in making this decision. Spain and Ireland were in full support but Holland and others were in ferment. 'I went home for the day and we spoke of little else. One wonders why the statement was made at all if it was not a definitive one.' With the parish priest very conveniently away the United States for a holiday it was left to Paul Hypher, who was on duty that day, to take all the calls of people wanting to discuss the matter. He was asked to make a comment in the press and it was printed as a statement by a ' Fr Z'. The Polish priest was not at all pleased since his name also began with the letter Z and disowned Paul's comments which were quite moderate in tone! By the beginning of August Cardinal Heenan issued a pastoral letter advising people not to abstain from the sacraments if they were in the position of using contraceptives, but it all seemed rather ambiguous. Joe Crehan on supply as usual that month, preached a very erudite sermon on the primary purposes of marriage. Malcom Muggeridge's programme was devoted to the subject. Charles Davis commented on it - now all bearded and still rather Catholic in his approach.

5th August: ' The controversy still rumbles on. Although at the moment one is still a bit doubtful. It does seem a grand call to humanity regarding the dignity and sanctity of human life which no doubt will further be eroded as time goes by.' It was however to take a terrible toll in some people's lives. Paul was called out to the tragic suicide of girl whom I had married two years ago. She had gassed herself and by her side was a news paper giving a report of the controversy. One of the parishioners in my district called in - she and her husband were a model family with several children. I had a frank discussion with her for some time and one realised that there were terrible problems when it came down to the practical living out of these ideals. The following day there appeared the famous letter to the Times commenting on the pope's declaration. One of the signatories was Fr Incledon the new chaplain at Fisher House. His views were also expressed in the Cambridge Evening News regarding the position of individual conscience. For the first time, for some years, my two uncles Reg and Wilfred met at the cottage and both of them, being very articulate, learned and knowledgeable and the fathers of large families, carried on for the rest of the day with an enlivening discussion on the subject until very late that evening when I had to get back to Cambridge.

7th August was yet another cool, foul day with torrential rain. 'One is becoming more and more personally involved in the unfolding crisis. Many Cambridge intellectuals wrote supporting Incledon's sermon. He has heard from the cardinal, almost agreeing with him. Now we wait to see if he is suspended. If he is then the prospect doesn't seem too good from one's own position and Paul is certainly wondering. We sit on the fence at any rate. If discipline is to be enforced merely for the sake of outward appearances and not for inner assent then something is wrong. It is extraordinary to think that conciliarism may rear its head again. Someone remarked to Paul that this could spark off a real reformation within the Church. No doubt the pope will be ultimately proved right and circumstances may make the present situation eventually irrelevant'. Such expressed the tension in my own mind.

8th August: 'More cloud and torrential rain which really sums up my mood. An *ad clerum* comes from the bishop on the subject in which he reiterates Cardinal Heenan's line, though his points on how to advise penitents really need some clarification- I found Newman's letter to the Duke of Norfolk on the Primacy of Conscience very much to the point.'

9th August: 'The weather is no better and the controversy rages on in the letter columns of the Times - quite extraordinary! The guttering gets blocked on the roof and the wet begins to seep through. So Paul, Jo Crehan and I get the ladders out and Paul clambers on the roof to unblock the offending pipe.'

11th August: 'We read Cardinal Heenan's letter at all the Masses; after Benediction at Hope one of the Ssters read the pastoral letter and the *ad clerum* to the assembled community in the convent chapel. Crehan as ever the academic historian, in his evening sermon drew parallels between the present crisis and that in the second century.

13th August: ' My day off and over to see Uncle Wilf at Ousden. The main topic of conversation all day was the crisis developing in the Church. The vicar general of Southwark was interviewed and sounded very harsh towards those priests who had spoken out publicly. Canon Diamond called in – but as yet no trouble on a large scale in our diocese'

14th August: 'On duty today and I had numbers of phone calls, including BBC Norwich, looking for Fr Incledon. On top of this a local academic phoned wanting me to sign his passport form. He was very upset when I told him that since I had not known him personally for three years I was unable to so do. He got very irate, saying that he was a personal friend of the canon. We used to get lots of these requests and it was particularly difficult in the shifting population of clergy and laity that is Cambridge .

17th August: 'The problem begins to rear its ugly head in the confessional'. One can say no more but it was to put one into a very difficult situation and state of mind. The following day I preached on the pope's forthcoming visit to Latin America and meanwhile there were rival demonstrations outside Westminster Cathedral regarding the Pill lead by a priest who had been suspended for his outspoken views. And so the controversy raged on with a Panorama documentary devoted to ' The Pill and the Irish' and an interview with a priest from Lima who proclaimed the marriage of Catholicism and Communism. But then, thankfully, the Church ceased to be headline news since the eyes of the world were now turned to the devastating events that were taking place in Eastern Europe - the invasion of Czechoslovakia by the Soviet Union and we watched in horror as the tragic events unfolded before our eyes on the television screens. However the controversy was not to go away and was a turning point for many in their relationship with the teaching authority of the Church. It affected ordinary people deeply and not necessarily those who were caught up in the practicalities. For example my uncle's old supervisor from Cambridge days now in his eighties and his unmarried daughter profoundly disagreed with the Pope's teaching. The general upheaval which led to many clergy resigning from the priesthood left many distressed. My mother, for one, was really in a state about the upheavals.'

This seemed to be a teaching that few really accepted and could it be that since it was not received wholeheartedly by the faithful could it be construed as not being infallible teaching? In the end as far as the confessional was concerned the problem just 'went away' as people no longer mentioned it or considered it a mortal sin. The perceived teaching authority of the Church had been so sapped in the eyes of ordinary people that they had made up their own minds and nothing that the pope or the clergy could say would really make any difference.

The controversy, then, like many others, 'disappeared' swept under the carpet and left unresolved. The Church's teaching, clear but seemingly irrelevant to most people's lives, only to be replaced in present times by a more damming indictment of the 'corruption' in the church mentioned by Fr McCabe in the light of the child abuse scandals.

In September terrible floods hit the region. At Dalham, near my own village of Lidgate, the waters were up to the bedroom windows and the rivers in the city had reached dangerous levels. It was at this time that the Sisters at Lady Margaret House 'came out ' in their new habits. There had been a great updating in nun's habits all round. Should they keep the old dress style, based on ninteenth century peasant garb, or move into the modern world with something a little more chic and trendy. The Hope Sisters, as already mentioned, had come out with a very smart modification of their habit. They still looked 'nun like' but you could now see that they had hair and legs and they looked quite normal. Sister Aiden bemoaned the changing fashion contemplating with anguish the two habits side by side on her bed. The Sisters at Bateman Street did the least - a slight modification of the wimple to show wisps of hair, a slight shortening of the skirts to reveal human ankles and something to do with their cuffs. But by and large they really looked much the same. With the Canonesses at Lady Margaret House we witnessed a transformation. One minute they were in ample flowing robes and veils half covering their foreheads and then it was all swept away and they appeared in what seemed to be cast offs from the Oxfam shop. Not having any veils they now had to think about their hair with hair-does and handbags. Mother St. Paul almost halved in size and Sr Thomas More still looking tall and distinguished sported a perm. The ordinary people were divided some liked the changes while others preferred a nun to 'look like a nun'.

Three new Eucharistic prayers came into operation at this time. It evoked little response from anyone except, not surprisingly, Dr Bennett, Professor of Medieval and Renaissance English and no doubt they flummoxed the Latin Mass Society. A reaction came shortly as the Canon used one of them– this was described as being 'for the intelligent'. But trouble was beginning to brew with the Latin Mass Society and the choir. Dr Richens tackled me about my homily on the new Eucharistic Prayers. I have no details of these comments!

Lunch with the Rev Hugo de Waal and his family at Dry Drayton proved a pleasant interlude and we managed to keep off The Pill controversy. However we did discuss possible cooperation at the new development at Bar Hill. He is certainly very Low Church and did not seem too concerned about who presided at the Eucharist or put much store by the theology of the Apostolic Succession. At the beginning of October the English Hierarchy issued a rather ambiguous statement on The Pill which pleased nobody though it did offer some relief to people. Certainly the Italian community were taking no notice of the controversy as there was a superabundance of babies at the maternity hospital on my next visit.

At Hope Nursing Home I was visiting a very distinguished patient whose importance I realised only much later. She was Dorothy Garrod, sometime Professor of Archaeology at the University. She was the first woman to hold an Oxbridge Chair and was famous for excavations on Mount Carmel. It was sad only to meet her in her final illness. I had prayed in the Bidding Prayers to, 'give strength to Dorothy Garrod'. This caused some amusement to the Sisters as she was proving somewhat difficult to control on occasions and the last thing she needed was 'strength'!

But October was to mark a time of personal sadness. My father's cousin Lilly Cross in the village had died suddenly and one of the other old villagers had died too. I went home for a half day to find that dad, who had been ailing for sometime, had had a slight stroke and lost the use of his right arm and his speech. During lunch he had another stroke and with difficulty we managed to get hold of Dr Batt. The canon allowed me to stay and so I kept an all night vigil with him. He said 'goodbye' to me with such finality that I wondered whether I would see him again. But it was back to work again for a few days until 16th October dawned which turned out to be particularly gruelling. Three sick calls all came in at once and it was difficult to prioritise with two at Addenbrookes and one at someone's home. On top of this a phone call came to say that dad had been taken ill again and rushed into Newmarket Hospital. When I got there late at night he was unconscious but I gave him the ministrations of the Church before going home. It was pity that I did not stay as, on arrival home, there was a phone call to say that he had died. Although he was nearly eighty and it was not unexpected it still came as a great shock to us all. My parents had been married only twenty eight years and for them life must have been a considerable struggle through the war years and trying to make ends meet with his work as wheelwright, carpenter and on occasion undertaker. The last few years had been so difficult with his declining health and it was fortunate that mother had the support of her two sisters. Mercifully I was given the week off to sort out family affairs and dad was laid to rest in the village churchyard not far from his parents and grandfather and the many friends at whose funerals he had officiated and whose coffins he had made. Both Canon Taylor and Brian Nightingale gave us support at his funeral. Many tributes came for him and he seems to have been well loved by people. Although our worlds were polls apart I never knew him to speak an angry word.

After some respite it was back to a world that had gone on without me and the first outing was a trip down to London with Canon Taylor for a meeting of the diocesan clergy at the Cathedral Hall at Westminster. The subject, one might have guessed, was – *Humanae Vitae*. Father Michael Richards was no doubt very good but I was still in no mood to really take things in. Although we had discussion groups there were no firm conclusions and some of us were still not too happy about things.

But the choir and the New Liturgy rumbled on. A letter from the choirmaster was delivered concerning the position of the choir during Mass. Since the temporary altar facing the people was positioned between the choir stalls this rather cramped their style. Dr Richens protested that since it had been announced that the altar was only an experiment it should now be removed forthwith so that we could return to normality. The Canon, however, was not to budge.

Was it divine intervention when the canon, returning the next day from a trip out with Fr Thompson from Huntingdon, skidded off the road and went through a hedge. Both were in hospital with concussion. The canon had a cracked nose and the car was a write off. But this event was to be followed by an unusual event. Professor Roy Calne had been pioneering kidney transplants in the city and one of his patients, one of the first to receive a new kidney had been working at the local petrol station. On visiting the isolation hospital I was kitted up with gown and mask to discover that he had developed a form of leprosy. A disease one did not expect to find in this country – as far I can remember he recovered and returned to work.

Mother was now alone at home and the aunts had returned to London for the winter so I went off to help her pack – jack the car up, turn off the water and shut the place down. It was all very sad and the cottage was cold and damp and dad's death had hardly sunk in. But I was glad that our Hungarian friend was able to drive her up to London where she would have the support of her sisters. Unfortunately, perhaps due to a nervous reaction she developed tinitus which plagued her for the rest of her life. But another disaster struck when aunt Elsie announced that she had discovered a lump on her breast. She had said nothing about it because of father's illness but it was now found to be malignant and so we were all in turmoil again. The operation was successful but there was quite a lot of hospital visiting down to the Miller hospital in Deptford on my days off. The train fare down to London was now £1.12.6 return and petrol had gone up by another 5d.

A couple of small domestic innovations came to pass by transforming what had been the communal television room into an office which entailed a lot of physical work and the housekeeper making our evening meal more flexible for up to now meals were at set times and we were expected to be in attendance. By now we had abandoned wearing cassocks in the house.

The Diocese now inaugurated study days on celebrating the new liturgy and one was organised for Clapham Park in Befordshire. We had a most enjoyable day rehearsing a four part Mass in English and at the Preparation of the Gifts we had a rather tasteful dance by some of the local maidens who bore the gifts to the altar.

We tried to celebrate Christmas after the Midnight Mass as usual. But the Canon would not join us – he needed his beauty sleep for the round of tomorrow. But we celebrated none the less with a wee dram and the usual barn back from Hope Nursing Home.

Mgr Gerald Moorcraft　　　　　**Mgr Harry Wace**

With Fr Brian Nightingale at Walsingham

CHAPTER FIVE

A NEW BISHOP ARRIVES
1969

The first of January had ceased to be a Holy Day of Obligation and this brought us some relief but we still celebrated the event in style at St Laurence's church with visiting clergy Tony Sketch, Bernard Nesden and Charles Davidson. It also marked the coming into operation of the new parish boundaries between our two parishes. The river now marked the boundary and we took over the small tin church at Fen Ditton which had been the original St Laurence's Church. On my first visit on the feast of the Epiphany I met Dr Russel Egget – the inventor of the Cambridge Slimming Loaf!

We were now organising a Mass at Comberton in the village hall so I went to make the acquaintance of the new incumbent at the parish church. I had quite a chat with his wife who said how difficult it was to reconcile her duties to her family with those of the Church and he, in spite of his family life, found life rather lonely – so celibates take note!

Outings for our altar servers continued and this year I was detailed to take some of them down to the spectacular Dick Whittington Ice Show at Wembley, along with Tony Sylvester. It turned out to be something of a nightmare especially as I was very new to driving. On the return journey thick fog descended, the thickest pea souper in years, and on a couple of occasions I lost my way and we did not arrive home will 1.45 am. With no mobile phones or means of communication the parents, needless to say, were frantic with worry.

Hong Kong flue was threatening and a shortage of vaccine was causing some concern with the press blowing things up into a major crisis. As a prelude to the Week of Prayer for Christian Unity I gave a talk at Bar Hill School. About thirty people attended and the short service of prayers and hymns was lead by Mr King, a Congregationalist. Five Catholics turned up. It was surprising how ill informed most people were including the Anglicans who wondered if I put much store by the Apostolic Succession. Mr King didn't believe much in creedal formulae either and seemed to want to forget the whole past history of the Church – so we were really starting from completely different basic premises. The question period rather got off the point – which was some relief – as a Catholic started questioning the extravagance of the proposed new inter denominational church. I think the ministers were just a bit deflated when they realised how 'orthodox' Catholics still were.

The actual Week of Prayer got off to a good start at Blackfriars where Ronald Speirs, the Presbyterian minister, Philips the Anglican and Alan

Keenan OFM were speakers. Speirs commented on how close the Presbyteri-an idea of the Eucharist was to ours. Another meeting at St Andrew's Baptist was a massive one with nearly 1000 people present – there was not much talk about unity but it was a great celebration. People must have been exhausted by this experience as there was a rather a poor turn out at the chemistry laboratories next to the church when Fr Henry St .John OP, one of the pioneers of the Church unity movement in this country spoke. His address was very good but I would think a bit too theological for the average person. The following day we had our Mass for Christian Unity to which a good number came -though rather poor from our own community- and the Separat-ed Brethren and their wives were invited into the rectory afterwards for the first time for refreshments. The week ended by attending a Serbian Orthodox Liturgy at St Benet's. The following day there was a Holy Hour of reparation because of the theft of the tabernacle and its contents from Great Billing Church.

For some time we had been thinking about forming a Parish Council. Paul Hypher came up with an elaborate plan and January climaxed with its launching at St Mary's Convent. I noted that, 'only about a hundred people turned up'! Dr Richens came up with a sensible amendment whereby the entire congregation should vote for the nominees. We were determined to push this one through willy nilly in order to get the people involved even if it turned out a fiasco.

February brought a surge of correspondence to the Canon's letter box regarding the liturgical changes and one letter from the choir master's wife complained that the clergy now projected too much of themselves while celebrating Mass. The Gregorian chant of the choir at sung Mass 'was intolerable and was more like the March to the Scaffold with unrelieved gloom and monotony'.

Scandals were hitting the Church and given full coverage in the newspa-pers: A Dominican priest went off with a black lady and a professor from Oscott College with a Mother Superior. The TV report that the chaplains at Amsterdam University wanted to marry was all in tune with the blizzards that were hitting the country at the time. This was the main topic of conversation at home and with my cousin's marriage having broken down after only two years it was not at all happy.

February 9th marked the elections for the first Parish Council. The voting took place during the sermon time at Mass and people seemed to enjoy the exercise – their first experience of democracy within the Church. Quite what Fr McKee, a visiting priest who said the 5 pm Mass, made of it, I don't know, since he was the organiser of the 'anti-neo modernists' group in Scotland. It was a pleasant evening counting the votes and we noted that Dr Richens and Dr Sanders, the President of Magdalene College, were both elected.

Evangelisation continued as I gave a talk on 'The Church in the Modern World' at Comberton Vicarage to a mixed group from different denominations. There followed a lively discussion and it can only do good in trying to break down the old prejudices between the Churches.

Lent was upon us and this time we had a Mission which was preached by two priests from the Catholic Missionary Society. They were Frs John Rawsthorne and Kevin O'Brien. They did great work preaching at all the Masses and doing a lot of parish visiting. This must have stood them in good stead as they were both, in years to come, to become bishops.

On 24th March the new Parish Council was inaugurated with Communion under both kinds. The whole structure was divided into various subcommittees. Dr Richens was elected chairman of the Pastoral – Ecumenical- Liturgy commission or PEL for short. Quite a tall order with such a wide coverage of subjects and I was deputed to be clergy representative. The meeting went off well a few days later and we met at Kathy Green's in Mill Road. We steered clear of the hot potato of Liturgy but everyone knew Dr Richens's position on that one anyway. In fact Dick Richens really tried to be quite 'with it'. I gave a resume of what was going on and what was needed regarding ecumenism and catechetics. The members of the commission were Bro Francis from De La Salle House, Florrie Prior, Kathy Green, Sr Scholastica IBVM, Mr Morgan, Eric Graef, and Mrs Bennett the wife of Professor Bennett.

The evening Mass for Palm Sunday, following the Italian Mass, was chaotic. The Italians had turned up *en masse* for the blessing of the palms and there was total disorder as the indigenous congregation came in – palms were strewn everywhere and there was uproar. The 5 o'clockers must have wondered whether they had come to the right church. We were regaled later in the evening by the choir's rendering of Liszt's Stations of the Cross. As with the plainsong the rendering was more akin to another March to the Scaffold.

April 1st marked yet another historic day with the announcement of the new auxiliary bishop for the Diocese (or was it all an April fool?!). He was to be a Mgr Alan Charles Clark, a former vice--rector of the English College in Rome and sometime parish priest of Blackheath; and this in spite of all the consultation we had had! We gathered he was a, 'safe, middle of the road sort of person', but also a member of CEPHAS. This was the Catholic Priests' Association set up to defend the Church against the 'neo-modernists'. Knowledge of this didn't exactly get the bishop off to a good start and he was regarded with some suspicion (though he later maintained he was only fifth columnist within the organisation!). Paul Taylor was not at all happy about

Bishop Alan Clark

the appointment and while at table Paul Hypher and I composed a suitable Limerick which went like this:

A papal domestic called Clark
Was Bishop'd quite out of the dark
You're far safer lead, without
dialogue Rome said,And from Alan's
not Flanagan's Barque

Fr Flannagan was the leader of CEPHAS and there was of course an allusion to the Flanagan and Allan comedy duo.

Good Friday was something of a nightmare. After an exhausting day hearing Confessions and hoping for an early night, the phone suddenly rang just before midnight. The Samaritans had a man who was threatening suicide and wanting to see a priest, and could they bring him down. Talk about passing the buck! Having delivered him they promptly informed me they were now off duty and were going home. So I was left with him for a couple of hours trying to reason with him. It seemed that he had been in hospital, so, having somehow confined him in the parlour, I went round to Addenbrookes where I was warmly welcome by the night staff about to celebrate Easter – they could not help – but they did get in touch with Fulbourn hospital whence he had discharged himself. They were unable do anything either as he had left voluntarily. In the end I phoned the police and persuaded them he was a real threat to himself and, very reluctantly, they came round and persuaded him to go with them to the station where they gave him a cell for the night. I must say that I was really at my wits end and felt like accompanying him down to the Cam and jumping into the river with him. With the all the confusion of Holy Week I don't know what the outcome was but hopefully it was a happy ending as there was no report in the newspapers of any local suicide. There was some consolation with the Easter Offering totalling £82.12.4.

The week off after Easter was really welcomed with the three having moved back to Lidgate for the summer. However, aunt Elsie's arm, after her mastectomy, seemed to be no better and she was in great pain and everyone was up the wall about it. Mother and I were planning to go to Rome again this year with Uncle Reg as he had never been to Italy before. Then disaster struck again when we learned that he had been for a check up and it was discovered that he had liver cancer– no doubt due to his heavy smoking. He was mother's favourite brother and it was a great blow to everyone.

Trouble was brewing again with the choir as we had introduced what they called 'mini-Vespers' which, according to the new Rite, consisted of a reduction from five psalms to only three. The homily was incorporated into the service but this didn't meet much with their approval either! ' Dr. Richens has made a comment that he thought that the readings should be in Latin at Mass, because it did not really matter if they were not understood by the congregation as they were a 'sort of incantation' over the people. One begins to wonder what they really understand Christianity to be.'

Canon Taylor prided himself that he didn't own a radio or listen to one – let alone watch the television. However with the trips to the moon and his scientific bent, he became hooked on the TV and was most embarrassed when found watching the box, jumping to his feet with a nervous cough and shrug of his shoulders. We weren't too happy about his artistic appreciation though. All the books in the dining room suddenly disappeared – flogged off. The carpet disappeared to be replaced with some horrible pale vinyl. It was just not in keeping with the room and the place really looked quite bleak.

The Hope Nuns were always good at cheering us up and on the bank holiday Monday we had a party down at the convent. There we danced with the Sisters! Brian cut quite a figure on the dance floor but I hadn't two steps to put together and hadn't done any dancing since the folk variety at primary school. Sr Aiden tried to teach me the Valeta and she said that I showed some promise!

The strange rules regarding Confirmation cropped up. I had special delegation as chaplain to the maternity hospital to administer the Sacrament in an emergency. I was called out to Addenbrookes where they were trying to resuscitate a baby. Since I was not official chaplain there I did not have the faculties to Confirm the infant and so I had to call on Paul to come round and confer the Sacrament!

I had been making arrangements for a monthly Mass at Comberton in the Village Hall and 15th June marked the first occasion. The Mass was quite well attended and we were rather short of seating.

My old headmaster from Laxton, Gerard Meath , who had been working at the Communications Centre at Hatch End, had now moved to Blackfriars as Prior. It was strange meeting him again on equal terms. He wanted the Dominicans to be integrated into the parish and we discussed using Blackfriars as a centre for conferences.

The annual clergy Retreat this year was at the Cenacle Convent in Burnham, Bucks. Paul Hypher gave me a lift. It was a very pleasant setting and there were a good number of clergy there. Apart from anything else it was an opportunity for clergy from this far flung diocese to meet each other. The retreat was lead by Abbot Passmore whose main theme was on prayer though he did take the opportunity to tear a strip off both the conservative and progressive wings of the Church. There was some relaxation as we watched the Investiture of the Prince of Wales on the Television.

But we were soon back to reality and an Irishman, on the cadge, had met with an unresponsive Canon. He then succeeded in kicking the front door off its lock. It was very difficult to see who was calling at the door and so a car wing mirror was installed just outside. This gave the housekeeper some sense of security when she went to open the front door to a caller.

'Bishop Clark made his first official visit to the parish. We had a deanery gathering and a Concelebration in English with the choir singing in Latin. The Mass was in honour of our martyrs Fisher and More and the Bishop preached on conscience – with obvious overtones. Brian and I were not too happy about his exposition and we had a heated argument afterwards until we were surprised by the bishop. I wonder if he overheard our comments – if so he now knows that we are 'dangerous'!!'

By mid July Uncle Reg was weakening so mother and I went down to Horsham to see him. He was quite philosophical about it all and took an interest in everything right up to the end when he was still annotating a volume of French Verse. He was well into developments in the Church and took an interest in everything and was studying the new *Missa Normativa* which had just been published for study. Stephen, who had received minor Orders at the English College, came home never to return, while aunt Marjorie, Uncle's wife, was very stoical and practical. He had been told that there was no hope and he took it all in good part saying that he was going to have to learn a musical instrument. He said he was all set to go and it was like waiting outside the headmaster's study to go in for an interview. He wanted me to read to him a passage from St John's Gospel and the story of the two disciples on the road to Emmaus. Like his first wife, Jessie, who was a great musician and member of the Royal Choral Society, when she was dying, he had been listening to Elgar's Dream of Gerontius. He was visited by Bishop Cashman shortly before his death on July 29th in 'the odour of sanctity' having just received Holy Communion and his family around him. His last words it seems were 'Holy, Holy, Holy.' His funeral was very joyful and we all wore white stoles. Five of us concelebrated and cousin Stephen played the organ. Later in the year we went to a Memorial Service in the Chapel at Christ's Hospital where he had taught all his working life. It was a most impressive service with a full chapel and choir and a moving eulogy preached by one of his colleagues. The choral rendering of Brahms's, 'How lovely is thy dwelling place' was quite overwhelming and I am afraid I was becoming quite overwrought. 'What with father, aunt and now uncle coming in quick succession there seems no end to the troubles. It is so difficult not having brothers and sisters and I am really wondering whether I should be earning my own living and trying to support mother.'

The PEL subcommittee continued to meet but Dr Richens was such a prophet of gloom and really quite impossible. We discussed the fabric of the church and he felt that the experiment with the temporary altar should now cease and we should return to the old High Altar. In some ways one could see his point of view as the canon did seem to be a bit dictatorial in spite of his democratic tendencies. However an architect had been employed to draw up a brief for the re-ordering of the church. In the face of this he was rather subdued as it was clear that this was the general wish of people that changes should be made.

The ill fated 'New Pentecost' scheme, already mentioned, resulted in the Hierarchy setting up the National Catholic Fund which was to finance the various commissions that were going to advise them on the future developments of the Church. A pastoral letter form the hierarchy read at all the Masses informed us of their plans.

One of those dreadful tragedies occurred which happened from time to time. Four Irishmen had been involved in a car crash. They had run into a wall at Bottisham Church on the A 45 and three of them had been killed while the other was left in a coma. I went down to the hospital – now the new Addenbrookes – to see him. There was no hope and so the medical staff were very anxious to obtain his kidneys. Professor Roy Calne came in to explain the situation and to get my backing. I said that it was OK but he had better tread carefully regarding the family who were coming over from Ireland as they might not be too happy about the procedure. In the event after a lot of toing and froing they gave their consent. It was a difficult funeral. Paul conducted the triple funeral and the survivor on his death was taken back to Ireland.

There were two rather charming eccentric sisters, P and C who dogged our steps from time to time and periodically went on the high wire. One day the medics arrived to collect C but she escaped their clutches and headed down Lensfied Road. Paul Hypher happened to be in the vicinity at the time and managed to fell her with a flying rugby tackle. On another occasion she was in hospital in rather a bad way and I was called round to anoint her. The staff in their zeal and obviously of an older generation stripped the bedclothes off her naked form so that I could anoint those parts of the body that had long since been removed from the Liturgy. 'That won't be necessary', says I, and proceeded to make a simple sign of the cross on her forehead with the holy oil. She recovered and we never exchanged details of this rather embarrassing encounter.

Father Sebastian Bullough OP had also died suddenly. I had a word with Fr Paschal at Blackfriars who said that he had practically died of a broken heart due to the changes in the Church. He would have enjoyed the full scale polyphonic Latin Mass we conducted that weekend and as a concession they enjoyed full scale Vespers in the evening with the five psalms. He might not have been too happy at our celebration on St Dominic's day with the brethren where a Dominican Nun, not wearing a habit, was seen smoking and addressed the Prior by his Christian name!

The Liturgical dramas continued at our sub committee meetings and we had nearly reached an impasse over the 10.45 Mass. We wanted to introduce some English singing and participation but it boiled down to the fact that Dr R found it impossible and impractical to do this.

Elsie had now taken to breeding budgerigars and was intent on giving me one, so I hunted around for a cage. The bird duly arrived and I named it Ichabod. He became a great talker and I successfully taught it the first half of the Hail Mary. He couldn't quite get the hang of the last few words which ended with a rather a rude noise.

Joe Creehan had supplied for the summer, as usual, and another Jesuit Fr McComber had also helped out. Peter Wynekus from our diocese, who had recently been ordained, came for some experience and I was able to take him round the parish. He was a keen astronomer so was able to share some experiences with my telescope on the tower, where there is a fine view of the city and Fenners cricket ground.

The wedding of the year took place on August 9th. It was between Tony Sylvester our MC and sacristan and Maria Murray, the sister of Tom, one of our church students. He was given the works with Mass at the High Altar and a full Richens polyphonic choir. Canon Diamond came over to celebrate the event.

With the holiday in Rome scuppered due to Uncle Reg's death, two of his boys, Stephen and Andrew came down to stay for a few days during the summer and I was able to take them out to see the sights. Paul Hypher rang to say that Brian Nightingale was being moved to his own parish at Swaffham. This was all rather sad as I had got to know him well over the last few years and thought a lot of him.

Back to the fray in September as more Liturgical changes were imminent. At Lady Margaret House we started things early and all the nuns came up round the altar for the Canon of the Mass. We also had a meeting at St Mary's to work out some scheme for catechetics. Gerard Meath, Sr Scholastica and Paul Hypher were the driving forces and Canon Taylor just let us get on with things. We met several times with parents at the convent and decided to set up a catechetical centre at Blackfriars. The idea stemmed from the promises that parents make at their child's baptism that they should be the 'first and best teachers of their children in the ways of faith'. We would run a series of lectures at Blackfriars on various aspects of the Faith. This we named CRESE or Catholic Religious Education Study Evenings. Their purpose was to train up catechists and then once a month we would have a 'Family Day' at St Mary's Convent. Here the children at non-catholic schools would be instructed by the catechists and the parents would be given ideas on how they might convey the Faith to their children during the coming week. In addition to our original group we co-opted some high powered academics to sort out the syllabus. There was Mary Thatcher from the Oriental Department - a very diminutive lady with great character, Dr Nora Wilson a lecturer at Homerton College, and Margaret Wileman the Principal of Hughes Hall.. One was amazed at Paul Hypher's energy and some of these meetings would go on late into the evening. All in all this was very successful although there were practical problems of maintaining impetus with changing personnel. It certainly involved the parents, some of whom really took to their responsibilities. Sr Scholastica showed just a little 'snobbery'– discovering how good one parent was teaching the children, commented, 'Oh Father – and he's only a plasterer'! – Well she was from good breeding!

At this time a young Scottish lad aged fourteen suddenly turned up wanting instruction in the Faith. We likened him to Bishop Grant who had come for instruction at that age while a student at the Perse School. He was certainly keen and was even seen at daily Mass before school. We really wanted him to wait until he was a bit older before he made this decision but he was determined and after his course of instruction he was duly received into the Church at Hope Nursing Home. The Sisters kept an eye on him in the succeeding years. Sadly he found, as he grew to maturity, some of the Church's teaching incompatible with his lifestyle and for a while he joined the Anglican Franciscans and, as so often happens, I lost touch with him in later years.

School Masses continued at St. Bede's – how I hated that regimented procedure with the altar stuck on the stage and the children *en masse* looking really bored as they sang their lack lustre hymns. St Mary's Convent was a little better with the school Masses and I was still going there once a week to instruct some of the teenagers from the local grammar schools. I had a lot of attitudes to change: 'What is the soul?' The classic answer came: ' A round white disc that gets covered with black spots when we sin.'!!

Brian Nightingale left to go to Swaffham in Norfolk. His going was great loss. He was to live in an old barn at the back of the church until he had built the new house and I visited him on occasion. The church had been a more or less do it yourself job by another character of diocese, Fr Gerry Langley. In later years as parish priest of Bury St Edmunds he attempted to put in a central heating system. This resulted in various pipes emerging from walls which never went anywhere. For a short time we had Fr Eddie Hill who had been recovering from a heart attack and so he wasn't able to do much.. Brian's replacement was Fr Tom Feighan. He was a very simple Irishman. At least he always gave that impression. How anyone understood him I don't know and he just couldn't stop talking in a very nervous hurried way. He was always a great source of irritation to Paul Taylor who had got to know him when in Peterborough and could only blame himself for his arrival at the Rectory. To add to the parish priest's irritation a Maltese priest, Benjamin Camillieri, was detailed to us to improve his English. It was all very unsettling when a change like this happened as it threw the whole organisation into chaos. At a staff meeting I was now deputed to take on Fulbourn Mental Hospital together with Brian's old area that covered Cherry Hinton, Fulbourn Village and right down to Linton. There was a catechism class at Fulbourn Village run by the Richardsons. I really wondered how I was going to be able to cope.

Dick Richens now came up with a stunning suggestion that we must have a referendum on Latin versus English. The Canon went along with this but the form devised was so complex that there was much confusion in the answers that came in that he was nearly apoplectic. At our PEL meeting we had an analysis which was very weighted in Dr R's favour; his conclusion was that there was a great demand for the Latin and little enthusiasm for singing in English. About this time the Latin Mass Society issued a document under the redoubtable Cardinal Ottaviani's name (whose motto was *'semper idem'* – always the same') attacking the 'new' Mass. It seems that we were all heretics denying practically every doctrine there was. It was ironic that a man so keen on obedience to the Pope should be attacking him and the Council in this way.

Fulbourn hospital, however, was my main concern. It had opened in 1858 rejoicing under the name of the County Pauper Lunatic Asylum for Cambridgeshire, the Isle of Ely and the Borough of Cambridge. It was one of those huge imposing Victorian Asylums with a warren of corridors and wards for the more permanent patients and new buildings where temporary and acute patients were treated. At its peak it held over five hundred patients and during the time I was there. During the 1960s, the hospital became internationally prominent for its pioneering therapeutic community, under Dr David Clark, who was the last holder of the title of Medical Superintendent, and later Consultant for the Cambridge Psychiatric Rehabilitation Service. This was largely lost on me at the time and the whole responsibility was very daunting as I had had no training in dealing with mental patients, apart from those that turned up on the rectory doorsteps. Again it was the 'drowning syndrome' and I really wondered what my role should be. As ever I had to find out for myself. One man on the loose in the foyer would always ask me how old I was, whether I was married and how many children I had but he had the amazing ability of being able to tell you on what day of the week any particular date in the calendar fell upon. This hospital was more forward looking than others in its use of drugs to control inmates and the doors were left largely unlocked. The huge wards with senile patients were very depressing. They just seemed to be there, waiting, as it were, on the conveyer belt to be shipped off into the next life. It was very sad to see elderly parishioners known outside that were now confined and very distressed in their new surroundings and I learned there was a category of patients known as 'dilapidated', since they were literally falling apart. People just seemed reduced to anonymity and some abandoned by relatives and friends. Some had been there all there lives as had the staff and it was very difficult sometimes to distinguish staff from patients. I had two or three regular Communicants, among them was Pat, a little hunchback lady whose version of the Lord's Prayer always included the invocation, 'thy King not come'. This compared well with some of the children's interpretations of our well known prayers - 'Blessed be the fruit of nylon Jesus' or 'Harold be thy name'. In Kent house, the more short stay department, much time was needed to converse with some patients but there just wasn't the time with all the other commitments one had. It took ages to walk round the hospital and very often by the time you had found the patients you wanted to see they had been taken off somewhere else for treatment. They had a full time Anglican Chaplain who was a little critical that I couldn't take part more in the community. A separate part of the complex was also the Ida Darwin hospital where there were terrible cases of incurable and deformed children. One admired the staff that had little to show for their efforts and all they could do was to keep the children clean, try to entertain them and give them a lot of love. One is not surprised that people advocated euthanasia. In the end I was just frustrated that I could only partially do a job and with little to show for the time I had put in. It was with some relief on my occasional day off at the cottage I could

255

use my hands in repair or construction work of a practical nature and let out my tensions.

November 9th: 'Tom in all innocence (?) said the Eucharistic Prayer of the Mass in English at the 10.45 am (we still kept the Canon in Latin at that Mass) and thereby caused consternation in the ranks – he must be our secret weapon!' We were getting letters criticising the way we celebrated Mass in the new rite. We were gradually coming round to the idea that we would have to put on an extra afternoon or evening Mass for the Latinists and so free the main morning Mass for an English sung version.

In the meantime a new Parish Priest had been installed at St Laurence's. He really seemed to be the old school Northern Irish type of priest. He found Cambridge very difficult to cope with and John Drury, who became his curate, on occasion received phone calls from way out in the fens asking him to collect his colleague who was 'somewhat worse for wear.'

December brought some bitter weather and snow and on top of that a flue epidemic swept the country. The Canon and Maureen went down with the bug and went into Hope Nursing Home for a spell. This had some advantage with them both being out of the way as the three of us curates were treated like Lords by the Sisters and we could do our own thing. Fr Denis Roberts, the Diocesan Treasurer, due to the flue died suddenly. This was a great shock to his two brother priests and not least to the rest of the diocese where the shortage of clergy was beginning to be a serious problem. 1969 had like 1968 been something of an *annus horribilis*.

Tony Sylvester
Sacristan & MC

CHAPTER SIX

PARISH COUNCILS AND LATIN MASSES
1970

The New Year brought the sad news of the death of Captain Huddlestone of Sawston Hall. He was a descendent of St Thomas More and the Hall had been a centre of Catholic resistance during the Penal Days and of outreach to the neighbourhood in happier times. His nephew, Timothy Russ, then study-ing at Oscott was eventually ordained a priest and came as an assistant priest in our neighbouring parish.

I soon became aware of how challenging the work at the mental hospital was to be in relating to patients. They required more than the administration of the Sacraments and although you were not a trained psychologist neverthe-less patients expected you to engage in conversation and to listen to what sometimes were very bizarre stories. With very little knowledge of mental illness it could be a very dangerous path to tread and I wished that I had had proper training in this work.

Fr Guy Pritchard, parish priest of Ely would, from time to time, have a mental breakdown due to his experiences as a prisoner of war in Burma. Because of Guy's illness we had to help out from time to time. He had the habit of developing problems at the busiest times of the year and responsibil-ity for his parish fell upon us. Another priest from Peterborough, Fr Reggie Atkinson was having similar problems and was being treated in the Hope Nursing Home. With his illness Fr Hill left us to take his place in Peterbor-ough. Things were becoming very difficult and the clergy were becoming more and more stretched. On top of this the local laundry refused to take albs or altar linen so Maureen had to wash them herself.

One morning, on opening the Church, I found to my horror that a young couple had been locked in overnight. How I missed them the night before when checking the place before locking up I don't know. 'Mrs Mann', as we called one good lady parishioner – she came in trousers and wore a cloth cap and hid behind a pillar at Mass – drew our attention to some 'wetness' in the straw by the crib – 'Fr it's yellow', she said. Poor things – thank heavens there was straw there and one was sure that the Holy Family did not mind their necessity.

The Canon was assured by Dr Richens that people came up to thirty miles to attend the Latin Vespers on a Sunday evening so he announced at the service that he would like to meet these people to have a chat – but no one came forward! Still I had my Christmas break and went home with two chickens and a cake thanks to the Hope Sisters.

My rota, one week, was saying Mass at Lady Margaret House in Grange Road. The Sisters were very hospitable but breakfast was a great trial. Whereas the Hope sisters would leave you in splendid isolation apart from the omnipresent Sr Aiden, breakfast at Grange Road was a communal affair where deep theological issues were tackled over your boiled egg. It was just too early for such stimulation.

The first part of the new Rite of Mass now sprang into operation at the various centres and was generally well received. However there was some consternation at the 10.45 am Latin Sung Mass when the Canon introduced it for the first time. This was the time when we lived by duplicated hand outs as the final editions of the various prayers had not yet been properly printed. Brian had made one or two nice *faux pas* – 'Would everyone please pick up their pink slips', and, 'We'll do number two for the Canon'. A slight titter went round the congregation! With the large new altar missal published one member of the Latinists brought along the whole missal to check up that we were following the correct procedures.

Unity Week came round again and there was an historic sermon by Cardinal Willebrands of the Vatican's Unity Secretariat at Great St Mary's Church. He had lots of interesting things to say and thought the Anglican Church might reunite with us while keeping its own distinctive Rite, similar to the arrangements with the Eastern Rite Churches. However it was couched in such theological language that I am sure most people would have found it difficult to follow.

Gerard Meath preached at our Unity Mass which was well supported. In the evening I had a former enclosed nun in solemn vows round to see me – she wanted to marry her first cousin who was a laicised priest. How many impediments here needed a dispensation? – My goodness we did get some problems in Cambridge. The week ended with a big gathering at St Andrew's Street Baptist and Catholics in London went on a pilgrimage of reparation to Smithfield where the Protestant Martyrs had been burned at the stake.

After several high powered committee meetings the first CRESE meeting took place at Blackfriars. Over a hundred people turned up and a very enlightening talk was given by the Scripture scholar Joe Rhymer on the developing idea of God in the Old and New Testaments. Afterwards people divided into groups to discuss the application of the talk to the various ages of children. With people worrying about children and relatives lapsing his interesting comment was that few of those who had been at school with him were still practising their faith, so it is no new phenomenon.

Come February we had introduced the rest of the new Liturgy, with some relief, though there were problems at the Linton Mass centre where one parishioner became very upset.

The Canon now became very excited about his plans for introducing Planned Giving or an envelope scheme for raising money in view of his proposals to re order the sanctuary to accommodate the renewed Liturgy. The amount given by the faithful was not at a very realistic level and we learned that Harry Wace at Kings Lynn had threatened to get a part time job if people didn't pay up more. We had a joint meeting of the finance committee and PEL to meet the architect regarding his plans. Needless to say Professor Bennett and Dr Richens shot him down but generally the people were in favour of the plan.

A pleasant interlude occurred following an invitation by Gerald Moorcraft to come over to the Cathedral with Nicholas Lash. I thought for a moment I was going to get my marching orders but it was a pleasant social occasion with the Bishop and Jim Marks, the catechetical director for the diocese. The Bishop seemed quite laid back, as was his won't, regarding the current diocesan problems. I was back in time to try and sort something out regarding the catechism classes at Fulbourn. In spite of my letter to parents there were no additional children and some didn't even bother to answer my letter. But the day ended on a cheerier note with a pleasant house mass at Trumpington.

The next CRESE talk was given by Fr Drostan McClaren OP. Unfortunately it was so intellectual that I am sure that it was lost on most people. Numbers were keeping up with about ninety people present and the discussion groups afterwards seemed to be much appreciated by the participants.

The blizzards of February had turned to rain and I had to go to the Carmel at Waterbeach to take a sick nun Holy Communion. It was in the forbidden *clausura* and it looked as though the Sisterhood were expecting the end at any time as she was all done up in a white sheet and looked quite ready for burial.

The Abbot of Downside had been giving a parish retreat which went down very well and I had been roped in to be the correspondent or secretary to the primary school managers. I suppose it was good experience for the future but it was deadly boring and the main topic of conversation was the outdoor toilets. This problem was never resolved at least while I was there. A new head teacher, by the name of Barry Jones, had now been appointed. He was a young man and a breath of fresh air after Mr Bates who had been at the school for as long as many people could remember.

My attempts at visiting patients at the Fulbourn Hospital were continuing to be incredibly frustrating. It was all right regarding the inmates who had been there since time immemorial but it was the transient population whom you could never pin down or find. In desperation one afternoon I just gave up and went for long pointless car ride to Saffron Walden and Sudbury. It really is difficult to know what to do as there is no one to give any advice. Canon Taylor was not much help as he had had no experience of mental hospitals either. One of our regular parishioners had become a patient – a lovely lady – and it was most distressing seeing her restrained in what I suppose was a padded cell and I was really upset for the rest of the day. The hospital is all right in small doses but it is just too much with one case after another. The parents in Fulbourn village were still quite unable to organise themselves for their catechism classes and I was in the absurd position of having to drive out the five miles to collect the children and deliver them to the catechist, Mrs Richardson, who lived only a few hundred yards away from where they lived. I became just a sort of clerical taxi service.

The blizzards continued into March and Professor Moule, who held the Lady Margaret Chair of Divinity, came to supper. He was a most charming man and delivered a talk, one of a series, from our pulpit.

The health of Enid Porter, one of my regular communicants and caretaker of the Folk Museum just across Magdalene Bridge, was deteriorating. She had a heart condition and her legs were very swollen but she still managed to sit in her little office to welcome visitors. She was a fascinating character and had written several books on the history of folk lore in the Cambridge area. On this occasion we discussed witchcraft and she informed me that an initiated witch came to our church on Sundays. She never revealed her identity and we never noticed any strange goings on or sign of an accompanying cat.

The PEL subcommittee meetings continued to meet regularly but were becoming a very unhappy occasions. Poor Richens had to read out a letter from the Canon criticising his management of affairs. He felt that people were afraid to approach the clergy and freedom of speech was being suppressed. Matters were getting out of proportion and irrelevant to anything that we were trying to do. Cathy Green's suggestion for a Children's Corner in the church came as a welcome diversion.

The question of sex-education in schools is no modern preoccupation since the Bishop issued a pastoral letter to be read at all the Masses at the weekend. The content of this I have no recollection.

The following day I had an unnerving experience. I was conscious in the night of the door to my room being opened and shut but fortunately I was not sufficiently awake to react but, subconsciously, did find it strange since the heavy door was quite tight fitting. On getting up the next morning I found that my clothes were missing! Was it a practical joke by the Canon? On coming down stairs I found Paul in a state of consternation. Someone had got in during the night. There was a ladder up at the window and my clothes were in a heap by the safe. Luckily my keys were not in my trousers and it was lucky that I didn't wake up. The mystery was never solved but we concluded that it must have been an inside job for the person to have known where the keys might have been. For some time I wondered whether the Canon had thought I had been sleep walking!

Guy Pritchard from Ely, as Holy Week approached, was beginning to have another nervous breakdown but luckily Tony Philpot was helping out. He had just returned from South America. He had volunteered to do five years, but after six months they could find him no work to do and so he came home!!

The snow continued and it was bitterly cold. The new Rite for the Easter Services was well received and the Easter Offering went down by £40. Obviously people were beginning to 'plan their giving'!

The plenary session of the parish council, after its first few months in operation, now discussed its constitution. People seemed very discouraged because the Canon was not really accepting the democratic element and wanted them just to rubber stamp his wishes. This of course was mainly to do with the Liturgy and one can understand the dilemma. If we put things to the vote there would probably be no change at all especially in the language of the Mass and so in some respects he just had to push things through.

We had volunteered to be drivers for the Simon Community soup run. So on one occasion I turned out in disguise to take out a couple of students and we were on the run until about 2.15 am. It was quite exciting clambering through derelict houses where some of the men were dossing in quite dreadful conditions. We stopped and chatted to one man who was living in a hut at the bottom of someone's garden but we left four others in a drunken stupor in an upstairs room in Victoria Road. Another had taken up his abode at the bottom of the steps at Great St Mary's church near the warm boiler house and we ended up in the market place looking under the tarpaulins. I was rather worried that cruising police cars might pick us up for loitering. Not having clericals on for 'protection' was quite an interesting experience and I don't think the students could quite make out who I was.

The next CRESE meeting was lead by Sr Margaret of Jesus of Corpus Christi College in London who spoke about the Redemption and we continued to have very good numbers. The following month it was Paul Hypher on Sacraments and Grace.

Charles Davidson was one of the great characters and elder statesmen of the diocese. He had been at Kirtling when I was brought along in my Moses basket so I felt some affinity with him. He was now, in his old age, chaplain

261

to the Carmelite Convent at Waterbeach. Here we celebrated the inauguration of the new 'face the grille' altar in their little chapel. We were entertained
to one of their 'dear little breakfasts' afterwards.

April 30th was another significant day as the new Mixed Marriage laws
were released. No longer was the non-catholic party required to make a
formal promise to bring up the children as Catholics though this remained a
requirement for the Catholic party. We were none too happy about this. What
point was there of requiring this of a totally lapsed Catholic especially if the
non-catholic party was the stronger of the two in the Christian faith. It really
didn't seem to make much sense. At least it was the first time that the clergy
had received the document before it was released to the press.

We were never short of tragedies. The Poles had a vibrant community
and on occasion would turn out in national dress. I was called out on an
emergency call to the hospital. A beautiful nineteen year old girl had collapsed and died just after the celebrations. And there she was in the mortuary
still in her national costume. The parents were in a distressed condition. What
could one say in circumstances like this ? – just to be there I suppose. Planned
giving also began on this day. The canon had had a series of lunches to
promote the scheme, the expense of which were rather criticised, and only
about half the envelopes came back on this first occasion. No helpers turned
up so the canon and I had the job of undoing each envelope and recording the
contents. In all there was £120 from the envelopes (£180 had been promised)
and £80 from the loose collection which I suppose wasn't too bad.

An important clergy meeting was to be held at Woodhall Conference
Centre and we had a deanery meeting to prepare for it. Although my contribution to proceedings was as usual rather incoherent we did get down to
discussing the possibility of married deacons and part time priests. Tony
Philpot together with Larry Howlin from St Neots had some useful things to
say but Larry along with Paul Hypher tended to dominate proceedings.
Canon Taylor is not a very good chairman in that regard.

A step forward was made at the latest meeting of PEL. Richens gave up
possible control over English singing at the 5 pm Mass so now I was given
the job of trying to do something about it. Already at Linton Mrs McGay had
got a small choir going and at the other two centres, St Bedes and Fulbourn.
I accompanied them on the piano during the Offertory for 'Come Holy Ghost'
and they all sang quite well. At last at a Fulbourn meeting they sorted out a
rota for parents to collect and deliver the children to the Sunday school, while
a chaplains' meeting at Bury hospital painted a depressing picture of future
developments for a new hospital with larger buildings which would be more
impersonal in tone.

To keep us in contact with the hospital we now have a bleep system. This was a sort of walkie talkie system that cost us £80 a year to hire but it did give us a little more freedom of movement.

One house Mass at the Cowie's in Fulbourn was followed by a very useful discussion about married deacons and they all thought that it was a very good idea.

In the middle of June, Bishop Clark came for his first Visitation of the parish and we found him quite congenial company. We even revealed to him the limerick that we had composed on his accession to the mitre. He took it in good part but was a little bemused.

However I was very fed up at the Fulbourn Mass Centre where few people rallied round to help to get the hall ready and made little effort in response. What struck me coming home were the crowds coming out of the Methodist Church being warmly greeted by the minister with a shake of the hand – do we find anything like that in our church? We tried to do this at OLEM but our greetings were not always met with much enthusiasm as people seemed to want to escape as quickly as possible. We ferried the bishop round the parish in relays. I took him to meet Miss Porter at the Folk Museum and also two new French widows recently added to my sick list – a Madame Walsh and Madame Glochner – real characters and the bishop was able to banter with them in French. We ended up at Elsie's and he was suitably impressed. He is a very good mimic – especially of the Canon driving his car (a night mare experience when he gets going at speed). He thought that large scale moves were imminent this year so I suppose I shall have to think about packing my bags. He thought that the Church would continue to loose a lot of members and our present situation would be a 'holding operation'. This was not surprising when I learned that the rota of parents I set up to bring children to catechism classes had collapsed already. They expect everything to be done for them.

The last meeting of CRESE took place – numbers were down to about fifty and Gerard Meath OP gave a talk on Liturgy and Prayer.

Although I was now chaplain at Fulbourn hospital I was still called round to the maternity hospital in an emergency. The latest emergency visit, just as I had sat down to supper,was the child of two seventeen year olds. It was very distressing watching it dying and the parents were distraught.

Mr Heath was elected Prime Minister and the woes of the Church continued to be in the public eye. Fr Wingfield-Digby a mature SJ left the order to get married and in Rome the Pope was confronted by over 1000 traditionalists demanding the restoration of the Tridentine Mass and asserting that the Church was perfect and needed no change– the poor old Holy Father pleases no one.

The Bishop's intimation about moves proved true as Paul Hypher announced that he was soon to be transferred somewhere - at least it may give me another year's grace. But what would we do about CRESE which was just finding its feet? There seems to be no stability and so how can we build up any sense of community?

'As if the Church had enough problems there were now serious difficulties brewing at home. The cottage roof was still bowing the walls out and an estimate of £3000 pounds was given by a local builder for repairs. One side of the cottage was buttressed up to prevent completely falling outwards. I couldn't see mother selling up. The problems of an only child in this profession! The simplest thing now would be if we all died off in quick succession.'

I was summoned round to a parishioner's house to collect some bottles for the fete – she had two garages and a colour TV and hadn't the energy to bring them round herself! – in the event they added to the overall profit of about £700. It had been a glorious day with temps up in the 90's and as usual the event was held round at St Mary's Convent.

The first national dock strike loomed as well as a final confrontation between the Canon and Dr Richens. While on my third memorable trip to Rome with mother the question seemed to have been resolved for on August 16th an extra 6.15 pm Sunday Evening Mass was inaugurated for the Latin devotees. Matters had come to a head when we tried to introduce an English version of the Responsorial Psalm at the 10.45 Mass– the choir would have nothing of it and resignations were threatened. Some people in fact preferred to go to the midday Mass in Polish rather than come to an English Mass! The 6.15 pm Mass was, however, to be in the new Rite. Dr Richens was not an out and out traditionalist and just wanted his Latin and was quite happy to accept the new *'Missa Normativa'* as it was called. He founded the ALL- or Association of Latin in the Liturgy as opposed to the LMS - the Latin Mass Society who took a hard line. In fact with the LNER (The Latin Never Ever – a group we invented) we were becoming more like the railway system which appealed to the canon, our railway devotee. He was quite convinced that the whole thing would die out very quickly – but how wrong could he be with the initial attendance of nearly 200 – and of course it went from strength to strength. 'He should have left things as they were', I recorded.

One of my tasks on a day off was to demolish 'The Little House' as we termed the outside privy. It had been standing there since time immemorial and was an essential requisite until mains water was installed in 1950s. I was to regret doing this as it was quite an historic building where we spent many hours meditating, contending with draughts and spiders, and reading the news print on the papers or telephone directories, which we used before Izal and the softer varieties were introduced. Now that we were on the main drainage such a primitive refuge was no longer necessary – but rhubarb was never the same again!

We now had a free hand at the 10.45 Mass to introduce some English singing and I was detailed to discuss the agenda with Ernie Peel our excellent organist. He was only too pleased now to escape the Latin Mass where relationships between choir master and organist had never been all sweet and light. And so on August 23rd when another Church scandal broke, that of so called 'nun running', we made out first tentative steps with some English singing. I introduced an opening hymn and a Gelineau Psalm and the people joined in very well indeed. The 6.15 Latin mass seemed to have dwindled a bit. However one or two comments came back – why can't we have some Latin music that we know and why no hymns that we can join in! You can't win! But these were obviously people who got more than they bargained for coming to a late Mass.

A new regular young priest studying at Downing College now made himself known. He was a New Zealander by the name of Justin Taylor of the Marist Congregation. He was a Kiwi with a very cut glass accent and proved himself very helpful and useful in the time that he was at college. He later reached the distinguished position of vice--Director of the *Ecole Biblique* in Jerusalem.

Elections for a new parish council were due. The canon after the attacks that he had received from various quarters conveniently went off on holiday to Florida and left it to Paul Hypher to organise things in his absence. This we did, but in hindsight, we realised that the whole set up was far too big and unwieldy – for instance how could one combine Pastoral, Liturgy and Ecumenism under one umbrella and there were far too many elected members with the *ex officio* members as well. However it was a positive start as we were really trying to give the laity a say in the day to day running of the Church. It was all very new and it was early days and we were feeling our way.

Even with our superfluity of clergy there were times when we were stretched to the limit and on occasion celebrated four Masses on the Sunday. Under the new dispensation we preached the homily at our own Masses. In times past one person had been delegated to preach at all the Masses on the Sunday. In some ways it was a pity as at least one had the chance of listening to one's fellow clergy and being inspired by them – now we had to be content to listening to our own voices all the time.

With the deterioration of the property at home my days off were spent doing my best to patch things up where in the past dad would have done things. The old stable roof had been causing concern and so it was up the ladder onto the roof removing the pantiles and installing some felt. It was rather precarious on the top of the ladder and it was a wonder that I didn't fall off. The thatch, too, on the main cottage was beginning to let in water near the chimney I really took my life in my hands and with one of dad's long ladders I clambered right up to the chimney pot to plug the offending hole. We had tried to get planning permission to sell part of the ground which would have helped with the finances but the application was turned down but in the end we managed to rustle up enough money to repair the roof and to have it re-thatched – a small fortune even in those days.

I was now required to go back to St Bede's to take a class again once a week. Why I am not sure. I think the head was under the impression that the clergy had some special charism which would do the trick. But it was something that I rather dreaded as I had no resources to hand and no syllabus to follow. On asking the group to get out their New Testaments, they looked at me blankly and said that there was probably one in the library.

Occasionally I had a class of forty to take. Sometimes they were quite receptive other times it was a bit of a nightmare and we usually came back to the current moral questions. What was most annoying was when classes were cancelled at the last minute or half the class was missing. At the last I was given what can only be described as the remedial class. Discipline was impossible and in the end I had to address them in small groups. This was what I suppose we were 'trained' for at Oscott when we were sent out on our Sunday afternoon catechism classes.

Meanwhile I had a got a little singing group together to lead the congregation at the 10.45am Mass. They came regularly for a practice each week and we were joined by Brother Thomas Campbell from De La Salle House. He was a pleasant man and someone that backed me up in what I was trying to do.

The 8th October marked the 80th anniversary of the dedication of the church so there were great celebrations. It was quite nostalgic as the Canon agreed to sing the Mass in Latin and at the old High Altar which pleased the Latin choir no end. However he was in no good mood inveighing against the bishop and the diocesan commissions which don't appear to be doing anything about anything!

The autumn session of CRESE began in great style with one hundred and thirty attending. The distinguished Scripture scholar Fr Henry Wansborough OSB from Ampleforth Abbey did the honours and spoke on the Bible.

The 16th October was a special day for the Carmelites at Waterbeach as St Teresa of Avila had been named a Doctor of the Church, the first woman to be honoured in this way. So in spite of the thick fog we all trooped off there for the celebrations. Bishop Clark presided and there were lavish refreshments afterwards. Fr Kennedy brought mum over and it was nice for her to meet a few especially Fr Henry St. John and Gerard Meath with whom she had only corresponded by letter when I was at school at Laxton. Another celebration was in progress on the way back and we were snarled up in the traffic of those who had come to witness Nijinski's last race at Newmarket. It was a good day, sunny and very warm for October. This was a build up to the other great celebration of the month - that of the Canonisation in Rome of the Forty Martyrs of England and Wales. The stops were pulled out for the 10.45 am Mass with deacon and subdeacon and the Master of St Edmund's House, Canon Sweeney preaching. We hung the portrait of the Martyrs in front of the altar and sang 'Faith of our Fathers' with great gusto. There was a 'solemn dirge' at the 6.15 pm when the choir sang the Litany of the Martyrs in Latin which we had proclaimed earlier. Mrs Huddlestone and her nephew Timothy Russ from Sawston came in for a little celebration after Mass – fitting being descendents of St Thomas More. She was most distressed about the possible fate of Sawston Hall and the talk of pulling out the chapel by the new occupants. The celebrations were completed by a hooly at Hope which was very jolly. Brian Nightingale came down from Swaffham and we danced and sang and played until midnight, bidding farewell too to Sr Carmel, the superior who was leaving for Ireland.

With demonstrations by students at the Senate House for the abolition of the Proctors and rehearsals by the Sawston Players for their forthcoming play, 'Murder in the Cathedral', there was never a dull moment. But it was sad day when on 27th Paul Hypher was removed to Stowmarket to his new parish. There was no one to welcome him at the other end and I felt somewhat bereft now having lost three good friends in as many years – 'it seems quite wrong that anyone should be just moved like this from one extreme to the other'. I certainly felt very much alone now as Tom Feighan and Tony Hogarth, who had now joined us, were such different characters. A week or two later I drove over to see Paul in his new abode. It didn't seem too bad with no parish debts and a warm house although it is bang on the main road. But of course Paul had been such a pivotal organiser of CRESE which was just getting off the ground and so he had to return to take charge for awhile to see that things did not completely collapse with his going. Canon Taylor cast a benevolent eye over matters but was never directly involved in its organisation. With Paul gone things became somewhat disorganised and the canon always seemed too busy for anything. Tom, although very good natured, was not really up to things and Tony Hogarth was beginning to have a mind of his own and rubbing the housekeeper up the wrong way. How things had changed!

Come Remembrance Sunday we had no Requiem Mass and instead a sermon on the Catholic Press. I noted: 'We do seem to be out of touch with what is going on in the real world around us.'

With the new Mixed Marriage rules just published we needed to sort things out at grass roots, so the inevitable deanery meeting took place. We all agreed that matters were not at all satisfactory and that representation would be made to the bishop especially regarding the promise that was required of the Catholic Party. We regarded it as Pelagian in tone as there was no mention of invoking God's grace – but simply:'I will do all in my power to bring up the children as Catholics......' we also devised an intensive visiting campaign for the following March. All this was overshadowed by the death of President de Gaulle and his funeral at Notre Dame where nearly all the world leaders were assembled.

The Parish Council and PEL lurched on and revivified with the presence of Doris Brown who decried the modern music at the 10.45, in spite of now being able to go to the 6.15 pm Latin Mass -you just can't win. Cathy Green was still pressing for her children's corner. But Dr Richens was very interested in what we were doing and actually set aside half of his music cupboard for the English Music – quite an ecumenical gesture!

The Canon loaded me with one of his marriages as he had too much to do. 'The partner of the marriage was having last minute nerves and there was not much I could do about it – frankly I can't blame him.'

In the middle of November we began to perish with cold as we had no heating in the house – the system seemed to have broken down. I was now deputed to look after the central heating and order the oil and turn the wheel in the cellar to put it on and off. But at least although it was in the middle November temps were still up to 60F.

And so another eventful year teetered to its end with the usual live crib minus the donkey as he was too old. A trip to Justin Taylor's rooms in Downing to listen to a stereo recording of the 'Marriage of Figaro' and our first all English Sung Midnight Mass. Our little choir were very pleased with themselves and we felt that we were beginning to make progress.

CHAPTER SEVEN

CONTROVERSY
1971

January started off bitterly cold with a break with the family down in London. The parish priest at Brockley was lamenting the fact that many surrounding parishes were still saying a Latin Mass with back to the people. By the end of the month temperatures were unseasonably mild in the upper 50sF

But it was soon back to normal with a class at St Bedes. 'I took down some New Testaments for the children who didn't appear to have come across them before! We were now in the position of discussing several subjects which they seemed to like better. They were generally in favour of divorce and having babies before marriage! Whether that was just trying to shock me, I don't know, but subsequent history in succeeding years seems to bear out their preferences! I heard some Confessions in that dreadful stock room corridor with the green curtain and plastic crucifix.

Back at base matters was beginning to hot up with the reprinted version of the plans for the reorganisation of the church being published, we could expect some more fireworks.

Unity week was soon upon us with the usual meeting in the adjoining chemistry laboratory theatre. The contributors this time round were the controversial Bishop, John Robinson (of *Honest to God* fame), John Coventry SJ and a Methodist. The topic was 'Evolution/Revolution'. The general view of the audience was that moves towards church unity were not going fast enough. Our contribution was a Mass for Christian Unity when we were joined by the neighbouring St Laurence's choir and Judith Arkwright sang the Responsorial Psalm. There were relatively few Catholics present but one or two vicars came in for refreshments afterwards. I was now experimenting with our little choir and had placed them someway down the side aisle to try to encourage the congregation to sing rather than have them up on the sanctuary.

The Fulbourn hospital round started again and I got talking to a poor soul whom I first thought was a member of the staff – she turned out to be a patient. But she was with it enough to say that she was 'with the Pope on the Pill and lights candles' – however she was against clerical celibacy. This conversation was conducted in an open ward in a rather loud voice.

The burdens on the local clergy were increased when the parish priest of St Laurence's had a breakdown and all the responsibility now rested on John Drury who on one or two occasions was summoned yet again into the fens to collect him from some local hostelry. Things weren't much better at Ely where a new Parish Priest, Brendan Peters had succeeded Fr Pritchard. He had retired due to ill health from Stowmarket but Brendan's mental health was far from stable as we would soon discover. Being of a radical nature he had removed all the old traditional plaster statues in his church (leaving the relic of St. Etheldreda's arm intact) and used them to help fill in the ornamental pond in the presbytery garden. It would be interesting to know what future archaeologists might make of their discovery! The poor Ely parishioners had had to endure a great deal and one felt that real changes were needed to cope with this sort of problem.

I was getting a few potential Converts and had now five on the go but it was difficult to know how to fit them all in. The classes that we had had for them had collapsed as attendance was so erratic and so it was down to individual tuition.

CRESE numbers had dropped to about sixty and we were beginning to wonder whether it was beginning to succumb to the 'Cambridge disease'. Paul Hypher spoke on this occasion on, 'The Resurrection'. We discussed the situation at our board meeting and wondered whether the venture could continue with all the changes in the clergy not least by the fact that Paul Hypher had to come over from Stowmarket to help keep the show on the road.

One of our stranger Cambridge characters now made an entrance. The Canon had already encountered the gentleman who had an important post at the Hospital – some sort of Voluntary Services Liaison Officer. During a business meeting in the presbytery he suddenly leant over to Paul, saying, 'I believe you love the Lord Jesus'. Somewhat embarrassed Paul coughed nervously, heaved his shoulders a little and that was that. However a few days later as we were going into lunch he rang the door bell and invited the canon to go with him down to the Cam for him 'to be dipped'. He had even come equipped with some swimming trunks for him! The gentleman haunted daily Mass for a while until one day he came up to the altar rails and presented himself for Communion. He obviously didn't know what to do and so I passed him by. After Mass he padded into the sacristy and demanded to known why I had refused him the Lord and then asked me a favour that he should be allowed to wash my feet. He said that he had been received into the Church the previous day. This was the first that I had heard of it until Fr Tom spilled the beans. Tom had quite simply given him a blessing! Needless to say it was not long before Mr S turned up in Fulbourn Hospital. Certainly people did seem to go slightly awry at the full moon and he had been banging on the door at about midnight some days before. We were always wary when the moon was in the ascendant. But it was appropriate as at this time the astronauts had landed and after a Holy Childhood Service at St Mary's

Convent I got back just in time to see the first moon walk. All this cheered us up no end as the postmen were still on strike while the petrol delivery men had just gone back. Rolls Royce had crashed and Fords were on strike as well, not to speak of the violence that was breaking out in Northern Ireland.

On February 5th the fireworks regarding the remodelling of the Sanctuary went off and up. The architect presented his plans in St Alban's school hall after the evening Mass. The pressure groups were there in force. These wanted no change at all and only a few spoke up to support some of the plan. The greatest outcry was caused when there was the suggestion of pulling down the ornate *baldachino* or canopy over the High Altar. Professor Bennett had even elicited the support of Sir John Betjamen. The cost of £17,000 really set the pigeons flying. The canon didn't come out of it too badly but there was the feeling that he had alienated a lot of people which was quite understandable. Some of 'The Town' present as opposed to 'The Gown' were horrified at the way the canon had been spoken to.

There was a fare report about proceedings in the Cambridge Evening News with photos and plans – but it does make us Catholics look an odd lot if that's all we can get into the news about. Mixed in with this was the move for coming up in a line to receive Holy Communion standing rather than kneeling at the altar rails and Mrs Richens had made the comment that it was 'wicked' to force people to stand. In the event the *baldachino* was left in its place and I think I can take some credit in persuading the Canon to leave some of the screen work and seating which he wanted to remove entirely.

If the £17000 needed for the renovations wasn't bad enough at a meeting the following day at Clapham Park we were informed that a devastating amount of the money would have to be found from the parishes over the next ten years for all the new development in the diocese.

15th February marked Decimal Day. 'It was a shame to see the old coinage go and one can't see the stupid ½ p lasting very long!' However for some time it was going to be very frustrating with having to count two separate coinages at the same time. An up to date coin sorting machine was eventually introduced which helped no end with the chore.

That great old warrior Mgr Davidson celebrated his 80th birthday and we had a suitable celebration at the University Arms. Both + Charles and + Leo came. The latter is sadly declining but there is still something of the old presence about him.'

We need not have worried about CRESE as my efforts at distributing letters and handouts paid off as well as the attraction of the speaker who was Sr Romaine one of the leading lights in the catechetical movement, who had given that rare lecture to us students at Oscott. Blackfriars Chapel was practically full for the gathering. However further tensions became clear because of her exposition and the 'new theology'. A farmer from my own village of Lidgate, whom I knew, was present and very vociferous in his questioning and his comment afterwards. He said that the whole thing was,'rank Modernism'.

A clergy Retreat Day tried to get our priorities right again. Tom gave a short dissertation on Our Lady after which the discussion was trying to foster contemporary devotion. We concluded that the new Liturgy had not yet settled down and it was too soon to see new patterns emerging but something should be done to encourage contemplative prayer now that the Liturgy was all activity.

I had been agonising over the talk that I was going to give to give at the next CRESE meeting which was on, 'The Church'. However it didn't go down too badly but perhaps rather too long and over egged with ideas. The farmer from Lidgate was also there and caused a bit of havoc in his group afterwards.

The Easter ceremonies went well with the new English choir doing their stuff and we really felt that we had made a breakthrough. I sang my own composition of the *Exultet*. Fortunately the Latin Choir had disappeared without trace and we learned later that they gone to Downham Market to assist Fr Baker, whom, as has been related earlier, was a staunch traditionalist and would have nothing to do with these modern contortions.

Discussions rumbled on with yet another parish meeting with discussion groups. The vocal 'Anti-change' lobby was there in force and were totally irreconcilable. One parishioner remarked that in thirty years he had never heard a parish priest addressed so rudely. According to the local papers, next day, the plans were going to be shelved and that a new church was going to be started at Cherry Hinton soon!

Myxamatosis was now raging in the country with dead and dying rabbits turning up all over the place. The class at St Bede's by May was getting desperate, so much so that I walked out in the middle of the class (with dignity I feel). 'One or two kids came and apologised afterwards. I then tested a few First Communicants. These were nearly all from non practising homes – one had only been to Mass twice. One is beginning to wonder what the point of it all is. I also gave a test to the Confirmation Class – their answers were appalling and one really wondered what on earth they are being taught.' Mr Kent seemed rather upset when I explained the problems to him and showed him their answers. I don't think we were really on the same wave length. Later he rang me back to say that the children now understood that the Holy Spirit was, 'part of God'. The Canon on being told was incandescent and there were heated conversations with the head teacher!

Another drama occurred when Sister Thomas More spoke at all the Masses and read a letter on the Religious Life, trying to promote vocations. At least four parishioners got up and walked out at the 6.15 Latin Mass and returned after she had finished speaking!! The idea of a woman, let alone a nun, addressing the congregation was just going too far for them.

. Bishop Clark came to Confirm the aforementioned candidates and attended our Deanery Meeting on the Bishop's Synod on the priesthood. We all agreed that the document was very poor and that celibacy was not essential to the priesthood, but on the basic issues of contemporary problems we don't really seem to be making a great deal of progress.

July 5th saw the arrival of Peter Hillebrand. He was an Australian deacon coming to Cambridge to supply for three months and to further his Japanese studies at the University. He turned out to be an extraordinary character. A former teacher at Geelong Grammar School, a brilliant organist and a convert from Anglicanism, he hated what Australian accent he had being very cultured, fastidious and flamboyant. He was not someone to fit easily into the present ecclesiastical mould and was not at all enamoured with the Irishness of the Australian clergy. He planned to get ordained in this country and say his first Mass at Hengrave Hall, but somehow this did not work out. On his return to Australia he wrote me a couple of long letters regarding the horrors of the Australian Church and the next we heard was that he had joined a schizmatic Archbishop Lefebvre's group and ordained by one of the schismatic Vietnamese Bishops. He soon rose high and was ordained a Bishop and lived in Kyoto. Something went wrong here too for he was re-ordained conditionally as a Bishop by another bishop, who himself had been re-consecrated conditionally. This was not the Levebvrist group but the 'sedevantists' who maintained there had been no validly elected Pope since John XX111! With hindsight all this was not surprising from getting to know him in Cambridge. He was not too happy with domestic arrangement and on the first night here he took me down to the *Still and Sugar Loaf* in town for a cup of tea, which outing became a regular feature for a few weeks. When Maureen, the house-keeper (whom he christened Mad Rene) learned of our excursions she would provide a flask of tea for us of an evening, which tradition continued for some years afterwards.

The local authorities were looking at the local schools situation and there were joint governors' meetings and there was some strong feeling about St Mary's Convent staying independent and creaming off the best girls. At this time our Christian Family Days were continuing to take shape and we even earned an article in the Clergy Review. These were largely geared towards children at the state schools with the idea that parents and children met each Saturday afternoon at the Convent. While the children received instruction from the catechists, the parents received instruction from the clergy and sisters with a view to putting them in the picture at an adult level regarding what the children were being taught and to help them as, 'the first and best teachers of their children in the ways of faith' as the new Baptism Rite put it. During the week they would try and continue the ideas with their children. We were aided by Sr Monica Wyard the diocesan catechetics director. Even writing some forty years later this seems a good idea. But as with other projects we launched in the parish it was the brain child of one or two people and was not taken up into the general policy of the parish for succeeding years or circumstances had changed that made them impractical. The parish priest gave his blessing but he had no involvement in the project and the enterprise gradually petered out. Sr Scholastica was always a great support especially at the tuck shop and with the arrival of Mother Clare, the new superior, a boost was given to CFD as well as to CRESE.

Tom Feighan left us in July and for a short time we had another Australian priest staying with us a Fr Caffrey.

Regular sick calls came and went. On one occasion a twelve foot deep ditch had collapsed on an Irish Labourer. He was dead on arrival at hospital and when I went round to give him the Last Sacraments he still had his boots on.

The Latin Mass now had a new family which provided us with some amusement. They sat in the front row. The girls were shrouded in black cloaks and stood and knelt at different times from everyone else. They looked like the Ring Wraiths from the *Lord of the Rings.* It was with some difficulty that I managed to keep a straight face when preaching my homily but managed to block them from my field of view by one of the carved statues on the end of the Ambo. In the event they turned out to be children of the Professor of Philosophy in the University – Elizabeth Anscombe; remembered for wearing a monacle, trousers and smoking cigars, and the literary editor of the great philosopher, Ludwig Wittgenstein. Her husband Peter Geach, another distinguished philosopher, never knelt with them but some rows back. Professor Bennett as already related brought with him the full version the *Missa Normativa* so that he could keep an eye on us, no doubt through the monacle he had taken to wearing. It certainly said something for their humility that they were prepared to sit at the feet of a humble curate such as myself and listen to what must have been sometimes very vacuous words. But their performance in the front row was disconcerting and continued when, on going to lock up the church of a night, one would almost fall of over a shrouded figure in the gloom making the Stations of the Cross.

Tony Sylvester the MC was still doing his stuff organising the Guild of St Stephen to which I was technically chaplain and we had another very pleasant outing to Walton on the Naze and a fish and chip supper was a fitting conclusion to a very enjoyable day.

At the end of July our replacement curate for Tom Feighan arrived. He was John Koenig. A tall, dark and handsome young priest hot from the English College in Rome, and like the other curates who had come and gone I had the responsibility of showing him the ropes. He was a very likeable chap and we got on well together.

Paul Hypher, now established at Stowmarket, was looking for a supply for one weekend and he asked me to go over and help out. To spy out the land I took mother and the aunts over to find the place – they didn't much like the look of it! When the weekend came mother came with me and we arrived in a torrential rain storm. We didn't like the place very much at all. It was very musty and stuffy and how Paul survived there I don't know. In the evening we did a rekky at RAF Wattisham where I would have to celebrate Mass the following day but on the way back, to allow a lorry to overtake us in a narrow road, I landed in the ditch. Fortunately a gang of men arrived on the scene and having told 'my wife' to get out of the car (!) they physically lifted the mini onto the road again. The Masses in Stowmarket went well with a couple of hymns at the main Mass but mother was rather horrified by the house and the state of the linen and she couldn't get out of the presbytery quick enough.

The summer holidays were spent as usual at home and the usual batch of friends and relatives came to stay with us. Mother was very energetic in helping me mix and lay some concrete for the paths and there were some dramatic scenes with the stubble burning around the house. It was very worrying and dangerous with the thatched cottage. Mother had the hose pipe out in the hope that it might do some good if a stray spark should ignite the thatch. The farm labourer who appeared to be in control of the inferno told us not to worry as the wind was not in our direction! As a special treat I took the Big Three over to Cambridge to see my room and the church. aunt's miniature chihuahua came too and promptly escaped into the Canon's room. However we managed to rescue her and eluded the Canon. We had another pleasant outing over to my old school at Laxton now converted into a home for retired Polish ladies and where a shrine had been set up in honour of Maximilian Kolbe who gave his life for a fellow prisoner in Auschwitz and whose cause for Beatification was at present going through the books.

A new term began in September. CRESE got underway and I gave another talk to about forty five people. CFD started as well and seemed to be successful and it was all the conscientious families that came. Monday classes continued at St Mary's Convent for the Perse boys as well as at St Bedes but John Drury and I had a 'confrontation' with the head about RE work in the school. He was happily quite amenable and his seeming neurosis about priests had developed in the past at other schools where the clergy were, as he said, 'for ever poking their noses into affairs that did not concern them.'

We still had our Monday morning house meetings where we looked at our diaries for the week ahead and discussed any parish problems that had come up however it became more and more frustrating as the Canon just bumbled from one thing to another without getting down to anything really in particular except detailing what his appointments were for the week and we just had to fit in our responsibilities with his. We went over the same old ground covered many times before. Young John was rather charismatic and much to the canon's amazement, with apostolic zeal, he shot off to Lincolnshire to help sort out some marriage problem – this really was not quite the done thing! We discussed the idea of making the waiting rooms a little bit more user friendly for visitors to the rectory – they really were like British Railways waiting rooms. He agreed in principle but we never got any where.

RAF or rather USAF Mildenhall were doing a public relations exercise and a clergy day was arranged for us to go over for a tour of the base. This proved very instructive since it was one of the nerve centres of NATO and would be a prime target in the event of a nuclear attack. Perhaps such a threat might have got the bishops going at the synod in Rome. They had rejected the ordination of married men out of hand. However Cardinal Heenan came up with the bright idea that the Vatican should have a jumble sale of all the old chalices to help the world poverty situation.

Over 50 clergy attended the funeral of Fr Owen Hardwicke at Newmarket. He had been quite a theologian but had been 'banished' by + Leo to the backwoods of Lawshall and Coldham Cottage. It struck me how high the average age of the clergy was. In ten years time most of them would be beyond it!

'I sometimes wonder whether I really am a Catholic coming across the very strange attitudes that some genuinely devout Catholics have.'

We were still trying to enliven the New Liturgy and a Folk Mass day was organised at Clapham Park. Gordon Rock took the session . The concluding Mass was very impressive and showed what could be done with some imagination. There was an Offertory dance and a mime of the Gospel and I was quite taken by the spontaneity and joyfulness of the music. There was Communion under both kinds and even in the hand.

The question of allowing Communion in the hand was becoming something of a problem. We had many foreign visitors at Mass who were accustomed to this in their own country and our local people were a little taken back. However the bishops declared that the possibilility of introducing Communion in the hand as well as fulfilling the Sunday Obligation on a Saturday evening was 'not opportune' - whatever that meant. Bishop Grant told us that we should give Communion in this way to anyone who requested it but we were not allowed to give any explanation about the practice from the pulpit. This was all very unsatisfactory. Just from a practical point of view Communion in the hand seemed sensible and returning to an ancient and dignified practice and far more hygienic. On several occasions I had nearly lost my fingers when people snatched at the Host and one's digits were covered with saliva. Sometimes people would not hold up their head when kneeling at the altar rails and it was a hit and miss affair trying to find the aperture and for people with ill fitting dentures it could be quite embarrassing opening their mouth more than a quarter of an inch! This put me in mind of the advice given at the seminary as to what you should do if the Host accidentally dropped down the cleavage of a female Communicant! The solution, heaven forbid, would not for the priest to do anything about it, but to take the lady concerned to the sacristy and ask her, very discreetly, to remove it herself. Holding the Communion plate under the chin by the server did not always achieve its end as invariably it would be tilted and anything falling on to it would slide off onto the floor. Communion in the hand seemed a much more sensible proposition.

Relations in the house had been getting rather tense especially with regard to Tony Hogarth who would not let the cleaners into his room. One morning coming downstairs the canon greeted me with the words 'She's gone'. Indeed Maureen had gone! Tony saw this as something of a victory and did some of the cooking in succeeding days as indeed I did too. We even resorted to getting a Chinese takeaway from across the road and with no one to open the door or answer the telephone we were kept on our toes. But it was not to last. Maureen had second thoughts and was back in a couple of days.

Among our visitors was Bishop Magambo from Fort Portal in Uganda who preached at all the Masses. He raised £130 and an anonymous donation for £500 came through the letter box. He had come to make contact with the Santal Mission Fund which was administered from Cambridge. This organisation was rather suspect and the News of the World did an expose. It seems that the fund had been creaming off an enormous amount of the takings for administrative purposes. However since the bishop was still getting a good contribution from them he was unaware of the problems and was quite happy with the amount that he received. Another visitor was Fr Simon Blake OP who came to sing the Latin Mass. He fascinated us with his accounts of his work in the Peace Movement. He was an ardent pacifist and considered that in these days of chemical warfare it is indefensible for a Christian to take part. He was one of the leaders of the march to Porton Down Chemical Warfare establishment to protest against developments there. He saw the task of the Church always to be against those in power in order to keep them on their toes. He suggested that if the bishops and priests had given some moral leadership some five years ago the present dreadful situation in Northern Ireland would not have arisen of which Mother Teresa had almost despaired in her recent visit there.

Our board meeting for CRESE discussed the programme for next year - 'The Church in the Modern World' seemed a good choice and we tried to work out whom we should invite to give the talks. Bishop Clark came to give the last talk of the year which was on the 'Miracles of Christ'.

Meanwhile John Koenig was taking the bit between his teeth and showed some initiative in calling a meeting together at Cherry Hinton to plan for the future building of a church there. When the canon got wind of this he was not at all pleased and had to take things into his own hands but least this had now put some pressure on him to act in this regard since the plot had been lying fallow for years and pressures came from the local Council to develop it.

Another Christmas was approaching and I joined CLAG (The Christian Life and Action Group), lead by Gerard Meath, carol singing at Whitefriars Old Peoples Home in Chesterton. This had grown into quite a strong little youth group.

John entered into the production of the Live Crib with enthusiasm. He walked our new donkey, 'Oswald', all the way from St Bedes and tethered him at the West Front of the church. Here he succeeded in knocking over the crib several times. John came up with the bright idea of stabling him in one of the garages with the car drawn across the front. Oswald's braying first thing in the morning caused some alarm to passers by in Hills Road.

Confessions were busy as usual and I had to say the Latin Mass. Most of the Latinists were there, but the general response by the people was very poor. The Mass appeared to be utterly devoid of devotion and it makes me more and more annoyed at having to say it as it is so unreal.

Midnight Mass had its usual drama which was as ever packed. A drunk was sitting by the pulpit and leapt up at one point shouting that it was all lies and that he was a homosexual. The congregation was frozen to their seats but as last someone persuaded him to move. Mass at Hope was concelebrated with ancient Canon Wainwright and all the nuns (in spite of the Bishop's letter) received Communion in the hand – except for two who did not agree. The Latin choir was let loose at the 10.45 Mass the next day as our English Choir resources had been used up at the midnight Mass. The people were regaled by an unaccompanied Latin sung Mass and there were several complaints by parents who had brought along young children. A good turkey lunch with all the trimmings and John Koenig, zealous chap that he was went down to Fisher House to help with the party that the Cyrene people had put on for the local tramps. I'm afraid I was too exhausted but did one good deed by going out to see Elsie at Coton who was all on her own for the festival.

On 29th it being the feast of St Thomas Becket, the Canon organised a clergy party. It was a great get together with the deanery priests and others coming. Paul and David Bagstaff our two Church students served. There followed a buffet lunch and drinks and as usual the clergy descended on the eats like a plague of locusts. Canon Diamond came as well as Brian Nightingale and Tom Feighan from Corby. He is now a beacon of liberalism there and actually succeeded in getting the parish priest to use a candle during baptisms. Fr Zawdiski, the old Polish priest, although partly paralysed by a stroke also came. But of course I was disturbed by a sick call to a poor blind soul at Fulbourn. I left her muttering prayers with no friends or relatives to be with her at her last moments. She was the 125th anointing I had done since first I came to Cambridge! But that was not the end for the night bell rang just as I was settling down. It was our 'ecstatic' Pole who had left his bicycle in the porch which had been locked. He warmly embraced me and his breath was decidedly laced with spirit. It was sometime before I could get him to the porch as he insisted on beginning his devotions at the altar before the Madonna. He nearly wept when he saw his bike and it was all thanks to Our Lord Jesus Christ who leads him and me and embracing me again he stumbled through the porch and out into the night.

The year ended with the joint Anglican/Catholic statement on substantial agreement on the Eucharist. This I am sure will stir up controversy among Catholic Conservatives and Evangelical Protestants. The canon and his brother seemed decidedly worried and said that for once they agreed with the Catholic Priests' Association's criticism which appeared in the Catholic papers today. It seems that there is a lot of compromise and woolly thinking, though it is difficult to judge without having seen the text. And on a happy note: £100 from the Christmas Offering, £25 for car tax, £10 petrol allowance, £17.50 for a quarter of the annual salary and also half the cost of general car expenses. What more could one want for the end of 1971?

CHAPTER EIGHT

COMINGS AND GOINGS
1972

The Church in England and Wales got off to a good start with the resignation of the whole teaching staff of Corpus Christi College. Cardinal Heenan had objected to certain lecturers mainly due to their stance on *Humanae Vitae.* 'The Sisters at St Mary's Convent are terribly upset. At least this college was trying to show a bit of imagination in their teaching. It is all very demoralising because it seems to call into question our programmes of CRESE and CFD. It had been hoped that the whole matter would have been kept secret. The Cardinal had wanted to hush up the resignation so as to avoid scandal – surely more scandal would have be caused by keeping silence. This secrecy business is almost an eighth sacrament and is just typical of Church authorities and one wonders from past experience whether they will ever learn. The Vatican too has cold shouldered the joint Catholic/Anglican statement on the Eucharist.'

Humanae Vitae reared its head again when a lady came about her son's marriage. He felt it hypocritical to come to Mass while not accepting this teaching, but he wanted approval to get married in a protestant church up north. 'There seems to be a lot of double think about the whole matter. On the one hand the Encyclical seems to have become a test of faith while on the other not accepting it doesn't prevent one practising as a Catholic. It is becoming very difficult to reason out the whole thing at all and seems so very dishonest.'

While clergy had their get togethers another important support group was meeting. This was for housekeepers who occasionally met for a jamboree. One can guess the topic of conversation at their meetings and I would have loved to have been a fly on the wall.

Peace Sunday was celebrated with many references to the Northern Ireland situation. Some positive things were happening there but: ' The canon provoked some protests from parishioners when he questioned the morality of internment without trial; this in fact had been condemned by the bishops. The protestors considered that his sermon supported the IRA. It is all a very complex situation and one wonders what the end of it all will be.'

The situation was brought home to me when I had a call out to a family at Comberton about whom a social worker had telephoned. The wife was nearly out of her mind as her husband was a soldier at the Long Kesh internment camp and was totally demoralised by it all. Social services were thinking of taking the children into care. 'The wife seemed quite pleased to see me but there was not much that I could say or do to help. It was rather horrifying to see that the children were playing with almost full sized machine guns complete with shooting noises. But no wonder people feel so lonely as I walked back through the soulless housing estate which could have been anywhere in a big city rather than in the middle of the countryside.'

'Elsie has become a sort of guru. When I visited her at Coton, like some Delphic Oracle, she uttered texts from the Scriptures relating to Peter's betrayal. It all seemed a bit obscure and I was wondering whether it was a veiled attack on the clergy for not being able to find her a companion or was it a more general commentary on the lack of charity among Christians in general and their lack of dedication? She also commented that I didn't say Mass with as much fervour as I did when first ordained - how she knew I don't know as she couldn't get to Mass - and that Cambridge was 'the ruin of young priests'. The latter was probably quite true noting my growing cynicism about ecclesiastical affairs.'

My post Christmas break as usual took me down to London and we went to see *Ryan's Daughter*. The sex bits were a bit embarrassing especially since I had my collar on. But there was also a trip over the Cutty Sark and Sir Francis Chichester's Gypsy Moth. 'My friend Denis Hall invited me over to his parish in Canning Town after a lunch at the Strand Palace eating all we wanted for £1.50. What a slummy damp place his presbytery is and quite a contrast from Cambridge. But he thrives there and is very happy. Pay as you enter buses have now been introduced which slows things up considerably.'

Our CRESE board meeting was held at Blackfriars and followed by a buffet supper with the brethren. Fr Henry St. John, one of the pioneers of the ecumenical movement and founder of Llanarth and Laxton schools came in - a grand old man for 80, as well as Kenelm Foster, another Dominican intellectual, somewhat eccentric and a world authority on the poet Dante. It was commented on, in relation to the Corpus Christi situation, that we have no theologians of international standing except Cardinal Newman and Bishop Butler and no centre of theological learning. It was considered a very sad business all round.

The treaty of Accession to the Common Market was signed and celebrated by the arrival at the end of January of +Leo at Hope for what was to be his final stay. 'We are going to be here for many months and We won't sit down for Mass because it is not reverent'. I could see that the Sisters were going to be in for some high jinks. As indeed they were as the poor old chap began to go senile and tried to leave the home in his underwear: 'They've taken away Our trousers and We can't say Mass'. And commenting on his bedtime conditions he was heard to remark, 'We wheezed all night.' But I did concelebrate Mass with him and said the words alongside him. On one occasion he succeeded in leaving the convent but he didn't get very far as he came round to the front of the house and rang the door bell, announcing, 'We have just arrived and are going to stay for some time'. Sr Aiden welcomed him in, offered him some sherry and he settled him down once more. How even mighty bishops come to a sad end.

The Week of Prayer for Christian Unity seemed to lack something this year and was poorly supported by parishioners. *Out of the Whirlwind* was the title of various sessions around town but there was not much sign of Pentecostal Spirit. The joint service in the church was a hotch potch of readings and hymns and several people walked out in disgust.

Bar Hill developments were continuing apace and while the Catholic Woman's League celebrated their 65th anniversary in the church under the guidance of its local indestructible leaders, the redoubtable Etheldreda Bradley and Doris Fasnacht, I attended a working party on Bar Hill's Community Church's relationship with our Church. The president of the Newman Society, John Urqhart chaired the meeting and Anglican and Free Church clergy were also present. Our Catholic input was pretty articulate for a change. We pointed out that we had problems of our own in being able to provide Mass there on a regular basis. We only wish that the bishops would agree to allow a Saturday evening Mass which would help no end in our ability to service the area. But the upshot was a series of meetings to follow. The next meeting was to be on Common Christian Witness and we discussed the possibilities of inviting some Belfast families over to give them a holiday as a joint Catholic/Protestant venture and to have a vigil of silent prayer locally.

The end of January saw the appalling shooting down by British troops of a number of protesters in Londonderry – everywhere is seething. This was aptly called 'Bloody Sunday.'

At Douglas House was a renal unit for those having dialysis. I was called to see a Portuguese patient, a patient of Professor Calne, who had died suddenly after receiving a kidney transplant. His parents were there who couldn't speak a word of English. They had already lost four children and this was the last one. His wife was out shopping and couldn't be found. So it was all very difficult until we could find an interpreter. The undertakers gave an estimate of £280 all in to get him embalmed and shipped back to Portugal in a sealed lead coffin but with his additional infectious disease it looked as though there were going to be problems. Evidently it worked out as we saw nothing of the funeral.

'We are in the midst of the miners' strike and power cuts begin to feature in our daily lives with cuts of up to six hours at a time on a rota basis and millions of people are laid off work. On at least one occasion the evening

Mass was said by the light of Tilley lamps with candles all over the altar and I addressed a black void from the pulpit. This added to the unadulterated gloom of the Latin Mass and it was an occasion of sin as I soaked them all with Holy Water at the *Asperges.* ' It seemed surprising that it was picking up so many people. During one power cut, during this Mass, the canon, with great glee, got the congregation to stand for Communion. Later he received a letter from Dr Richens requesting advice on what the female choristers should wear during the Mass. Because of this innovation of females being allowed onto the sanctuary several of the Latin Mass types had ceased to come and now come to an English Mass instead!! There are some, though, that preferred to come to the Mass in Polish rather than the Mass in their native tongue.

At St. Bede's School, John Drury and I were called to distribute the ashes for Ash Wednesday. The Head had wanted us to go round the classes and dab the ashes on the children's head without any ceremony but we insisted on a proper Liturgy. We couldn't use the hall due to exams. Instead one hundred and fifty children were packed into Mrs Whipp's domestic science room. There was uproar and the deputy, Colin Ball , shouted at them to 'say a prayer'. When this failed in desperation a teacher shouted – 'remember you are in the presence of the ashes'. That did the trick – reverence for The Ashes must have been strong for these kids! John Drury and I had a get together about the situation as he was not at all happy. The upshot of it all was that the Canon had an almighty set too with the headmaster about religious education in the school.

To bring a little light relief into the gloomy situation John Koenig and I used to stay up late on a Friday evening to watch the horror movies, just as in Canon Diamond's day we used to watch the wrestling, to take our mind off the hours spent in the Confessional. Big Daddy and Giant Haystacks knocking the stuffing out of their opponents were now replaced by the *Curse of Frankenstein* and *Dracula's Daughter.*

We learned that Tony Hogarth was to be moved and we would be reduced to three clergy. So we divided up the districts again. It now meant that each one of us would be responsible for about 1,000 families each. 'The situation is getting quite of hand. This means that we have twice as many families as say Paul Hypher at Stowmarket in addition to all the schools and hospitals we are responsible for. With Tony's departure 'a cloud has lifted' to quote the canon. Tony was a pleasant enough chap but he had a will of his own and didn't fit easily into a communal environment. We now had additional sick Communions – and since they were not able to receive on the same day this made our routine doubley difficult. 'We really do need either a deacon or lay person to be able to take Communion to these people. With fewer clergy it means more duty days in the house because the housekeeper does not like to be alone. One understands her problems with all the undesirables coming to the door but surely the rest of the work can't be held up because of this.'

The Cherry Hinton Committee were now getting to work on planning for a new church and the group went off to Weedon and Rickmansworth to see how dual purpose buildings function there.

Unusually I had a baptism on a Monday. It was for an Italian family and was the usual social occasion. They couldn't come on the Sunday because of the ice cream business. The English photographer commented with some surprise that the Creed that we used was the same as that in the C/E!

CRESE was now going the same way as all things Cambridge with a fall in attendance –an excellent talk was given by Derek Lance from St Thomas's School in Birmingham. He was well up in modern catechetical methods and was later ordained and joined the diocese. It wasn't for lack of advertising but none of the teachers from our Catholic schools came - the ones who could have benefited most. As it was the numbers were right down and mainly consisted of nuns. One began to wonder if the comments from the United States that the new 'Jesus' movement was the 'last flush on the cheeks of a dying Christianity'.

The battling Doris Brown whose Catholic Reading Circle was still struggling along had now taken over the stocking of the bookstall. She was very keen to sell 'The Keys of Peter' and 'Faith'. These were organs of the two very right wing priests' associations and it was really quite frightening reading the editorials and articles in these publications. They were rather like the propaganda broadsheets produced by the Communists.

I had recently been to a celebration of the Jewish Seder Meal at Stowmarket organised by Paul Hypher and this seemed to be an excellent way of trying to get to know our Jewish brethren. I thought it would be a good idea to celebrate a Christian version with the grammar school children at the Monday school at the convent. It was great fun researching it and sorting out the appropriate foods. The celebration went well and one could see that in the context of a family get together it would be ideal. I also celebrated one at the Connell's house in Cherry Hinton. A number of people came and it was very well appreciated. Here I made acquaintance of the Mitten family. Simon and Jacqueline were to become quite big noises in astronomical circles and I would later celebrate Mass for them in their home at Bar Hill. Tony Hogarth had arranged a folk Mass, the pieces of which we managed to pick up after his sudden departure, and with the help of the school music teacher we made it something of a success.

Another home crisis developed. aunt Elsie had to go into hospital to have another lump removed which fortunately turned out to be benign but this put the wind up everyone. On her return home there was a problem with her wound opening up again so it was all rather distressing for everyone. On top of that aunt Win, at Lidgate, had nearly burned down the cottage when the fat fryer caught fire but she had the presence of mind to turn off the electricity but throwing water all over the place was not exactly the most sensible thing to do. What with these domestic problems, with Ulster riots, the various strikes, the discovery of a body of a missing Irish girl in the local Barnwell pits, the ongoing crisis in Vietnam and now a vicar on the radio calling abortion 'creative' there is no wonder that life was really beginning to get me down. As well as this the crisis in the Church continued. Another of our clergy, Paul Casapieri, had left the priesthood. This was a real a surprise and quite unexpected. As he was a local man, the press were phoning up all the time trying to glean information, but luckily I had none. The press are real sharks. Another distressed priest from somewhere in France called in looking for employment in Cambridge. It seems he had been suspended over there and so there was nothing I could do in the circumstances.

The canon's brother Bernard, a Jesuit from Mount St Mary's, also came and helped out on occasions. He was a big help with the Holy Week services. He was quite a different character from Paul, being much more friendly and lively. For once the weekend passed off without any high drama.

'The Easter offering was welcome just as men of the road started demanding help at the door again. One man, a well dressed black bearded Irishman, was particularly nasty when I wouldn't give him any money. Another one came to the door at the same time. He was completely plastered and glazed eyed with a bottle poking out of his pocket. The bearded man said I would be in hell before he would be – what is one supposed to do for these people?'

Peter Hillebrand departed after Easter for Genoa. We kept in touch for some time with vivid accounts of his experiences in SE Asia but then as so often happens communications ceased apart from a card from Kyoto with a flambyant signature and the rest of his extraordinary story as already related.

'The Bishop in his pastoral letter for Good Shepherd Sunday painted too rosy a picture about the number of students we have studying for the priesthood – twenty nine in all. On analysis the situation wasn't really all that good for our growing needs.'

Father Thomas Gilby OP was elected prior of Blackfriars and so very sadly we had to say goodbye to Gerard Meath who had been such a support in our CRESE evenings and generally in the parish. Paul Hypher came over to give a talk on 'The Church'

The classes at St Bede's had reached a nadir so I got in touch with the head teacher asking to be relieved of these responsibilities. He wasn't too happy as it seemed they have a shortage of RE teachers – which isn't saying much for a Catholic school. However I kept on the 'Monday School' at St Mary's and the three boys that I had – Michael Sweeney, Wasek Brodski and Andrew Cheffins from the Perse were a different kettle of fish and I felt I was getting somewhere with them. 'None of the children from our Catholic Family Days, except one, were passed for their First Communions by the Canon – so that was not too encouraging for the enterprise and on top of that Sr Monica is being given a new job in the diocese and is being relieved of her Cambridge duties – they might consult us about these things before acting, considering that she was such a lynch pin in the set up.'

A cheerful meal at the Old Rectory at Caldecott with Mr and Mrs Stidworthy together with S Gorley Putt, senior tutor at Christ's College cheered me up. But it was all very high powered conversation and I didn't get much of a word in.

The Mass count around this time was 50 at Linton, 156 at St Bede's and 66 at Fulbourn.

'A Choirs' Festival, organised by the Church Music Association elicited a good turn out from all over the diocese and the rehearsal and the Mass went like a bomb. It was a pity that Richens and his choir backed out of it – was he at the back listening? The new Latin Missal vanished and we suspect a campaign by the Latin Mass Society to destroy all the new missals in order to re-establish the Tridentine Rite.'

The ecumenical baptism went off well at Bar Hill with the Presbyterian minister staying. People were most friendly and one remarked with surprise how our ceremony was so like theirs.

'Fr Corbishley SJ addressed the Newman Society meeting at Lady Margaret's. His subject was 'Ecclesiastical Power'. The questions afterwards showed how far behind the laity really are in many ways in understanding the present changes in the Church. One commented that all the old signs posts had been torn down and nothing had been put in their place – they still wanted the Church to tell them when something was a mortal sin. It was largely a question of the laity not wanting to accept responsibility'.

16th May: '31 today so I suppose I should be beginning to feel old! I did wake up with a dreadful muscular pain in my back that luckily wore off during the day. I succumbed to pressure by the head teacher and so I am still keeping one class on at St Bede's. I reduced the kids to silence as I related Dr Barbet's account of the horrors of the crucifixion. But you can't do that at every class. I joined a field trip to Thetford Forest with my class and it was some consolation that they seemed almost as unteachable in this interesting practical method as in my class'.

30th May: 'The Duke of Windsor dies and old memories were awakened among many people for whom the abdication of 1936 was still a momentou event'.

Visits to Fulbourn hospital had their moments when one Asian patient screamed out when she saw me that all I was interested in was her money, which didn't go to the poor but into my pocket. One psychiatrist said that I had better talk to one patient about 'the Pope's encyclical'. In the event she didn't get round to mentioning it, which was something of a relief.

'Paul Hypher asked me to supply at Stowmarket again. I stayed at Ixworth Abbey with the Rowe family. Joy is very high powered and her husband, Alan, very musical and a G.P. with five children and goes to medical conferences on the continent related to the Common Market. It was very chaotic when I arrived as they were in the middle of a birthday party. The grandparents also turned up. Grandpa was also a retired doctor and a botanist of some distinction about to do a lecture tour in the States. Paul's house was in rather a mess and I don't like it very much at all. There was not much food in the house and I'm glad that I'm not staying there, but the people were very friendly'.

'The bishop comes to lunch to discuss the proposed Cherry Hinton church and about a priest living there. He didn't look at all well. I hope perhaps that I might be the priest to be moved there when it is built.'

'June turned out to be the coldest since 1916; something to do with the icebergs floating too far south, whereas in Norway they are having a heat wave. In fact it was warmer last 21st December than it was on 21st June this year.'

The July fete at St Mary's Convent which made £800, was held inside because of the dreadful weather. There was a near tragedy when Tony Sylvester's little boy nearly drowned in the ornamental pond.

The Haverhill parish had acquired the Corn Exchange with its ever growing population and mother and I went to its official opening with a Mass celebrated by Bishop Clark and Father Ray Kerby, the parish priest. But summer holidays were upon us again and I had a trip down to St David's with Paul Hypher for a few days staying at a cottage owned by the Rowes. It was really enjoyable seeing new sights but Paul, being a night bird hardly stirred before midday and so I had to do most of my touring on my own. The trip was capped by a voyage to Caldey Island in the thick mist and hardly saw a thing! We visited the Passionist House on the cliffs. The community there were entertaining a mixed group of youngsters from the Troubles in Ireland for a holiday; trying to build something positive out of the mayhem.

Back to work in August and the weather was no better. All seemed quiet except someone seemed to have tried to burn down the temporary altar in my absence – whether this was a fanatical Latin Mass devotee or someone who had flipped their lid, which was not uncommon in the city, who knows. Anyway Cambridge was taking on a new look with the demolition in progress of the south side of Petty Cury to be replaced by a disastrous piece of modern architecture. Elsie was in no great shakes – she had had all her teeth removed without general anaesthetic. She thought this was a cleaner job than routing round her teeth with a darning needle. 'The canon aired his worries about the shortage of priests and how it will affect us here and the rationing we have to consider regarding the Mass centres – it's all rather depressing and no really constructive solutions to the problems are suggested'.

One of the marriages I had been preparing was that of Dr Lovatt, the senior tutor at Peterhouse and his fiance Miss Screech who were getting married in the college Chapel. This was all very complicated and I had discussion with Dr Edward Norman the chaplain. In the event the wedding took place with my taking the vows and Dr Norman saying something that made it legal for the C/E. There was a posh reception in the combination rooms afterwards. I thought Dr Norman had certain Catholic leanings and many years later he became a Catholic.

And now there was appalling terrorism at the Olympic Games with the murder of the Israeli athletes. There were further troubles with the expulsion of the Ugandan Asians by Idi Amin and many of them were housed at the old RAF base at Stradishall near my village. They waived and smiled at us as we went by and eventually we provided them with clothes parcels etc.

Paul Hypher came over to help organise the new session of CRESE and this time round we were to discuss the Joint Statement on the Eucharist. A sort of breakaway group was also formed called FEF – 'Further education in the faith' which was headed up by Stella Cracknell, a young, dynamic and forward looking teacher at the school, Brother Thomas and Mother Clare.

'A new priest has joined. He is Fr Gerard Thornton, a Redemptorist, a man in his late fifties. He has had one of the pioneering operations for replacements hips and travelled around in a special little adapted machine. His weaving among Cambridge traffic is very alarming. Because of his gait John has nicknamed him 'Loppy''. He was very friendly but sparks would fly between himself and the canon as they were of a similar age and both rather fixed in their own ways. Gerry was good company and a very pastoral man doing a lot of visiting but a little old fashioned. So there was a lot of huffing and puffing, jerking shoulders, and nervous coughs from the Canon! Counting the collection on a Monday morning, which we were still doing, often became a theatre of friction between the two. Gerry was appalled at some of the living conditions in Cambridge commenting that they were as bad as any he had seen in Liverpool.

One of our little altar servers had developed cancer and there was a big move to try and fly him to the controversial Dr Issels clinic in Switzerland. The canon was not very keen to promote this. It was very embarrassing as other churches were doing just that. In the event he died and his funeral before a packed congregation was full of emotion.

I had a big drive at Fulbourn hospital and spent some four hours there. I discovered that there were about fifty Catholic resident patients.

Saturday 7th September saw the opening of the new Church Centre at Bar Hill. This was a concelebrated Eucharist by the Bishop of Ely assisted by the Rev Hugo de Waal and the Presbyterian Minister. It was a very interesting service and a little embarrassing when I had to pass on the Communion bread when it came round. The remains of the consecrated loaves were stacked in newspaper in a box at the back of the church – so much for our united statement on the Eucharist! A lady fainted which added to the drama.

I received an invitation from the Dean to preach in Peterhouse College Chapel in January. However I was rather windy and managed to extricate myself from the event.

I preached the most rapid sermon in my life at the Latin Mass so that the Sue Ryder concert could take place. This was a magnificent affair and given by survivors of the Holocaust. The Canon boycotted the event as he hadn't been properly consulted about it and sadly the whole organisation leading up to it was a complete shambles.

Bishop Clark arrived for his official visitation of the parish and we had a meeting of all the local clergy to try and sort out our problems. Needless to say we came to no firm decisions. The only comment was that we should use 'epikeia' on supplying Mass on weekdays for people unable to get to Mass on Sundays. 'It was felt that the whole question of ministry needed a radical appraisal in the light of our present circumstances and just papering over the cracks and further stretching our resources was not the answer – unfortunately the Bishop didn't seem to cotton on to this very well- I suppose he has to tow the Bishops' party line on this one. There was Confirmation in the evening for about sixty eight children. I took him round the sick and the housebound and he wondered if I wanted a move. I tried to put him in the picture about my family circumstances and responsibilities. He seems a very pleasant and amenable man to talk to'.

Monday morning sessions with the Canon continued to be very frustrating. It was almost impossible for us to work out a routine of work and priorities as he would suddenly change his and expect us to fall in with his plans. There was really a feeling that what the curates did didn't really matter.

We did suggest that we might invite some Ugandan Asians from Stradishall over to tea but this didn't go down very well because of the housekeeper. After this frustration attending a production of Britten's *Noye's Flood* by school children at Chesterton Church lifted the spirits somewhat.

Another year came to an end quietly. John Koenig had taken over organising CRESE and numbers had been in the sixties. People responded well to the discussions on the ARCIC agreement, but one wondered about unity when the Rev Isitt said that baptism achieved no special change in our relationship with God. FEF with the bubbly Mother Clare was also proving to be very valuable.

Fr Gerry Thornton

**Mother, Sr Aiden, Sr Michael at
closure of Waterbeach Carmel**

CHAPTER NINE

MORE RESPONSIBILITIES
1973

The New Year began with two historic events the joining of the EEC and the beginning of work on the new altar and the sanctuary and so the temporary altar was placed outside the Communion rails during this period. The former attracted little celebration although one in four took the day off and as to the latter one could guess the reactions of some people. An additional pain was a flood in the boiler house and I had to spend some time bailing out water. The water board eventually discovered the cause - a burst water main some four feet down in the car park.

With Father Peters ill again at Ely we had to help out there and a trip to the Tower Hospital to anoint an RAF Officer who had had a heart attack. I was just about to light my two little candles - when he shouted out 'don't - there are oxygen cylinders in here'. I suppose the whole place could have gone up with a big bang - anyway the excitement didn't bring on another seizure thank heavens. With CRESE resuming Bishop Clark came over to talk about his part in the ARCIC agreed statement.

Ecumenical relations grew with a Mass celebrated in the new chapel at Bar Hill. No Protestants came to Communion and the Rev Hugo said he saw value in abstaining from Communion on such occasions. However he revealed that when he was in Holland he concelebrated with the Abbe Pierre.

With one of our worthy parishioners up in court for pinching ladies' posteriors in church, the excitement was intensified by the Canon proudly presenting us with a twenty seven foot long roll of paper from his adding machine with the year's accounts thereon and the men began moving the monumental brass of Canon Scott from the sanctuary to the Sacred Heart Chapel.

A homily I preached on celibacy and the married diaconate elicited some response in the person of Dr Saunders, President of Magdalene College, who said that he was interested but whether he took it any further forward I do not know. A vocations *fervorino* by several visiting priests at St Bede's was a happy occasion ending in a concelebrated Mass.

One of our key choir members, Violet Britcher, died rather suddenly as did Mama Bazzini, the matriarch of the Italian Community. There was a good turn out of Italians for the funeral and they all joined in very well however her daughters had become Jehovah's Witnesses and I felt a hard core of resistance on the left hand side of the congregation. I read the bit about the 144000 from the book of Revelation and hoped that this impressed them. The undertakers regaled me afterwards with the story of funerals they had taken with the sect.

Aunt Elsie had now been diagnosed with cataract but was resigned to the fact that she would probably be dead before they needed to do anything about them.

The next deanery meeting was held at Sawston and chaired by David Thompson. Everyone had plenty to say about everything apart from what we were meant to be discussing which was adult religious education. Everything was all right as it ever had been in the individual parishes and really the brethren did not see the need for any change but there were unanimous protests about the usual lack of consultation by the Bishop – or the fiction of it.

I recognised a face in the congregation which was that of John Ginger. He was the struggling author, a friend of Brother David Lawson OP whom we had met at Captain Jack Leslie's monastery at Allatri near Rome. He had written at least two novels, *Nothing and Shade* and *The Retreat to Yetunda*. He was here teaching at Homerton and so I arranged to see him and had a very pleasant hour or so chatting with him.

During March disaster struck when the Canon returned from Peterborough with a dose of shingles and before long he was in The Hope. It was in a nasty position over his bald head and narrowly missing his eye. I heard, indirectly, that I had been appointed *Vicarius Substitutus*, but there was no word from Northampton of encouragement or concern about the situation. The Canon had gone so far as to hand over to me the accounts and the cheque book! Life then began to become very hectic and only the three of us to get on with things. The first was a school managers' meeting which I succeeded in getting through reasonably well. On top of this the new altar came into operation and everyone generally thought that it was satisfactory. The original altar table was to have sat on a multitude of collumns. These had been reduced in number and it looked much better. The Latin choir of course had to cause chaos by disobeying orders and were scattered all over the sanctuary steps and caused congestion and my first stiff letter was sent rather speedily to the choir master. In the end the choir took up a position between the old high altar and what become known as the 'Canon's Playpen' or 'Wind Break'. This was the raised area at the back of the altar accommodating the celebrant's chair and surrounded by a low wall. The weekday Masses were now in the south transept which made it much more intimate and so there cannot be any more lurking behind pillars by members of the congregation. However the microphone system, in spite of being renovated, was not much improved. At the time even some of the older parishioners wondered why we had not moved the choir stalls – but that would be for phase two?

A notable event was the death of Fr Henry St John OP the great pioneer ecumenist and founder of Llanarth school. He had been in the Hope Nursing Home for sometime and I was privileged to have a short talk with him before he died. He said it was the school that had made him and that there they had tried to live as a community with common ideals. His still great wish was for union between the Anglicans and the Catholic Church and that he could never have been anything other than a priest. His funeral was on March 14th and it was a pity that he did not have something grander that recognised his contribution to the ecumenical movement but there was a good turn out by all the Dominicans I had known at school including former Fr Hugh Nash who had now married. The interment was in the city cemetery somewhere alongside Fr Sebastian Bullough OP. It was good to hear the old Dominican chant again after all these years. A week or so later I went down to St Dominic's Church in Haverstock Hill for a memorial Mass but again there was rather a poor turn out.

The continuing violence in N Ireland and the recent Old Bailey bombings put us continually on the alert. A call from the police station one evening announced that someone had put a call through to the station that an unattended suitcase had been left in the church porch and could they come round and check it out. An officer arrived but there was no sign of any suitcase. The next day sure enough two suitcases were discovered so I phoned the police who returned and a well spoken constable said, 'best not to touch them sir',and he stood guard until two sergeants arrived to check things out. They appreciated that we all wanted to 'get there' (presumably Heaven) but not 'too quickly'! A few minutes later they came back and to my amazement they said 'we have shaken them up a bit sir, and they seem to be all right'. They took the suitcases away no doubt to blow them up on some piece of waste ground. About lunch time two people turned up asking what had happened to their suitcases- poor things, ever trusting, they thought that their property would be safe if they left it in the church. All I could do was refer them to the police but never discovered if they ever retrieved their belongings!

There was now chaos in the house as the sacristy was being redecorated but nothing compared to the chaos in the country with the hospital and ancillary workers going on strike with a real danger to patients, the gasmen continued their go slow and the train drivers continued their one day strikes with the civil servants climbing on the band wagon as well.

'My experience of being acting parish priest does not fill me with much enthusiasm for the job especially with all the irrelevant material I have to deal with – letters and bills without end. The system really needs reorganising. I am really quite surprised how unconcerned the 'authorities' appear to be. The bishop's secretary is still writing to the Canon under the illusion that he is still doing correspondence. Although improving, he is certainly in no fit state yet to resume responsibilities. The Vicar General and secretary eventually go to see him but they didn't darken the doors of the rectory here. Just to add to problems John K goes down with a bug after giving a Mission at St. Bede's and so does Brendan Peters at Ely yet again. So everything is very much on a knife edge'. And on top of this the big day of the consecration of the new altar loomed.

It was only at the last moment that the Diocese sent me a copy of the rite for the blessing of the new altar and we just about managed to run off some copies for the people. In connection with this I had been invited to dinner with Mr Philp and his wife who had been sometime financial advisor to the Westminster Diocese. Being a Knight of St Gregory he wanted to discuss the finer points of escorting the Bishop for the ceremony – about which I knew nothing. He was surprised at the rather casual attitude to things in the diocese and gave his suggestions for a better financial administration of this parish.

The great day came on the ninth of April and about thirty clergy including the two bishops and Canon Taylor, straight from convalescence, duly arrived. There was a buffet before and after in the school hall for the parishioners. Everything was quite chaotic as no one really knew what was going on. In the end I did not concelebrate – it was just as well. I nearly reached my wits end when the man who was to lay the bed of cement in the altar for the fixing of the altar stone containing the relics of the saints did not turn up. Fortunately I had some experience in such matters having helped my father on many occasions to mix loads of concrete – however there was no sand available and in the end all I could do was to mix a very sticky mess of neat cement – so the relics were well and truly fixed and no pickaxe would be able to prize them out now. Neither bishop enquired as to how we were coping – I hardly think it was from their complete confidence in our administration but probably it was a question of no news being good news. I did happen go meet the bishop who did smile and say – 'I expect you are glad that that is over'. There was not a terribly good turn out by parishioners but quite a number came from St Laurence's parish. For the next week the Canon lay doggo in the house until he went off to America for three weeks recuperation. Life was certainly more relaxed when he was away.

Having survived the consecration of the altar, Friday the thirteenth of April was something of a black day with Michael Kennedy from Newmarket suffering a stroke and dying a few days later. We would all miss him as he always showed great kindness to our family – they were very cut up about it. And on top of this the news broke that Patrick Fell from Oscott days, who had been at my first Mass and now a curate in Coventry was being questioned by the police in connection with bomb blasts in London of a couple of weeks ago.

And if this was not enough Maureen set light to a saucepan of oil on the stove and the place was filled with a pall of dense black smoke and a nasty fire was just avoided by our quick action. And to add to my worries on going home for the day to check out the cottage and cut the grass I found the bathroom flooded and so had to go over again to dry things out.

Holy Week was upon us and this more than compensated for the misery of the last few days. Our FEF group organised a very successful Seder Meal at De La Salle House and I had decided to try and make the forthcoming Liturgies memorable – while the Canon's away the curates will play!

Palm Sunday was a beautiful spring day and for the very first time we started our procession from the courtyard in front of the rectory – instead of the rather meaningless meander around the inside of the Church. We managed to empty the church before hand and it was very impressive walking along Hills Road and in through the west doors of the church. Of course by this time the building had filled up with late comers and the regulars were done out of their seats – so they might not be so keen to do it next year – if the Canon has one!!

The first three days were very hectic hearing Confessions and Richard Incledon the chaplain at Fisher House preached at the morning and evening Masses as a sort of mini retreat. In the middle of this was Michael Kennedy's funeral at Newmarket. It was a very moving occasion with eighty six priests concelebrating with the two bishops and the church packed to overflowing – a fitting tribute to a much loved man.

The Carmelite nuns at Waterbeach were on the point of leaving their convent after many years to amalgamate with the convent at Chichester so I went over to empty the tabernacle after saying Mass for them. It was very sad having breakfast for the last time in the bare parlour which had been familiar to me since childhood. I had an audience with all the Sisterhood and they informed me it was going to be run as an old peoples' home and that the new owners would keep one of the grills in place as a memorial to the Sisters – an ideal location for climbing plants! On another day I celebrated Mass for the last time for the Carmelites at St Mary's Convent. I breakfasted with them and sat between Mother Clare and Mother Mary St John DC. Such intimacy, after so many years being divided by grills and spikes, was an experience for both of us. My friend, Sr Mary Carmel of Jesus didn't have much of a look in. Afterwards I took the three sisters over to Waterbeach to finish their packing and took photos as they went to Chichester in their curtained mini-bus where an end game began for them. A few years later that convent, too, and what was left of the community amalgamated with a convent in Cornwall. A chapter of my life ended and mother would miss them. By the time I got back the tool shed near the rectory had gone up in flames and the fire brigade had to be called – just in time before the garages were lost as well - there were two fire engines and about a dozen fire men.

On Maundy Thursday we introduced an Offertory procession with goods for the poor and parishioners really turned up trumps. I thought the procession with a variety of produce, tinned or otherwise, would never finish. There was last minute panic about getting enough men to have their feet washed and some were very reluctant when first asked but we made it in the end.

I fetched mother over for the ceremonies. This was first time that she had really participated in all of them and so it was great for her. She stayed at the rectory and everyone made her most welcome. She was rather amused at the statue of Our Lady in the dining room which we had encircled with all the Canon's choice wines and liquors. The Good Friday Liturgy which was packed as usual was followed by a Procession of Witness through the City with about three hundred people from the different churches in town. We stopped for readings and prayers on the way and ended up at our church

Holy Saturday was a gloomy and wet day and we thought we were going to have to call off the Easter Fire - but it went off with great vigour. Tony, the sacristan, had piled, I don't know what, onto the fire which was in the car park next to the church and there was something of a worry that it might get out of control. Dr Saunders found himself trapped between the wall and the fire and there was some concern about the proximity of the oil tank. It was a spectacular event and no one called in the fire brigade, however there was something of an anti-climax when on processing to the west doors we found that someone had forgotten to unlock them. This was a 'first' for the parish and one wonders if the Canon will continue next year. John Koenig sang the *Exultet* by candlelight and there was a baby to baptise and the whole thing took two and half hours which was somewhat longer than usual. Our little English choir was a credit and everyone seemed to enjoy the celebration with one or two appreciative letters afterwards.

It was all go the next day on the country run and mother accompanied me and after a good lunch with Bernard Taylor we went around to Kings College Chapel for Evensong which was inspirational.

There was however one event to mar the celebrations. 'At the evening Latin Mass there was chaos at Communion – some were standing and some were kneeling and there was a lot of pushing and shoving. John Koenig who was rather tired and tensed up spoke his mind at the end of Mass and this provoked a letter next day from professor Bennett attacking the reasons I had given in the bulletin earlier for standing for Communion. He thought the clergy were putting too much pressure on them to stand. In a tense conversation on the phone a few days later I finished by saying that all the options were open and that an announcement, clarifying procedures, would be made at the next evening Mass. In the event Gerry Thornton forgot to make the announcement and everyone knelt for Communion! I spent my day off at home venting my spleen on the logs of wood I was chopping. – one for Bennett – one for Richens. The whole thing is too sad for words!'

The Canon returned sometime at the beginning of May and I can't say that I was sorry. He was still not a hundred per cent and the first thing he did was to appoint a non-catholic teacher at St Albans school. And meanwhile the Watergate scandal was breaking. Having just come back from the States the Canon was able to fill us in with some first hand details.

There was still concern about the shortage of vocations and students to the priesthood and we had a pretty dreadful pastoral letter from the Bishop on the subject. Dreadful in the sense that it was just the usual pious platitudes without really facing up to the real issues and asking people to help solve the difficulties.

CRESE was now becoming rather depleted and it was with some relief that I delivered my talk about the relationship between the baptised and the un-baptised.

My thirty second birthday saw me buying a television for £49. This seemed like a lurch towards materialism and I began to feel that I should really go off and live like St Francis. It was very difficult trying to sort out the practical side of Christianity and what were the priorities in one's life for so much of what we do in the parish seemed so irrelevant to Christianity - a walk in the botanical gardens to clear my head failed to resolve my problems.

'A deanery conference on helping parents with their children's First Communions concluded with a tour of the new Polish Centre at Chesterton. It is a pity that our people at Cherry Hinton would not work with the Polish Community as by now we would have had a church centre down there. The Poles have a very nice house now and can use it for all sorts of ventures'.

When Bishop Clark and his brother came over for a wedding we broached the subject of Dr Saunders as a potential Deacon. But he was against ordaining a seventy year old and suggested that he might do as an Acolyte.

June was flaming for nearly a fortnight with the hottest temperatures for two years but it also brought the threat of serious water shortages. There were violent storms one day and more rain in twenty four hours than ever recorded before.

The Canon seemed to be making slow progress but frustrated when told by Harry Wace that it took him over a year to recover from shingles. I actually did some parish visiting for a change but people in the posh end of Cambridge didn't even seem to know much of what was going on here and didn't even know that the Canon had been ill.

For some time I had been preparing another ecumenical talk and this I delivered at a house group in Little Eversden on the borders of the parish. It was a general talk on the Catholic Church and in the end I felt I had more in common with the Quakers than the Methodists!

'The Latinists try to insinuate an extra Latin Mass for the feast of Corpus Christi so the pot is set to boil again.'

My father, not long before he died, had been constrained to write his autobiography. He set too with a will which was remarkable and it was a fascinating account of a world long gone. His younger brother Charles's new wife in Canada wrote to say how impressed they had been and they were having big discussions on getting it published. One can just imagine a cult growing in Canada and people flocking over to Lidgate to visit his shrine – how old dad would have chuckled. They wanted mother to go over to Canada, all expenses paid, to talk things over. Reports of bombs on the QE2 and a spate of high jackings made that trip rather uninviting.

The constitution of the senate of priests was the subject for the next clergy meeting. 'The exercise was largely a waste of time though there were some useful contributions from Justin Taylor and Nick Lash. The point made by Brendan Peters and agreed by everyone else was that people were generally just a bit cynical about discussing the subject since the Bishop doesn't consult people and no doubt had made up his mind about procedures already. Fr Trochim, the Polish Priest, pointed out that we were discussing matters of principle and that we would have other bishops in the future'.

Remedial work had now finished on the church spire and the final project was gilding the weathervane cock on the top. They found on removing it that there was a .22 bullet inside which must have been fired from the ground!

Miss Brown continued her apostolic work on the bookstall by displaying the very conservative catechism by Fr Ripley SJ, unapproved by the hierarchy, and published under his own steam. Anyway she seemed very pleased by her acquisition and had been mustering as many books on Authority and *Humanae Vitae* as she could.

Barricades in Belfast and possible civil war made a depressing background to Pentecost Sunday. I tried to preach on the Holy Spirit at all Masses including the convent. Talking about fire and wind made little impression and John came back from Comberton very depressed at their lack of participation. To add to this gloom the *Pieta* in St. Peters in Rome had been bashed by some maniac and a television programme warned of the extinction of the Manatee in Florida.

Flaming June continued with some torrential rain which brought sheets of water cascading into the spare room and we were half the night baling it out. With the Canon away again I had to do the Addenbrookes visiting. This was really exhausting climbing those many steep staircases and visiting all the wards and the usual frustration of never always going at the right time. This was in addition to Fulbourn Hospital where one poor woman announced that she was expecting a child by the Duke of Gloucester..

The fete was quite a success with the usual £1000 or so being raised but the stalls didn't seem all that much to attract people. Gerry Thornton passed his test at last and now he would be able to drive a properly adapted car instead of the little three wheeler which was surely a nightmare for other motorists on the streets of the city.Tony Philpot took up his cure at the Newmarket Parish in succession to Michael Kennedy.

At Comberton Mass centre I meet Dr Juan Mascaro who seemed a very scholarly man. He had translated the Upanishads which I had just been reading. He presented me with a signed copy of his latest book on extracts from the world religions.

We were going to have a live broadcast from the church but in the end we had to call it off largely because of the influx of foreigners during the holidays and our choir going away for the break. The media was full of the Portuguese Prime Minister's visit to London. There was a great row especially in the light of Fr Adrian Hastings's revelations about the massacres in Mozambique. There was uproar in Parliament.

'Negotiations have been successfully concluded for our use of Trumpington parish church. We are not allowed to have Mass facing the people as the Anglican Bishop of Ely will not permit a table to be brought in – this is to be for a trial period of three months;it will be tremendous using their historic church'.

Both 'Loppy' and I were getting more and more dissatisfied with arrangements here with no positive leadership from the Canon. Maureen went away for the week and I succeeded in doing most of the cooking much to people's surprise.

Another of our visitors was Bishop Paul from Cambodia and a nun whom we named Sister Mini because of her diminutive size. Sadly they were to vanish without trace in the genocide in that tragic country.

The summer was marred with the death of the wife of the architect, Cedric Brown, in a car crash and Paul went and spent the night with the poor fellow. But holidays were upon us with more remedial work at home in the old stable where we had Mass each day and over to see mother's old friends at Leigh on Sea. A trip out to the Maplin Sands to see the proposed site of the new London airport and to Prittlewell Priory made a welcome change. On the only day of decent weather we took a trip to Walsingham and Cley followed by a visit to the shrine of St Uncumber at Worstead, the patron saint of those who wish to 'uncumber themselves of their husbands' – there she was with a bushy black beard resplendent on the Rood Screen. Fr Fulcher from Stoke by Nayland died suddenly and so my chances of a move increased somewhat.

The first farewells to clergy now took place with the end of the summer. We said farewell to Justin Taylor with a do at the Polish Club. It was sad to see him go after five years helping out at OLEM and on top of that the news had broken that John Koenig was to be seconded into the Diplomatic Service in Rome. He just didn't really seem to be the type! So we had another great send off for him with Mass at St Laurence's. I had quite a chat with Brendan Peters from Ely who was very disgruntled about the state of Diocese and I was inclined to agree. 'It seems that John may not be replaced and with the Canon, Maureen and Gerry Thornton going away on holiday, John and I were left to hold the fort and supplied with 'meals on wheels' by Sr Aiden from The Hope. Brian Nightingale had been transferred to Hadleigh and came over very depressed by the condition of the property there.

On a positive note I was given quite an intelligent class at St Bede's – the first since coming to Cambridge – they responded in mum stupefaction to my efforts – or was it boredom? However our Catholic Family Days continued into decline and they were transferred to St Alban's School next door and sadly very few parents turned up for the first session. With John going the CRESE chairmanship now passed to me and for the first session we had Derek Lance giving an inspiring talk on 'Prayer and Young People'. About forty people turned up which was not bad going. The following one was given by Ann Bidder, a Quaker, on 'Prayer'

The Retreat was held at the Cenacle and so I had a long drive down to Burnham Beeches. It was given by an American Picpus Father who threw heart and soul into it and advised shared prayer, and urged the clergy to show more friendship to each other and to invite one another round for a 'jar'.

'A new Middle East War now dominates the scene with threats of oil being cut off and rationing. There have been the biggest tank battles in modern warfare and all this against the possible impeachment of the American President and with a nuclear alert into the bargain. The Mass readings seemed strangely relevant with extracts from Joel on The Last Times. Patrick Fell now came up for trial and it seems that he was heavily implicated in the terror plans for Coventry with Frank Stagg. It hardly seemed possible. In the event he was sentenced to twelve years in prison.'

Now that I was responsible for the eastern area of the parish I planned to divide Cherry Hinton into areas and called my scheme 'Church 2000'. I sounded people out about setting up a group in each area for discussion, house Masses and contacting people at a more local level in this huge rather impersonal area. Everyone seemed quite favourable though, knowing Cambridge, I was rather sceptical until things actually happened. Groups were eventually set up centred on the Mountains, the Connells and the Hunts at Fulbourn and from time to time we had discussion groups and house Masses which drew in people who might not normally be involved. This was a pastoral endeavour and sometimes it worked, sometimes not.

Midsummer Common saw its annual fair and the Circus Big Top. One of the clowns came round seeking the baptism of his baby and so we had a delightful afternoon while Gerry Thornton baptised the same under the Big Top surrounded by all he paraphernalia of the circus.

At the end of September Francis Selman arrived. He was a deacon at the time and a nice quiet chap whom I remembered as a couple of years below me at school. Being the intellectual type he soon made friends with the Professor Anscombe. In later years he became a lecturer to Church students at Allen Hall in London.

Phase two of the Church alterations was now published. Gone were the plans to remove the *baldachino* and the altar rails and the proposals were a logical extension of the last with the removal of the choir stalls and screens. However the back of the apse had been repainted a sort of off white which did not look at all in keeping. The plans evoked the usual half dozen emotive replies and someone scrawled 'Famine in Ethiopia' over the plans in the porch. Ructions, however, increased and the Bishop agreed to come and address a parish meeting. His visit nearer Christmas took the wind out of their sails and at the same time there was a general call for a church at Cherry Hinton

But the feeling that western civilisation was tottering to its end was confirmed by the worsening of the power crisis at home with the electrical engineers going slow and there was now talk about the railways joining in and with the oil crisis there was the possibility of a ban on Sunday motoring. On top of this the church and house heating broke down due to a leaky valve. The one cheerful note was a getting together of potential group leaders at Cherry Hinton at Peter and Josie Mountain's.

We did have lighter moments when poor demented Harold – a big man with a shock of white hair started wandering too and fro across the sanctuary during Mass– one moment shouting out 'The Lord be with you...' and then in the next breath the various unmentionables of the male anatomy. On another occasion while the Canon had been distributing Communion he found his way into the Presidential Chair behind the altar – you should have seen the expression Paul's face! At about the same time, at the end of the sung Mass, a lady got up and at the top of her voice declared that she had solved the problem of married priests – once the Pope had allowed birth control then all the priests could get married without the responsibility of children! We do get 'em here.

With Christmas upon us there were problems getting volunteers for the live crib. There was a bitterly cold snap and I slipped over in the snow and gave my back something of a bash. There was now panic buying of petrol and ration books were issued should the worse come to the worse. The Deanery meeting to discuss plans for the Jubilee Year were not met with much enthusiasm in the light of the current situation but we were regaled at Alconbury Air Base by the Americans with an enormous steak for lunch. Meanwhile tensions in the house were increasing between the Canon and Gerry Thornton ....

CHAPTER TEN

LAYING FOUNDATIONS AND FAREWELLS
1974

The new year dawned on my ninth year at OLEM and I become one of the longest serving curates in living memory with the realisation that this surely must be my last year here. It dawned inauspiciously with most people on a three day week and not taking the new Bank Holiday for January 1st. The miners were still on strike and it looked as though the railways were going to close down altogether. We had a sort of petrol rationing by being only allowed to do 50 mph on all roads. With the Canon away Loppy and I had another discussion apropos of an article in a colour supplement about 'part-time priests' – that is those who have little to do all day apart from writing a few letters and making a few visits and the frustrations of curates who do not have any real responsibility or those responsibilities not being recognised by the parish priest. And now recorded yet again - nothing annoyed us more than when having fixed up a round of Communions and visits the Parish Priest suddenly announces that we shall have to stand in for him since he had various commitments. Were not our commitments just as important?

The Comet Kahoutek was going to give amateur astronomers a bit of excitement and I had my telescope at the ready in the Trumpet gallery of the Tower – but there was thick cloud and in the event the whole thing was a damp squib.

'For the first time in my career I found I had no marriages on the books. I can't say that I am really sorry. The whole marriage preparation is a real burden especially when it is a Mixed Marriage and there being no real support from the Catholic Marriage Council to deal with the practical aspects. It seems that we clergy are supposed to know all the answers. I think on the whole I prefer funerals! The couples usually come with insoluble problems and more and more people wanting to marry divorcees. I met a young Catholic Indian girl at the Hope who said that her marriage was a totally 'arranged' one and that she didn't see her husband until the wedding ceremony. Although this didn't seem a valid union to me it surely did away for the necessity of marriage preparation. One of the benefits of this meeting was that I did learn how to put on a sari'.

Our post Christmas breaks were in full swing. The Canon returned as jumpy and nervous as ever and I passed a pleasant week in London looking up my ancestors in the Record Office and with a trip to the cinema with Dennis Hall to see *The Day of the Jackal* but there was that horrible feeling of the possibility of an IRA bomb going off as only recently Madame Tussaud's had been attacked. Dennis had just spent a month in San Francisco – some people seem to have all the luck!

My first sick call of the year was a 1am call to Addenbrookes to a lady who was dying of a very painful stomach tumour and with a hundred mile an hour gale hitting us with torrential rain and thunderstorms I made a quick visit to Lidgate to make sure that the house hadn't been blown down and that Cousin Win was OK.

Ecumenical contacts started again with lunch at David Walser's out at Linton rectory together with the new URC man. The latter had been a Presbyterian and was having problems allowing a non-ordained man to take the Communion service. David, who was a celibate, was very pastorally minded. He provided us with an excellent pheasant lunch complete with lead shot and we discussed what possible things we could do together.

As part of the Week of Prayer a Festival of Praise had been organised at the URC. We had been having rehearsals for parts of *Messiah*. There weren't many tenors and I was stuck next to the sopranos and felt rather isolated – I don't think that they thought much of my efforts. However it was a resounding success with the Salvation Army accompanying with their usual gusto

'We have a new visitor in the person of Fr Peter Milward SJ who stays for a couple of months. He lectures in the University in Japan. It was interesting to hear the respect the Japanese have for the Church and the many requests he has to assist at non-catholic Japanese marriages'.

'The Canon, with great glee, has extracted the RE syllabus from St Bedes and is writing a critique of it. It really is dreadful. Almost as bad as the new class of children I am fated to teach. None of them had heard of the Week of Prayer for Christian Unity which we were just beginning. The Canon preached at a joint Communion Service at the Methodist Church. I attended a united service at the URC in Cherry Hinton Road where David Ford preached. A much more leisurely service than ours. We always have to get through in such a rush to get on to the next Mass centre.'

To aid my efforts at visiting I had bought myself a fold up bike for £20. This meant I could drive off some distance with the bike in the boot and then use it for local visits. However my first attempts were not very successful as the streets were so dark since the lights had been turned off due to the strike so I didn't get very far.

'The Canon's eye is playing up badly again and I think he fears the return of the shingles. This doesn't help to mollify his tetchiness'.

The house groups in Cherry Hinton were beginning to get going with a social at the Connell's. It got people together and they all seemed keen to get involved though there were the usual sceptics who said that they had seen in all before. This was followed a week later by a meeting at the Mountain's. They were all enthusiastic which was the heartening thing – there is so much talent and good will in Cambridge. Again a little while later we had a Mass at the Connell's with the co-ordinating families. It was a very valuable meeting and practical problems will soon present themselves. It's a pity that the Canon doesn't come along to get some idea of what it is all about.

The Week of Prayer, with the unusually mild weather for January, the mildest since 1932, ended with a Unity Mass at our church and with Communion under both kinds. We are sure that a few 'separated brethren' communicated. Gerry Thornton was particularly riled when the Canon invited the guests into 'my house' for refreshments. Was it not also the home of the curates?

Our intellects were stimulated by a trip to the Divinity School to hear a lecture by the famous Dominican Fr Yves Congar OP– one of the architects of the Vatican Council. He was lecturing on the occasion of the 700th anniversary of St. Thomas Aquinas and the subject was his approach to Ecumenism. His talk was difficult to follow due to his French accent but one gleaned a few interesting ideas.

'The IRA bombings continue to dominate our lives with some appalling atrocities. Patrick Fell has now been transferred to a top security jail and has lost his privilege of saying Mass. And now an election is called against the background of a full scale miners' strike. We really wonder what we are coming to. But we had some good news in that the Bishop was consulting us regarding the appointment of a new Dean and so with enthusiasm I put pen to paper to state my views and excitement was further engendered when the Canon returned from the White House, (the Bishop's residence at Poringland near Norwich), with the news that the dividing of the diocese was now on the agenda together with an overall plan for the country'.

Our next Deanery meeting was at Buckden Towers to discuss the *Church 2000* document. Hugh Byron pursued his line with conservative zeal and Larry Howlin had a great deal to say. The discussion was largely depressing in the way that things seem to be breaking down but Timothy Russ injected an optimistic note and I was surprised that the Canon asked me to say something about the groups I had been organising in Cherry Hinton. 'Looking back some four years I see that many of the resolutions we passed at this meeting were practically the same as those we passed all those years ago!'

The controversial Jesuit, Daniel Berrigan was giving a lecture at Kings College that evening but unfortunately I missed it after loosing myself in the complex. Alexander Solzhenitsyn was expelled from from the Soviet Union because of his latest book.

'The Canon is pleased with his new edition of the English Breviary but it seems a bit steep at £11.50 a volume. He has just returned from the Chapter meeting at Northampton full of the same complaints about the system of consultation that we have about him ! Our deanery recommendations about ordaining permanent deacons were just brushed aside by Alan Clark and Charles Grant, it seems, concurred. One just despairs of anything. Vent my frustrations in a letter to John Koenig now learning his diplomatic stuff in Rome'. In a letter to me he recalls that his colleagues in the diplomatic service just cannot believe his tales about his Cambridge experiences.

'Preach on love of enemies at all the Masses and at the Latin Mass had a silent Eucharistic Prayer to enable Richens to sing a split polyphonic Sanctus/Benedictus – all very wrong and the whole thing makes me squirm now – with no participation from the congregation'.

With the growing crisis regarding the clergy, we were called on to help out in other parishes. I went over to Ely again and also to Bassingbourn Barracks near Royston. There were not many at Mass but I was invited through to the Officers' mess afterwards for a drink and a meeting with some of the top brass.

'Francis Selman is very ascetical. He rarely wears an overcoat even on winter days when he goes off on his bike and comes back looking frozen stiff. However he had a meal with Elizabeth Anscombe and her family and on his return regaled us with a hilarious description of their unorthodox life style. They have requested a Mass to be said for Rene and Ludwig (Descartes and Wittgenstein). The crisis of the election comes to a head with Mr Heath resigning and the Labour government being installed under Harold Wilson'.

One of my great hobbies had been model making and I had been working for some time on Herod's Temple. I did quite a lot of research and it looked quite impressive. The construction of this, like the original, would go on for some time if not forty years and I eventually found it quite useful as a visual aid. However with the advent of Alec Garard and his fantastic model at Fressingfield in Suffolk mine looked rather a humble effort and thirty years later after attacks by mice in the garden shed I decided to do an AD 70 on it and it all went up in flames! However it was not without its drama as, one day, my Stanley knife slipped thereby cutting off the tip of a finger. Blood was everywhere and a dash down to A and E proved necessary. The Canon was horrified seeing my arm in a sling and incapacitated for awhile.

The general feeling of things falling apart were emphasised with half the choir likely to be away for Easter and only thirteen families turning up for the Catholic Family Days when over one hundred signed up a couple of years ago. However CRESE forged ahead with a committee meeting at Nora Wilson's. The programme for next year was going to be a consideration of the pastoral impact the Church in Cambridge is having.

During Lent we instituted a series of Station Masses which involved having a special Lenten Mass in a different parish or location each week. This was quite well supported and helped the different communities to get to know each other. On one occasion a group of us walked, as a pilgrimage, to St Laurence's in the next parish for Mass. We were directed very efficiently by their MC Richard Conrad who was later to distinguish himself as a scholarly Dominican and Prior of his Community. We thought at the time there was something unusual about him !

'During Confessions one Saturday a man came in at the back of the church and shouted out, 'Pray for more heat – I don't know how you lot can kneel here in this cold!'

Bits of the clock face that protruded from the church tower had been falling on passers by and scaffolding had to be erected for its repairs. This was too much of a temptation for one young drunken undergraduate. He shinned up the scaffolding and pulled off the hands of the clock. He faced a hefty bill and was later sent down.

Bell ringers came from far and wide to practise on our fine ring of bells. This however was not appreciated by the neighbours who would on occasion ring up in protest and asking ever so impolitely when those *** bells were going to stop. We could not hear them in the rectory and our reply was usually - 'Bells, what bells ?!'

A new argument arose at our Monday staff meeting. The Canon suggested that we were eating too much – especially cheese. We gave as good as we got and suggested that Maureen was not as economical as she might be. But it is difficult to see where we could cut down – the answer is for the Canon to cut down on the housekeeping.

Our groups were continuing to more or less work and at a meeting of the group leaders Leon Peters lead a Liturgy of the Word followed by a two hour discussion on where we were going which was extremely valuable and rewarding. I wrote up a report for the Canon – it would have been nice to have had some positive encouragement for one's efforts.

At Holy Week time: 'I had a rather jolly Passover meal with the Monday school boys at St. Mary's Convent – lying on the floor and with cakes and lemonade. It was rather spoiled when they started throwing darts on to the flower beds outside and Sr Imelda came storming up to address the situation. As a lead up to the Holy Week at the Family Day get together we did a telescoped version of Holy Week starting with a Palms Procession followed by washing of feet, veneration of the Cross and Paschal Candle. They all seemed to enjoy it. On Palm Sunday itself I went to the Cracknell's for a seder meal which John Drury looked in on towards the end'.

'The house Mass at Jim and Patsy Mulhern's one evening attracted about seventeen people and it all seemed very promising – but how full of complaints the parish is. No doubt complaints about the clergy were aired when the congress of housekeepers met under the auspices of Maureen. That must surely have been the main topic of conversation. The clergy thought it best to vacate the premises for meals. Loppy went to the hospital, Francis to Hope and I had a Singapore Chou Mein in my room'.

Holy Week was again a very full programme with Fr Marcellus OFM preaching. I went to Linton for a United Service of hymns and prayers in a packed church. It was all very worthwhile though the URC and Salvation Army absented themselves due to 'pressure of work' ! The Canon reluctantly consented to having a fire and procession as last year – he can't see the point of this, thereby exhibiting his somewhat philistine tendencies. It all went without a hitch including the baptism of a baby and the new English choir performed well, though being half deaf at the time I hardly appreciated it. But there was little celebration afterwards and we had to content ourselves with a cup of tea and then bed. Although the Easter meal was very good there were no signs of the customary liquors afterwards – however all was well when presented with our cut from the Easter Offering which was the princely sum of £114.05.

'The Canon drops veiled hints about possible moves and he will sound out the Bishop next week. It seems there are five new priests to be placed and so we are obviously in the line of fire. He spoke of my getting a parish straight away after leaving here but that seems fairly unlikely as there are a number of senior ones in my year. However I dread the thought of going as a curate elsewhere'.

'With the Canon going away for a week's break, tension in the house was lifted and I had an interesting talk with Francis at supper about the likely decline in western civilisation and the possibility that we are heading for a new dark age – from his reading of ancient history he thought perhaps we were'.

The Cherry Hinton Groups were in full swing again and I arranged for a seder meal at De La Salle House with the group leaders. It was a great success with my new revised rite and we went on talking until midnight.

Having had pheasant with David Walser at the rectory in Linton at our last clergy fraternal, the next meeting was at the manse where we were served mince beef pie and water – one wonder what we shall get at the Sally Army next time round. We had an interesting discussion and they all agreed on some idea of Purgatory – because of cases of ghosts and hauntings. The Captain was very sincere and full of the spirit.

By now mother had returned from London to the cottage and very dispirited by the state of the place with the birds already beginning to attack the thatch at the back. We picked up the old Austin from Collin who said the sight of her car on the move again was a sure sign that Spring had arrived. Aunt Win next door was now eighty and her cottage was in quite good shape so we thought that eventually we might move next door. My week's break was a bit dismal as the hot water tank went wrong and we found that it had never been fitted with a proper drainage tap meaning it had never been properly drained when we went away. I spent some time trying to bale out half a bucket of limescale from the tank. However we cheered up a bit by going to the cinema in Cambridge to see the *The Great Gatsby* – a most odd film. Mother's seventieth birthday was celebrated by a trip down to London to see the aunts. Uncle Wilf was staying over at Ousden and so we spent a final evening putting the Church to rights with him and listening to all his troubles about cousin David who had such severe diabetes. On return to work I started writing my talk on 'The Resurrection' for CRESE. The board meeting concerned planning next year's programme which was going to be, 'You and your Parish'. The gathering was lightened my Mother Clare who is a real scream as she described the school trip to Italy with John Koenig and Sr Barbara and a hair raising trek up to the cone of Vesuvius. But there was something of a blow when Brother Thomas announced that he would soon be leaving.

'The house groups have restarted with one held at the Richardson's at Fulbourn. This was not so well attended but there was a wide ranging and useful comments afterwards which ended in a discussion, of all things, on water divining. Richard Hunt was quite sceptical until he was persuaded to try with a couple of metal rods over a tea cup. There was some result which he found rather disconcerting. A few days later we had another house Mass at Linton. This went very well and people seemed keen to become involved – but again the Canon didn't express much interest when I mentioned it to him – but anyway perhaps one is laying the foundations for future development'.

Juan Mascaro, whom I had recently met at Comberton, and an expert on eastern religions gave a fascinating talk at the next CRESE meeting on 'Eastern Mysticism' and we were even treated to him singing from the Upanishads in sanscrit. This meeting was better attended than the inaugural united service for Christian Aid Week at Linton Parish Church when only three Catholics participated! A few days later we had our promised lunch at the Salvation Army – a real working class lunch of sausages and mash but we found we were all facing much the same problems in our different church communities.

'My thirty third birthday is marked by an horrific massacre of Israeli teenagers. Work continues on adapting the sanctuary. The final two choir screens are removed with great effort and the far transept is opened up. I think it will look quite good'.

Ulster continued to teeter on the brink of chaos and the following day twenty eight people were blown up in Dublin and a hundred seriously injured with a car bomb going off at Heathrow. 'I was called round to the hospital to see a man who had been concussed after a fall. The horror was that he had lost his wife and a father in the sectarian murders in Ulster and his six year old son had had both his legs blown off. Much to the jubilation of the Loyalists the power sharing executive in Ulster collapses and so what next?'

'The question of deacons came up again at our next deanery meeting held at Ely. As already recorded the Canon had brought up the idea at the Chapter meeting when it had been dismissed without reason. We also discussed the lay distribution of Holy Communion and this was supported by everyone. But we were all most dissatisfied by the state of affairs and will continue to press for an answer – consultation – rhubarb!'

Once again a period of depression set in about what I was supposed to be doing and whether I should change my employment with the present circumstances as they are. The wind of moves being in the air still didn't help and Mgr Davidson continued to plot where I might be sent next- the latest was Thetford. But there was some consolation with the success of the House Groups in Cherry Hinton and the next one at the Mountain's attracted some sixteen people and we talked into the early hours of the morning.

'On June 4th I went with Tim Russ on a trip to Oscott. It was nice to see the old place again and especially Ken Collins who is now Professor of Scripture. He hasn't changed much in the last twelve years and we had a good natter about old times. Frank Thomas is now rector and Peter Hocken is also lecturing. The spirit in the house seemed quite good and David Bagstaff and Tom Murray were on good form. They seem to be working much harder than when we were there and involved in much more outside work.'

'The Canon reveals that only a third of the teachers at St Bedes are Catholics and one wonders how they can regard it still as a Catholic School. This accounts of my having to go in and take RE classes'.

After the trip to Oscott it was the trip to the Old Howardian reunion at Laxton. This was to celebrate the fiftieth anniversary of the transfer of the school to Laxton from Hawkesyard. There was a reasonable turn out and I concelebrated with Fr Vincent. None of my year was present but there were some familiar faces. It seemed strange seeing them with their wives and children.

10th June: 'OLEM is filled with what might be the *Shekeina* cloud in the Jerusalem Temple as they try to sand off the maroon paint in the apse. The apse was eventually painted cream and did not look as well as it did previously. That evening I visited a lady who had dreadful hang ups about the liturgical changes and the 'wrecking' of the church. Although the arguments were largely emotional nevertheless they were pretty intense and it all seemed so sad. The Latin Sunday evening Mass continues to flourish and numbers of young people participate'.

And so at the end of June we came to the last session of CRESE for the year and this was given by Margaret Wileman, principal of Hughes Hall. Her subject was the 'Spirituality of Charles de Foucauld'.

A gentleman came in with details of his marriage which, with dispensation, was to take place elsewhere in the city. His name was Prokoviev. He showed me his birth certificate and sure enough his father was one, Sergei – composer!

I had a disturbing cremation to do. It was a last minute one and so I knew nothing of the man concerned. We were often called out to do these last minute services for people of whom we knew nothing. I felt the atmosphere was rather charged and it was only afterwards that I learned that he had been a game keeper who had been involve in a duel with another game-keeper and had received the bullet. Another distressing event was the funeral of Hilary Bown. I had only been to see her recently and the day after a car mounted the pavement and she was killed. It was a difficult service as her husband Professer Bown was an atheist – but we managed somehow. This wasn't the first time that I seemed to have been the harbinger of the Grim Reaper who struck shortly after I had visited!

'The annual Retreat was at the Cenacle at Burnham, Bucks again. There were only about a dozen of us this time and the programme was organised by Gerard Meath and Paul Hypher. +Charles gave a rather rambling introduction on, 'The signs of the times'. These Retreats make me rather too depressed and introspective, more so than for a long time. I contribute little or nothing to any discussion that takes place still having little confidence in myself and a fear of making myself look a fool. The talks on the other hand were excellent with Julian Filochowski of CIIR holding forth on the facts of World Poverty and the exploitation of the Third World. Lional Swain on, 'In God's Image and likeness' which was a very fine survey of Scripture and provoked a lively discussion. This was followed by shared, spontaneous prayer which I am afraid I can't cope with'. Although we had a friendly chat with the Bishop the next day and my mood somewhat lightened, he made no mention of any possible 'move'. Bishop Mahon of Justice and Peace, certainly material for Westminster, gave an inspiring *fervorino* at the finish.

Back to the grindstone and having prepared a good class for St Bedes I only to got down to the school to find they had gone to Walsingham – no one had bothered to tell me – so went shopping instead . But there was a Catholic Family Day meeting with Sr Monica and a feeling that the programme needed revamping. There was the same planning meeting too for CRESE and I sorted out a programme for next year and began to deliver leaflets; I actually did some useful parish visiting for a change!

The mounting problems of children at non-catholic schools and catering for the religious instruction continued and I preached on this subject at all the Masses. We reckoned that there were at least five hundred such children and the dire need for more catechists. In the end we roped in about sixteen volunteers.

Another Mass at the Mountains attracted about twenty people including some teenagers and as usual we talked into the early hours.

'The Canon tried to gain more information about the autumn 'moves' but got no joy from the Bishop. He was told that the proposed division of the diocese would not affect the expected moves this autumn. I continue to despair. IRA bombs continue with one injuring a number of tourists at the Tower of London and there is a military coup in Cyprus with Archbishop Makarios escaping'.

Brother Thomas Campbell who had contributed so much to parish life – to our new choir and the House Groups was given a nice farewell 'do' in the club, but in the middle of it all an emergency call came from the rectory to say that a drunk had got into the house and Maureen needed rescuing – why hadn't she put a catch on the door?

21st July we read a pastoral letter from the Bishop regarding the distribution of Communion by lay people – this was a surprise move by the bishop. There was also an *ad clerum* on the question of consultation re clergy moves - this was an excellent development.

27th July. And then in happened! There was a tap on my Confessional and Bishop Clark appeared. In about two seconds over a cup of tea and in a cheery fashion he informed me that I was to be transferred to St George's, Norwich. He felt that I needed more experience of parish life and that the Canon was relying on me too much ! The others came in and there was no chance for further discussion – he would ring me when it was finalised. I took it fairly well at the time – but when it sank in later I realised the brutality of the announcement – so much for consultation or discussion or how I felt about things. It seemed so contrary to what one had been expecting from the recent *ad clerum*. So I resolved to write to the Bishop. Looking back and reading the letter it seemed quite a good balanced one! I certainly mentioned the problems of responsibilities for my aging relatives and my unhappiness in the way the announcement had been made. The Bishop's reply was very courteous, regretting the, 'seemingly abrupt and unfeeling declaration of intent' and asked me to 'overlook what must have appeared as almost calculating in its brutality'. He thanked me for not saying 'no' and described the possibilities that lay at Norwich with its new parish priest. 'Forgive my 'approach' he concluded, but 'much long term hurt comes from unclarity. But I don't what clarity to destroy charity'. Of course this was all secret and not to be divulged to anyone. My reply to the Bishop did appeal to know who was going to follow in my footsteps as there was so much in the pipe line that needed discussing with him, but I don't think at this stage even the Bishop knew who was coming. A mysterious Dutch priest turned up on the doorstep whom Maureen, who had got wind of the moves, was convinced was my successor. She was right but he thought it was only going to be an opportunity to study and when he found that it was going to be a real pastoral appointment he went off intent on writing to Bishop Clark.

And amid all my personal excitement and disorientation the Watergate Scandal broke in the United States with all it succeeding drama. But my own drama had not quite run its course. 'With summer holidays approaching I spoke to Sister Scholastica about the possibility of being put up at the Bar Convent in York for a few days. She made the necessary contacts and all was planned for a stay first at their holiday home at Whitby and then at York. So this will be a change to get mother away as well to a new place myself'.

The short break we had in Yorkshire was marvellous and the first time that mother and I had stayed in that area. We visited a lot of the beauty spots but my concern was mother's walking ability and she seemed in considerable pain and difficulty getting about, but we managed a walk around the walls of York and trip into the Dales.

After these very pleasant August days with mother in Yorkshire, I returned to receive a phone call from Canon Taylor. He sounded quite distressed about the impending move. It seems he had been to see the Bishop but had received little joy from him. He said that he had resigned as Dean in protest about the lack of consultation – I don't think that even he had been approached about matters. The family were now quite upset. I nearly considered thinking about a transfer to the Brentwood Diocese. I wrote a frank letter to +Charles Grant. I welcomed the breakthrough of his *ad clerum* regarding consultation of the clergy in the matter of appointments – but the seeming arbitrary way I had been dealt with rather shattered my confidence. I felt that the Church was supposed to be a 'family' in which the father would be more cognisant of the personal needs and anxieties of its members. I lamented the numbers of curates who had been suddenly moved from Cambridge, which discontinuity made me despair of achieving anything of value and I wondered whether our repeated discussions at deanery and other clergy meetings about consultation and co-responsibility were relevant at all – which was a recipe for frustration and disillusion. Well I had never been so frank with a bishop before. But as I would painfully learn in years to come it would make precious little difference.

But this was not to be the end of my letter writing spree with authorities – or hardly the beginning! At the beginning of September I learned that Gerard Thornton had been given his cards by the Bishop. John Koenig, who had returned from Rome, and I were up in arms about this one. All he had received was a letter through the post with no personal contact at all – nothing seemed to have been learned from my recent personal problems. The poor chap was quite devastated. So it was another missive off to the Bishop on his behalf. The reply from +Clark – and it was never a word from +Charles, was that he had been led to understand that things were not at all happy in the house. Well as earlier recorded there had been quite a personality clash between him and the Canon. Paul had ordered a franking machine for the post. We knew nothing of this until a special delivery arrived at the door which Gerry Thornton was to sign for. But he pleaded no knowledge of this order and sent it away again. His argument was that such a major expenditure by the parish should have at least been a matter for discussion among the clergy. The Canon was incandescent and this did not really help in their relationship! In the end Gerald went to see the Bishop and matters were brought to happy conclusion and we celebrated the outcome by going to see the film, *The Exorcist* . We would have been spared a lot of angst if there had been a person to person discussion instead of seemingly arbitrary high handed behaviour. He left at the same time as I and ended up in Luton in a situation that was none too happy there – but he died full of years and did useful pastoral work.

Now it was the dismal task of making the move public and beginning to clear up my bits and pieces and saying good-by to everyone. However I seemed to be in a state of suspended animation as I had no idea when I was supposed to be moving. The full sanctuary was now in operation and it seemed to be working well.

There was more dismal news when Cardinal Heenan suffered a stroke in Cambridge and I wondered whether I would have to anoint a Cardinal. Not so long before I had had to delegate Cardinal Conway of Ireland to officiate at a marriage in Fisher House. It was also reported that Fr Paddy Oates had also suffered a stroke. We had supper at St Laurence's with John Drury who gave me some assurance that Norwich was a 'good place'. Our groups continued till the last moment with an excellent meeting at the Mulherns and at Fulbourn and once again discussing into the early hours.

Things at last started moving on September 17th with a phone call from Fr Bob Manley from St George's, Norwich, who seemed very friendly. He seemed to be expecting me in a fortnight's time. Tony Rogers, my successor, came over from Northampton. He seemed a good chap and of like mind though how people will take to his long hair I don't know!

The following day I drove up to Norwich with my bike on the back of the car and with mother and the aunts to see the new parish. Fr Bob gave us a friendly welcome and Roy Gathercole, the curate, seemed pleasant enough. It was a modern house and the family were quite happy about things. We then had a nice trip round the Broads and the coast and to Martham where grandfather had worked in a post office back in the 1880's

David Miles Board, of the Catholic Information Office, gave an excellent talk at my last CRESE meeting on 'The Parish family – the Community'.

Nine years was a long time for a curate to remain in Cambridge - perhaps the authorities didn't know what to do with me. It was 'in at the deep end' at the start however I gained a tremendous amount of experience and and it was a far cry from my first tentative knock on the rectory door. Successes or failures are in God's hands but it is interesting to recall that I assisted at 108 marriages, 295 baptisms plus 43 emergency baptisms at the hospital, received nine converts into the Church, Anointed 122 sick people and conducted 72 funerals. It is rather sad perhaps that, in succeeding years, I have met up with only two couples that I married and no one that I baptised. As for those who have died, hopefully, I shall meet up with them in the next life!

'So Cambridge life begins to dissolve around me as I pack the last of my books. A sick call to the hospital at 2.30 am to Mrs Peters's husband left me rather shattered the next day after not getting to bed until 4.30 am but I was just about alert to say good-by again to John Koenig, who was moving to pastures new. Not surprisingly, his career as a Vatican diplomat did not get off the ground. So one by one we shall soon all be gone'.

And so it was all partings and one or two parties. On 30th Tony Rogers arrived and the canon went off to a Chapter meeting. A last 6.15 pm Latin Mass and an unemotional farewell to Dr Richens. For the first time a man of the road spat at me at the front door but I just managed to shut the door in time. On October 2nd the end came and in many ways I was glad to be gone.

CHAPTER ELEVEN

PASTURES NEW
1974

OCTOBER

All packed up and so it was off to pastures new –to St. George's Church in Sprowston Road, Norwich. What a contrast this was to be with Cambridge – from an 'inner city' parish to one lying in the sleepy suburbs of Norwich, with a church built in the sixties in the old basilica style by Sebastian Comper, son of the famous Sir Ninian whose only other church in East Anglia was in Newmarket. A church built just at the wrong time as all the liturgical reforms were coming into play. Norwich was famous for its shoe factories and it was mainly from workers subscribing to the 'Turniptops' money raising gamble that the church had been built. In fact it turned out to be far more expensive than first anticipated as when the site was surveyed it was found to be built over limekilns and great piles had to be driven into the ground to support the structure. The presbytery was ultra-modern by the standards of those days and every creak and groan could be heard as you moved around the house. However this was a great improvement on the old damp flint house that was sometimes the presbytery further down the road and the church replaced the still extant small church at St George's, Fishergate.

I was given a very warm welcome by the parish priest Bob Manley and his effervescent and somewhat mannish housekeeper Nancy Reynolds who was known as Judy. It all seemed a far cry from the rather more formal set up at English Martyrs. To cap it there was 'Ben', the Norwich terrier, who greeted friend and foe alike with Christian joy and excitement and the command 'in the garden' would send him scurrying off onto the large lawn at the back to chase non - existent rabbits. Roy Gathercole was to be my fellow curate. Roy was a convert from the Church of England, rather academic and serious but he possessed a good sense of humour and was very learned and linguistically blessed. I replaced Francis McDermott, a charismatic Irishman, who took up a new post at High Wycombe.

I was broken in gently until I found my feet. The church is placed on the edge of Mousehold Heath, that delightful wild area of heathland right in the centre of the city and overlooking it and there one might be miles away in the countryside. This was a place featured in George Borrow's 19th century tales of gypsies and a place to rage and fulminate when things weren't going so well in the parish.

Bob was a delightful and very complex character in his mid fifties – such a contrast with Paul Taylor. He was exuberant and enthusiastic and full

316

of ideas for stirring the parish out of a certain lethargy as he perceived it, after the many dedicated years of his predecessor Fr Chris Roberts who had built the church. However he was none too pleased with his appointment. His previous parish had been Gorlestone where he had been very happy and St George's he found rather difficult. He was a mixture of the old and the new with something of a yearning for the old Liturgy and the Latin which was to manifest itself from time to time. He could be very kind, generous and down to earth with a great sense of humour and fun. His added responsibility as chaplain to Anglia Television brought him into contact with the ' real' world rather than that of the Church which gave him a pastoral sensitivity to people. He was great friends with Peter Freeman, the Anglican Chaplain, who would be a frequent visitor. He was also the official chaplain at Norwich prison which work he pursued very conscientiously and his articles in the local press were very popular.The other members of the staff were 'Jack' the handyman who lived in the old presbytery and the various church workers such as the Howlings and the Handleys who were servers and sacristans and who would later become deacons. He also had a secretary Hazel - someone we could have well done with in Cambridge

On the first Sunday I was to discover that the church had a fine choir which had been founded by Tony Roberts – one of the famous trio of brother priests – with the choir master and organist being Geoffrey Laycock well known in the field of church music. The Mass was a mixture of Latin and English. Later in the evening I presided at Benediction and for the first time for as long as I could remember I lead a public decade of the Rosary.

There were no schools in the parish – they were the other side of town – so that was one responsibility I would miss. However we had instruction classes on a Sunday afternoon for children at non-catholic schools and two nuns from Notre Dame School came over to help. There were no general hospitals. Instead there were two mental hospitals - one at Hellesdon and the other at Thorpe with a children's hospital at Little Plumpstead. In addition we had responsibility for Norwich Prison. There was a Mass centre at Hellesden, one at Thorpe, at Hoveton in the Broads as well as one at the original church at Fishergate.

Crowds of people came to Frank McDermot's farewell do and they were very friendly and welcoming but I could see that I would have a job stepping into his shoes. This was especially so since Bob immediately asked me to run the youth club, presumably because I was still in the younger bracket. With absolutely no experience of this, I really didn't know where I was going to start and it was back to the 'drowning' syndrome again.

Presbytery hospitality was at the forefront of life. It was expressed by good meals, a session watching the television in the evening and any excuse to celebrate by bringing out a wee dram or two. It was certainly a more homely place than I had been used to for the last nine years.

However some things remained the same. We still had to count the collection on a Monday morning and without the benefit of the counting machine we had in Cambridge and there was also the question of Duty Days and each of us was to have two each. Bob also made the practical suggestion that he should pay us £100 a quarter to cover all our needs including car insurance and petrol. This seemed very enlightened compared with many places.

Problems at home though didn't go away and now I was sixty miles or more from the family compared with my close proximity at Cambridge. My first day off consisted in climbing right up inside the ridge of thatch of the cottage and trying to plug up a few holes near the chimney. It was amazing to see that the main rafters of the roof looked as though they had been cut out of the local hedgerows – which they probably had been. If I had had a heart attack up there heaven knows how any one would have got me out. mother and the aunts were very tired and depressed about the place.

During the first week we travelled over to St John's, the main parish church. This was of cathedral proportions on the other side of the city. The former parish priest had been Tony Roberts's, cousin, Gerard, and Norwich had become something of a family fiefdom. I can't say I liked St John's. It is dark and cavernous and with very heavy gothic revival architecture compared with the lighter version at English Martyrs. The Bishop presided and we were quite pleasant to each other in spite of our earlier correspondence. The subject was 'Ground plan', the document issued about the future structures of the diocese and it was generally agreed that it would be a good idea to divide the diocese. I met several new clergy from this side of the diocese among them being Fr Bert Wyatt, the one legged priest from North Walsham who was quite a character and Canon McBride who was parish priest of St. John's. He was a great friend of Frank Diamond with whom he used to holiday but the contrast in character could not be more different. The Canon, a Scot, was rather a rough diamond and I was glad that he was not my new parish priest.

I was on duty for the rest of the day but not much happened so I found a book entitled: 'How to run a youth club' and Bob also gave me the responsibility for the organising the Mass Intentions..

The Mass centre at Hellesdon was dedicated to St Boniface. It was in a sort of prefab building- rather dark, gloomy and cold. Later the whole place had a make over which greatly improved the atmosphere. The sacristan Bill Stannard loyally and efficiently set things up on each occasion and during the week when we had a regular service. The only other excitement was the cliff hanger of the general election when Labour got in by a whisker.

However although there were some promising things a sense of depression began to set in as to really what I was supposed to be doing and the relevance of the whole 'system' as we have it to the mission of the Church. It was such a contrast with the 'activity' at English Martyrs – here nothing seemed to happen and there were not the same pressures as at OLEM. I was also unsettled in not knowing how long I was likely to be there with the possibility of getting my own parish in the not too distant future. Worries about the family didn't help and there was a general sense of unreality. I looked in at the Youth Club for an hour or so. It met in the well appointed hall next to the church where people were encouraged to go for refreshments after Mass but few availed themselves. It was ironic that, whereas in Cambridge we were beginning to get potential helpers to run a club but no premises, here in Norwich we had the premises but no Youth Leaders. So where were going to go from here?

16th October : 'I am on my on my own in the house. Bob is down at Anglia Television recording Sir Bernard Miles and Roy is away at Clapham Park for the clergy 'play school' as it is called – or post ordination study. I hear that a Fr Rolls who was due to take up an appointment in Cambridge has had another heart attack even before he arrived so that does not look too promising. I actually get a beggar at the door and was quite pleased to see someone. The policy is to give each one 26p. 'Ben' always puts us to shame as he greets them in such a warm way. We also have Mass for the over 60s'.

We had a weekday Mass at Hellesdon Hospital and I had to pick up two elderly gentlemen on the way. There were the usual characters that appear in a long stay mental hospital. Enid was prominent full of her knowledge of local clergy of different persuasions. She would go through the whole list of clergy every time we met – how is Rev Rye?..Rev? Rev?......

17th: 'Dr Ellis calls and I am signed up on his books and receive a flue injection. Bishop Grant is ill again and Sister Benildus arrives. She is the new catechetical expert sent to reorganise the diocese and wanted to organise a youth day at Hengrave Hall. Bob ran a mile as he had known her as a teacher at Gorleston and found her rather formidable. He leaves us to greet her'. Later she became known as Sr Maeve.

St. George's Parish was pretty extensive and our furthest flung centre was out at Hoveton on the Broads. Here was a well established community and a brick built church which was packed during the holiday period. Mrs Grace, the local factotum, had everything under her control and ran the religious instruction there. She was of a somewhat conservative turn of mind but everything was well organised.

319

19th : 'All we seem to do is eat and relax here – the food is certainly good and ample and Roy and I have trays to have our supper on in order to watch the television which is an up to date colour model. I am sure the laity would be scandalised by our affluence. Fr Roberts, the former parish priest, calls in to do a wedding and he seems very unhappy about the parish under its new management, reflecting the general dissatisfaction that many seem to have. But I suppose this is always the case when a new parish priest takes over who is so different in personality and outlook from his predecessor and who has hardly been in the parish two minutes'.

21st : 'As the roads are quieter this end of town I decided to go and buy a new bicycle for the princely sum of £33 as my old one was beginning to fall apart. On my new steed I was able to cycle to Hellesdon hospital to do some visiting. It's funny meeting a Catholic with a broad Norfolk accent as one expects them all to be non-conformists!'

22nd : 'At our house meeting we get down to brass tacks regarding parish policy – what are we to do about religious education for the children and, for instance, Bob is not too happy about all the non-spiritually productive organisations in the parish like darts and cribbage etc. People flock in to these gatherings but rather neglect church activities. At any rate the youth club had a disco that evening – the noise was fierce and it really isn't my scene'.

23rd :'Bob's secretary from Anglia rings up asking me to go on a training day at the television centre in three weeks time. A few years ago I managed to get out of this but not any more! It's as well that I have bought a bike as there is talk of petrol going up by 10p next week and could reach £1 a gallon by next year!'

Sunday: 'Mass at Fishergate church, near the centre of town, takes me back in time to Mass with back to the people and not a lot of participation.. One of the congregations, a deputy head at one of the schools, has a habit, during the administration of Communion of coming up to the candle stand, which stands right next to the altar rails and cleaning it! It makes such a distracting sound and is a source of irritation to us all'.

25th October: 'Bob has been down to London for a few days break but has been taken ill there. Judy then reveals that he suffers from all sorts of maladies – oh dear! On his return it looks as though he may have a kidney stone and we had to to get a Franciscan priest in from Woodford in Essex to supply.

31st :'The Halloween party cheers us up a little and there was the traditional bobbing for apples and people generally having a good time'.

Family woes were not far from my mind and I was able to give some assistance when the new back boiler was put in but then news came from

London that aunt Elsie had developed a very bad chest with all the responsibility devolving on sister Dorothy. It is as well that mother would soon be returning to London to help out and I had all the business of trying to close the cottage down for the winter and put the car into moth balls.

NOVEMBER

5th : 'A twenty mile trip to Blofield Hall and Little Plumstead to pick up two half demented souls to take them to Mass. They were about the only people there which is not very encouraging. Later in the evening I went over to Cambridge for my farewell party at English Martyrs. I had the misfortune of having to share the occasion with Gerry Thornton who had also moved. Misfortune, as I had to share the farewell collection with him which amounted to £250. I suppose I mustn't grumble. It seems that Gerry gets no car allowance at Luton where he is now stationed and it all has to come out of his own pocket. We have a concelebrated Mass and quite a few people came but there were very few in the hall for the party. Sr Monica Wyard now seems to be organising things on the RE front and there are groups springing up all over the place. Tony Rogers already seems to have achieved a lot and we talked into the early hours. Things are more informal now – and the Canon is now addressed as 'Paul''.

7th : 'Bob is beginning to get up for meals but is still none too well. I attend a board meeting at Hellesdon hospital which gives an interesting insight into the running of the establishment and meet some of the staff. However visiting patients there is utterly frustrating, just as it was at Fulbourn Hospital. One can just never find them. I managed to get round about twenty wards. After all that exertion I came home exhausted. However to cheer us up Bishop Clark called in. He said he thought I looked well but bemoaned the fact that there were quite a lot of sick and recalcitrant clergy to deal with at the moment. The recalcitrant being Fr Baker at Downham Market. There are also problems on the other side of the diocese with a former colleague from OLEM having left High Wycombe. Not so long after another priest had resigned from the parish and on top of this there were still IRA bombs going off – here luckily so far we seem to be on the margins. He informed us that Bishop Grant was due to go for a gall stone operation today but his heart started playing up so they have had to postpone the operation'.

9th: 'Bob, very generously, gives me permission to stay a couple of nights when I went down to London to see the folks and he gave me £10 towards expenses. The car journey took about three hours and the roads were pretty good most of the way though it is a bit of bind trying to negotiate Ipswich since as yet there is no by pass. The family seemed to be on the mend and it was good to be away for a short time'.

16th : 'A really depressing day and about the worst session of self questioning I have had for a long time. I have a dreary trip round the other wards at the Mental Hospital and really wonder what positive work I can do. I try to do some home visiting – one moved, one dead, and one wouldn't let me in, though two were more encouraging. I also try to fix up with a dentist but they aren't taking on any new patients so I will have to stick with my Cambridge man'.

18th: ' I have a new experience today. Bob takes me to the prison where he is chaplain. It seems that I shall have to fill in for him when he is away. It was all rather daunting being thrown in again at the deep end without any preparation and with remembrances of my experiences at primary school. The torrential rain made the trip there all the more dreary but it was much as I had expected it to be. The place is very old fashioned and 'prison like'. Mass is celebrated in our chapel which is three cells knocked into one – very much the poorer relative of the Anglicans who have rather a nice purpose built chapel. About eight or so men come and Bob lead a chatty discussion afterwards. I think I recognised one old lag who was a regular at the door in Cambridge. Somehow it all had an air of unreality about it – and I found that they actually do sew mail bags. Afterwards each man was given cigarette'.

19th: 'I get the train down to London this time as the car journey is so tiring and stay the night – it was £5.60 return and 30p on the underground. A not too happy time as aunt Elsie has discovered another lump so all this worry is about to descend once more – it is a cursed disease. I wish I was that much nearer be of some help'.

21st: 'My worries are nothing, I suppose, compared with the IRA bomb blast that rocked Birmingham City centre killing 19 people and the worst peacetime atrocity. There seems to be no end to the carnage. I try to do some house to house visiting and one widow kept me talking for ages on the doorstep which I am told is the usual custom in Norwich. The torrential rain continues causing serious flooding in the south. Aunt goes in for her operation but in the meantime water cascaded through the front room window and mother and aunt Dorothy were there at 3 am in the morning trying to bail it out'.

22nd: 'The priest in the Earlham parish refuses to continue the chaplain-cy at the Norfolk and Norwich hospital and so St John's takes it on – minus a curate. Bob suggests that we do it. Another example of bad planning'.

23rd: 'I make my debut at the prison in lieu of Bob. I was told that it was easier to get out of the prison than to get in and this proves to be true. The man at the porters lodge was reluctant to let me in as I had, as yet, no official pass. I was a little nervous as I was lead through the different locked gates until I had access to our three cells and was rather wary as I looked out the wine for the Mass lest I be set upon. In the event the men were friendly and we had a useful discussion afterwards. They were very moral condemning the ills of society – which was part of the reason why they were inside.. The Anglican chaplain looked in for a moment. Later, back at the church,I had a funeral to officiate at. Like the previous two no one seemed to have much of a clue what it was all about and this was the first time in my experience that not one person joined in with the Our Father.'

25th: 'Down to London by car and make a couple of visits with mum to the Miller Hospital in Deptford to see aunt Elsie. She seems to be making progress, but the whole thing is making me very depressed and dejected and not quite knowing what to do. At least Judy is very kind and sympathetic'.

26th: 'Preparations are now going ahead for the carol service at the Mental Hospital. I think it is going to be interminable. Meet the other chaplains – the Rev Rye from Barnham Broom and the Rev Barny Broom from somewhere else – they ought to swap parishes. In the evening we went to the Catenian Lunch at the Royal. The Catholic business men and their wives were all there in their best bib and tucker but it was a largely indifferent meal and all a bit of a bore. I have the embarrassing experience of someone picking up my wineglass by mistake. The Bishop graced us with his presence and urged us all to work together in these difficult times'.

Sunday: 'We have another Mass centre at Thorpe where they have a nice purpose built church. This is combined with a trip to Hoveton. I read the Bishops' statement about the current IRA attacks in London and Ireland. It's extraordinary how people here arrive late and continue to drift in right up until the offertory. I suppose it's still the old mentality of making sure that you are there for the Offertory lest you commit a mortal sin. The importance of the Liturgy of the Word still hasn't had an impact here yet. We are also helping out at St John's as they are short of a curate and I had to go over to Notre Dame High School to say Mass for the nuns. They still have a lectern outside the sanctuary for the sisters to read from as this is still the rule and at St John's the people are still not yet allowed to receive Communion in the hand. There was some compensation today as it was Judy's birthday and so we had more than enough to eat and drink'.

DECEMBER

2nd : 'Roy and I agree that we had far too much to eat and drink yesterday and with the threatened economic catastrophe round the corner we needed to make the most of it'.

3rd : 'My identity wasn't questioned at my second visit to the prison, but the porter had a job finding any keys for me this time and when he did there was a problem finding a chain to attach them to. In the event he couldn't find one so I had to clutch the keys to myself for dear life lest a quick fingered inmate wrest them from me. The Mass went well and the prisoners were a delight ! It strikes me that they have more freedoms – television, visits etc – than we ever had at the seminary! I look in at the youth club on the way back but find it all rather uninspiring – like much else here'.

4th: 'My big day at Anglia TV. About half a dozen parsons had gathered for the training course. We started with a brief interview before the cameras when I suggested that a underground system might be ideal for Norwich. We then did a two and a half minute solo on some secular subject. Mine was the life cycle of the Large Blue Butterfly. I received some constructive criticism and Canon Freeman and a Methodist said that I had improved considerably on the second attempt. We then went to the control room to see how an actual epilogue was put together and I was impressed by the meticulous care that was put in for such a small contribution. I walked back to the presbytery, exhausted after the experience and Bob returned later completely whacked out. It seems so unfair that he has the responsibility of both a large parish and this chaplaincy to the Television Centre. I found the experience very useful as it trained me to use an economy of words in putting over ideas and was a very good discipline. This was only the trial run and I have been signed up to do some real epilogues'.

5th: 'To celebrate Judy's birthday we go for a slap up meal at Dino's, an Italian restaurant, and for the first time have a huge bowl of mussels. We look in at the medieval church that Bob hopes to buy to replace the old Fishergate Church'.

6th: 'I am finding picking up the two old gentlemen from their nursing home for Mass at the mental hospital very frustrating. It was especially so today when having waited an eternity for one to turn up announced that the day before he had been on a twenty mile cycle ride and so was rather tired! Why he can't bike to Mass then I have no idea! One sometimes feels that they think they are doing us a favour in being able to pick them up! Another annual meal we have to contend with is that of the Ladies' Guild. There was the feeling of being devoured by them , but it was a pleasant evening and they were all nice people. On return we found that Geoffrey Laycock wants to resign as organist and choirmaster – now's my opportunity?'

'We have two crematoria to service. One was at Horsham St Faith's which was the first to be opened in this country where the coffin descends rather than going through the curtains. The one at Earlham road is more modern. On my next visit there the Polish Priest from Cambridge, Fr Trochim was conducting the service and he was able to bring me up to date with happenings in Cambridge. It seems that Canon Taylor is more on edge than ever and he, Trochim, is running my English choir. The crematorium attendant said that they were getting so many cremations that they were having to do them as they went along. So this energetic man was pulling the curtains, adjusting the hi-fi for the music and dashing behind the scenes to keep the fires on the move.'

8th : 'Half a dozen people attend the sponsored silence in the hall and Judy says that it is impossible to get anyone to do anything in this parish.. Only twenty five turned up to a parish social even though they had a band that played on relentlessly. One parishioner lamented the 'general apathy in the parish'. I seem to have heard that before somewhere! Bob keeps talking about handing in his resignation to the Bishop on the 18th – the anniversary of this appointment here – it doesn't do much to boost one's enthusiasm about the place. Perhaps it is not surprising that things are as they are due to the current economic gloom.'

13th: 'This Friday was a really black day interest rates are running at twenty per cent – the highest ever. Despite that I went to enquire about the price of pianos – a new one was about £470 and a reconditioned one at £270. Eventually I did buy one which I parked in the sacristy and it was a great joy to go in there and let off steam on the first piano I had ever owned'.

14th: 'With the economy being as it is we are now restricted to driving at 50 mph on the roads and I had to remember this on a trip over to Cambridge to a dental appointment and have a chat with Tony Rogers at OLEM about life. It was a chance to visit cousin Win at Lidgate who is now causing some worry as her legs are playing her up and she forgets to turn off the electric. However the pest control man had been in and twenty one rats have been successfully eliminated'.

15th: 'Not all is doom and gloom, although the IRA are still active and it is dangerous to leave one's bike unattended, for we were invited to Cocktails, Cabaret and Conversation with the East Anglia discussion group at Notre Dame Convent. The Poringland players supplied the cabaret. Fr Little OSB was also there from Beccles and we were told that he had received 'baptism in the Spirit'.

4th Sunday of Advent: 'We have our Carol service and Graham Bell, the announcer from Anglia TV did the readings. John Swinfield, also from Anglia and his Catholic wife came along too. This fairly lack lustre affair was nothing compared with the interminable offering at Hellesdon hospital where I had to say the introductory prayer'.

Christmas Day: 'And so my first Christmas at St George's and I am given the honour of being the celebrant at the Midnight Mass which was quite well attended. Bob preached and I wondered whether he was having a dig at me when he spoke about people spending two or three hundred pounds on themselves – in reference to my piano?'

I was at the outstations for the day but it enabled me to go down to London having sandwiches en route. This was the first Christmas at home for about 15 years. But for the people of Darwin things were very different as their city was destroyed by a terrible tornado.

31st: 'The year ends with a bang. Bob ever hospitable invites all the local clergy including the Bishop over for a New Year's Eve party. It was a superb turkey meal but I felt very uneasy about the general conversation when it got on to talk about various aspects of the Church. It all seemed so irrelevant to the world outside. The Bishop mentioned something about an Industrial Chaplaincy in the area – I hope it's not going to be the case of getting landed with a another responsibility without any preparation'.

Living it up at St. George's
Roy and Me

CHAPTER TWELVE

I NEARLY GET MY FIRST PARISH
1975

JANUARY

We marked the inauguration of the Holy Year with a Pontifical Mass at St John's. Bob and Roy agreed with me that it was interminable and quite dreary. One wondered really what the Bishop's homily meant to anyone and the sung plainsong Kyrie seemed out of place. Well if that didn't uplift and inspire us then watching the film *The Charge of the Light Brigade* with some alcoholic sustenance on our return did just that. In some chat after the ceremony Bishop Clark didn't see any future for smaller groupings in the Church as a possible long term development. We all agreed that it would be pretty disastrous if he were transferred to Westminster as the bookies seem to suggest.

5th: 'The IRA menace is never far away and Roy has an anonymous phone call threatening to blow us all up tomorrow and the police came round to check things out. So what with that and postage going up to 7p things are not too bright'.

6th: 'Epiphany was celebrated with a glass of Green Chartreuse after a sung Mass at which Plainsong Mass 12 was rendered – not even Richens sang that particular setting– it was quite unbeknown to me. The congregation are still not responding to the *Mysterium Fidei* or to the *Embolism*. Festivities were not yet complete as it was over to the elegance of the White House at Poringland where we enjoyed fellowship with other clergy members of the Deanery'.

7th: 'The exceptionally mild weather continues and nature seems quite confused with the spring flowers coming out all over the place – and in January too.'

'I rather like eavesdropping on conversations and on my return trip from seeing the folks in London a group of high powered men were discussing the Anglican Church. It appeared that one was surveyor at St Paul's Cathedral and York Minister. One was heard to say that he thought that in twenty years the Anglican Church would turn into a little sect'.

12th: I am quite alone in the house with both Bob and Roy away. It must be dreadful living alone without anyone to talk to – a one horse mission for the next thirty years is not a very inviting prospect – no wonder half the clergy are eccentric. In fact Roy and I had been going through the clergy we regarded as eccentric the other day'.

I travelled over to Cambridge to see how CRESE was going and stayed with John Drury at St Laurence's. The session was good and was given by Fr

Michael Hollings. He gave us a fascinating insight into his parish at Southall and his work with the down and outs to whom he gave hospitality in the presbytery – not everyone could take this. Certainly Canon Taylor only recently had the experience of being attacked by a dosser in the rectory and the night shelter is moving just round the corner from the church.

14th: 'A fellow curate of Bob's comes to lunch, Fr George Grace recently appointed to Huntingdon. They reminisce about clergy of old and the long sagas of last year's appointments – mine it seems was not the only one! Another priest from my year has left – so that makes three curates leaving in three months! – not to speak of those who have retired or crocked up'.

18th: The Unity Service for the Week of Prayer at Mile Cross Methodist was invigorated by the Sally Army Songsters who raised the roof. An Anglican preached and the Captain kept saying 'Amen' all through the sermon and my Bidding Prayers. We had our own celebration at the church with some songs splendidly delivered by five men from the cathedral choir and ending with a hymn which I accompanied. To get away from it all for awhile I went for a ride out to Yarmouth and then to the Roman Burgh Castle at which I arrived after a long muddy walk from St Fursey's Church. The wind was so piercing that I didn't stay long, but the Roman ruins were spectacular.'

I had another trip down to Anglia Television to watch them recording some epilogues. This time it was the scripture scholar Joseph Rhymer. This gave me more insight into what I would experience shortly and during an excellent meal Mr Rhymer was quite convinced that Israel and Egypt were likely to destroy each other through nuclear attack this year and nobody would bat an eyelid.

Bob meanwhile had returned from giving a course on communications in Lincoln – he was very depressed and kept talking of resigning. However things were a little more cheerful watching the enthronement of Dr Coggan as 101st Archbishop of Canterbury with all the top Vatican brass there – Cardinals Suenans, Willibrand and Marty. Coggan's sermon was quite positive and inspirational. Once Bob was out of the way Roy and I had a heart to heart chat about the same old problems – too many jobs and not being able to tackle any one properly.

During my new year's break in London mother and I made our first trip to Canterbury. There was torrential rain but it was quite mild. It was a pity that the cathedral was covered in scaffolding but none the less it was very impressive. On our way back we looked in at Aylesford Priory which I hadn't visited since a trip from primary school. A trip up to the records office in Portugal Street revealed that my great grandfather farmed 100 acres at Great Bradley. The flat had been converted to natural gas but aunt Dorothy began suffering from shortness of breath and it turned out that the fitting was faulty and it had been leaking. She makes an excellent 'canary'.

FEBRUARY

5th 'Now that Geoffrey Laycock has retired from running the choir I am doing my best to keep things going by teaching the congregation new music and running the choir. We seem to be getting on quite well. With Holy Week in the offing again we all discuss plans with the MC. Something of a bad dream again with the strange mixture of tradition and progressiveness that Bob has'.

10th: 'We do have some marriages here. I do rather dread some aspects of the preparation course. The catholic girl was 16 and uninstructed, knowing practically nothing about the Catholic faith. It seems quite wrong to load her with all that is required of her by the Church's law – but there is the declaration that she has to make – to 'remain true to her faith as God laws demand etc etc.''

Roy and I had a meeting with the Society of St Vincent de Paul and the question of their being commissioned to take Holy Communion to the sick arose . Only one was really keen and the rest would only do it if required to do so and two or three could not do so in conscience. Evidently we have got a long way to go in helping people to appreciate these new responsibilities.

15th: 'I actually did some visiting today. I visit about a dozen families. All but three had moved but met some rather interesting locals in a rather deprived area. And this was going to be the pattern of visiting with most families having moved away and those that were left were lapsed and kept one on the doorstep – one in fact was waving a carving knife. It is difficult to know what one can do to evangelise these families and certainly our visiting lists are all hopelessly out of date.'

I was advised at the next cremation by the undertaker that the lady in question would 'readily cremate' as she 'had lived life to the full and was on the gin until the end'! One might say that about the clergy too as it was any excuse for a drop – this we enjoyed after a dinner with the teachers from the schools over the river. Bob as usual was the life and soul of the party and needless to say we came home by taxi.

20th: 'Bob is nothing if not an enthusiast and he wants to go ahead straight away with house Masses and a youth vigil. I feel that we need a bit more time to settle in and get to know people a bit better.'

Our next Deanery conference was at St John's and we were graced by the Bishop's presence. The main topic of discussion was what we thought the Bishop ought to do about preaching the Gospel in the modern world. Needless to say we didn't get far but we ended up with a concelebrated Mass attended by various local civic leaders and heads of religious bodies to remember the late Duke of Norfolk whose father had built the church – in thanksgiving for a happy marriage.

Occasionally we would help out at the school in the other parish and we started off Lent by administering the ashes. Bob vowed to go onto tomato juice during Lent but come Sunday we succumbed- anyway it is agreed that the Sundays do not constitute part of Lent and so the temptation being too strong it was a little sherry and 'Southern Comfort'.

I now had to put my mind to organising the youth vigil. I was somewhat in the dark so went over to Notre Dame school to elicit help from one of the younger nuns. But she wasn't much help and didn't seem to have much idea how to organise one either. I also visited the Williams family who were stalwarts of the club and various other things. They did not show much enthusiasm but would rally round and help.

My next visit to the prison although uneventful consisted in having to sign the Official Secrets Act and to get my pass. I learned that two prisoners at least were being discriminated against over pay because they come to Mass in spite of assurances by the Governor. On return Bob had finished getting together his first Parish Report. This seemed a very good idea as it informed the parish about all the various facets of parish life - especially income and expenditure.

So it was to work on three projects – the All night Vigil, my talks for the Epilogues at Anglia and more marriage instructions. I got on quite well with the latest engaged couple but they began to look embarrassed when I brought religion into it.

My first house Mass was at Mrs Grace's at Hoveton. About six came but the discussion afterwards was chaotic. One man there was an ardent Latinist who had some very contradictory ideas. While professing loyalty to the Church on the one hand he wasn't for having any of the changes the Church was bringing in. The trouble is many people have no idea about the reasons behind the changes- which we were trying to emphasise at Cambridge. They seem to think that it is just change for changes sake. It was all just a bit depressing and one just doesn't know what people really believe.. Judy, the housekeeper, certainly doesn't like the alterations and come the Thursday Mass which I said as Bob was away she wanted me, as he does, to celebrate in the Lady Chapel with back to the people and the Epistle and Gospel in Latin. I didn't comply with the latter. She hates the Sign of Peace which is strange as she is such an outgoing person and moves as far away from people as possible at this point.

My texts for the epilogues were now complete and so hand them in. I get to work typing up a Seder Service for the Vigil and one of the nuns brought in some visual aids to use.

A Salvatorian priest preached the annual appeal for the missions. He refused to say more than two Masses (rightly so) but I was landed with having to say four which really was against all the rules. Mass at the prison but only three attended.

MARCH

3rd: 'I am still trying to do some parish visiting. I managed one evening to visit twenty homes. This sounds impressive but this was because most of them had moved and the remainder weren't a little bit interested but there was a surprising welcome from one or two.'

5th: 'My debut at Anglia Television. We started with coffee in the board room with Canon Freeman and Graham Bell and then on to the make up room. Then I did my two party pieces. It turned out not to be as nerve racking as I thought though it was a bit odd not having any audience except the camera crew. At least we had an excellent lunch at the Royal where a Methodist minister also recording epilogues gave a gloomy prospect of the political future – leaving the Common Market, collapse of the present government with a third party emerging. We shall see. There was enough tragedy about with the terrible Moorgate train disaster without having to dwell on further catastrophes.'

10th: 'Mass at the prison. One or two men thought a clerical collar would be a good disguise for a burglary. And if that was not madness enough we hear that Fr Guy Pritchard has been certified and sent to Hellesden Hospital. I went to see him later and chatted for about half an hour.'

16th: 'At Mass I talk about the various textual changes coming in the English version of the Creed. It's strange that Great Britain should be the last to get into line with the rest of the English speaking world. Now we say 'We believe' instead of 'I' – in line with the Council of Ephesus in 431 AD'.

19th: 'My big night for the epilogue arrives and my debut on the tele. Just as we sat down to watch I got a sick call to Wroxham to see Mr Neave who was dying. So I never got to see myself on the box'.

22nd: 'My preparation for the Vigil comes to fruition. About twenty five youngsters stayed the course. We started off with the Seder Meal with a proper meal in the middle. This was followed by Oberamagau slides of the stations of the cross, J.C. Superstar, thoughts on the world's problems, personal responsibility, Confessions and ending with Mass at dawn. A chap who works at the theatre set up some good effects. So my efforts all seemed worthwhile and people seemed to get something out of it. However the

331

unleavened bread we used at the Seder and also at the dawn Mass proved to be rather 'primitive' and the left overs in the tabernacle took sometime to finish.'

Mgr Charles Davidson one of the great characters of the diocese and who remembered me in the Moses Basket at Kirtling had died and so I attended his funeral in Cambridge There were about 80 clergy present and both the bishops. Bishop Grant had a kindly word and actually thanked me for my letter of six months ago (presumably regarding Gerry Thornton) – he said that it had had it desired effect and so I am glad that I wrote it and Bishop Clark actually asked me how things were going.

And so it was Holy Week again and the Chrism Mass was celebrated at St John's at midday. I found it long and tedious and uninspiring. Our evening Mass went well and we had Communion under both kinds – of course we had to celebrate afterwards. At the Good Friday liturgy Roy presided and I was Deacon. We read the Passion in three parts with the choir singing the crowd parts in English. Thick snow arrived for Easter Sunday but it was gone again very quickly.

APRIL

1st: 'An historic day with the funeral of + Leo Parker and so of course we all converged on the Cathedral at Northampton for the event. The ceremony was very impressive and Cardinal Heenan, looking very florid and hardly able to struggle along himself, was there and Bishop Grant presided. The ten bishops present were a sorry looking sight – poor old boys. There ought to be a compulsory retirement age of 65 for bishops. +Leo had received special permission from the Home Office to be buried in the Cathedral as its enlargement had been very much his creation and he was interred in the Blessed Sacrament Chapel. We later went to inspect and were surprised that the coffin was only about three feet down. The celebrations were followed by a pleasant buffet. + Leo for all his foibles was a very pastoral bishop and although many parish priests were in terror of his Visitations I always felt that he took a personal interest in me. Perhaps he is the last of the Prince Bishops'.

2nd: 'Back to visiting again and call on a fourteen year old at the David Rice mental hospital. She was too advanced for her years and regarded religion as 'a lot of squit'. Fr Guy was in bed and so took him Communion. Some of the families I visited were really 'inadequate' and living in quite squalid conditions but in spite of this they all seemed happy. One lady was now bedridden after an operation designed to reduce her thirty two stone. But this was nothing compared with the horrors continuing in Vietnam when the first relief plane load of orphans crashes killing the lot of them. The problem of evil brought out in all its starkness. 'Why does God always seem to play into the enemy's hands' says Bob'.

5th: 'Coming up to Ascension, Judy informs me that the Paschal Candle must be removed on this feast – of course this has now been changed to stay on till Pentecost – but best not to fall out over a candle! It's funny that those who appeal to the discipline of the pre-Council Church won't accept the present discipline. Though some strange things seem to happen in some places when a parishioner informed me that when he went to Mass in Manchester people received Communion 'in an envelope' !? Paul Jarvis, a parishioner and talented cartoonist could have made a great sketch of that one. As it was there was a famous one of a Christmas cake with Bob, Roy and me portrayed as little figures standing on the top of it'.

A farewell Mass was celebrated for Geoffrey Laycock after ten years work running the choir and the music. There was a presentation for him but £27 seemed excessively mean after all the work he has put in here.

Days off became very fraught again. Aunt Elsie was taken ill while I was down in London with pains in her chest and vomiting and she was taken off to hospital while mother and I followed in the car. All this is putting considerable strain on everyone and especially mother who gets so worried and het up about things. Aunt Dorothy for all her eighty years and frailty is a tower of strength. This rather scuppered mother's return to the country but I was able to take some of her luggage back with me. A heavy fall of snow didn't help matters and I was none too happy having to do my one hundred and two miles trek back to Norwich. After several days of great concern she pulled through once again and I only wish that I wasn't so far away. Then we had the budget with 2% on income tax and car tax up from £15 to £40 with the £200 million cut in oversees aid which seemed particularly mean – not to speak of inflation reaching 21%

For Judy's 55th birthday we all trooped off to Dino's to have our usual slap lunch. Canon Freeman also came together with his atheist wife who was obsessed with cats. It was perhaps not surprising that a few days later Bob had another 'cholic' and the doctor was called in. He delighted in showing us a very bloody bottled specimen. This didn't stop us celebrating a few days later Bob's sister's birthday who had died in 1927.

My days off were now trying to get the house in order for mother's return. Luckily there was some nice sunny and warm weather and I was able to decorate the bathroom and cut the grass which was in a terrible state.

We now introduced, at last, an Offertory procession at St Boniface's while Mass at Fishergate still with back to the people continued to be irritating with the congregation reciting their parts at different times and the deputy head continuing to come up to light candles during communion and cleaning and scraping up the wax.

Another interesting experience was a trip down to Anglia Television to watch a production of Sale of the Century compered by Nicholas Parsons whom we met beforehand. The clergy being beyond reproach acted as judges should there be any contentious answers. Saigon falls and thirty years of this dreadful war has now come to an end.

Bob goes off to an International Television Convention in Brighton and so it is back to the prison again. Over a dozen men came – they were all new bar one and they all participated well but I find it rather difficult to make small talk afterwards. The prison warder asked if I wanted him to stay – I said no, though in the face of the numbers I wouldn't have minded. Bob told me afterwards that this was because there were a couple in for sexual offences and other prisoners might have turned on them.

MAY

My week away was nearly put off with Bob going for yet another meeting but luckily he was back in time for me to go home to sort the family out now that they had returned to the country. It seemed strange on a trip to Cambridge with no through traffic in town due to the opening of the bypass but I was a little worried lest I was identified as the Cambridge rapist as I am about his size. He has already attacked a number of women and there was great concern.

The next *ad clerum* from the bishop was a little more positive as it reported on giving a subsidy to priests who have a long way to travel to visit their aged parents – perhaps I have had some influence! At the next deanery meeting the priest from Lowestoft was getting very worried by the Sisters' constant demand there for Communion under both kinds!! Our car allowance went up to £350 which was good and the usual slap up buffet concluded affairs.

Due to Judy's comments mentioned earlier the paschal candle had been removed on Ascension Thursday but then reappeared again for Whitsunday – the parish priest had at last realised its symbolic significance!

One of my regular communicants was a Cyril De'ath who was completely blind. His house was pretty bare and miserable but I suppose that was really of no concern to him and he had people coming in to keep an eye on him. He was a nice simple straight forward chap who had no complaints about his disability – but tragedy struck him on the news that his nephew had been blown up by an IRA bomb in Belfast – the carnage just goes on and on.. An ailing Pole with a brain tumour was my next port of call and the wife of a company director who was bitterly complaining about the gypsies encamped near their establishment.

30th: 'Who should turn up to do a baptism but Michael Jones-Frank from Oscott days. He is now a naval chaplain – appropriate as his nickname at college had always been 'The Admiral'. When he leaves the service he is going to be an artist as he can't see himself fitting in 'the system'

JUNE
2nd : 'The coldest June day since records began and there were heavy snow showers in some parts of the country. All the seasons seem to be getting muddled up. I get my new Renault 4 with its eccentric gear change system. I got £620 on my mini and will have to find the balance of £750 - the menace of inflation. I was presented at the garage with a bouquet of flowers 'for my wife' – I should have said 'don't you realise that I am an eschatological sign?'!'

The Common Market referendum received a comfortable majority and I preached a short homily on the 'European dimension'. It coincided appropriately with the feast of St Boniface, the patron of the church, which we duly celebrated at Hellesden.

News then reached us that Fr Hubert Richards had left the priesthood – the last of the Corpus Christi group – a sad reflection on the ecclesiastical set up in this country – he has done a lot to popularise Scripture study by his books.

23rd : 'Another trip to the prison as Bob had to go into hospital for a cystoscopy - they found warts on his bladder and so had to operate straight away to cauterise them – poor chap and I went to see him in the Norfolk and Norwich where he seemed reasonably bright. Judy thinks he will be a semi-invalid from now on. One wonders why he wasn't left at Gorleston where he had been happy. In the meantime Fr Peter Williams OFM comes all the way up from London to supply. At the prison I visited a man who had been shot in both legs. A rather daunting experience when the cell door shuts behind you and you wonder whether he might attack you and not be able to get out in time.'

It was prison again the following week and the reading appropriately enough was St Peter's escape from prison especially in the context of the easy escape routes from Norwich prison by the inmates.

On top of all this a broadcast Mass had been arranged supervised by Rev Hubert Hoskins. With Bob being away I had to preside at the Mass itself. In the event it all went very well. I received a certain amount of 'fan mail' afterwards including a namesake – an eccentric gentleman whom I was to meet sometime later and also a second cousin who for many years would send me a cake on my birthday.

The ministers' fraternal was held at the presbytery and a good cross section of Baptists, URC, Methodist and C/E. But the prospect of real unity would seem to be very remote with such diverse views. One wonders what further progress can really be made when it comes down to the average minister and congregation.

A visit to Hoveton turned up a family who had lapsed because of the Irish situation and the apparent silence of the hierarchy in not condemning the violence. One meets so few people who have any idea of the what the Church is all about – apart from 'duty' and the Sacramental Service.

I had built a polythene tunnel greenhouse at home and by now the courgettes and the tomatoes had practically taken over the whole show.

JULY

1st: 'Another sad piece of news came in about this time that Nicholas Lash had applied for laicisation. He is one of our most brilliant theologians but he continued in this role, eventually becoming the first Catholic to hold a chair of theology in the University of Cambridge– there doesn't seem to be any immediate explanation for things. All our good people seem to be leaving'.

The Bishop calls to see Bob who is not so well again. He informs us that his condition is malignant and will have to go for a three monthly check up –poor chap.

It seems that St John's Parish Council has written to Bishop Grant advising him that the church needs a new roof as the lead is wearing out after a hundred years and it is going to cost ¼ million pounds. They suggested moving to a smaller church but received no reply from the Bishop. In the end they sent him telegrams. O this general malaise and inactivity is quite sickening.

18th : 'A happy day for once with the ordination to the diaconate of David Bagstaff at OLEM. I went by the new Newmarket bypass. I had tea in the scullery at Hope Nursing Home with Sr Aiden –just like old times. The ongoing sagas at the church continue and Bishop Grant comes to celebrate the ordination but there was no enquiry about Bob's health or how I was coping. All the old team was there and also twelve lay people were commissioned to administer Holy Communion – surprisingly some of the more traditional types. The organ which had been cleaned sounded glorious'.

Liturgical discontent continued with one lady attacking Bob for introducing standing for Communion and another said that a friend had left the Church because he had said in a sermon that you don't have to come to Confession every time before going to Communion.

21st: 'Trip to the prison but had to have a 'dry' Mass as I had forgotten the altar breads – it didn't occur to me to ask the Anglican chaplain for help. Bob informs me that this has been the unhappiest year he has experienced in the priesthood'.

22nd: 'I have an interesting get together with the Brewster family at Hoveton. Mr Brewster takes guided tours around the Broads and Mr Bates who was also there is a public prosecutor so it was a lively evening and didn't get home until midnight. A rather crusty major does the reading from time to time. He read a passage from the prophet Malachi, except his rendering of it was 'the prophet Malarchy'. We have an up and coming young organist, Nick Walmsley, the son of the family to whom I take communion, and is also something of a composer, so that is encouraging for the future'.

A university student at Thorpe said that I had preached a bad sermon so we had a chat afterwards and was relived to find that it was a misunderstanding. One wonders how many other homilies go the same way. It's a pity we don't get more of this criticism and an opportunity to discuss the sermon with the congregation.

AUGUST

I sometimes feel we are just Mass machines churning out religion. It was certainly like this on the feast of the Assumption with services at 7, 12.15, 6.30 and 7.30. And then I had a potential convert – a Jehovah's Witness girl – unfortunately she didn't stay the course but it was interesting while it lasted.

With August came some holiday and worries continued about the state of the cottage. 'It is going to cost some £2000 to have the roof rethatched and the end bedroom window is beginning to decay. Usually dad has done all these repairs and the cost of getting someone in was going to be impossible. I tried to get a ready made window in Cambridge but they were all too big so in the end I managed to knock one together with my innate carpentry skills and with various ropes etc hauled it into place – I was quite pleased with my efforts. But even more of a worry is mother's walking ability which seems to be the onset of arthritis but she is being very stubborn about it. I can see that I shall have to get leave of absence to look after them all.'

I was now becoming very frustrated and uncertain about my position and decided to draw up an assessment of my present situation and state of mind:

August: 'Norwich has its compensations. I must start on an optimistic line. The presbytery set up is excellent and the quarters are most comfortable. The house-keeper is a gem, albeit a formidable one. My fellow curate, too, is most pleasant. The parish priest most kind, very human and understanding, but, sad to say, afflicted, since he has been here, with various ailments. He is not happy in a large parish and looks forward to the day when he can leave. He says that the eighteen months he has been here have been the unhappiest time in his priesthood. We could make a very good team. If the presbytery set up here could be transferred to Cambridge the situation would be ideal.

However, the general feeling I have is one of drift. It would be nice if people would say from time to time - 'that's a good idea; anything I can do to help?' I won't say the people are unfriendly - far from it - but so few seem to have any idea what the Church is all about. They flock to the whist drives and bingo, the 'pig and whistle' and the socials - though even the latter are really only supported by a hard core. But when it comes to 'active participation' as a Christian community then it's very hard going. There's resistance all along the line. The choir - so steeped in tradition - really don't want any changes and adapt - but who can blame them? People drift in late for Mass and drift out early. The Ladies' Guild and the SVP Would rather miss Communion than have it administered by a lay- person. Things like the Third World group are poorly supported. The Ladies' guild seems more concerned with making corn dollies and learning new recipes than with the apostolate. The Christian education of our young people is in a poor state and really no nearer a solution as we come up to another term minus a nun. The youth club, such as it is, has folded up - not surprisingly since I have no experience of youth clubs and have very little interest in sporting activities. Anyway are we supposed to be providing entertainment? Ecumenism is best forgotten. Apart from the annual event, supported by a minority, there is little real interest.

It's very easy to suffer from an identity crisis especially when people think you are the electricity or gas man, or have come to to fix the new fridge. You might, indeed, be a creature from outer space for the difference it makes. What is one supposed to be doing apart from merely keeping the plant going? Go out into the highways and byways and start preaching? It was with a deep sense of embarrassment this morning as a man was doing just that in the centre of Norwich. Doctrinally he seemed sound enough but the only reaction was that people hurried by.

What have I learned since being here? That Cambridge is by no means the most frustrating of places - in fact it was positively flourishing. There are my visits to the prison which, although very interesting, is something I don't think I could stomach on a regular basis; a broadcast Mass, two epilogues on TV; a disappointing attempt at a folk Mass; a fairly rewarding all night vigil; the purchase of a piano on which I have unleashed my frustrations. But I feel that I am somewhere near a cross roads; I have never been so near giving things up as I have been this year. Drift! But perhaps reflecting the general drift in society at the moment with no one really seeming to know where they are going or how to get there.'

A new saga in the diocese was developing in the diocese with Fr Baker of Downham Market refusing to say the new Mass in English and Canon Taylor was interviewed on the radio about his possible removal. In the event the saga just went on and on with Fr Baker remaining in the old presbytery and acting as chaplain to some other like minded people. It proved very difficult for the new parish priest who was appointed. Since Fr Baker was still living in the presbytery he had to find other accommodation. On one occasion there was a protest by some two hundred and fifty people in support of Fr Baker and the Tridentine Mass and he received considerable news coverage.

SEPTEMBER
On return from holiday my first duty was a trip to the prison. I visited a pleasant chap in a cell. He, it seems, had nearly slit someone's throat with a piece of glass. He had a rosary tastefully draped over a nude pin up. I was rather horrified to see a young teenager on remand with all these old lags.

16th : 'Some sad news with the sudden death of my cousin David. He it seems had fallen into a diabetic coma and with a bit of sugar he could have been saved. This lead to Uncle Wilf selling up the cottage at Ousden and returning home to Maidenhead. We shall miss our visits to him and our stimulating discussions.'

'I am now responsible for running the choir. It is not easy as they are still very much inclined to the Latin and are reluctant to do anything in English at the sung Mass. So I just have to put up with that and get them going with the new Liturgy in Latin. What is difficult is that they seem totally unaware of what the Church is trying to achieve with the reforms. I sometimes get the impression that they think I am introducing new things off my own bat.'

22nd : 'Prison Mass again. It is always so daunting walking up to the prison gates and feel like running away on occasion. It's very embarrassing asking for the keys which the porter still finds difficulty in finding. At least this time at the Mass I had to control my mirth when one of the prisoners pronounced 'Hittites' as 'High Titties'!'

23rd: 'And now a new experience in marriage counselling. A few weeks ago I had married two seventy five year olds. Now they were having problems and I was summoned round to try and sort them out ! They were really at each others throats and there was little I, with my tender years and inexperience, could do to sort out these two aged lovers apart from sitting and listening to their mutual recriminations.'

'Not only is Bob ailing but Roy has now been struck down with something similar. This time it's a phlebolith and he is in some considerable pain so with the two of them in this state things are none too cheerful.'

Communion sick rounds could be sometimes very disconcerting. I sometimes felt that people considered they were doing me a favour by allowing me to bring them Communion rather than for their spiritual benefit. On one occasion no sooner had I put the host in the person's mouth than the lady shot up in bed and asked if I wanted a cup of tea

29th: 'Prison again. Bob having recovered from his migraine which takes him out of action from time to time was off to the Crown Court to give support to a prisoner who was awaiting trial. While waiting he found himself unknowingly talking to the Cambridge rapist who shortly afterwards got life imprisonment. The most extraordinary case since Jack the Ripper they say.'

A documentary on the television highlighted the new seminary at Econe which is training a new generation of priests to bring the 'Old Mass' to people wherever they want it. One such priest said that they were the true Church and the Pope and Cardinals had apostatised. Even Bishop Grant said that he was beginning to get worried about things.

OCTOBER

6th: ' My days off now seem to be concerned with doing remedial work on the cottage. Climbing onto the roof and into the very small roof space to try and plug gaps in the straw. Sparrows were getting into the roof next door and became very distraught when I started wiring up their entrances. Mother's legs are now really becoming a source of concern.'

A Spaniard called in about his proposed marriage. He wanted to marry a divorced non-catholic and I was supposed to provide him with a document formally excommunicating him so that his civil marriage would be recognised in Spain – I was glad I could pass that buck to the Spanish Church in London to sort out!

9th: 'I have now acquired an ecclesiastical cloak – very useful for the warmth and for graveside burials. It came from Dr Frank Cleobury, a relative of the Dean cousins. He had been an Anglican Divine and interned for conscientious objection during the First War. His sister, Elsie, had become a Catholic together with other members of the family. Frank's grandson, Stephen, later became director of music at Kings College. I went round to see them as they lived the other side of Norwich. He gave me some pastoral advice on preaching the essential doctrines of the Faith. He was a convert from the Baptists to Anglicanism and his sister from Baptists to Catholicism.'

10th: 'I endeavoured to anoint a lady in hospital but she stopped me in no uncertain terms – and an eighty year old parishioner tells me that this is a dead parish and gives me 25p for a Mass stipend.'

NOVEMBER

7th: 'Cardinal Heenan dies – certainly a great character and popular among ordinary folk. Bishop Clark seems to be in the running as his successor – one hopes not! Our catechetical efforts with the children do not seem to be bearing much fruit. One child when asked what he could tell me about Holy Communion said that it was that piece of soggy bread that you get and which you suck and must not chew !!! What have we come to?'

8th: 'I am in Bob's bad books. He now blows his top in one of his occasional outbursts – I can only put it down to his ongoing illness. He ranted about my doing nothing about the youth club or having prepared songs for Confirmation. I'm afraid I was rather sharp in return. This was followed by another clobbering for not having filled in a couple of god-parents names at a baptism. I am slipping. But things were soon put right and Bob apologised for getting on my back. On top of this another disaster strikes when + Alan calls me aside and informs me that I am being sent to Thrapston to live in a caravan in the New Year. Will they never learn after all the carry on of last year?'

10th: 'It transpired that Bob had known this for sometime and had gleaned the information from the other side of the diocese. In fact Alan Clark didn't know where I was going until Bob had informed him! I must say Bob was fuming and may have accounted for the outburst the other day. I just don't know what I am going to do now – its marginally nearer home than here but the prospect of living in a caravan is something I find difficult to face and on top of that it is in the other side of the diocese which, when the diocese divides will place me 'on the wrong side' and this after the consultation by the Bishop asking us on which side we would prefer to be . Should I ask for transfer to Brentwood? I daren't tell the family at the moment. I wrote to +Charles saying that I had heard rumours of a move – because as yet I had heard nothing official. I soon got a phone call from Derrick Morgan, the secretary, saying that he was sorry that things had leaked out. A typically disarming phone call soon followed from + Charles saying that there was talk about building a house or getting a mobile home. But our conversation was cut short – it sounded as though someone was jamming the line! My colleagues were amused and they are coming to jeer at me at Thrapston.'

24th: 'Prison. On checking up at home I find that aunt Win was in the process of having a blackout – well if she will heave around pails of coal at 82 and still go out in the early morning to weed the front bank.'

25th : 'Bob, on his way back from Northampton, calls in at Thrapston. It really sounds awful and I am in a quandary. It seems now that they are expecting a change over on the 28th December! What a time to expect anyone to move. I had to let the family know and they were rather upset though I didn't let on about the caravan. I set to composing letters to the Bishop. Aunt Dot seemed remarkably placid and was praying away for me. However I inspected a mobile home on a site and got some brochures and they look rather attractive but I will be going over there in a few days to check things out for myself – after the Bishop had rung me up asking me if I had made a decision.'

I spoke to Alan Clark when he came to do the parish Visitation and expressed again my wish to stay in the new Diocese, however he thought I ought to go until September but with the division of the diocese imminent it might not be so easy to cross back again. Sad to say one feels that +Alan is not to be trusted and so said Paul Taylor and Bob. He did suggest Diss as a possibility and was convinced that Warlock would be going to Westminster. I took the bishop on his usual round to visit my district and the sick therein and on the trip to Hoveton he lost his *zucchetto* in a howling gale and I had to chase it down the main road someway before it landed in a puddle, but there was no further mention of my caravan move.

The following day I made my historic trip to Thrapston to check out the place. It was a brilliant sunny day until, within half a mile of the town, an ominous black cloud appeared on the horizon – a sure omen. Stan Condon, the parish priest seemed to be something of a bohemian. His caravan sort of grew out of the ground and was cold and draughty and with little room. The lavatory was in the sacristy in the adjoining church which was quite modern. He had a shower in his bedroom and two boxer dogs. He took me to nearby Raunds to meet his mother for lunch. She feeds him and does his washing. The bishop has asked him to take over the parish at Bedford. It's extraordinary that nothing has been done about his accommodation in the ten years he has been here. On top of his living conditions the window of the caravan and the sacristy had been wired over as there was a demented lady who was going round with an axe and chopping them out. Well that was just about it. Not feeling called to the life of a missionary priest, I posted my letter to the bishop declining his invitation to reside there. From there I had a dreadful three and a half hours journey back to the family in London getting caught up in the rush hour on the north circular road. They were rather shocked by my description of conditions there –and to think they wanted me to move in four weeks time just after Christmas. After a couple of days at home I returned to Norwich but there had been no communication from the bishop. We joked about Thrapston and Bob thought the situation there was appalling. He had beeen over there himself to to check it out with his Anglican colleague, Canon Freeman. He was shattered to think that the bishop could expect any one his priests to live in such conditions.

DECEMBER

Well I had no response from the bishops – neither of them. Not surprising I suppose since Alan Clark had to go into hospital for an emergency prostate operation and Charles Grant was going in soon for his cataracts – so we are a body with no heads. However we did have a message from

+ Charles for New Missions Sunday asking for £140,000 for the Church just down the road. I must say it rather stuck in my throat.

On my way to Lidgate on my day off I spied out the land at Diss – wishful thinking I fear. I did a bit of remedial work at home and looked in next door on cousin Win who seemed reasonably OK for her eighty two years and then to see aunt Eva. Poor thing she is now aged ninety and living in some squalor and still with no running hot water. She was trying to toast some bread and was nibbling it round the edges. She seemed quite pleased to see me but there is not much one can do for her as she is so independent.

Mother was now going for physiotherapy with osteoarthritis in the hips but it was not surprising as the temperature in the flat barely touched 50F. They have no central heating except a gas fire and with the ceiling unusually lofty the heat is lost. I went round trying to put draught excluders to doors and windows.

During the week before Christmas we celebrated Canon McBride's thirty second anniversary of his ordination at St. John's. Bob had taken to his bed again (pre Christmas nerves, said Judy) and so did not accompany us. We sensibly took a taxi there and back. Mgr Diamond was there as they were great friends, but there was not a single allusion to Thrapston. But there, as has been recorded elsewhere the Mgr even has secrets from himself! The visiting clergy spoke of the hard times they had had in their early careers – how they survived I don't know – but I suppose they were made of sterner stuff than I. But it was a slap up meal and plenty of good cheer.

The Sunday before Christmas: 'Our Carol service with David Self from Anglia TV reading the lessons. To Hoveton for a repeat performance. Just before Christmas the Bishop's circular to the clergy came round but there was still no news of a Thrapston appointment.'

Christmas Day: 'Masses are packed out – one wonders where they all come from and at Thorpe and Hoveton everyone joined in and sang well. We had a record collection of £700 and that was more than the parish across the river. Then with sandwiches I was away down to London in a record two and a half hours. It was good to see them for a couple of days and nice to celebrate aunt Elsie's seventy ninth birthday but mother's condition is giving great cause for concern as she struggles round. She's very philosophical and struggling bravely on but finding it more and more difficult to walk.'

29th: ' All I can say is thank heavens I am not going to Thrapston today as I should have been and was happy to count the Christmas Collection where our share was a bumper £250 each. The bets are now being placed for a successor to Cardinal Heenan and Bishop Clark is a hot favourite by Ladbrookes. Even Fr Baker's name had been put forward!'

For a change, for my day off, I went off to Diss to see Rev Whalley, the former Anglican rector of Lidgate. He was as eccentric as ever but seemed pleased to see me and asked after his old parishioners. From there it was a tour round Eye before going on to Stowmarket in the hopes of seeing Paul Hypher, but he was out. On return I discovered that my old music teacher at Laxton, Rafael Gabriel Gomer, who had died recently, had left me £10 and a brass crucifix – what a nice thought. There was great excitement as Bob and Judy were putting the finishing touches together for the clergy party tomorrow. We saw the New Year in with a drop of the hard stuff – 1975 was not to be the year when I became a parish priest!

Thrapston - Stan Condon & The Caravan

CHAPTER THIRTEEN

NEW DIOCESE, NEW PARISH
1976

JANUARY

About a dozen came to the clergy New Year's Day party including Bishop Clark (he made no mention at all about the Thrapston episode – far too preoccupied with the possibility of his own move no doubt!) As usual it was an excellent meal provided by Judy and followed by coffee and liqueurs – the Green Chartreuse being the favourite. The conversation was far from inspiring ranging through *Humanae Vitae* to Downham Market and a certain amount of clergy 'character assassinations'. I was surprised how conservative Swaffham is with the other end of the scale at Costessy, while for the chaplain at UEA everything is in black and white. It all seemed to reflect the general malaise and lack of direction facing the clergy at the moment. I really can't see Alan being the new Archbishop of Westminster he just hasn't enough charisma. Guy Pritchard was wheeled in from the local nursing home where he is at present living. I phoned up home and they were disappointed that I had heard nothing from the Bishop. However there are rumours that Tom Feighan is being sent there – too good natured to say no I fear. There was also the rumour that Clark might get Cardinal Willebrand's job on the Secretariat for Christian Unity – which may account for the surprise he expressed when someone said he thought that Willebrands would keep both jobs.

It being the end of the International Year of Women I thought I ought to say something on the subject on the Sunday. However we were soon to be nearly blown away and violent hurricane like winds hit the country with speeds of over 100 mph. We thought the house was going to blow away and there was extensive damage to be seen and debris scattered on the road to Hoveton. With worry about the cottage Bob let me off to go home to check on things. Luckily we escaped the worst but the big Bramley apple tree had been blown down as well as the tree by the pond. In other places there were massive trees uprooted and it is surprising how selective the winds were. Cousin Win had survived but it was some days before her electricity was restored.

10th: 'I was able to give some useful to advise to a patient who had attempted suicide in the hospital. His mother had told him that on recovering and going to Confession if he mentioned his problem he would be excommunicated. What dreadful misconceptions some people have. Derek Lance called in for a chat. He is obviously experiencing difficulties settling in at St

John's. Curates who are experienced men of the world are still treated as children by the Church authorities.'

12th: 'The children reassembled for the Sunday school and I was appalled by the basic ignorance that children have of details from the Gospels - but there we have a job competing with Dr Who and Danger Man etc. They are just not growing up with the background of the Faith in their homes.

14th: 'My day off consisted in trying to saw up some of the fallen trees at home – very energetic but I feel better for it as we get precious little exercise otherwise. The man came to put down poison for the rats. Quite what I shall eventually do with the property I just don't know.'

16th: 'Fr Eric Doyle OFM stays the night while making a recording at Anglia TV. He often does a late night slot with two other clergy which is a very popular programme. We talk into the early hours of the morning. He says that Clark is still hotly tipped for Westminster and Willerbrands or Villot as the next Pope. He thinks that Paul Vl the greatest Pope since Pius V and in many ways much more personable than John XX111.'

'The Vatican document on Sexual Ethics reiterating the traditional teaching of the Church is published. One feels it gives people such a clobbering that it would not be very helpful to individuals. The bishop in fact sent a missive to be read out at all Masses commenting on the document – it was not terribly helpful and we are not reading it here nor duplicating it for wider distribution. Why make any more song and dance on this utterance – it just gives the impression that the Church is sex-obsessed. It has got a very bad press coverage and causing some controversy.'

18th: 'Aunt Eva dies at the age of 90. Poor soul she can't have had a very happy life having spent many years in virtual isolation and not very friendly to people, and living in such basic conditions. As a child I always somewhat dreaded my Sunday afternoon visits to her with my dad. She always reminded me a bit of Miss Havisham.'

19th: 'Another trip to the prison for Bob. He informs me afterwards that there had been two murderers present in the congregation. It is as well that I didn't know of this before hand. The rumour mill has it now that I am going to Shefford and my chances of going to Diss have been dashed as Bob McCormick is now going there.'

20th : 'I attended an ecumenical service at Hoveton and about sixty people were present. The vicar thought my theology (not knowing that I had worked in Cambridge) was influenced by Cambridge divines – especially Christ's College! Bob said that Alan was very preoccupied and that the Westminster announcement was imminent.'

On my way to aunt Eva's funeral I called in at OLEM where Canon Taylor was facing a new crisis regarding free school transport. If it was withdrawn he thought the school would be finished. John Drury had suddenly lost his curate, Timothy Russ, and was likely to get a 'problem priest' from Liverpool.

My post Christmas break was again fraught. It was bitterly cold at the flat and I went round trying to plug up the draughts I had missed last time. Mother's hips were deteriorating and the doctor at the hospital wondered how she has been able to carry on in her present state. The treatment has done her no good and she will probably have to go to Guy's hospital within a year to have something done. The trouble now is that she keeps dozing off a lot and one only hopes that it is the tablets and nothing more serious. Naturally everyone was very worried about the future. However to cheer me up I met up with Denis Hall and went to see the film, *Jaws* up in the city. However there was a certain anxiety as the IRA were still planting bombs and there was always the fear of an attack on a public place such as a cinema. Things were not much more cheerful back at Norwich with Bob still having treatment for his 'warts' that are continuing to bleed. All very depressing and distressing and it certainly doesn't help morale in the house or in the parish.

28th: 'With Bob convalescing, after another trip to the hospital, I was deputed to go to the prison again. I find the walk down to the main gates always very daunting and causing quite a few butterflies. The performance at the porter's lodge is very irritating as they never seem to have a key available and always reluctant for me to have one. The smell of carbolic, the cheery 'trusties' doing odd jobs, the locking and unlocking of gates and climbing up several iron stairs to our dreary cell chapel all adds to the atmosphere. Unlocking the cupboard with the vestments and the wine I have one eye over my shoulder lest I be attacked by an inmate and then trying to find something to lead the discussion afterwards can be very difficult. I am never too sure of the cigarettes I bring in for them to have a drag after Mass, as to whether it was legal, in view of the notice at the entrance to the prison, but Bob assured me it was all OK. On this occasion I was locked in by the warder which I found rather discomforting and especially the lack of courtesy in the middle of Mass when one 'screw' put his head round the door asking for a prisoner. But as usual it was a flying visit and I don't think that I would like having to do this every week.'

The time spent in these institutions was again raised when the hospital chaplain at Hellesden rang wanting to get me involved in all sorts of things and enter fully into their team work. This was akin the situation at Fulbourn in Cambridge days but one just didn't have that time to give when one was responsible for so many other things in the parish. The chaplains there spend some twelve hours a week there on average. I then had my first night call at

1 am with an ex-Broadmoor patient ringing. I didn't record the reason but it must have been a call for Bob.

We were still called to meet the pupil nurses at the hospital with the other chaplains. Much to their chagrin, I thought, we got straight down to 'Last Rites' so had to hold forth on that subject. It seems that the nurses have no formal instructions about what do about calling for a priest in case of death.

30th: 'Canon Roberts, the cousin of Tony Roberts, who was PP at St John's has died and so more moves can be expected. Bob says he had received a letter from the Bishop saying that a move for him was more certain. He wonders how Paul Hypher might do here – it would be funny if I became his curate. But as he said 'put not your trust in princes'.'

FEBRUARY

Some visiting was quite exciting. One family had a whole collection of toads, lizards and a delightful pole cat that walked all over me. Did I smell for the next few days?! At least that was one positive contact- with the family that is – but nearly all the rest had moved or died.

At the next deanery meeting all the brethren agreed that we wanted less 'legislation'. We were dissatisfied with the location for retreats and pressed for smaller gatherings. Bob wanted the bishop to be more of a spiritual pastor than he is at the moment.

With Archbishop Warlock now appointed to Liverpool odds were now shortening for Clark or Michael Hollings to be the next Archbishop of Westminster. No doubt the parish priest would find out a bit more as he headed for his so called 'sleasy' hotel in London to slum it for a period of convalescence. Anyway Roy and I lived it up while he was away. It seems that he has more definite news of his possibly moving in November.

17th: ' The big news breaks. Abbot Hume of Ampleforth is to be the new Archbishop of Westminster much to everyone's surprise. This will be to a complete break with the old school of the English College. At least we will have a man of spirituality and he comes over with a very warm personality. Certainly the national press seem very favourable, but the Catholic press seems rather muted in their reaction.'

MARCH

As a cold February ended the IRA troubles continued with hunger strikes. Mother had trips to Guys hospital to try an experimental tablet for her arthritis and at the next prison Mass the lads attacked the corrupt nature of society – very upstanding comments! This latter was very much in tune with Solzynitzin's interview who painted a gloomy picture of the future for the west. It was not a question of whether Russia would change its policy but that the West was likely to dramatically collapse. He poured scorn on détente and spoke of the need for a great moral renewal as opposed to mere pragmatism.

3rd: 'The question of General Absolution comes up for discussion. Our Senate of priests was rather divided on the issue but it was interesting that two dioceses with conservative prelates – Nottingham and Shrewsbury are pressing ahead with the scheme. On my next visit to the prison I had to visit a Jamaican in the hospital block who had murdered his wife. He seemed quite a pleasant chap but very unbalanced. One wonders really what use prison is for most of these fellows.'

9th: 'Poor Bob is now prone to great outbursts of anger for no apparent reason. It is very disconcerting but luckily the mood just as quickly changes and he was soon full of the news that the Diocese is to be divided and there is to be two weeks of consultation. The odd thing is that we have no bishop. Poor old Clark doesn't even remain as a sort of substitute. It's rather sad after the press having made him a Cardinal but I should imagine he will be appointed as the first bishop of the new diocese. Bob is busy with press handouts and is working out some statistics as it seems that we have the smallest number of clergy of any diocese in the country. However having got out all these press statements he is informed that the event will not take place until Saturday. Bishop Clark is 90% sure of his appointment and is naming his secretary and Vicar General. Bob says he fears that he may loose his opportunity to refuse a Canonry if offered him!'

10th: 'A very civilised parish meeting to discuss the parish report - none of the dreadful histrionics and abuse of the Cambridge meetings. Bob was an expert chairing the meeting.

12th: ' Nearly half way to my silver jubilee. In London to celebrate aunt Dorothy's eighty first birthday and celebrate it with a good curry dinner and a bottle of *asti* - so that sent them to sleep for the rest of the day.'

16th: 'A deanery day of recollection at Walsingham and about twenty clergy took part. The bishop gave a good but wordy talk. The village seem so unreal and totally dead compared with the pilgrimage season. A discussion on General Absolution - certainly controversial especially having to confess mortal sins a later date after receiving the Absolution. The Bishop kept falling back on, 'Rome says' or 'the mind of Rome'. Prime Minister Wilson suddenly resigns.

18th: 'I am now feeling in a real state of depression and dejection about family affairs as I hear that aunt Dorothy has now developed heart trouble and that the doctor at Guys to whom mother is going for treatment is surprised that the tablets for her arthritis aren't having an effect. I visited a cottage where an elderly lady was dying and being looked after by her son – it put me very much in mind of my own situation.'

20th: 'Bishop Clark rings to seek advice about music for the enthronement – he obviously feels home and dry! Stereo broadcasting is now available in East Anglia –what a miracle of technology. Although the new bishop's identity seems a forgone conclusion we were still asked to write to the Apostolic Delegate, Archbishop Heim to make suggestions for the same. I wrote and suggested Tony Philpot. The clergy at Cambridge had also sent in their reservations about Alan.'

24th: 'Celebrate a class Mass with the children at St Thomas More school on the other side of town. It makes such a change when the Mass is well prepared and the children participated with great enthusiasm. An historic day as the expected announcement of the new Diocese is promulgated, but +Charles remains bishop until a new bishop is appointed. Bishop Clark has already been talking about the members of his new curia and installing a lift at St John's to take him to his new offices on the top floor so he obviously thinks that he is the man for the job. Fr Gerard Meath OP comes to give a day of recollection. He is now working at Hatch End in the Communications department there – all rather nostalgic seeing him again and he is really a great chap.'

25th: 'A happy day, for once, as we watched on the colour television the enthronement of Basil Hume as the new Archbishop of Westminster. We wondered what Clark must have been thinking. Afterwards the new Archbishop went with his monks to Westminster Abbey to sing Latin Vespers.'

26th: 'An Indian Baptist Pastor staying with the Anglicans up the road visits us. He has sixty six parishes. No wonder he asked us if our parish covered the whole of East Anglia. The Telegraph reports that Clark has already been appointed to the Diocese. Bob comes back depressed from his planning meeting. He picked up information that the Apostolic Delegate had said at Hume's installation that Clark had such overwhelming support from people that he would be 'in' –and this before the consultation period had officially ended. I dreamt last night that I was unemployed.'

27th: 'My car has its 9000 mile service. The bill came to £30.33! £20 of this was labour costs. Eric Doyle gives a Lenten lecture at the Anglican Cathedral about the future of the Church to which we go. I am sure he would upset the RCs if they could follow the drift of his argument. Another dreadful bomb goes off on an underground station at West Ham – no doubt the work of the IRA.'

26th: 'I had a busy and tiring day at home trying to clear up the debris from the storms. I called over to Ousden to see Uncle Wilf who was down for a few days. He summoned up some of the old spirit to attack the malaise in the Church – its outdated structures etc – though he still prefers the Tridentine Mass. Bob was very critical of the Bishop's talk the other day and didn't think much of its spiritual content. Derek Lance it seems is opting for the Northampton diocese as Clark, if he becomes Ordinary, hasn't given him the job of catechetics director.

MARCH

1st: It was down to London to check up on the oldies. The aunts were improving but mother's legs are not and they keep giving way. Aunt Dorothy was in the middle of telling me about the mandate her mother had given to protect my mother – but I never heard the end of the story as we were interrupted – there is so much I don't know about the family. The tablets mother has been taking, experimentally, seem to have been hopeless and it also seems that she has decided against seeing the surgeon about a possible hip operation , whether this was her own decision or subtle persuasion by the others I don't know but she said she would stick with the new tablets for another month before going back on the old ones. However I did learn on my next visit that when she was about twelve years old aunt Dorothy had been experimented on for a possible cure for TB and this had disastrous effects on her metabolism and this is now catching up with her. As part of her treatment mother had been going to the local baths for some hydrotherapy but with little effect. She really has got great determination and pluck.'

2nd: 'I actually have a reply from the Apostolic Delegate in response to the consultation regarding the new bishop and so has Bob! However that all seems rather late in the day as it seems 99% certain that Alan is to be the new Ordinary and that Tony Philpot may be the new Vicar General. It also transpires that Michael Hollings is also being vetted and that Hume wants to be called 'Father' and is enquiring as to what provisions are being made for resigned clergy and broken marriages.'

10th: 'In preparation for Holy Week we did an exchange of clergy for hearing Confessions. We went down to our soon to be made cathedral and sat through a solid three hours of Confessions. I also helped to give day of recollection to twenty girls at Notre Dame school.

13th: 'Over to Lidgate and find the new rector, Arnold Freeman, bringing Communion to cousin Win. He invited me to preach in the village church at the end of May - what about 'a prophet not being honoured in his own country'? He wanted the sermon to be on Our Lady and to last about twenty minutes. This seemed to give new strength to Win who at 82 is still out at the crack of dawn doing the weeding, moving her raspberry canes and even two old mangles! I spent the rest of day demolishing the old greenhouse, bringing in coal and wood and cutting the grass.'

17th: 'Holy Week and Easter went quite well and we tried the new English version of the *Exultet*. Fr Rees Jones, formerly of Diss joined us again. It's dreadful to think that if you get a stroke and lose your parish you have to hike about looking for somewhere to live.'

21st: 'Celebrate a cremation. It is so difficult when one knows nothing of the person concerned or the family - one is just a functionary.'

26th: 'St George's Day. The parish has a scouts and guides troop with which I have never had contact but they have their traditional parade at the evening Mass.

27th: 'At long last the first Bishop of East Anglia is announced – who should it be but Alan Clark! Let's hope he doesn't push people around too much and does some good.'

MAY

With the advent of May the weather began to turn really warm and into the 80F mark and we have the first meagre spot of rain for ages. I went to London and see a marvellous exhibition of Constable's paintings at the Tate Gallery brought in from all over the world. Security was tight and bags were searched. I then walked back to Victoria and then decide to walk all the way home having bought a bun at Woolworths for my lunch and kept a meths drinker company in Bessborough Gardens. It struck me how wonderful it was to be free and to be able to go where one wanted to - the Thames looked marvellous with a heat haze over it. I trudged as far as New Cross before getting a bus for the last leg of the journey. I only wished I had someone to talk to regarding my various problems.

On my return to Norwich there was little excitement except that there was a note suggesting that we all contributed to a crosier for the Bishop – one which he had already chosen.

9th: 'Bob is in a funny mood again. He accuses Roy and me of being 'legalists'. We can't quite understand what he is getting at – especially since we gather he asked permission to say a Tridentine Mass on the occasion of his jubilee. He is a funny mixture of old and new. It seems he caused something of a storm last week at Hoveton when he introduced Communion standing. However, come his jubilee, he had his extraordinary celebration of the old rite –down to the big six candles, the Last Gospel and Prayers for Russia. There was quite a full church and people soon slipped back into the old ways of kneeling. However it all seemed very unreal and over cheese and wine afterwards many people were happy that we had moved into the new Rite.'

11th : 'The rector of Lidgate's suggestion that I should preach in the village church seems to have caused something of a stir. I wish I had been a fly on the wall at their Parish Council meeting. It seems most people had pushed me through the village in a pram as a baby! So now I shall have to get down to work to do some research into John Lydgate who wrote a poem on Our Lady. This I do at the city records office and find it all quite fascinating. This research, a few days later, took me to Hatfield Broad Oak in Essex to see the site where he had been Prior after picking mother up for her return journey to Lidgate. I stayed a couple of nights to settle her in but she is beginning to find the stairs something of a trial. She is getting so terribly stiff now and keeps dozing off. I tried to have a serious talk about future plans for the cottage but I really didn't get very far on the topic. I did a trial run of my sermon in the church – the pulpit seemed too vertiginous and I couldn't see over the lectern and so I hope that we can come to some other arrangement. On return to Norwich we learned, in spite of rumours to the contrary, that 'yesterday's men' had been appointed to the responsibility of Vicar General – Canon McBride and Chancellor – Paul Taylor.'

17th: 'Mass at the prison enabled some prisoners to lament the fact that the library at Norwich prison was by no means as good as at Wormwood Scrubs but they quite realised that life there was a holiday camp compared with that endured by Alexander Solzhenitsyn in the Gulag. On my next visit a week later one man seemed to know a lot about Swedish Gaols which were so much more civilised that British ones.'

30th: 'My historic sermon in the village church at Lidgate took place - the first since the Reformation. I had to use the Jacobean pulpit which was rather a tight fit and the reading stand seemed tied on by a piece of string. The tension mounted as the congregation arrived consisting of various relatives, associates and acquaintances. In all about forty came - not bad considering the usual attendance is about five. The rector wore a tatty Roman cotta while I wore a clean Anglican surplice! I was escorted to a privileged position in the chancel and luckily I could not be seen and I was able to squirm all the during the service that followed - no wonder people don't come to church! Evensong was interminable and it was three quarters of an hour before I eventually got into the pulpit where I gave my oration on Christian Unity, John Lydgate and Our Lady. The rector gave thanks for the Roman Catholic Church that had brought Christianity to these shores and at the end of the service he announced that, as a mark of Unity, all Catholics present should join with him in saying the Hail Mary. Needless to say the response was small, although there were one or two in the congregation, including auntie Marjorie, Uncle Reg's widow, who was staying with us. There was tea and biscuits in the village hall afterwards and I did the rounds. I wonder what my ancestors would have thought of it all.'

JUNE

Communion in the hand had now been introduced in the parish. It all went very smoothly. Nearly everyone received the Sacrament in this way at the out stations and about half in the other places – it was interesting that it was mainly the 'oldies' who preferred the new way while the youngsters stuck to protruding their tongues. In Cambridge one irate parishioners protested about the practice alluding to the fact that a priest's hands had been consecrated to touch the sacred elements. Paul replied, 'And who, madam, consecrated your tongue?'

2nd Today saw the historic installation of Alan Clark as the first bishop of East Anglia and the largest parish church in England becoming a Cathedral. The whole panoply of Church and State were there and there was eager anticipation for the arrival of the Apostolic Delegate and the new Archbishop of Westminster, recently created a Cardinal. ' It was a magnificent sight as they all processed down the aisle. The Cardinal has great dignity and composure and the people seem to have taken him to their hearts. Bishop Grant, our erstwhile bishop looking very frail took up his position in front of me opposite the Cardinal. Our new Ordinary seemed in a great hurry to reach his episcopal throne after the Papal Bull of appointment was read out by the new Chancellor, Canon Taylor. He was greeted by various dignitaries and a note of spontaneity entered in when the Bishop of Norwich, Maurice Wood, greeted him 'from the heart'. The Bishop preached but his style is difficult to stay with and I was glad that a priest next to me agreed. Mary Berry (late Sr Thomas More of the Canonesses of St Augustine) provided the plainsong which did not add much to the proceedings and I together with several others clutched a ciborium to Communicate the laity at various points in the cathedral. The press and media were present and there was good coverage. The reception followed. In the evening we returned for another Mass for those who were not able to attend in the morning. Bishop Clark's sermon was more relaxed that in the morning. I knelt quite near the Cardinal. In the reception afterwards he stood on a chair in the middle of the marquee to speak to people - though he was tall enough without that. He was very informal and natural and just what we needed. Bob organised the interview on Anglia TV the next day with the Cardinal. He came over very well as a personality and took a slightly different emphasis from Clark on 'structures'.'

6th: Whitsunday. A trip to the Broads for the annual blessing. There was some hymn singing with the local clergy and the Bishop of Norwich in the car park at Hoveton. We then boarded the chaplain's launch with the Bishop in true biblical style standing in the prow waving his crosier at the bewildered half naked sunbathers bedecking their boats as we passed. A quick duck down at Wroxham Bridge prevented him losing his mitre and at the end of the excursion he preached a very pleasant sermon.'

After the next visit to the prison where one of our number had been recently recaptured after escaping and a very moral discussion on violence, I went to the University of East Anglia with Roy to lunch with Desmond McMorrow, the chaplain – a good lunch for 90p. I wonder what staff make of this northern Irish Vincentian !

The temperature continued to rise with 86 degrees in the shade – the hottest for twenty four years. I met the rector, Arnold Freeman, on my trip home who said that the sermon had gone down very well and this 'will sew the seeds of understanding'.

10th: 'Something positive came from a meeting of the hospital chaplains with psychiatric medics. Dr Abel was particularly good – at least it helped to break down prejudices – except the more hostile doctors weren't there. Dr Abel had already psychoanalysed our new Cardinal – 'real spirituality and goodness shines through.'

We all had a personal letter from Alan Clark after his elevation to East Anglia. Roy and I are quite convinced that he writes the original in Latin and then translates it into English

The 'Father Baker Case' is beginning to cause problems and the new Vicar General is sent to Downham Market to try and sort things out. His mission is to attempt to persuade Father Baker not to go on tour around East Anglia with the Tridentine Mass. But sadly the situation was never resolved. Fr Baker continued to live in the old presbytery while continuing to maintain the Old Liturgy. This caused great tension and sadness all around. The arguments became quite acrimonious and he described the Bishop in the daily press as this, 'pathetic, disastrous bishop'. He was technically removed from office and the new parish priest had to live elsewhere while he became a focus of dissent, albeit marginal, in the diocese for those protesting at the Liturgical reforms. He set up a Mass centre in Norwich and the Bishop issued a rather unintelligible letter to be read in all the churches. One priest refused to read the letter saying that 'enough rocks and been thrown'. I suppose he had to make a statement but what good it will do I have my doubts. Unfortunately the bishop didn't issue a statement to the media and all day the phone was ringing from the press looking for Bob, being the media contact. Fr Baker ended his days first as a member of Archbishop Lefebvre's dissident group and then of the *'sede vacantists'*, those who refused to accept the legitimacy of any of the Popes since Pius X11. He had tried his vocation with the Dominicans and for awhile was a curate at Newmarket when we first got to know him back in the 1950's. However Fr Baker was not the only problem. Some clergy refused to administer the Host to people in the hands if they requested it and at Thetford a notice went up saying that Communion would only administered on the tongue.

14th: 'Both prisoners and I were very upset at my next visit to the prison when on two occasions a warder interrupted the Mass looking for a prisoner. As one man put it – it's about the only time in the week when we can get a bit of peace and quiet.'

I continued to try and do some pastoral visiting – which usually ended in frustration. On one occasion a lady let me in – said nothing, plonked me down on the settee and I had to wait until she had finished the latest episode of Coronation Street before she spoke to me – so far now does the media dominate people's lives.

A break came with a Study Conference at Clapham Park in Bedfordshire. Gerard Meath OP chaired the discussions which were on Moral Theology and lead by Fr Brendan Soan. Of course the contraception issue was tackled and he saw it as an ideal to be worked towards. Paul Hypher had heard that the bishop would not be making any moves this year- so I can see myself stuck in Norwich for a bit longer – Paul couldn't understand the bishop's introductory letter much either.

JULY
5th: 'Deep discussions on the meaning of life at the prison. And the temperatures continue to soar - 95 degrees and 90 in my room and it is almost unbearable. The situation is getting quite serious in the country with the grass quite brown, forest and heath fires and the crops almost ripened. The heat seems to have got to Bob as I received a lash of his tongue for having missed choir practice and one or two other minor things – I was 'inefficient, irresponsible and forgetful'. Ah well there's many a true word but it left me in a most unhappy and introspective mood for the rest of the day.

10th: 'The ordination of David Bagstaff at English Martyrs in Cambridge. This was a very happy occasion for the parish and I felt I had helped him a little along the way with my Latin and Greek lessons! It was good to see Frank Thomas, rector of Oscott, and Ken Collins and also Sister Scholastica from St. Mary's whose Community have now taken over the De La Salle House in Brookside as an annexe.'

14th: 'Today I warm a little to the bishop! I had to taxi him to Blakeney for the funeral of a retired Westminster priest. On the way back he theorised about moving me in the autumn – 'How about Sudbury?', he said! We shall see! Bob seemed to be aware of things and we discussed the clergy situation where matters seen to be heading for crisis proportions and no one seems to be terribly concerned about it. We even have someone travelling from the Cathedral to supply at Peterborough.'

At short notice I was landed to take a deposition from a witness relating to a marriage case – what a lot of old nonsense some of the questions were. I had to follow this up by visiting one of the parties but his mother said the problem had now been solved as he was marrying in the United Reformed Church.

Bob's mood is now getting almost unbearable and the tension in the house in unbearable too and it was all we could do to get through lunch. I had a word with Judy and she said that things do get like this from time to time. No doubt his illness and the proposed changes in the household make it difficult for him. However like a summer storm the mood soon passed and I was off to suss out the ground at Sudbury – should plans materialise. It would be ideal as it was near home and in a lovely position by the river. This cheerful news was heightened by the excitement of the Americans landing a craft on Mars and sending back brilliant pictures. How this contrasted with home news that unemployment was now the worst since the war.

Summer holidays were round again so off home. The project this time was putting some felt on the stable roof, which involved removing all the pantiles. This was rather a precarious job as I had to climb up a ladder and perch myself on the ridge but it made a pleasant change from my normal work. In the middle of this the Parish Priest, Tony Philpot, rang up asking whether the family would like Bishop Clark to visit them during his official Visitation. They could hardly say 'no' and in the event the visit went off well and he was very chatty, but there was no mention of my possible move to Sudbury.

We went out for several car trips. Sure enough pinned up on the door at the Thetford church was a notice saying: 'Communion in this church is given only on the tongue', and then rather incongruously: 'please use the mat'. I did get a few days away to stay with my cousin Andrew down in Horsham. He had just been awarded his ARCO and doing well at St Andrew's University. From there I was able to go over to Chichester to see how the Carmelites who had been at Waterbeach were getting on and I was able to have an audience with Sr Mary of Carmel our old friend. It's an ageing community there but they all seem to have settled in well. Trips to Winchester, Stonehenge and back to St. Leonard's to view my old primary school, all shut up and looking very decrepit.

It was about time I was shriven so I took the opportunity of going to Bury St. Edmunds. It was a two sided Confessional. I should have known better as I had operated one at OLEM. I knelt down, heard what I thought was a blessing, and then reeled off my list only to be dismayed when I heard the shutter pulled back and greeted by the priest. The voice I had heard was on the other side and so I had to go through the whole list again!

My conscience was pricked somewhat when I learned that my former colleague from OLEM, Tom Feighan, had been appointed to Thrapston instead of me. I expect he took the commission very meekly and obediently but I felt he had rather been put upon because he was not likely to say no. And what was the rector of Oscott's continual message to us

students ? - 'obedience to your your bishop'. Perhaps I had failed the test. Still feeling rather guilty about my refusal to go to Thrapston I made another trip over there. There I found poor Tom eking out a rather ghastly existence in the caravan. He looked unkempt and uncared for and I can't see how the bishop, who hasn't been over to see him, can sleep easily in his own bed at night. His name was on the housing list – but there was a long wait. The family were pretty shocked and I am glad I did refuse.

It had been a nice summer break with glorious weather - but with mum dozing off at a moment's notice, the aunts getting quite worked up about it and with aunt Dorothy getting very frail and aunt Elsie not far behind, the future was beginning to look a bit bleak.

Back at base, after the holiday, there was still no news of being moved and we had a young Spanish Priest, Fr Oriel staying with us to supply. David Bagstaff had moved to our new cathedral of St John the Baptist. But putting his ear to the ground he could glean nothing of any developments. The Bishop was out of the country until September and so I was not likely to hear anything. It was all very unsettling for everyone concerned.

Bob had organised a Harvest Festival for Hoveton. There one or two objected that they had never had one before and the whole thing was very 'protestant'.

The drought was now getting critical and in some parts the water has been cut off with the prospect of standpipes in the street. There have been several serious forest fires too, while in China and the Philippines there have been earthquakes and a large volcano is about to blow – so 'The End' can't be far off !

18th: At last!! ' The phone goes and it's the Bishop to give me the news that I am going to Sudbury. Deo Gratias! They were all quite excited at home It seems that I shall be on my own there and succeeding Fr John Cureton who has been there for many years. At least being on my own will not lead to the interesting combinations of clergy that the late +Leo devised. He put a Fr Nut with a Fr Squirrel, a Fr Bustin with a Fr Howlin and he sent Canon Peacock off to retire at 'Fox Den'.

Eric Doyle OFM came up again for another stint of recording at Anglia TV. We had a long discussion into the early hours about such contentious subjects as sex, the Resurrection and women priests. We contemplated the disastrous effects on people that some teaching by moralists have had and the guilt complexes that people have endured because of this teaching particularly in the realms of sexuality. Eric was a great man and tragically died at an early age of cancer not so many years hence.

23rd: 'A minister for drought has now been appointed and unemployment has reached over one and a half million - the worst on record and the source of the Thames dries up. The heat is almost unbearable. Bob not so well and goes to bed with bronchitis

Our Lady & St John, Sudbury

24th: 'Took a trip down to Sudbury with the folks. Looked in at the church - very small but well kept. A dreadful organist practising - she'll have to go! Beautiful setting and surrounding countryside. Went on to Great Cornard where there is a Mass centre. Not so good here as it is a centre for the London overspill.'

26th: 'Down to Sudbury again and call in to see the parish priest who is moving up to Sheringham. It's a rather strange sort of house and back staircase to the basement where the housekeeper lives. She has a tiny little room upstairs and am not too keen on her close proximity to mine. She doesn't know whether she is going or not. Fr Cureton gave me all sorts of bewildering information especially about the dreaded school and the proposed appointment of a new head teacher. He hasn't informed his parishioners yet and he doesn't yet know when he is going because Canon Hulme at Sheringham is still on holiday

28th: 'Torrential rain!!'

29th: 'Archbishop Lefebvre says a banned Tridentine Mass before seven thousand people in Lille. A speech full of politics and vitriol - he called the new Rite - a bastard Mass and bastard Sacraments and the Pope is in heresy. Poor Pope Paul. Let's hope the Vatican plays it cool.'

SEPTEMBER

1st: 'Bob returns from hospital after his operation and seem reasonably all right. I am sure my move is just what he needs at the moment! The parish priest of Lowestoft is ill and his curate is not much better - Canon McBride from the cathedral rings to elicit our help. One of the choir members doesn't think that it is worth restarting the choir again in the autumn - so I leave it at its last gasp.'

3rd: 'Bob shows me how to balance the books - after all I am now going to have to learn how to do this all by myself. I spend most of the day attempting to do just that. We really ought to have had a course of accounting at college. Riots in South Africa - one can see a terrible inferno there before long.'

4th: 'Ring up Fr Cureton but he still has heard no news as to when the moves are likely to take place. The Harvest Festival went well at Hoveton and dispelled the 'protestant' jibes. Bob said a few kind embarrassing words at the Masses about my moving.

6th: 'Last Mass at the prison and for the first time I am asked for my pass. A collection had been taken for me at the church and it came to a staggering £327!

7th: 'The parish priest retires to his bed and the doctor is called.'

8th: 'Heavily laden with books and bicycle I drive down to Sudbury and deposit them there. Have a good chat with the housekeeper, Miss Dunne, who it seems is going. She wonders how on earth I am going to cope on my own. In the evening over to Cambridge and concelebrate with other clergy for Canon Taylor's brother Bernard's Silver Jubilee. Nice to see John Koenig and Fr 'Loppy' Thornton.

10th: 'My successor in the person of Fr Bede Edwards - a former Carmelite - comes over and I show him the ropes and this gives me an opportunity to say good bye to my sick round of parishioners.

11th: 'At last I hear when I am moving and there are sad farewells at the various Sunday Masses and even some applause. The mystique of the priest-hood is all very strange. People were all very friendly.

16th: 'A farewell meal at Coltishall Hall Hotel - and excellent meal of Prawns Orientale and we return home for one of Bob's Gaelic coffees.

17th: ' And so the Norwich interlude draws to a close. It all seems very strange. The choir present me with some very nice wine glasses and a bottle of wine and the parish priest gives me an electric kettle and I give him a tape of *Carmina Burana.*. Hear from the local Council that they have turned mother's application for planning permission for part of the garden - so more worries on finance there.'

18th: 'A very tiring and confusing day. After Mass out at Hoveton finally pack up the car and after sad farewell I head off for Sudbury where Fr Cureton was in a state of confusion and trying to pack. I was then treated to a welter of information about the parish that made my head spin- schools, catechetics, convent etc.'

But I leave the rest to a sequel. In the end I was pleased to have gone to Norwich and to have met and worked with Bob Manley and Roy Gathercole - two very fine priests and the inimitable Judy. In some ways I was lucky to have got my first parish after only ten years of ordination. Sometimes clergy have had to wait until almost retirement before they got their own patch. I have been dropped in at the deep end on many occasions so far - and no doubt more will follow!

Cartoon by Paul Jarvis for Christmas Newsletter
Me Bob Roy